A CENTURY OF CONTROVERSY
Ethnological Issues from 1860 to 1960

A CENTURY OF CONTROVERSY

Ethnological Issues from 1860 to 1960

Elman R. Service

Department of Anthropology
University of California, Santa Barbara

1985

ACADEMIC PRESS, INC.

(Harcourt Brace Jovanovich, Publishers)

Orlando   San Diego   New York   London
Toronto   Montreal   Sydney   Tokyo

Paperback cover: "Natives of Oonalashka, and their Habitations," steel engraving from the work of John Webber, in Captain James Cook and Captain James King, *A Voyage to the Pacific Ocean in the years 1776, 1777, 1778, 1779 and 1780*, atlas volume, 1784. From the Hill Collection, Mandeville Department of Special Collections, Central University Library, University of California, San Diego.

Passages from the following are reprinted by permission of the publishers:

Benedict, Ruth, *Patterns of Culture*, copyright © 1962, by Houghton Mifflin Company.
Durkheim, Emile, *The Elementary Forms of Religious Life*, copyright © 1966, by Free Press.
Carneiro, Robert L. (ed.), *The Evolution of Society: Selections from Herbert Spencer's Principles of Sociology*, copyright © 1967, by the University of Chicago Press.
Hocart, A. M., *Kings and Councillors*, copyright © 1970, by the University of Chicago Press.
Kroeber, A. L., *The Nature of Culture*, copyright © 1952, by the University of Chicago Press.
Radcliffe-Brown, A. R., *Structure and Function in Primitive Society*, copyright © 1952, by Free Press.
Resek, Carl, *Lewis Henry Morgan: American Scholar*, copyright © 1960, by the University of Chicago Press.
White, Leslie, "The Concept of Culture," in *American Anthropologist* 61(2): 227–251, 1959, by the American Anthropological Association.

ACADEMIC PRESS, INC.
Orlando, Florida 32887

United Kingdom Edition published by
ACADEMIC PRESS INC. (LONDON) LTD.
24–28 Oval Road, London NW1 7DX

LIBRARY OF CONGRESS CATALOGING IN PUBLICATION DATA

Service, Elman Rogers, Date
    A century of controversy.

    Includes index.
    1. Ethnology—Philosophy.   2. Ethnology—History.
I. Title.
GN 345.S46 1985   306   84-21596
ISBN 0-12-637380-9
ISBN 0-12-637382-5 (pbk.)

PRINTED IN THE UNITED STATES OF AMERICA

85 86 87 88   9 8 7 6 5 4 3 2 1

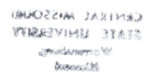

Contents

V. ECONOMIC LIFE OF PRIMITIVE PEOPLES

VI. SOCIETY AND CULTURE

VII. A BROADER CONTROVERSY

Preface

This book is an assessment of the history of ethnology in terms of its intellectual progress as such, rather than of the life histories of the various personalities involved. The title was chosen to suggest that the major concern is the clash, mix, syntheses, and rejections of ideas themselves, as they related to certain major problems in the theoretical development of the discipline. Perhaps this sounds like an obvious aim, but because this kind of selectivity is in fact unusual, an explication is needed.

Histories of anthropology and ethnology usually classify persons in terms of "schools of thought," a useful device, because anthropology became professionally academic, and because disciple-ism, despotism, and collegial rivalries and alliances became important factors in forming schools significant to the acceptance or rejection of ideas. But earlier, what is now usually called the 19th Century Evolutionist School really was not a school at all in this sense of the word. Spencer, Maine, Tylor, Lang, Bachofen, McLennan, Lubbock, Morgan, and others of the time were all evolutionists of a sort, yet not much alike—and with no evident tribal loyalties. They argued with one another, or agreed, free of modern professional or trade-union considerations. And since then, of course, there have also been numerous important individuals who neither founded nor belonged to any school.

Closely allied with the schools classification is what could be called the Great-Man, or First-Cause, or Founder-as-Case-Study approach, or some such. That is, those taken to be the Original Thinkers, such as Tylor, Durkheim, Malinowski, Radcliffe-Brown, and Boas, have all been given frequent biographical treatment as case histories in the development of cultural and ethnological theory. The analyses of schools in general, and their founders in particular, are of course relevant and enlightening; we need them and more of their kind in the future. But for whatever its value, the present work diverges greatly from such emphasis. This does not mean that important individuals are ignored here; the attempt is to elevate or reduce them only in terms of their contribution to the development of certain major issues. This also means that only the minimal relevant biographical information is given about these individuals—often none. This is not to disparage the histories organized around individuals or schools; it is only to note that the present effort is quite different. Jacob Gruber makes a reasonable plea for the preservation of personal biographical and auto-biographical materials so valuable for a reconstruction of the intellectual history of our very young science. As he says, "In the study of men, we must realize the importance of the men who study (1966: 27)." I believe this is true, and I do not counterpoise my work to that which he recommends. I offer the present book, not to replace the biographical, but to concentrate on what has not received enough attention, the intercourse of the written arguments as such. As this is neither a conventional history of anthropology nor an attempt at an analytical "sociology of knowledge," I have not rehashed what the burgeoning number of contemporary historians have already said about the past of ethnology. To do so would unnecessarily complicate the text and not serve the intended purpose.

This research was originally begun for empirical reasons, to see what could be ascertained, as impersonally and objectively as possible, about the progress of our discipline. But the attempt at objectivity created the imposing problem of selecting major problems to be considered; what one of us might think of as a major issue another might think minor, or not an issue at all. I decided, finally, to let history make the selections. That is, I regard as major issues those that began early and have persisted significantly until at least 1960. But of course, the choices are still bound to seem to some idiosyncratic and ill-chosen; one can only aim at and hope for a fairly broad consensus among the readership.

Why begin in 1860? J. W. Burrow, historian of Victorian social theory, had this to say:

> It was the third quarter of the century which saw revival, after half a century of relative neglect, of interest in primitive society. It was in the sixties of the 19th century that a systematic, well-documented comparative social anthropology was born, and an interest in the manner, customs, institution and beliefs of primitive and oriental peoples ceased to be confined to travellers, antiquarians and satirists, and to take the study of them seriously became no longer merely a proof of eccentricity. (1966: 80)

Andrew Lang stated in his biographical chapter on E. B. Tylor in the *Festschrift* for Tylor: "It is to be noted that in 1860–70, a fresh scientific interest in matters anthropological was 'in the air'" (Thomas 1906: 1–2). Lang went on to describe the 1860s as a "generation of heroes," naming Tylor, Lord Avebury (Lubbock), McLennan, and Maine. In an address titled "The History and Present Orientation of Cultural Anthropology," A. L. Kroeber also chose 1860 as the date the discipline became an organized, coherent endeavor (Kroeber 1952: Chap. 17). There were no ethnological museums before 1860, no university chairs or courses in ethnology, no provisions for field research and no regular publications. To be sure, there were a few anthropological organizations before 1860, of which the American Ethnological Society, founded in 1842, and La Société des Observateurs de l'Homme, founded 1797, come most readily to mind. And to be sure, there have been, for as long as we have written records, interesting works that can be called ethnological in the descriptive sense, but they were not parts of a recognized discipline and represented no common scientific ideology. More noteworthy was the presence of important ethnological questions with philosophical answers during the periods of British and French Enlightenment. But probably humans have always been interested in themselves and their neighbors; the *philosophes* of the Enlightenment expressed their interests better than their predecessors had done, however, and in more reasonable ways. The philosophical anthropology of those times reads very well today (try Adam Ferguson's *An Essay on the History of Civil Society*, 1767). But the main controversies of the 1800s up to the 1860s that could be called anthropological—such as polygenists versus monogenists,[1] degradationists versus evolutionists—hold no interest for anthropologists today. The controversies that have held the most continuing modern relevance had their beginnings in the 1860s.

If the idea of a beginning point of 1860 has merit, it suggests an additional comment. Kroeber, particularly, felt that the advent of institutional forms of organization is the hallmark of an evolving discipline. We may accept this idea, in the main, but could it not also be true that along with the impetus to institutionalization there arises a countervailing problem? There is the obvious fact that any organization is always somewhat hierarchical, thus somewhat oligarchical, so that individuals may come to have politicized relationships. If intellectual progress is fostered by organizations, it may also be hampered by the personnel problems related to hierarchy. At any rate, for better or

---

[1] In Britain, The Ethnological Society was founded in 1843, splitting to form an offshoot, The Anthropological Society, in 1863. Relations between the two societies were bitter, centering primarily on conflict between the ethnologists' belief in monogenesis (under the primary influence of J. C. Prichard) and the polygenist anthropologists' racist ideas (Burrow 1966: 118–127).

worse, part of the history of ethnology must be related to the great increase in its institutionalization between 1860 and 1960.

The reasons for not bringing this history up to date, to 1985 instead of 1960, are several. 1960 is a better cutoff date because we need that much perspective. Also, it seems that the major controversies that began in our early years really reached full maturity by the 1950s. Particularly, several of the newer innovations appeared or were receiving important commentary by the 1950s: Lévi-Strauss' (1949) *Les structures elémentaires de la parenté*, Kirchhoff's *Principles of Clanship* (1955), Leach's (1951, 1954) social–political studies in highland Burma, Polyanyi's restructuring of primitive economics (1957), Childe's version of Marxist evolutionism in political anthropology (1936, 1942), Steward's "ecology" and "multilineal evolution" (1955), and White's "culturological" determinism (1949, 1959) all brought refinements or new dimensions to many of the older problems. For many reasons, therefore, 1960 seems like a good time to finish this kind of intellectual inventory.

There is a further kind of innovation in the present approach. Instead of taking a slice through one given time span, or generation, in order to treat all the major contemporary thought of that time (i.e., late nineteenth-century ethnology), and instead of isolating nations and schools (i.e., British Social Anthropology) in their contribution to all issues, a very different route is taken. Separate topics, such as kinship terminology or totem and taboo, are treated one by one through each of their individual historical careers. There are two reasons for this procedure: (1) to promote understanding of these major events in their most meaningful context, that is, the history of the dialectical interplay of the thoughts themselves, and (2) as a pedagogical means for imparting understanding of the separate topics as such.

This latter point needs further discussion because of its probable unfamiliarity. Let us take a standard example, what to many beginning students of ethnology is a difficult if not baffling subject: kinship. Beginning historically may lead to an easier and better understanding than dumping students into the middle of the contemporary efforts to make so many various and often minor contributions. In this historical approach one begins at the beginning, when the problem seems (to us, now) very simple. For example, Morgan's solution to the problem posed by the classificatory kinship terminologies was finally accomplished, to his taste, after a long time and a lot of work, but we can see it today in its obvious simplicity. McLennan's rebuttal can also be seen today as simple. Then came the revival of the argument in somewhat different form by Rivers and Kroeber, and since then, and finally snowballing, came the articles, the misunderstandings, the schools of thought, the neologisms and new kinds of diagrams, until today a student quails at the prospect of reading and trying to understand them all. But if, instead of a total immersion in all of this subject's contemporary manifestations, the student is introduced to it historically, little by little, comprehension can be greatly eased, as well as increased. But this cannot be proved by further discussion at this point.

*   *   *

A few readers may wonder why I have used the word *ethnological* in the title rather than *cultural* or *social anthropological*. This was done because the choice between cultural and social is itself a controversy. A whole school, that of British Social Anthropology as founded by A. R. Radcliffe-Brown, has discarded the concept of culture as an abstraction. And the Boasian meanings attached to the word *culture* are also controversial, even among American cultural anthropologists.

Radcliffe-Brown (1923) also argued that *social anthropology* should replace the term *ethnology*, because the latter had been associated with studies of "conjectural history." Although it is true that some ethnologists sometimes did conjectural history, not all did, nor do today, and there is no etymological or historical reason to identify one in terms of the other. A. C. Haddon's *History of Anthropology* states that although *ethnology* was once synonymous with *anthropology*, "with the development of the subject, its [ethnology's] scope became gradually defined, until it is now generally restricted to the comparative and genetic study of human culture and of man as a social animal" (1910: 120–121).

Ethnology and *ethnography* were defined by Elizée Reclus in the eleventh edition of the *Encyclopaedia Britannica* in 1910, long before Rivers had incurred Radcliffe-Brown's ire with his conjectural history, as "the whole history of the material and intellectual development of man." The latest edition of the *Encyclopaedia Britannica* defines *ethnography* more or less as above but has no entry for *ethnology*. The latest *International Encyclopedia of the Social Sciences* article "Ethnology," by Harold Driver, says: "Ethnology is generally regarded as one of the major subdivisions of cultural anthropology, the others being anthropological archaeology and anthropological linguistics" (1968: 178). I use *ethnology* in this sense.

*   *   *

I am happy to acknowledge the help of the following friends who with thoughtful care criticized all or large parts of the rough manuscript: Donald Brown, Thomas Harding, Elvin Hatch, and Albert Spaulding at the University of California, Santa Barbara, and Robert Carneiro of the American Museum of Natural History. Two student friends, William Olmstead and David Earle, prepared the index and read the page proofs. Their capable assistance with these normally thankless tasks was much appreciated.

I

TO SET THE STAGE

Part I departs to some degree from the decision to deal with controversies rather than individual biographies. In particular, it seemed useful to give more attention to Lewis H. Morgan's career than others because, as the more or less accidental source of some of our more enduring and important controversies, Morgan's work demands close scrutiny. Also, Morgan has been maligned, revered, and misunderstood more than any single figure in the history of our discipline, and this too suggests a need for more treatment in depth. But I have tried to stay true to the plan by discussing only the features of his personal career that are directly relevant to an understanding of the development of his ideas.

1

Introduction

In compiling a list of major issues of interest to modern ethnology, I was struck to find that most were born in the latter half of the nineteenth century. Of still greater interest was the discovery that most of the broadest issues were broached in the 1860s particularly, and some in the 1870s. Two related philosophical or theoretical poses that characterized the prominent ethnological thinkers of this period, and earlier, are related to this phenomenon. One of these was the prevalent positivism, the other the belief in human progress as a form of social, cultural, and mental evolution.

The positivism of those scientists such as Spencer, Maine, McLennan, Tylor, Morgan, and others was simply a belief in the universality of natural causation. Whereas the actions of mankind once seemed disconnected from the rest of nature, by mid-nineteenth century it became increasingly accepted that man was a part of the cosmic order—and Charles Darwin was by no means the originator of this perspective. Of course there were many thinkers outside the field of ethnology who held such a view long before (Comte and James Mill are prominent examples).

A conception of the progressive unfolding of human and social potentialities—evolution in the broad sense—was in large part related to the triumph over the theological partisans of degradationism, the belief that man had "fallen from grace" rather than risen from lowly beginnings. The rise of progressivism fitted neatly with the increasing intellectual interest in primitive peoples, now being described scientifically (in the sense of natural history) in many faraway parts of the globe by missionaries, botanists, museum collectors, geographers, ship's doctors, and "gentleman adventurers" of many types. The major scientific interest of armchair ethnologists (the nineteenth-century evolutionists, Morgan excepted, did not themselves undertake fieldwork) was in arranging these fascinating reports about primitive peoples in layers of culture from the most primitive to the most evolved, with a particularly strong emphasis on the origins of various institutions.

But these layers of development were arranged in terms of development only; they did not involve a perspective on the rise of particular societies as such—as structures or organizations—nor did they include any conception of adaptation. The effort to correct this one-sidedness was a salient concern of some twentieth-century ethnologists.

The most controversial of the nineteenth-century evolutionists turned out to be Lewis H. Morgan, whose *Ancient Society* (1877) attracted the close attention and approbation of Karl Marx and Friedrich Engels. Of course, many of the ensuing controversies were due to the fervent pro and con attitudes toward Marxism within the developing science of ethnology. This is not to say that these attitudes were always political and polemical; some were, undoubtedly, but others were probably indirectly or unconsciously influenced by the strong opinions of those who were political.

Chapters 2 and 3 are devoted to Morgan, since his work was so significant as a source of early controversy. But the decade of the 1860s in Western Europe and Great Britain witnessed a new ferment of opinion about the evolution of society well in advance of Morgan's works of 1871 and 1877. The 1860s were preeminently spirited by the earlier theories of Lyell, Spencer, Darwin, Müller, and others, and in this atmosphere we find several eminent scholars dealing more closely with the subject of ethnology. Sir Henry Maine and John F. McLennan in Great Britain, Johann J. Bachofen in Switzerland, and Fustel de Coulanges in France are among the most important of these for the present work because of their controversial opinions on several of the topics to be treated herein. In particular, we want to note briefly the respects in which the works of Lewis H. Morgan were anticipated by them.

In the main, we find that before Morgan there was a general interest in societal evolution, especially as manifested in the gross distinction between primitive, or ancient, forms of society and modern civilization. But, in addition, more specific ideas about the primordial forms of the family were argued.

Sir Henry Maine

In 1861 Maine published his landmark history of jurisprudence, *Ancient Law*, intending not merely to present a treatise on the history of classical law but aiming chiefly "to indicate some of the earliest ideas of mankind, as they are reflected in *Ancient Law*, and to point out the relation of those ideas to modern thought" (Maine 1861:v).

Maine, it should be noted at the outset, thought that the original form of the family was patriarchal, since the ancient Indo–European evidences of law were clearly of this sort. Moreover, he notes that the earliest states were founded on the premise that the members were all of one stock, descendants of one primordial family. But since evidence abounded that societies also grow by accretion—mainly through adoptions and confederations—the assumption that the family grew into the *gens*, then into the tribe, and then tribes into a commonwealth or state is a "legal fiction" to which incoming groups must accommodate themselves (1861:109). This is the unifying effect of both the fiction and actuality of *kinship*—"the scale on which the proximity of relatives to each other is calculated in archaic jurisprudence" (1861:121).

At this point Maine brings up the primacy of the patriarchal principle as it was manifested in ancient kinship. The Roman terms *agnatic* and *cognatic*, he says, can be used to account for the two major kinds of kinship, ancient and modern. Cognatic relationship is the familiar modern kind; "it is the relationship arising through common descent from the same pair of married persons, whether the descent be traced through males or females" (1861:121). Agnates, on the other hand, are those who trace their connection exclusively through males.

Why shut out the descendants of female members? Here Maine supplies an interesting point, which, as we shall see, is a very different assumption about kinship from that of Morgan. He says: "The foundation of agnation is not the marriage of Father and Mother, but the authority of the Father. . . . In truth, in the primitive view, relationship is exactly limited by Patria Potestas. Where the Potestas begins, the kinship begins. . . . Where the Potestas ends, kinship ends" (1861:123).[1]

Maine's view of kinship has it as a much more artificial, humanly contrived system than Morgan's, who thought of kinship as straightforwardly biological–genealogical. Morgan, we shall see, thus saw marriage as only a man-made device, and thus as variable, while the biological fact of descent from pairs was the true kinship. A cognatic system, therefore, was the natural genealogical system, and the descent from married pairs (monogamy) was the normal civilized form of kinship. Deviations from this among primitive societies occurred because the societies were less evolved in their marriage rules. Basic to Maine's view, by contrast, was the idea of legal fictions—rules of inheritance, adoptions, rights and obligations, private law, and so forth—

---

[1]*Patria Potestas* means "the life-long authority of the Father or other ancestor over the person and property of his descendants" (Maine 1861:112).

as the variable determinants of kinship. Now, in hindsight, this seems remarkably sophisticated compared to Morgan's view, even though we may not subscribe to the particulars of the theory of the actual primacy of *Patria Potestas* outside of the Indo–European historical sphere.

Maine also anticipated Morgan in seeing significant—that is, qualitative—distinctions between primitive society and civilized society. These distinctions were of two orders, organizational and legal. The first of these was the distinction of the *kinship* organization of primitive society from the *territorial* organization of civil society. The second was the change in the character of personal relations from *status* to *contract*.

The kinship principle, in Maine's view, was a political organization based on *Patria Potestas* and was the organizing principle to primitive society. Submission to it and membership in it was in terms of kinship statuses. As nations developed, membership (citizenship) became based on territorial boundaries.[2] Kinship, based on the agnatic organization, waned in the larger scene and became smaller and more cognatic (or as we might say today, more *isolated* and *nuclear*).

The distinction between status and contract is more special, but it is not difficult to comprehend. The distinction has to do with individual persons and their rights and obligations to one another. In primitive society these relationships are of familial statuses and are maintained and adjudicated by patriarchal familial authority. Let us use Maine's own words:

> The movement of the progressive societies has been uniform in one respect. Through all its course it has been distinguished by the gradual dissolution of family dependency and the growth of individual obligation in its place. The individual is steadily substituted for the family, as the unit of which civil laws take account. . . . Nor is it difficult to see what is the tie between man and man which replaces by degrees those forms of reciprocity in rights and duties which have their origin in the family. It is contract. (1861:139–141)

Maine made another distinction between the two kinds of societies that anticipated Morgan, but it has failed to capture attention. Morgan spoke of *primitive communism* in a very favorable way and ended his *Ancient Society* with a ringing denunciation of private property that attracted the acute attention of Marx and Engels. But Maine had also

---

[2]Sometimes an objection is made by modern anthropologists that many primitive societies take great cognizance of their territories and defend recognized boundaries (as do many animal species). But this is not Maine's point. He was talking about internal *organizing principles*, and in *relative terms*. Even a firmly territorial group, if it is primitive, is mostly organized—subdivided and joined—in terms of kinship (though not necessarily agnatic kinship).

emphasized that the "Village Community of India," for example, was probably a survival of a widespread stage of ancient society "at once an organized patriarchal society and an assemblage of co-proprietors" (1861:216).[3]

JOHANN J. BACHOFEN

Bachofen's *Das Mutterrecht* appropriately appeared in the same year as Maine's *Ancient Law*, 1861; they were both jurists and scholars of early Indo–European history, but they came to exactly opposite conclusions about the nature of the early family system. Contrary to Maine's idea of *Patria Potestas*, Bachofen argued for a universal primitive stage of "mother-rule," or matriarchy. A considerable number of scattered references to matrilineal inheritance of names among lowly primitive tribes convinced him of this.

The only way to make sense of what to him was so unusual a mode of reckoning kinship was to postulate stages in the evolution of marriage and the family. First there was a stage of *hetaerism*, mere promiscuity. Since under such conditions the father of a child would be unknown, relationship was traced only through mothers, eventually giving them power not only over their own offspring but in the society at large. But marriage and family finally required that the role of males be enlarged, not only economically but also politically, and the rule of men replaced the matriarchate.

JOHN FURGESON McLENNAN

Four years later, McLennan described in his *Primitive Marriage* (1865) a theory of the evolution of the family that also included the stage of matrilineal descent associated with the early period of sexual promiscuity. McLennan, much more than his predecessors, studied the available ethnographic evidence carefully in the belief that data from contemporary primitive peoples would shed light on the early stages of social evolution. The surprisingly widespread evidence of mock bride-capture at weddings interested him above all, and he felt that these ceremonial forms of resistance by the bride's family were survivals of an early stage of actual capture of females.

[3]Maine devoted a whole chapter to this topic in *Ancient Law* (1861:chap. 8) and in 1871 published *Village Communities in the East and West*, carrying on with the theme of communal property versus private property as salient characteristics of primitive versus civil society. Consider how changed subsequent ethnological history would have been if Marx had cherished Maine for this and remained ignorant of Morgan!

Another set of data from widely separated peoples detailed the practice of female infanticide. McLennan reasoned that the earliest, rudest stage of society was also a precarious one in which daughters would be a liability in a mobile hunting society. But *wives* were a necessity: hence the practice of taking women captive from enemy groups because of the local shortage of women. The surprising fact of Tibetan polyandry was also adduced as evidence of this shortage, in this case solved within the group by having several men share a single wife. The fact that some primitive rules of marriage required that wives be acquired from outside the society (as in wife-capture) and others from within the society (as in polyandry) led McLennan to coin two words that have become important concepts in anthropology: *exogamy* for the former rule, *endogamy* for the latter.

As primitive societies became agricultural, less nomadic, and the subsistence less precarious, female infanticide could be abandoned. But this kind of economy increased the significance of property, especially in land, so that its inheritance became important, as did males themselves, who typically were in charge of agricultural work. These points recur in Morgan's *Ancient Society* (1877) and impressed Marx and Engels because of their interest in "materialist" (usually economic) causes of evolution.[4] It may have been such parallels to his own thought that so embittered McLennan and caused him later to attempt to refute aspects of Morgan, especially the uses made of kinship terminology, which he might logically have modified rather than rejected.[5] These arguments are described at some length in later pages.

[4]They were impressed by other aspects of Morgan's work as well, as we noted earlier, especially his description of primitive communism and the economic causes of the origin of the state. These are discussed later.

[5]In 1866, Morgan wrote to Joseph Henry of the Smithsonian Institution, asking him to get on with the publication of *Systems of Consanguinity and Affinity of the Human Family* (1870): "It is absolutely necessary that I should be relieved from it and turn my attention to other matters. For nearly nine years I have given this subject almost my entire time, and it will demand more or less of my time until it is printed. It is also necessary for another reason, that I should be forestalled in some of its conclusions. This has already occurred as to one or two points by McLennan's *Primitive Marriage*" (1960:92).

It is relevant to note that Morgan gives credit to Bachofen's researches on the matrilineal primacy in *Ancient Society* (1877: 297–298) but had not mentioned him in *Systems*. In a friendly letter to Bachofen noting his agreement with him, Morgan wrote, December 25, 1874: "My first notice of your investigations was in Prof. Curtius' *History of Greece*. I there found that you were examining a class of facts closely allied to those upon which I had been for some time engaged. I have now your Mother-right." (Morgan 1877:Editor's note 5, 297).

Numa Denis Fustel de Coulanges

We find that of the few anticipators of some of Morgan's ideas, Fustel de Coulanges should command the most interest, but for some reason he has not done so. He is normally given credit for having used documents and philological evidence with great skill in reconstructing the society of the ancient Mediterranean world. This is to say, as well, that he did not have (or at least did not use) the evidence from the primitive world that might have helped him to reconstruct early times after the fashion of McLennan and Morgan. His reconstruction led to the discovery that the ancient classical world was a world of theocracy in which religion dominated not only politics but every facet of everyday life. We no longer doubt this, but in Fustel de Coulanges's time and in his intellectual circles the usual image of the ancient world was a legacy of the eighteenth-century Age of Reason, of deism, skepticism, and humanism: the classical world was pictured as one of great secular philosophy, with reason and light the dominant factors in the life of the society. Fustel de Coulanges's book, *The Ancient City* (*La cité antique*), made a tremendous stir among classicists when it appeared in 1864 and so convincingly corrected the current view.

For present purposes, it should be emphasized that Fustel de Coulanges raised some very important, but more specific, issues that also claimed Morgan's attention later. In fact, Morgan used *The Ancient City* as one of his sources on the nature of early Roman and Greek social organization, although he failed to understand some fundamental characteristics of kinship as described by Fustel de Coulanges.

First of all, Fustel de Coulanges (1864:126–131) established an ascending order of kinship institutions something like Maine's: families proliferate into the *gens*, which are then allied to one another in the *phratry*, then into *tribe*, and finally into *city*. But this latter *city* was different from a society formed by proliferation of kin groups; it was, significantly, also made by alliance and confederation of unlike groups.[6] It was therefore obliged for a long time to respect the religious and civil independence of its component tribes.

Fustel de Coulanges's discussion of the ancient family and gens is of direct significance to our present enterprise. One of Morgan's greatest mistakes, we shall see, was to equate the Iroquoian clan with the gens

---

[6]*Civitas* and *Urbs*, both translated as *cité* in French, or "city" in English, were not synonymous to the ancients. *Civitas* refers to the religious and political *association*; *Urbs* was the *place* of assembly and the sanctuary of the association (Fustel de Coulanges 1864:134). Both, it should be emphasized, were profoundly religious in character.

of early Greece and Rome. It is difficult to fault him, however, since to him the fundamental similarity was astonishing: they were both large associations of related families (of which we moderns take so little account). Such a resemblance between American Indians and ancient peoples of the classical lands had also excited Lafitau, and it would continue to engage the attention of philosophers from the time of the Enlightenment until today.

But Morgan missed a fundamental difference between the Greco–Roman gens and the clan that he knew in America. In the former, the component families are arranged hierarchically around a central core of a hereditary theocratic priest–chiefship. The various gentes of the tribe are arranged hierarchically around one aristocratic gens. In the Iroquoian clan, however, the families are similar segments, each having equal descent from a common ancestor and equal power within the clan, and the various clans are also equal to one other—constituted "democratically," as Morgan put it. This problem area should be underlined because it not only gave rise to a number of misinterpretations by Morgan's followers of important American Indian societies (most notably Bandelier's report on the Aztec) but also muddled Americanist studies of kinship throughout its history—even affecting interpretations of the origin of the state. The major damage was done when Morgan's interpretation became engraved in Marxist theology, obviously, but it should be emphasized that damage also was done in academic studies not related to Marxism. But more of this later.

There is another very important and interesting point at which Morgan could have learned something that might have corrected another mistaken assumption that was to plague anthropology, in some quarters at least, to this very day. The contending schools of thought about kinship differ in their basic assumptions about the family itself, mainly in the answers they give to two questions: What is *marriage?* (its purpose and function); and What do kinship terms *mean?* (What do they have to do with kinship organization, which varies with different forms of marriage?)

To Morgan, as we shall see more fully in the next chapter, marriage regulated sexual conduct and therefore the continuity of the biological family. To Fustel de Coulanges, however:

> Marriage, then, was obligatory. Its aim was not pleasure; its principal object was not the union of two beings who were pleased with each other, and who wished to go united through the pleasures and the trials of life. The effect of marriage, in the eyes of religion and of the laws, was the union of two beings in the same domestic worship, in order to produce from them a third who would be qualified to continue the worship. (1864:51)

If that is the fundament of marriage, what, then, is *kinship?* What do the terms of relationship signify? Fustel de Coulanges quotes Plato (1864:56) to the effect that "kinship is the community of the same domestic gods." The foundation of kinship was not birth, he argues, but worship (1864:57). If this is so, it may be properly asked, what can such words as *father* and *mother* mean? Fustel de Coulanges's answer is interesting, especially in that at such an early date he took a side of the question that was later to form, wholly independently, a basic criticism of the very assumptions of Morgan's reasoning.

Father, Fustel de Coulanges says (1864:89), was not simply a genealogical term. *Pater*, etymologically in Latin, Greek, and Sanscrit, was a title applied to gods like Jupiter, Neptune, Apollo, Bacchus, Vulcan, and Pluto. None of these was considered a father in the genealogical sense. Indeed, the title *mater* was even applied to such virgin goddesses as Minerva, Diana, and Vesta. Neither paternity nor maternity, in our modern sense, was implied by those words. The users of the old Indo–European languages used *pater* for any man whom they desired to honor: "It contained in itself not the idea of paternity, but that of power, authority, majestic dignity" (1864:90). Begetter was signified by an entirely different word, *genitor* (male), and *genitrix* (female).

SUMMARY

As a preamble to the next two chapters, which attempt to describe both the positive, useful discoveries as well as the mistakes and weaknesses of Lewis H. Morgan's work, it may be well to briefly review the ways in which both aspects were presaged in the 1860s. There was disagreement among Maine, Bachofen, McLennan, and Fustel de Coulanges as to the nature of the earliest society and its form of marriage, the nature of the evolutionary transformations of society (especially from primitive society, or *societas*, to civilization, or *civitas*), and the actual meaning and function of kinship terminology—on which Morgan's whole majestic edifice depended.

Maine and Fustel de Coulanges both accepted as the original basis of society the probability of the marriage of single pairs to form the nuclear family. Then, basing their researches on early Indo–European data, they posited patriarchy as the political ingredient and the gens as the broad kinship-based larger subdivision of primitive society. Bachofen and McLennan, for their part, both saw sexual promiscuity as the earliest matrix out of which marriage and kinship grew; such kinship would be based on matrilineal descent, since particular fathers would be unknown until the later evolutionary advent of monogamy. Mor-

gan, we shall see, unfortunately was drawn to accept the latter view.[7]
At the same time, he found Fustel de Coulanges' materials on the gens
acceptable, and he equated this social form with the clan organization
so common among the American Indians that he knew—a mistake,
but an understandable one.

Morgan was on sounder ground when he posited the nature of property and the social–political–legal nature of *societas* as "primitive
communism" and of *civitas* as based importantly on government,
along with increased commerce and writing. Here he most resembled
Maine (though he did not cite him in this regard).

But it was Morgan's unique contribution to use his discovery of the
vastly different forms of kinship nomenclatures around the world to
buttress his theory of societal evolution. Here lay the most confusing
and complex source of controversy in the whole scheme. None of his
predecessors of the 1860s had his wealth of materials on this subject,
but there were, nevertheless, some interesting thoughts on the meaning of kinship terms. Both Maine and Fustel de Coulanges, while considering only the Indo–European forms, took pains to point out the
legal, cultural–religious, social–political aspects of kinship terms—
that, in other words, distinct *social statuses* were the significances,
not genealogical, biological positions. This was to become the club
that McLennan wielded against Morgan in the 1870s. The problem of
the significance and social function of kinship nomenclatures has been
a feature of such basic theoretical controversies as the above-men-
tioned McLennan–Morgan, and later Rivers–Kroeber, Radcliffe-
Brown–Rivers, Radcliffe-Brown–Kroeber, Malinowshi–Rivers, Malinowski–Radcliffe-Brown, Dumont–Radcliffe-Brown, Murdock–Lévi-
Strauss, and many others of lesser renown.

---

[7]Paradoxically, he carried on a friendly correspondence about it with Bachofen but
had an acrimonious dispute with McLennan. This is pursued in Chapters 2 and 3.

2

The Classificatory
Kinship System

> We devised means that no one should ever be able to know his own child,
> but that all should imagine themselves to be of one family, and should regard
> as brothers and sisters those who were within a certain limit of age; and those
> who were of an elder generation they were to regard as parents and grand-
> parents, and those who were of a younger generation as children and grand-
> children.[1]

Thus did Plato's ideal Republic recognize the essential opposition of
genealogy to the larger society, the conflict of family loyalties with
political unity. One doubts, though, that Plato knew of the actual
existence of that most generalized of kinship nomenclatures, the one
we now call Hawaiian, or generational. The above passage describes it
perfectly, but of course he could easily have imagined it from his well-
developed functional sensitivity to aspects of society and politics. In
this respect the passage succinctly points up a problem that has been
central to the study of primitive kinship: the relationships (or lack of
relationship) of kinship nomenclature to the political and organizational aspects of the wider society.

Knowledge of the existence of the classificatory nomenclatures[2] did
not at first arouse much interest until it was used to challenge current
notions about the origin and evolution of society. As early as the first
century A.D., Nicolaus Damascenus noted this mode of kinship terminology among the Galactophagi (Bachofen 1861:21), but he made nothing more out of it. In a report of travels in Brazil in 1587, Gabriel Soares
de Souza described a classificatory nomenclature, evidently of the

[1]From Plato's *Republic*, quoted with an interesting commentary by Andrew Lang
(1878:22).

[2]We shall accept, as is fairly customary, Morgan's use of the word *classificatory* as a
system which merges in terminology a person's lineal relatives (of the nuclear family,
such as father, mother, brother, sister, son, and daughter) with more distant collateral
relatives in each generation.

13

Tupinambá, in a brief passage (1587:316–317). In 1666 a vocabulary of Island Carib Indians by Raymond Breton revealed a classificatory terminology; and a half-breed Creek Indian wrote about his mother's people (about 1830–1835), describing a sort of "Crow" (classificatory) terminology (Stiggins, n.d.).

But all of the above are merely incidental fragments, which attracted no intellectual attention so far as can be ascertained today. It was Father Joseph Lafitau (1724), a missionary among the Iroquois, who first saw further significance to the classificatory system. He thought, with considerable prescience, that American Indian tribal customs of kinship nomenclature would shed light on the social organization of the "tribes" of the Old Testament (see Lafitau, Appendix A). But still no one related these kinds of data to societal evolution—at least to any important effect—until Lewis H. Morgan's massive assault on the problem in one of the most seminal and original works in all of the history of social science, his *Systems of Consanguinity and Affinity of the Human Family* (1870), and its sequel, the more widely influential *Ancient Society* (1877). (See Appendix B for chronology of Morgan's publications.)

W. H. R. Rivers said of Morgan's work:

> I do not know of any discovery in the whole range of science which can be more certainly put to the credit of one man than that of the classificatory system of relationship by Lewis Morgan. By this I mean, not merely was he the first to point out clearly the existence of this mode of denoting relationship, but it was he who collected the vast mass of material by which the essential characters of the system were demonstrated, and it was he who was the first to recognize the great theoretical importance of his new discovery. (1914b:4–5)

It is certainly true that Morgan "discovered" this system all by himself, obviously unaware of predecessors like Lafitau, and he gave it to anthropology by writing a massive book about its implications. Lafitau was in somewhat the position of Gregor Mendel in genetics, too far ahead of his time. Evidently Andrew Lang (1878) was the first anthropological writer to credit Lafitau with this discovery, though to little avail. Lowie's article "Kinship" in the *Encyclopaedia of the Social Sciences* (1937) does not mention Lafitau, and more curiously, the article in the same *Encyclopaedia*, "Lafitau," by John Cooper, does not mention the discovery of the classificatory system.[3]

Prior to Morgan's publications, the Aristotelian theory of the origin

---

[3]It may be thought rather extraordinary that Morgan did not cover the literature on the Iroquois thoroughly enough to discover Lafitau's work, but it should be pointed out that there were only a very few and inadequate bibliographical resources in Morgan's day (compared to Lowie's and Cooper's).

and evolution of society was almost universally accepted by scientific-
and historically minded intellectuals (but not by Bachofen and McLennan). Succinctly put, this theory held that societies begin with the
family household, a natural unit composed of the father, mother, and
their descendants. The father is the patriarch, the master of the personnel and goods of this embryonic community. In time, his eldest son
succeeds him in a continuing process of succession and proliferation
that leads to the association of families related in the male line and
ruled by the primogenitural descendants of the original patriarch. This
group has been called, variously, the *clan*, the *gens* (Latin), or the *yeros*
(Greek). As the population increases with the generations, the more
distant relatives split off and form new clans, and since they have not
lost the sense of primitive kinship, together they all form a *tribe*. When
this process continues, the next development is to unite related tribes
under a *king*, the purest descendant of the original founding family.
Within all of these stages, however, the "natural" family remains as
the basic building block, united with others by increasingly attenuated
kinship ties (Lang 1878:18).

As more information about the social organization of primitive peoples came to the attention of Euro–American thinkers, a mounting but
piecemeal distrust of some of the elements of the above ideas came
into being. These discoveries were: the classificatory kinship nomenclature; exogamic marriage, incest taboos, and the frequently allied
totemism; evidence of early matrilineal descent (and, some said, a
primordial matriarchate); and, finally, evidence of a political (institutional) and economic basis for the great transformation from primitive
society (*societas*) to civil society (*civitas*) instead of the simple growth
from the patriarchal family through intermediate stages to kingdoms
and nations, which are simply larger and more complex developments.

Morgan's *Ancient Society* (1877), more than any ethnological work
of the last century, presented controversial opinions on all of these
problems, but far more important in the history of his own thought
was his discovery of the classificatory kinship nomenclature. His explanation of this led to his entire scheme of social evolution.

For the first time, with Morgan, ethnological fieldwork and historical data from illiterate primitive peoples were combined with intellectual training and scientific aims toward understanding all of human
society—the uniquely ethnological intellectual mixture. It all began
with Morgan's totally unprecedented thought about primitive kinship
systems. It was an exciting intellectual life that he led after his discovery and, although its significance has become considerably shadowed
in our century, he was honored by the attention of many of the great

figures of his day. Henry Schoolcraft said that he was America's greatest authority on Indians; Henry Adams cited his work as the "foundation of all future American historical scholarship."[4] And, as we shall see in more detail later, prominent European and British intellectuals were interested, among them Karl Marx and Friedrich Engels, who modified their own revolutionary theories in the light of Morgan's researches.

Morgan was born in Aurora, New York, in 1818, took a law degree from Union College in Albany, and settled in Rochester, New York, in 1844 to practice his profession. In those early years Morgan developed a romantic interest in the American Indian so profound that he succeeded in causing a secret fraternity that he had long belonged to ("The Order of the Gordian Knot") to change from a society modeled on a Greek myth into one based on the customs of the Iroquois. In roughly the same years, Morgan also transformed the Rochester branch of the fraternity from a "boyish" group enjoying secret rituals into a more scholarly, intellectual organization devoted to furthering knowledge of Indian customs. And particularly in the 1840s, the society gave legal and economic aid to help defend the Seneca Iroquois (of the nearby Tonawanda reservation) against the Ogden Company of land speculators, which was endeavoring to have them removed to a reservation in the West. Ely Parker, an educated young Seneca, became a close friend of Morgan's during these litigations and Morgan thus had an excellent informant and entrée into the Seneca tribe's confidence. Morgan and his friends, advised by much correspondence with Henry Schoolcraft, pursued their studies of the Indians energetically. Although the fraternity began to break up in 1847, mostly because several members moved to other cities, Morgan continued his own ethnological pursuits and wrote and lectured tirelessly as the "foremost Iroquois authority in the country" (Resek 1960:39). In 1851 he brought his findings together in what was perhaps the first full-length ethnological monograph written about an American Indian society, *The League of the Ho-de-no-sau-nee, or Iroquois,* to be based on firsthand "field" experience (Lafitau's was firsthand but not a full-length description).

It should be noted that there is one particular respect in which Morgan's work was, at this time, deficient from a modern trained ethnologist's point of view. Morgan was enthusiastic about "his" Indians and frequently compared their institutions to classical models, especially those of the Greeks. But at that time he knew nothing of

---

[4]Resek 1960:vii. Unless otherwise noted, the biographical data are from this source.

primitive society in general nor even of other American Indians. This deficiency was noted by Francis Parkman in his review of *The League of the Iroquois*. Morgan's ignorance, Parkman said (1851:424), "leads him to regard as the peculiar distinction of the Iroquois, that which is in fact common to many other tribes." This lack was to be strikingly remedied, at first only accidentally, but eventually by his own arduous field trips to the American West and Canada and a voluminous correspondence with travelers and missionaries in far quarters of the earth.

Morgan's earlier parochialism was modified first when he became an investor in, and one of the directors of, a Rochester-based company called the Iron Mountain Rail Road Company. This project was designed to transport ore from the Iron Mountain Mine in Michigan's upper peninsula to the port town of Marquette on the southern shore of Lake Superior. (The newly opened canal and locks at Sault Sainte Marie connected Lake Superior to Lake Huron and thus to the eastern Great Lakes and the Erie Canal.) Beginning in 1855, Morgan was to make many business trips to Marquette, and from this enterprise he secured a modest fortune that eventually enabled him to devote full time to his kinship studies. But it was the presence of Ojibway Indians near Marquette that was more immediately relevant to his intellectual history.

Meanwhile, also in 1855, Morgan read a paper before "The Club"[5] that detailed what he called "The Laws of Descent of the Iroquois." In it he noted that descent was through the female line, a characteristic that seemed so striking to him that he never got over his preoccupation with it. His other observation was that their political institutions were founded on "family relationships" only: "In fact their celebrated League was but an elaboration of these relationships into a complex, and even stupendous system of civil polity."[6] This was Morgan's main point in the paper, and it was certainly a very important one for those years. For our present purpose, the importance of the paper is that Morgan described the Iroquoian classificatory system, of which the main significance (to him, then) was that it could include the membership of the whole confederacy as one family. In comparing this system with either our civil or canon law, he said in his introductory paragraph, "the collateral lines, with the Iroquois, were finally brought into, and merged in the lineal; while in the other cases, every remove from the common ancestor, separated the collateral lines from the

---

[5]Morgan was a leading spirit in forming a new scholarly club of Rochester intellectuals. Derogators called them "the pundits," and the group adopted the name.

[6]This paper eventually appeared in the *Proceedings* of the American Association for the Advancement of Science for 1857 (1858).

lineal, until after a few generations actual relationship ceased among collaterals." This statement, made in 1855, was essentially the basic distinction he was to draw later (1870) between the "classificatory" and "descriptive" system of kinship terminology. Morgan's object at this time was to present the idea that such domestic institutions (he also called them "primary institutions") have a high degree of permanency; "not even language itself will be found to be more stable than the domestic institutions within certain limits." Because of this stability, Morgan argued, history could in some part be reconstructed and, in particular, a world-wide comparison of such institutions might solve the "great problem of the origin of our Indian races."

There are good reasons for dwelling on this point about the relative stability of these domestic institutions that would make them useful for historical reconstruction, for later on we shall see that he also developed a theory of their changes—their evolution through stages. But in the 1850s he was just beginning to formulate an argument about the nature of kinship and kin terminology that grew out of his deep concern with Iroquois life.

On one of his business visits to Marquette in 1858, Morgan was to have an experience that altered his whole conception of kinship and of the scientific significance of the great dissimilarity between the Iroquoian and Indo–European terminological systems. In Marquette, Morgan became acquainted with a local fur merchant whose wife was an Ojibway Indian. From them and their children Morgan learned that the Ojibway used a system for designating relatives which was fundamentally similar to that of the Iroquois in its classificatory characteristics. Since the two societies represented entirely different language stocks, the system of nomenclature revealed a basic underlying pattern of "primary ideas" much more ancient than the separation of the distinct languages.

On returning to Rochester, Morgan reviewed published sources on the Dakota and the Creek Indians and discovered indications of the classificatory system among them. He was, of course, greatly excited by these evidences, for should it be found that the American Indians as an entire race participated in the same system, perhaps further researches in the rest of the world might discover evidence of ancient relationships of the Indians to foreign races. A particularly likely region would be Eastern Asia, of course. Morgan soon began to send a questionnaire to Indian agents and missionaries, mostly in the western U.S., and to a few persons in Oceania, the Far East, India, and Africa.[7]

---

[7]The foregoing account of Morgan's actions are from White's (1957) article, "How Morgan Came to Write *Systems of Consanguinity and Affinity*."

Perhaps the most succinct rendering of Morgan's reasoning about this problem is in his own letter covering the questionnaire he sent out under a U.S. Congressman's postal frank (intended to lend authority to the letter):

> It has occurred to me, after careful examination of the system of consanguinity and descent of the Iroquois that we may yet be able, by means of it, to solve the question whether our Indians are of Asiatic origin. Language changes its vocabulary and modifies its grammatical structure in the progress of ages, thus eluding the inquiries which philologists have pressed it to answer; but a system of consanguinity, once matured and brought into working operation is in the nature of things, more unchangeable than language; not in the names employed as a vocabulary of relationship, but in the ideas which underlie the system itself. The Indo–European nations have one system identical in its principal features. . . . That of the Iroquois is originally clearly defined, and the reverse of the former. It is at least to be presumed that it has an antiquity coeval. (Resek 1960:74)

Morgan's original "schedules" (questionnaires) comprised more than 200 queries about kinship designations, going so far even as to ask the name of the "daughter of a brother to the son of the son of the son of the brother's sister." The schedules were intended to be self-correcting by having the same kin term elicited in several ways. But it should be noted here—and remembered—that the questionnaire was based on the assumption that the terms were in fact attempts to designate the actual genealogical and conjugal–affinal "natural" relationships; that is, that "father" meant *genitor* rather than *pater* in the sense of Fustel de Coulanges's distinction. Thus was the basic question begged in the very means of collecting the original data.

Not long after receiving encouraging replies to his schedules in 1859, Morgan went on his first of four summer field trips, this time to the tribes settled in Kansas and Nebraska. He counted this trip a great success, for he completed 11 schedules in 11 different languages, and nearly all of them clearly implied the Iroquoian system. Upon his return to Rochester he found more schedules in his mail, and their import was entirely to secure the "unity of the Indian race" with respect to kinship terminologies and therefore, he thought, with respect to historical identity. It remained important now, however, to discover relevant information from the rest of the world, especially Asia.

In August of the same summer Morgan read a paper in Springfield, Massachusetts, before a meeting of the American Association for the Advancement of Science, called "System of Consanguinity of the Red Race, in its Relations to Ethnology" (1859). A few excerpts from that noteworthy paper should point up the quality of Morgan's thought at that most critical time in his intellectual experience.

Morgan first notes that "underneath any scheme or code of relationship we may frame, there lies a numerical system which is universal, and unchangeable. All of the descendants of an original pair stand to each other in certain fixed relations, the nearness or remoteness of which is a mere matter of computation." But how, then, can there be variations in the ways in which various peoples do their computing? This is possible, he averred, because there is an intermingling of "foreign blood" within each generation due to marriage, uniting the blood of both father and mother in a descendant. This involves a possible choice as to whether to calculate descent in the male or female line. Thus the Hebrews decided to calculate descent in the male line, the Iroquois in the female. Both of these are very ancient, and for very good reason:

> "It is . . . an interesting fact that every individual is himself of the centre of the system: the ego, from whom the degree is reckoned, and to whom the relationship returns:—the point around which the circle of kindred revolves. It is my father, my mother, my uncle, my nephew, my grandson. Every one, therefore, is compelled to understand and to use it for himself. Hence, when a system is perfected, and its nomenclature settled, it will from the nature of the case, be very slow to change. There is perhaps, nothing in the whole range of man's absolute necessities so little liable to mutation as his system of relationship." (1859:3)

Morgan's major discovery up to this point is now laid before us: the possible historical significance of the critical differences in types of kinship systems, given their great degree of permanency. The major divergences are, first, the aforementioned choice between a male and female descent line and, second, the difference between the Indo–European system of relationship terminology (later to be called by Morgan the "descriptive" system) and the American Indian system (later to be called the "classificatory" system).

The Indo–European nations share a system "identical in its principal features" (thus attesting to its great antiquity), the characteristic feature being "the existence of a lineal and of collateral lines, the latter of which perpetually diverges from the former . . . [after a few generations] terminating in a total dispersion of blood, and in the loss of the great fact of consanguinity, except as it was preserved by the national tie" (1859:4).

The American Indian system classifies relatives in a form "nearly the reverse of this." Collateral lines do not diverge beyond first cousin, after which (in the grandchild's generation) they are all brought into and merged with the lineal line. Thus the whole tribe remains, for countless generations, founded on consanguinity, and the terminology

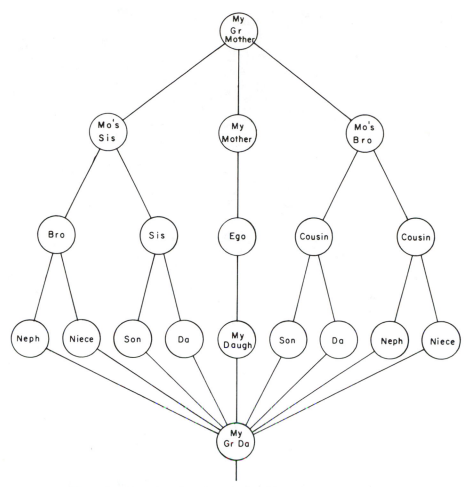

Figure 1. Iroquoian classificatory kinship system, after Morgan.

of consanguinity includes every member. These "primary ideas" are so divergent from the Indo–European that, were they more firmly established as fully coterminous with all American Indians, it would then be possible to find elsewhere the distant relatives of those Indians on some other continent. Figures 1 and 2 illustrate the Iroquoian and Indo–European classificatory kinship systems.

At the end of the manuscript is a brief paragraph, signed in Morgan's handwriting: "Note—The foregoing paper was read just as it stands here before the Association for the Advancement of Science at Springfield in August 1859. Shortly after my return from Springfield I re-

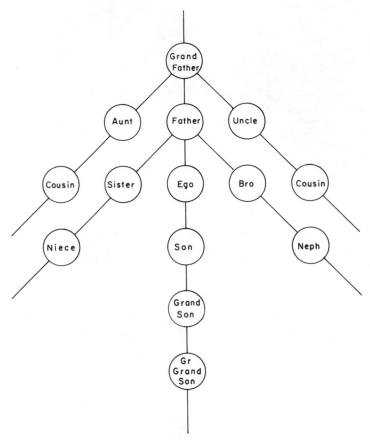

Figure 2. Indo–European classificatory kinship system, after Morgan.

ceived Dr. Scudder's letter and obtained my first clear evidence of the Asiatic origin of the American Indian Race."

Dr. Henry W. Scudder was an American missionary of Arcot, India, who was then visiting in New York. Hearing of him, Morgan had sent him a schedule, and now, as Morgan notes, he had returned it, showing that the Tamil kinship system was identical with the Iroquois. Morgan's excitement was great, expectably, but as he wrote over 20 years later, this greatly changed the scope of the research and the amount of labor still to be accomplished. "It seemed imperative," he said, "to include the entire human family within the scope of the research, and to work out this comprehensive plan as fully as might be possible" (1870:5).

That fall (1859) the Smithsonian Institution agreed to print Morgan's schedules and covering letters on their letterhead, and they also acquired from Lewis Cass, secretary of state, a letter to American diplomats in foreign countries asking their cooperation in circulating the questionnaire.[8] This venture must be considered a success, for some 200 kinship classifications were studied by Morgan in the next four years. Some were gathered on his own summer field trips.

Morgan gave up his law practice completely to devote all of his energies to his massive compilation to be called *Systems of Consanguinity and Affinity of the Human Family.* After three years of labor he sent it to the Smithsonian Institution in 1865. Joseph Henry, the director, could not make sense of it and sent it to the Reverend Joshua McIlvaine, a fellow Pundit member and close friend of Morgan's from Rochester who at the time was teaching ethnology and philology at Princeton. It was this friend who had, a year earlier, suggested in a letter to Morgan that "promiscuous intercourse" may have prevailed in antiquity more extensively than commonly supposed. Now, in trying to help Morgan get the manuscript published, the clergyman pressed Morgan to accept the promiscuity theory of the origin of the classificatory system. Resek (1960:96) points out that McIlvaine felt that Aryan–Semitic society (which had the "descriptive" system) was superior to Asian and tribal societies generally (with their "classificatory system"). To argue that the Aryan–Semitic system was founded on monogamy and the others on promiscuity was simply further evidence of the moral inferiority of the latter. To Morgan's considerable credit, he wrestled with this hypothesis for three years, trying to find better evidence for the classificatory system than the moral superiority argument.

It was finally his fear that McLennan, the Scottish lawyer, would establish priority in the field that pushed Morgan into acceptance of the evolutionary explanation of the kinship systems. McLennan had, as noted earlier, published his *Primitive Marriage* in 1865, and this contained an explanation of the widespread primitive custom of marriage-by-capture. To recapitulate it briefly, the custom of female infanticide in very ancient times had led to polyandry because of the shortage of

---

[8]The questionnaire with the covering letters by Joseph Henry of the Smithsonian and Cass was published as a "Circular in Reference to the Degrees of Relationship Among Different Nations" by the Smithsonian Institution in 1862.

The questionnaire method of acquiring information about Indians was already well established. Jefferson's "Instructions" to Lewis and Clark and Lewis Cass's 64-page "Inquiries," published in 1823, as well as Henry Schoolcraft's questionnaire subsequently, were undoubtedly all well known to Morgan. Morgan's was the first ever to attempt to cover the world, however (Hallowell 1960:40–50).

women, which in turn was supplemented or replaced by marriage-by-capture, itself reinforced by the rule of exogamy. With polyandrous marriage, McLennan argued, blood relationship would be known only through the mother, thus the many evidences of ancient matriliny. (One of the proofs he cited was Morgan's own circular, which showed that Iroquois children did not distinguish their father from their father's brothers.) It is easy to imagine the spur this put to Morgan, particularly since he, not McLennan, was in possession of such an enormous amount of data relating to this very subject.

Morgan finally read his paper, "A Conjectural Solution to the Origin of the Classificatory System of Relationships," before the Academy of Arts and Sciences in Boston in 1867 (published in the Academy's *Proceedings* in 1868). The intellectual success of this venture led to the final acceptance of *Systems*, with a new chapter explaining the evolution of the family via marriage rules and the effect of the successive stages on the systems of relationship nomenclature.[9]

Before further elucidating Morgan's views on kinship systems, it should be repeated that his main aim had been to explain the origin of the classificatory system in terms of family organization, for that was the strange—the unexpected—system in Morgan's experience and to his listeners at the Academy meeting. To most people, including Morgan, our own system, being descriptive, seemed natural, that is, more accurate of genealogy and needing no explanation. But in his talk, Morgan briefly ventured an explanation of how the classificatory system changed to the descriptive. This was a logical requirement of the evolutionary scheme but one which only Morgan recognized. If all of mankind once lived in the tribal state and failed, because of the classificatory system, to distinguish their sons from nephews, and nephews from strangers, "it will be sufficient to remark, that, if such were the fact, the rights of property and the succession to estates would have insured its overthrow. These are the only conceivable agencies sufficiently potent to accomplish so great a change." (This idea, completely novel for its time, received fuller treatment toward the end of *Ancient Society* [1877], and read there by Marx and Engels, conveyed great interest to them, and thus eventually to a great part of the intellectual world.)

While Morgan was on a 14-month tour of Great Britain and Europe in 1870–1871 with his wife and son, his monumental *Systems* was published and soon read by Darwin, McLennan, and Sir John Lubbock

---

[9]Since Joseph Henry so suddenly accepted *Systems* once it had the moral evolution chapter added, it is relevant to note that he had been a colleague of McIlvaine's at Princeton, then a Presybterian theological seminary.

(later to become Lord Avebury). Morgan was kindly received by them and, later, he visited briefly with Maine and Thomas Huxley. All were friendly and appreciative of the uniqueness of the book (although later some were critical, especially McLennan, who, as we shall see, was to attack its very foundations). Maine mostly ignored the book, although he finally dismissed the classificatory system as due to an "imperfection of mental grasp on the part of savages" (1883:290). At this point, it may be well to present a brief account of the huge book's simple explanation of the evolution of the family.

As noted earlier, to Morgan the greatest significance of his findings was the discovery of the fundamental dichotomy between the classificatory and descriptive systems and the fact that, outside the Aryan–Semitic historical sphere, most of the world, especially of primitive peoples, embraced the former. This classificatory system, he found, had various permutations including the important fact that some were more classificatory than others. Thus his first discovery, the system of the Iroquois, was, while widespread in the primitive world, not so fully classifying as some others. These others, which he identified from his schedules as Malayan (also found in Polynesia, and in today's ethnology texts called *Hawaiian* or *generational*), made distinctions among relatives only on the basis of sex and generation. All male relatives in Ego's parental generation were called by the same term as Ego's own father; all female relatives in the parental generation were classed with mother; own generation relatives were undistinguished from brother and sister; all relatives of the next descending generation were classed with son and daughter (recall Plato's scheme in the epigraph to this chapter).

Such a system, Morgan reasoned, must have resulted from an earlier time when marriages (and consequent family types) corresponded to it—just as the descriptive system corresponds to a monogamous marriage and household. If so, any man designated "father" might have married, or did actually marry, any woman Ego calls "mother." Thus the postulated marriage system created what he called the Consanguine Family, whereby brothers as a group intermarried a group of sisters. This postulation makes particularly good sense if it is assumed, as did Morgan and others, that the earliest human groups were simply "promiscuous hordes" without any marriage customs at all. The group marriage, therefore, can be seen as an early stage growing out of promiscuity, on its way toward eventual modern monogamy.

The Iroquoian type of nomenclature is the next most prominent general stage between the extremes of the Malayan type and the descriptive. The gens, or clan, when it is the Iroquoian type known to Morgan, prohibits marriage among its members (practicing "exogamy," in McLennan's phrasing). This "Gonowanian" (or Iroquoian) type, Morgan thought, was characteristic of American Indians (and the Tamil of south India). Because of clan exogamy, which prevents marriage among clan members who would be called "brother" and "sister," the nomenclature has a definitive characteristic: Ego calls mother and all her classificatory sisters by the same term, but her brother (and all his classificatory brothers) are called by a distinctive term (like "uncle"), whereas in the Malayan system, he would be called "father." A similar bifurcation occurs on Ego's father's side: Ego calls him and all his classificatory brothers by the same name, but father's sister (and all classificatory sisters) are not called "mother," as the Malayan system would have it, but by a distinctive term (like "aunt").

Morgan's experience with the Iroquois was crucial because the family form suggested a transition from group marriage. That is, numerous nuclear families forming a lineage related in the female line lived together in a longhouse. Their individual family sleeping cubicles and few possessions suggested an incompletely or recently achieved monogamy, for all those living in the longhouse were "father" and "mother" to Ego, and the people in Ego's generation were "brother" and "sister." The aforementioned "aunts" and "uncles" and their children (Ego's cross-cousins) lived elsewhere. What was more sensible than to regard this as a transitional system between group marriage and monogamy?

Sensible, that is, if one thinks as did Morgan that the system of nomenclature had the express purpose of making a genealogical, or quasi-genealogical, set of identifications. "Father" and "mother" are the crucial terms in this scheme, and all others—those to be "aunts" or "uncles," "brothers" or "sisters," "cousins" and "nephews"—follow from this "primary institution," the family form as related to the marriage rule.

This is only the briefest introduction to Morgan's complexly expressed ideas. In subsequent pages we deal more fully with their final formulation in *Ancient Society* (1877). In that work, Morgan answers criticisms and introduces new materials from Australia—materials at first glance puzzling but very exciting—provided by his first disciple, the Reverend Lorimer Fison.

Fison, educated in classics and theology at Cambridge University, had emigrated from England to Australia to search for gold. After a few unsuccessful years he joined the Wesleyan church and established a missionary school in Fiji in 1864. The arrival of Morgan's circular aroused him intellectually, for he was already aware of, and puzzled by, the peculiarities of the local kinship nomenclature. In 1869, he sent descriptions of the Fijian and Tongan Islanders' social organization that showed great ethnological skill. The material was late, and was included only in the Appendix to *Systems*, but a long and cordial correspondence was begun between Fison and Morgan.[10]

In 1871 Fison returned to New South Wales and began an investigation of the family system of the Kamilaroi tribe. He soon became acquainted with A. W. Howitt, a famous explorer of Australia and at that time the police magistrate for the district of Gippsland. Howitt engaged himself as did Fison, in sending Morgan's schedules to various people in Australia, but the results were so disappointing that the two men increasingly set about gathering data themselves at first hand. Howitt's major interest in Gippsland was the Kurnai tribe, into which he was adopted. Fison and Howitt together finally wrote a monograph, *Kamilaroi and Kurnai, Group Marriage and Relationship, and Marriage by Elopement* (1880), but Morgan had acquired their findings earlier by correspondence, and he was highly intrigued, for it seemed as though he had finally come across remnants of group marriage among people easily judged to be near the bottom of the evolutionary scale. This may have been the primary push after the publication of *Systems* toward the writing of his more general and more thoroughly evolutionary book, *Ancient Society* (1877).[11]

As Morgan finally interpreted the Kamilaroi in *Ancient Society*, he thought there was evidence for the earlier presence of "the family organization on the basis of sex"—groups of brothers holding their wives in common and groups of sisters sharing their husbands—that was in the process of being overridden by the organization of society into gentes consisting of clans with female descent. Morgan assumed that the Kamilaroi kinship system was characteristic of Australia (it was in fact fairly typical in its general features).

The crucial data that seemed to argue for the organization upon sex was the presence of eight named categories of people that Morgan called "marriage classes." They were named as follows:

Male	Female
Ippai	Ippata
Kumbo	Buta
Murri	Mata
Kubbi	Kapota

[10]See Stern (1930) for interesting selections from the letters of Fison and his collaborator, A. W. Howitt, to Morgan.

[11]Another important impetus was Morgan's desire to meet the many criticisms of *Systems* that were appearing. McLennan's criticism of Morgan's kinship terms was the most acrimonious—and the most trenchant. Other criticisms of Morgan's work, such as of his treatment of the classical gens, are noted in Chapter 9.

This is not really an eight-class system, however. Fison, on reading his newly acquired copy of *Ancient Society* in 1878, wrote immediately to Morgan that there were really only four classes, and female affixes were employed when it was desirable to denote the sexual difference: "I am forced to the conclusion that the termination 'tha' [sic] in 'Ipatha' etc. is nothing more than the feminine form of 'Ipai' [sic] and that Ipatha is not a class by herself but a woman of the Ipai class. . . . This does not affect your conclusion" (Stern 1930:269). Fison's note is welcome not only to correct the record but also because it enables us to simplify the discussion to follow.

All of the Ippais are brother and sister to each other, no matter what gens they belong to; likewise with the Kumbos, Murris, and Kubbis. If an Ippai man and an Ippai woman (Ippata) meet "who have never seen each other before, they address each other as brother and sister" (Morgan 1877:52). Since this organization ignores gens membership, which is based on kinship, it is thus "more archaic . . . than any form of society hitherto known" (1877:52).

Each of the four classes can marry into only one of the others,

$$
\begin{array}{lcl}
\text{Ippai (Ippata)} & = & \text{Kubbi (Kapota)} \\
\text{Kumbo (Buta)} & = & \text{Murri (Mata)}
\end{array}
$$

The intermarrying groups address each other as husband and wife (or spouse). Morgan took this to mean that there used to be actual marriages of the whole group of siblings to the other group of siblings and that that was the first step up from promiscuity, an extended form of polygyny and polyandry.

Morgan next notes that children pass into a named class different from either parent. Thus:

$$
\begin{array}{ccc}
\text{Ippai} & = & \text{Kubbi} \\
\text{Murri} & &
\end{array}
$$

$$
\begin{array}{ccc}
\text{Kumbo} & = & \text{Murri} \\
\text{Kubbi} & &
\end{array}
$$

The fact that this system was widespread and seemed to cut across gens (lineage) membership, and that the gens was small and simple compared to the Iroquoian gens probably also reinforced Morgan's idea that the gens was the more recent of the two. Here it may be well to point out that other significances can (and will) be attached to some of the above data. One in particular was noted above which later will have greater relevance. This is Morgan's statement that people may use the class system "who have never seen each other before. . . ." Fison, in the letter cited above, said:

Not only have the four class names been found from West to East across the continent but we have ascertained that their marital rights extend over all the tribes who have them—e.g.—that an Ipai's claim to the class of women who are free to him in his own tribe would be recognized in a tribe 1000 miles distant from his own if he were to visit them even though the languages are as widely apart as is French from English. It is the most astounding system of communism the world has ever known. (Stern 1930:270)

Without debating now, but merely to forecast the possibility of taking a radically different view, we may note that some impressive later ethnologists in Australia have stated that the social context for the use of class nomenclature *is* distinct from the use of kinship (gens) terms. A. R. Radcliffe-Brown has pointed out (1930–1931:436) that the class names are used among strangers when the kinship connection, which is based on individual relationships, is too remote to be traced. In effect, A. P. Elkin (1954:101) also says this, for the spread of the class terms is due to their being a means of "summarizing kinship": they are used at huge intertribal gatherings among strangers "so that mutual behavior can be organized and respected during the time of meeting."

Saying that the class terms "summarize kinship" rather than conflict with it suggests that we take another look at the four "marriage classes" of the Kamilaroi. The simplest as well as the most basic universal components of status and role in family life are generation and sex, as between mother, father, son and daughter, and brother and sister. Those ingredients of the nuclear family are matched by one more: affinal statuses as created by marriage. If the four-class system is in fact a "summary," or the Australian family writ large, then generation (parents' and children's) and affinal status are the two intersecting criteria that form the four compartments (sex being designated by the affixes).

Fison and Howitt did some fantastically good reporting; their data clearly laid the basis for the above interpretation rather than Morgan's. But they had no other guide, and they remained loyal to their friend and teacher, now increasingly beset by critics. In reflecting on his findings, Fison in particular was quite explicit at times with explanations of the class system that now seem not to support Morgan at all— something, understandably enough, he did not see at the time. He says, for example: "The simplest, and probably the earliest, form of class division among the Australian aborigines is the separation of the community into two intermarrying classes, each having a distinctive title, which is taken by every one of its members" (Fison and Howitt 1880:33).

If Fison had only known that such a "moiety" system of affinal halves of a community is very widespread in the primitive world, and at widely varying evolutionary levels, he might have been able to see more easily that this was not related to "group marriage" at all, but was merely a way of objectifying at large a fundamental status differentiation, that of affines. Individual marriages not only bring relatives of the married couple closer but also into a *new kind* of relationship; successive individual marriages between members of the two groups strengthen and exaggerate the affinal status—which of course is reflected in the structured forms of interpersonal behavior, just as are the named status positions reflecting generational and sexual distinctions.

Morgan thought that kinship terms—and the "class" categories that summarize and objectify their major ingredients—were denotative, not of general kinds of social status, but of actual genealogical relationships alone. This simple assumption of the meaning of kinship and class terminology was the cause of his ponderous and complex scheme of marriage systems that was supposed to account for them.[12] But we hasten to remark that although this is a simple idea, to criticize it is to bring up one of the most difficult of philosophical problems, one not agreed upon to this day. It is the semantic problem: the relation of language to reality; more specifically, it has to do with the locus of explanation, where to look for the meaning of kinship terms. Do you find the meaning "in the heads" of the people, and is it in their heads as a simple reflection of something directly perceived? If the answer to

---

[12]An assiduous reader might want to know what the successive forms of the family were that created the "systems of consanguinity" (kinship nomenclatures). They are as follows (Morgan 1877:420–429):

1. The *Consanguine Family*, founded on the intermarriages of brothers and sisters, own and collateral, in a group.
2. The *Punaluan Family*, founded on the intermarriage of several sisters, own and collateral, with each others' husbands, in a group; but the husbands need not be kinsmen. If a group of brothers have wives in common, the wives need not be kin. It is still "group marriage," in either case.
3. The *Syndyasmian* or *Pairing Family*, founded on marriage between single pairs but without exclusive cohabitation.
4. The *Patriarchal Family*, founded on the marriage of one man to several wives.
5. The *Monogamian Family*, founded on the marriage of single pairs with exclusive cohabitation.

The *Consanguine Family* gives rise to the *Malayan System* of consanguinity. The *Punaluan Family* is organized into exogamous gentes giving rise to the *Turanian* and *Gonowanian* (Iroquoian-like) systems.

The gradual movement toward the *Monogamian Family* through stages 3 and 4 (stage 4 is rather exceptional, being found only in pastoral tribes) finally overthrows the classificatory systems in favor of the Aryan, Semitic, and Uralian systems, which are alike descriptively.

this is yes, then all you have to do is ask an informant your genealogical question and he or she probably knows the answer. And this was indeed Morgan's method. We find no instance of his wondering about actual behavior, even among his close confidants, the Seneca Iroquois. Nor, to his mind, would behavior have been relevant.

It would seen that there has been a major misunderstanding of Morgan's position. For example, the main authority on Morgan, Leslie A. White, has said:

> Every society of human beings is divided into social classes or groups, which, with reference to any individual in the society, are designated with kinship terms such as "uncle," "sister," "mother-in-law," etc. One's behavior toward one's fellows varies, depending upon the category of relationship in which the person stands. Since the categories are labeled with kinship terms, a close functional relationship obtains between kinship nomenclature and social organization and behavior. These are the views and postulates upon which a modern school of social anthropology bases much of its work. They were discovered, elucidated and established by Morgan many decades ago.[13] (1948:144)

But Morgan plainly meant that the kinship terms were biological ("consanguineal") and that the only "human"—that is, cultural—intervention was the rules of marriage (moral rules that were "primary ideas"), and it was this and only this that changed the form of the family. To be sure, the arrival of the gens, and finally the inheritance of property, were to influence the marriage rules and thus the form of the consanguineal group, but the labels for the relatives—the kinship nomenclature—had only one purpose and one meaning, to designate *true* blood, "natural" (Morgan's word) relatives, and these were basically parents and children.

Morgan was very clear about this, especially in *Ancient Society*, written when he was aware of the misunderstandings of his nearly unreadable *Systems*. But even before *Ancient Society* he tried to be plain about it ¬eplying to the charge that the classificatory nomenclatures that *Systems* describes are "arbitrary" and "artificial," Morgan says: "The system [in this case the Turanian] itself, as thus explained, is found to be simple and natural instead of an arbitrary and artificial creation of human intelligence" (1875:86).

The above seems to be the first printed reply of Morgan's to a basic criticism made of *Systems*. In this case it concerned Sir John Lubbock's misunderstanding of what Morgan thought kinship systems were all

---

[13]A member of that school, Fred Eggan, quotes this paragraph with approval in an article on Morgan that similarly misunderstands him (Eggan 1960:197). On this and other misunderstandings of Morgan, see Service (1981).

about.[14] But John F. McLennan's later criticism attracted more attention and exasperated Morgan more, so much so that he devoted a 12-page appendix in *Ancient Society* to debating him.

The development of Morgan's thought about the significance of classificatory kinship was not complete until he finally wrote *Ancient Society*. In it he described his full theory of the nature of social evolution, which included not only kinship terminology and forms of marriage but stages of social organization in general and of government, and even the relation of the rise of private property to this complex evolution. The next chapter will be devoted to an analysis of *Ancient Society* by itself.

APPENDIX A

Extract from LaFitau
Moeurs des sauvages Amériquains,
comparées aux moeurs des premiers temps (1724)

Dans les coûtumes des Iroquois, nous trouvons des maniéres de parenté un peu différentes à la vérité de celles de Hébreux et des Chaldéens, mais qui conviennent avec elles en ce point, qu'elles peuvent fonder des équivoques dans les termes, et servir par cet endroit-là même, pour corriger les idées que nous portent à l'esprit ces mêmes termes, quand nous les trouvons dans les Historiens, parce que nous ignorons, et que ces Auteurs ignoroient eux-mêmes comme nous, les sens différens qu'ils avoient chex les peuples, dont ils ont parlé.

Pour rendre ceci sensible par l'application, il faut scavoir que parmi les Iroquois, et parmi les Hurons, tous les enfans d'une Cabane regardent comme leurs meres, toutes les soeurs de leurs meres, et comme leurs oncles, tous les freres de leurs meres: par la même raison, ils donnent le nom de Peres à tous les fréres de leurs péres et de tantes à routes les soeurs de leurs peres. Tous les enfans du côté de la mere et de ses soeurs, du pere et de ses fréres, se regardent entr'eux egalement comme freres et soeurs; mais par rapport aux enfans de leurs oncles et de leurs tantes, c'est-à-dire, des fréres de leurs meres, et des soeurs de leurs péres, ils ne les traitent que sur le pied de cousins, quoiqu'ils soient dans le même degré de parenté, que ceux qu'ils regardent comme leurs fréres et leurs soeurs. Dans la troisiéme génération cela change; les grands oncles et les grandes tantes redeviennent grands-péres et grandes-méres de enfans de ceux qu'ils appelloient neveux et niéces. Cela se continue toûjours ainsi endescendant, selon la même régle.

De cette facon il est facile de concevoir, comment les Chaldéens et les Rois Parthes pouvoient épouser leurs méres, C'est-a-dire, des tantes souvent moins âgées que leurs neveux, au lieu que si c'eût été une nécessité, que les Rois

[14]In *Nature*, March 25, June 3, June 17, and August 19, 1875.

Parthes devinssent les époux de leur propre mere, c'eût été une nécessité que le même personne eût été la mere et l'épouse de tous les Rois Parthes, ce que est contre le bon sens. Il est facile de concevoir comment les Egyptiens et quelques autres peuples pouvoient épouser leurs soeurs, c'est-à-dire, des cousines germaines, ou bien même des parentes dans un degré encore plus éloigné. (Volume II, pp. 243–244)

'Among the customs of the Iroquois, we find systems of kinship which are in truth slightly different from those of the Hebrews and the Chaldeans, but which agree with them in this, that they can create ambiguities in vocabulary, and therefore they can be used to correct the connotations that some terms bring to mind, when we encounter them in historical writings, because we do not know, and neither did the writers, that these terms had different meanings among the people being described.'

'To make this clear by a concrete example, one must know that among the Iroquois, and among the Hurons, all the children in a House [Longhouse] look upon all the sisters of their mothers as their mothers, and all the brothers of their mothers as their uncles: for the same reason, they call Fathers all the brothers of their fathers, and aunts all the sisters of their fathers. All the children on the side of the mother and her sisters, of the father and his brothers, consider each other brothers and sisters; however in relation to the children of their uncles and their aunts, that is, the brothers of their mothers, and the sisters of their fathers, they behave toward them as their cousins only, although these cousins are as closely related to them as are those they regard as their brothers and sisters. At the third generation, things are changed: the great-uncles and great-aunts become again grandfathers and grandmothers of the children of those whom they call nephew and nieces. It is always done in this way generation after generation, according to the same rule.'

'In this manner it is easy to understand how the Chaldeans and the kings of Parthia could marry their mothers, that is, some aunts often younger than their nephews, rather than if it had been required that the kings of Parthia become the husbands of their own mother, it would have been necessary that the same person be the mother and the wife of all the kings of Parthia, which is against common sense. It is easy to understand how the Egyptians and a few other people could marry their sisters, that is, their first cousins, or even less closely related womenfolk.' (translation by Service)

APPENDIX B

Chronology of Morgan's Investigations
and Major Publications on Kinship

1. 1846: First encountered the classificatory system among the Seneca. Published an account of same in *League of the Ho-de-no-sau-nee, or Iroquois* (1851:85–87).
2. 1856: The American Association for the Advancement of Science meeting in Albany "quickened his interest in ethnology."
3. 1857: Prepared "Laws of Descent and Consanguinity of the Iroquois" for the American Association for the Advancement of Science meeting in Montreal.
4. 1858: Discovered that the Ojibway system of terminology was the same as that of the Iroquois.
5. 1859: Read "System of consanguinity of the red race, in its Relation to Ethnology," American Association for the Advancement of Science, 1859.
6. 1860, 1861, 1862: Field trips in quest of kinship nomenclatures.
7. 1868: "A Conjectural Solution to the Origin of the Classificatory System of Relationships." *Proceedings: American Academy of Arts and Sciences* 7:436–477.
8. 1870–1871: *Systems of Consanguinity and Affinity of the Human Family.*
9. 1872: "Australian Kinship, from the Original Memoranda of Rev. Lorimer Fison." *Proceedings: American Academy of Arts and Sciences* 8:412–438.
10. 1877: *Ancient Society.*
11. 1880: "Introduction" to Fison and Howitt's *Kamilaroi and Kurnai.*

3

Morgan's *Ancient Society* (1877)

Beginning with his rather accidental discovery of the classificatory system of kin terminology, Morgan progressed through scholarship, field trips, personal advice (such as that of McIlvaine), and voluminous correspondence to finally erect a logical, unified edifice of theory stemming from that system. In *Ancient Society* (1877), he presented an evolutionary theory, which not only explained the classificatory and descriptive systems and the associated forms of the family but also a sociopolitical scheme of the evolution of social structures, and finally of property and inheritance. Although all these were finally united in Morgan's mind, his critics attacked them piecemeal, and they have taken largely separate trajectories in the history of thought in ethnology.

This is to say that Morgan's ideas about kinship terminology—what it means, what its function is, how or why it takes such different patterns—turned into a rather specialized kind of study and thus can be treated as a particular current in ethnology with its own record of intellectual successes and failures. Similarly, his ideas on the evolution of social structure—of the *societas–civitas* distinction and its related questions on the origin of and nature of the state, and particularly of the nature of the gens—have made a separate record of controversy. The last part of the book, "Growth of the Idea of Property," made the greatest and most lasting impression because it was taken up by Marx and Engels, and thus in our intellectual history a particular pro and con fervency has become associated with it.

In this chapter, Morgan's ideas are presented carefully but with little analysis and no criticism, inasmuch as subsequent chapters detail the arguments and advances successively made over Morgan's beginnings. We shall follow the topics in the order presented in *Ancient Society:* government, family, and property; but Morgan's Part I, dealing with

35

the general scheme of evolution, is left until last in the expectation that it can be more simply presented and more easily comprehended at that point.

GROWTH OF THE IDEA OF GOVERNMENT

Morgan thought that the extreme classificatory system that he called the Malayan demanded the prior "organization of society on the basis of sex." By this he meant that originally, in the lower status of savagery, there was a "community of husbands and wives" as the central principle of the social system (1877:49). This kind of organization—husbands calling one another brother, and wives calling one another sister—was slowly to give way to an organization of exogamous unilineal kin groups, or gentes. Morgan considered the Australian system described by Fison and Howitt to be a striking example of an intermediate stage between the sex classes and the gentes stage. The so-called system of marriage classes, whose membership was not that of unilineal descent but of sex only (he thought), seemed older than and distinct from the smallish, inchoate Australian gentes of unilineal kinship. (The Australian case will be more fully discussed when we deal later in this chapter with Morgan's "Growth of the Idea of the Family.") The gens, however, as a form of social and political organization, was so very widespread in the primitive and ancient classical world that Morgan treated it as a major stage in the development of government and civilization. As he put it:

> The experience of mankind . . . has developed but two plans of government . . . both were definite and systematic organizations of society. The first and most ancient was a *social organization,* founded upon gentes, phratries and tribes. The second and latest in time was a *political organization,* founded upon territory and upon property. . . . The two plans were fundamentally different. One belongs to ancient society, and the other to modern. (1877:60)

Morgan's first and most striking encounter with the gens was during his years of studying the Iroquois. The Iroquoian "clan" (as modern anthropologists call it) was an organization of matrilineally related families, all politically and economically equal to each other. That is, they exhibited (in Morgan's phrase) "liberty, equality, and fraternity"—they were "democratic." This is a crucial aspect of Morgan's view of primitive and ancient society, and one which, as we shall see, involved him in controversies of significance in both anthropological and Marxist thought. Groups of Iroquoian clans, believing themselves to have hived off from a parent clan, constituted a phratry, and several of these taken together constituted a tribe. By dint of much study,

Morgan eventually saw the same thing in Greece and in the Roman *gens, curia,* and *tribe.* The Irish *sept,* the Scottish *clan,* the *phara* of the Albanians, and the Sanskritic *ganas* were likewise similar to the Iroquoian organization, which Morgan finally decided was common to all American Indians as well as many Africans and Asians.

"A gens, therefore, is a body of consanguinei descended from the same common ancestor, distinguished by a gentile name, and bound together by affinities of blood" (1877:61). Further, it is unilineal (therefore including only half of the descendants), counting via the female line only in the "archiac period," and exogamous. And, as noted elsewhere, Morgan thought gentes were all egalitarian ("democratical") in organization, without any state. It may be well to be reminded that Fustel de Coulanges's *The Ancient City* has presented the early Greek, Latin, and Sanskritic organizations as patrilineal (patriarchal), not exogamous, and hierarchical rather than egalitarian.[1] These two opposed characterizations are the first of several important disputes about the nature of primitive social structure, particularly with respect to the gens (or clan).

As noted earlier, one of Morgan's aims in writing *Ancient Society* was to make use of materials he was not aware of when he published *Systems* in 1871 or that had appeared subsequently. Although Bachofen's *Das Mutterrecht* was published in 1861, Morgan does not mention it in *Systems* and evidently did not acquire a copy until 1874, when he began a fruitful correspondence with the Swiss jurist that lasted until the last year of his life.[2] The relationship was one of mutual approval since they had independently come to the same conclusion about social evolution, that the female authority and matrilineality had long preceded patriarchy and patrilineality. Morgan also cites Sir Henry Maine on Celtic gentes and mentions his "brilliant researches" on law and the primacy of the patriarchal family,[3] which he believed he had now refuted (Morgan 1877:305, 428). He also took occasion to incorporate a "Note" in *Ancient Society* to reply at length to McLennan's acrimonious attack on *Systems* that Morgan had read when *An-*

---

[1]Morgan referred to Fustel de Coulanges' work on the religious aspects of the Grecian gens as "admirably treated" (1877:203, 208), but nowhere does he seem aware of the fundamental departure he is making in other crucial respects from Fustel de Coulanges' interpretation. And nowhere in the several commentaries on Morgan's work is this discrepancy noted; not even by Leslie White, who carefully documented Morgan's error in attributing an egalitarian clan to the hierarchical Aztec (see especially White 1940:1–108).

[2]This relationship is detailed in White's long editorial footnote in Morgan (1877:297).

[3]Morgan is presumably referring to *Ancient Law,* but he doesn't cite the work.

cient Society was in press. This is discussed later in the section called
"Growth of the Idea of the Family."

Morgan's idea that the gens represented the first political institution
in human society and that it anticipated the family–household form of
organization was completely novel for its time. The Aristotelian view
of the succession of institutions was accepted almost without exception: that is, that the patriarchal family–household was the first and
primary institution and that larger kin groups, phratries, tribes, and
confederacies were products of continued population growth. To Morgan, the gens was first and the patriarchal family last, completely reversing the Aristotelian scheme. This was probably the most surprising of Morgan's findings about the nature of the gens, but there were
others that also elicited much criticism. It may be well to list them in
summary form at this point, for all were to reappear in important
theoretical contexts over many years.

1. The gens was *exogamic.* So important was this in Morgan's
    thought that it was as though the main function of the gens was
    to break up the ancient, primordial system of group marriage by
    preventing the intermarriage of brothers and sisters.
2. The gens traced descent, and its membership, *unilineally,* and
    the first stage of this was *matrilineal.*
3. The gens was *egalitarian,* with no state-like political base of
    differential political power. Gentile society was a form of *so-
    cietas* rather than *civitas.*
4. The gens was *communistic* with respect to important forms of
    property.

Chapter 9 consists of a full discussion of the subsequent research and
argumentation related to the nature of the basic parts of the social
structure—the descent groups—of primitive society. All of these were
clearly stimulated by or directly related to Morgan's ideas.

GROWTH OF THE IDEA OF THE FAMILY

In this, the third part of *Ancient Society,* Morgan described the evolution of the family and its associated kinds of kinship systems. This
part of the book is much more succinct than Part II, inasmuch as he
had nothing much to add or change from *Systems.* Here we need only
briefly summarize it since it was already discussed in Chapter 2.

1. *Promiscuous Intercourse.* This is the "bottom of the scale—the
lowest conceivable stage of savagery. . . . Ignorant of marriage, and
living probably in a horde, he [ancient man] was not only a savage, but
possessed a feeble intellect and a feebler moral sense" (1877:422).

As evidence for this long-lost condition of lowest savagery, Morgan states that the consanguine family and the Malayan kinship terms logically presuppose an antecedent state of promiscuity. Therefore, the argument rests on the evidence for these latter two institutions.

2. *The Consanguine Family.* This is the first stage of the evolution of the family. As an institution it is based on the morality of restricting original, random promiscuity to sexual intercourse only within the group. The group is formed in the first place by a "compact" on the part of several males to collaborate in subsistence activities and defense. These males also hold their women in common. In time, therefore, the descendants are all consanguineally related. All members of a given generation are "brothers" and "sisters," and the consanguine family is thus based on the intermarriage of brothers and sisters, own and collateral, in a group.

3. *The Malayan System of Consanguinity.* This system (today called generational or Hawaiian) simply segments the society on the basis of generation and sex. All relatives of Ego are grandfather–grandmother, father–mother, brother–sister, son–daughter, grandson–granddaughter.

Such systems exist in the primitive world as well as in Plato's imagination and presumably have long outlasted the family form that brought them about. Because Morgan could conceive of no significance or function of kinship terms other than to denote actual consanguineal and affinal relatives, the Malayan system on his view could have had no other possible origin than group marriage, with the consequent inability of the members to distinguish genealogical relationship other than on the basis of sex and generation.

4. *The Punaluan[4] Custom.* The generalized form of group marriage forming the consanguine family was eventually restricted to marriage of several brothers to each other's wives in a group and similarly of several sisters to each other's husbands in a group. The conception of brother and sister included cousins even to the third degree. The significance of the Punaluan rule was that own brothers and sisters could not marry each other. The reason for this prohibition was that the "evils" of brother–sister sexual relations "could not forever escape human observation" (1877:359).

To Morgan, the best surviving evidence of this marriage rule was the Australian "marriage classes" (specifically the system of the Kamilaroi). The notable characteristic of the classes is that in each gener-

[4]Morgan derived this term from the Hawaiian custom of *punalua*. See below.

ation there are two classes of relatives; the members of one must marry into the other but must not marry into their own. Morgan saw that this prohibited marriage between brothers and sisters and sanctioned it between cousins (actually between what we now call cross-cousins). The Hawaiians did not have the named classes of the Australians but did have a frequently used term of relationship to designate a form of polygamy whereby two or more brothers had wives in common and two or more sisters had husbands in common. Morgan decided that there once must have been a true stage of marriage and associated family form, basing this partly on the evidence—there were the Australian and Hawaiian survivals of it—but also on the following logic: If there had been a state of promiscuity succeeded by group marriage, and if our own monogamous family is the latest stage, then certainly the prohibition of marriage between own brothers and sisters must have been the first and most obvious way to make a moral improvement over undifferentiated group marriage.[5]

5. *Organization into Gentes.* The gentile organization has already been discussed, but the influence of it on kinship terminology and the evolution of the family should be mentioned here. Two of the fundamental rules of the early gens were already evident in the Australian case: the prohibition of marriage between brothers and sisters and descent in the female line. (Morgan thought that descent had to be in the female line because the identity of the actual father would not be known.) With the foundation of the gens thus established—that is, as the germ of a unilineal descent group—"it then required an exercise of intelligence to turn this natural punaluan group into an organization, restricted to these mothers, their children, and descendents in the female line" (1877:366).

6. *The Turanian or Gonowanian[6] System of Consanguinity.* This system of kinship nomenclature is usually found together with gentile organization. Here (1877:367–368) Morgan makes an important point, distinguishing the evolutionary behavior of the nomenclatural system from that of the family. The family is "active," advancing from lower to higher forms as society itself evolves from lower to higher conditions. "Systems of consanguinity, on the contrary, are 'passive'; recording the progress made by the family at long intervals apart, and

---

[5]A great deal of the evidence in Morgan's possession consisted of travelers' tales and missionaries' accounts of "savage promiscuity." Many of the descriptions seem likely to have been related (in terminology and behavior) to the widespread primitive customs of sororate and levirate.

[6]Morgan called this system *Gonowanian* when referring to American Indians, otherwise retaining *Turanian*.

only changing radically when the family has radically changed." This idea is used to explain the lack of correspondence between the system and the actual form of the family. The Hawaiians, for example, have the Malayan (generational) system appropriate for the consanguine family, when they have actually the Punaluan beginnings of the gentile organization. But these beginnings were not yet sufficient to overthrow it.

The Turanian system is a simple modification of the Malayan caused by the exogamic rules of the gentile organization. In the Malayan system, for example, all relatives in my generation are "brother" or "sister" and my brothers' "wives" are also my own. All of the children of these "wives," and of my "sisters," are my "sons" or "daughters." Among the Seneca Indians (always Morgan's favorite illustration), all of my (male ego) brothers' wives remain my own, as above, and their children are also my own "sons" and "daughters," but all of the children of my sisters become "nephews" and "nieces" because, under the law of gentile exogamy, these women cannot be my "wives" (nor "wives" of my "brothers"). With myself a female, the obverse occurs, and the children of my several "brothers" are my "nephews" and "nieces." Every generation is bifurcated in this way by the sexual (descent-line) distinctions—Morgan had discovered what we call today the distinction between cross- and parallel-cousins, the indicative feature of the bifurcate-merging system.

7. *The Syndyasmian[7] Family*. Morgan noted that many of the "more advanced" tribes of the state of savagery had begun to restrain their polygamous tendencies as the husband began to recognize one of a number of his wives as the principal one. Eventually (in the stage of barbarism) the marriage of single pairs was usual and the Syndyasmian family was created. This was not yet the true monogamy of civilization, for the obligations of husband and wife were not strictly observed and, as was characteristic of the American Indians, they were both quite free to divorce and seek new mates. The family form was not yet sufficiently strong nor structured consistently enough to make paternity a certainty and to overthrow the Turanian (Gonowanian) system of consanguinity—only true monogamy was able to do that.

8. *The Patriarchal Family*. This kind of family, historically somewhat evanescent, was associated largely with pastoral life. It consisted of a single male head and "exclusive cohabitation," with only inciden-

[7]Morgan coined this word from the Greek word meaning "to pair" and "adjoining two together".

tal polygamy. This family form was best illustrated by the ancient Hebrews and Latins. This form of society did not create a new system of consanguinity.

9. *The Monogamian Family.* One of the most surprising results of Morgan's scheme was to have monogamy the latest—actually the modern—stage when it had been consistently placed at the very origin of society by the prevailing theories. Morgan believed that the new influence of private property and above all, the establishing of the inheritance of property in the children of its owner, were the principal cause of the need to have greater certainty of the paternity of children. "The growth of the idea of property in the human mind commenced in feebleness and ended in becoming its master passion" (1877:426). (Further discussion of this point is reserved for a later section.)

The descriptive system of consanguinity, the main indicator of which is the separation of each line of descent from its ever-renewing collateral lines, was the final adjustment of the family to the monogamian form of marriage and the individual possession and inheritance of property. The Aryan, Semitic, and Uralian systems are very similar and all grow naturally out of this kind of family and its property. The system seemed descriptive to Morgan because "it expresses, and must by necessity express, the actual facts of consanguinity as they appeared to the common mind when the system was formed" (1877:427).

GROWTH OF THE IDEA OF PROPERTY

Part IV of *Ancient Society* is brief, consisting of only 23 pages on "The Three Rules of Inheritance." Nevertheless, its place at the very end of the book gives Morgan's idea about property such prominence that some comment should have resulted. As has been noted, Morgan thought of the significance of individual property in breaking up primitive social organization as early as 1855 in a speech to the Pundits; he again addressed the subject in 1867 when he read his paper, "A Conjectural Solution to the Origin of Classificatory System of Relationships" (published in 1868). It is a remarkable paradox that Morgan's idea, which was to have such a great influence on Marx and Engels and through them on the whole intellectual world, seems to have made no impression whatever prior to 1884 when Engels published his discussion of it in *The Origin of the Family, Private Property and the State.*

As Engels stressed in this book, "Morgan in his own way had discovered afresh in America the materialist conception of history discovered by Marx forty years ago, and in his comparison of barbarism and civilization it had led him, in the main points, to the same conclusions as Marx" (1884:5). But of all reviews of *Ancient Society* known to me and of all the comments made by famous scholars,[8] only one, Frank Leslie's *Illustrated Newspaper* (July 27, 1878), commented even briefly on Morgan's emphasis on the relation of property to modern civilization. It is especially puzzling because the idea was summed up resoundingly near the end of the book. The paragraph is worth quoting in full:

> Since the advent of civilization, the outgrowth of property has been so immense, its forms so diversified, its uses so expanding and its management so intelligent in the interests of its owners, that it has become, on the part of the people, an unmanageable power. The human mind stands bewildered in the presence of its own creation. The time will come, nevertheless, when human intelligence will rise to the mastery over property, and define the relations of the state to the property it protects, as well as the obligations and the limits of the rights of its owners. The interests of society are paramount to individual interests, and the two must be brought into just and harmonious relations. A mere property career is not the final destiny of mankind, if progress is to be the law of the future as it has been of the past. The time which has passed away since civilization began is but a fragment of the past duration of man's existence; and but a fragment of the ages yet to come. The dissolution of society bids fair to become the termination of a career of which property is the end and aim; because such a career contains the elements of self-destruction. Democracy in government, brotherhood in society, equality in rights and privileges, and universal education, foreshadow the next higher plane of society to which experience, intelligence and knowledge are steadily tending. It will be a revival, in a higher form, of the liberty, equality, and fraternity of the ancient gentes. (1877:467)

This is undoubtedly the most frequently quoted statement Morgan ever made. It, more than any other passage, influenced Marx and Engels to believe that Morgan had not only discovered a materialist conception of history but was also forecasting a future socialist utopia on the basis of a scientific evolutionism.[9] One important feature of that evolutionism was the exciting news (to Marx and Engels) that by far the greatest part of human history, everywhere, was spent in commu-

[8]Such as Henry Adams, Spencer, Darwin, J. W. Powell, McLennan, Bachofen, Lubbock, Tylor, and Maine.

[9]Eleanor Leacock, in the introduction to Part I of her annotated edition of *Ancient Society*, points up the problem of attributing "materialism" to Morgan (because he talks so heatedly of the evils of property) in this way: "That the causes of our difficulties lies not in the nature of man, but in our social commitment to property, is the profoundly important message. However, to say no more than that human intelligence will rise to the mastery over property, since 'experience, intelligence and knowledge are steadily tending' toward full democracy and brotherhood, begs the question: What are the realities of historical process that enable, or even impel, mankind to move from where he is to where he can or wants to be?" (1963:I:viii).

nistic forms of social order: that the private property aspect of civilization was only localized and evanescent, not a major stage of social
evolution at all. It is appropriate that we should now turn to a fuller
consideration of Morgan's evolutionary theory.

MORGAN'S THEORY OF EVOLUTION

It should be noted, perhaps even strongly emphasized, that in its first
version Morgan's grand synthesis, *Systems*, was not an evolutionary
treatise. During all the time he was collecting data and working out his
ideas with such voluminous correspondence, his aim in its broadest
import consisted solely of amassing proof that the American Indians
had originally come from Asia, as was demonstrated by the similarity
in the two regions of the "systems of consanguinity." This reasoning
assumed resistance of the systems to any kind of change and thus was
fundamental to the logic of his investigation into the provenience of
the American Indian. In other words, Morgan was not originally an
evolutionist or even a functionalist with respect to such social institutions.

The manuscript of *Systems* as sent to the Smithsonian in 1865 was
incomprehensible to Joseph Henry, the director. He expressed his
doubts to Morgan's friend, the Reverend Joshua McIlvaine, who was
then teaching at Princeton. McIlvaine knew Morgan's work thoroughly and had discerned a greater significance for it than the matter of
the Asian–American historical tie. That significance began with Morgan's discovery that there were two polar kinds of kinship systems in
the world, the classificatory and the descriptive, the latter being the
"unifying principle" for the Indo–European and Semitic nations, the
former for all the rest of the world—including (significantly for McIlvaine) primitive peoples such as the American Indians. Why should
one part of the world distinguish between the offspring of several
brothers or sisters and the other part of the world not? This might be a
vastly important question and Morgan, although the discoverer of the
dichotomy, had not really addressed himself to it.

McIlvaine's role in changing Morgan's ideas was described in his
own words in his address at Morgan's funeral:

> During all these years, he had not the least conception of any process of
> thought in which [the classificatory system] could have originated, or of any-
> thing which could have caused it so universally to prevail. He treated it as
> something which must throw great light upon pre-historic man, but what light
> he had not discovered. Before the work was finished, however, he obtained
> [from McIlvaine] and adopted a hypothesis which, vigorously applied to its

peculiarities, he found would account for, explain, and render them all intelligible. . . . The reason why people called those their fathers who would not be their fathers now, was because they either were their fathers or were undistinguishable from their fathers, by reason of a common cohabitation with their mothers. . . . The reason why they called them their brothers and sisters who would not be such now, was, either because they actually were such, or were undistinguishable from them by reason of the common cohabitation of their parents with each other. And so of all the other relationships of the system.

The adoption of this explanation of the vast body of facts which he had gathered, worked a complete revolution in the mind of our friend.[10]

Since philologists had for a long time agreed that words and grammatical forms would outlive the functional conditions that had originally brought them about, McIlvaine had proposed to Morgan that the strange-seeming classificatory kinship systems were survivals of earlier forms of marriage and family. The question then became: What was the original state of affairs and what were the stages in the evolution of the family that would explain the variety of unexpected systems of consanguinity?

Resek (1960:94) points out that anthropological literature contains a controversy over McIlvaine's influence on Morgan, particularly in regard to the evolutionary theory. Bernhard J. Stern, in the first biography of Morgan, *Lewis H. Morgan, Social Evolutionist* (1931), pictures the clergyman as influencing Morgan *against* Darwinism (1931:22–29). L. A. White disputes this vigorously in his article "Morgan's Attitude toward Religion and Science" (1944), denying the influence of McIlvaine and his religion and proclaiming Morgan a Darwinist. Resek says that "both authors misconstrued the relationship between the two, which was extremely fruitful" (1960:94). Resek is plainly right about McIlvaine's influence. Moreover, Morgan did not begin his study as an evolutionist; the ideas he borrowed from McIlvaine were not Darwinist, and the result was a peculiar mélange that defies classification as either anti- or pro-Darwinist.

Actually, the influence of philology as a model for cultural evolutionary theory was probably always much greater than biology—even after Darwin's publications. Combined with Lyell's enormous influence in geology after 1830, comparative philology provided a widely acceptable, uncontroversial model for social or cultural evolution. As we saw above, it was McIlvaine's philology that was the direct basis for

[10]Resek (1960:95). This statement is overly modest, for McIlvaine had been to considerable pains to get Morgan to see this—as Morgan acknowledges in a letter to Joseph Henry of the Smithsonian. At that time neither McIlvaine nor Morgan had knowledge of Bachofen's *Das Mutterrecht*, which also proposed original promiscuity.

the explanation of differing systems of consanguinity (which consisted, after all, of words), and as we saw earlier, Fustel de Coulanges's
influential *The Ancient City* was constructed out of comparative philology. J. W. Burrow says in his history of Victorian social theory that
"the overall impression one received is that the subjects which combine to form modern anthropology owed more, methodologically, to
geology and comparative philology than to evolutionary biology"
(1966:110).

McIlvaine's evolutionary scheme that Morgan borrowed was not
concerned with natural selection, nor structural adaptation, nor with
functional interrelationships; it was, along with the philological methodology, simply moralistic, mentalistic, and racist. The Aryan and
Semitic language–races, with whom the descriptive system was associated, were morally superior to all the others of the world. These
others not only lacked the Judeo–Christian heritage but also, naturally
enough, lacked the monogamous family and the associated sexual–
moral code. The clergyman was not a Darwinist in still another sense;
for example, after reading *The Descent of Man*, he wrote Morgan:
"Man has come up from a low state and there is a splendid future
before him. But he never came from the beast."

It is evident from the correspondence between Morgan and McIlvaine (Resek 1960:96) that, although Morgan did not accept the
Darwinian conception, he still was not such a fervent believer in
"Christ the Redeemer" as his friend would have liked. His goals and
beliefs were much those of the natural sciences and philology of his
day: beyond that he seems to have conformed to the prevalent deism.
The most significant aspect of Protestant Christianity shared by the
two men was their stern morality, which they naturally attributed to
Judeo–Christian traditions.

Morgan thought about McIlvaine's theory of promiscuity as the
cause of the classificatory system for three years and then rather hur-
riedly wrote his 1868 paper, "A Conjectural Solution to the Origin of
the Classificatory System of Relationships," which detailed the stages
of marriage and family that caused the systems of consanguinity. It
should be of interest that not only was this a response to McLennan's
threat of priority on certain points but it was also an attempt to redo
the manuscript of *Systems* to make it more suitable to the Smithsonian.[11]

[11]Joseph Henry still held back the manuscript. His comment to Morgan should arouse
the sympathetic interest of any modern anthropology student who attempts to master
the tome: "The first impression of one who has been engaged in physical research is that,
in proportion to the conclusions arrived at, the quantity of your material is very large"
(Resek 1960:96–97).

After the appearance of *Systems* in 1871, Morgan became gradually immersed in the writing of *Ancient Society* and was able to think out more completely a scheme of evolution and attempt to present it as a coherent whole. He was impressed with Darwin's natural history work (and, as was noted earlier, had visited him to pay his earnest respects), but he was not really a Darwinist with respect to human social evolution. Today, we accord to Darwin and thus "Darwinism" the theory of natural selection and adaptation.[12] In Darwin's own day, however, much more excitement was caused by his idea of man's kinship with other animals and perhaps above all (certainly among religious Christians of the time) by the idea of *evolution* itself—*ascent* from low to high estate as opposed to the "degradation theory" that primitive peoples had fallen from a state of grace.

Morgan, it is apparent from his writings, accepted evolution only in this very general sense of progress from low beginnings to higher states of technology, thought, morality, and so on. As he once correctly pointed out, *human* evolution through stages of savagery and barbarism to civilization was a conception as old as Horace and Lucretius. But he did not believe in man's kinship with the animals. Man was divinely created although he had to evolve his mind and institutions from "extreme rudeness."[13] It may seem amazing that Morgan held to a conception of such extreme savagery as exhibited by a stage of "original promiscuity" and yet did not conceive of this as suggestive of kinship to the apes. But Morgan was part of an eighteenth- and nineteenth-century intellectual rationalism that understood and accepted human material progress and social reform (two different things) but not a full-scaled evolutionism of the Darwinian sort that encompassed all animal species, including human beings. Morgan's evolutionism, if it deserved that name, was very limited and not at all original. His most truly original contribution was his suggestion of the role of private property in destroying the classificatory kinship system, but this was not an aspect of his evolutionary theory. In fact, as we shall see shortly, it could be considered antievolutionary.

Morgan sometimes asserts that God was behind it all. For example, the final sentence of *Ancient Society* states, with respect to our primi-

---

[12]To be sure, a few times in *Ancient Society* Morgan used the popular Darwinisms "natural selection" and "struggle for existence," but not in the Darwinian sense by which the fittest obliterated or replaced the less fit. Morgan did not use "natural selection" in connection with a mechanism or explanation of evolution at all, except in the sense that good ideas were likely to take precedence over bad ones because of human judgment (but more on this later). His uses of "struggle" served merely to emphasize that times were hard for early man—he had "rude beginnings."

[13]This view is most fully expressed in *The American Beaver and His Works* (1868).

tive ancestors, that "their labors, their trials and their successes were a part of the plan of the Supreme Intelligence to develop a barbarian out of a savage, and a civilized man out of this barbarian" (1877:468). But with such obligatory statements of his times and status out of the way, Morgan records other kinds of conclusions about the evolution toward civilization. They are quite contradictory and only a few will be cited now in order to emphasize the futility of trying to find orderliness in his theory by extracting statements from his own context. More care is required.

Frequently Morgan makes "racist" or biologistic explanations of cultural advance. For example, in the final paragraph of *Ancient Society* (in the same paragraph as the above sentence about the "plan of the Supreme Intelligence") we read: "The Aryan family represents the central stream of human progress, because it produced the highest type of mankind, and because it has proved its intrinsic superiority by gradually assuming the control of the earth."

But sometimes the racism is countered by the "psychic unity" argument so frequently used by cultural evolutionists. Again near the end of the book, Morgan says:

> With one principle of intelligence and one physical form, in virtue of a common origin, the results of human experience have been substantially the same in all time and areas in the same ethnical status. . . . A common principle of intelligence meets us in the savage, in the barbarian, and in civilized man. (1877:467)

But this is said only in order to combat the polygenesis theory of man's origins.

Sometimes Morgan sounds like the arch-materialist, even technological determinist, that Marx and Engels and others since have found in him. This was particularly due to his statements about the role of property and his tendency to demark ethnical periods in terms of technological events. Here again we may quote from the final paragraph of *Ancient Society* (because this locus suggests care, emphasis, and finality):

> The hindrances that held mankind in savagery were great, and surmounted with difficulty. After reaching the Middle Status of barbarism, civilization hung in the balance while barbarians were feeling their way, by experiments with the native metals, toward the process of smelting iron ore. Until iron and its uses were known, civilization was impossible. (1877:468)

But most of his statements emphasize mentality, as in the case of the "great fermentation of the human mind which ushered in civilization" (1877:390). This kind of causality is prominently displayed in the titles to several of the parts of *Ancient Society:* "Growth of the Idea of Government"; "Growth of the Idea of the Family"; "Growth of the Idea of Property."

Morgan himself offers us some guidance through this maze early in the book with the idea that there are two kinds of evolution:

> As we re-ascend along the several lines of progress toward the primitive ages of mankind and eliminate one after the other, in the order in which they appeared, inventions and discoveries on the one hand, and institutions on the other, we are enabled to perceive that the former stand to each other in progressive, and the latter in unfolding relations. While the former class have had a connection, more or less direct, the latter have been developed from a few primary germs of thought. Modern institutions plant their roots in the period of barbarism, into which their germs were transmitted from the previous period of savagery. They have had a lineal descent through the ages, with the streams of the blood, as well as a logical development. (1877:12)

The very organization of *Ancient Society* testifies to Morgan's thoroughgoing allegiance to this dichotomized scheme of evolution. Part I deals with inventions and discoveries in relation to his seven "ethnical periods" (Savagery, divided into Lower, Middle and Upper Status; Barbarism, similarly subdivided; and Civilization). Parts II, III, and IV are concerned with the growth of the ideas of the institutions of government, family, and property.

On the face of it, it would appear that Morgan is a materialistic determinist when he deals with inventions and discoveries and accords them such significance in marking the ethnical periods. However, he seems mentalistic when he discusses the unfolding of institutions in terms of the development of intelligence. That is, Morgan sometimes gave a mentalistic account of social evolution and sometimes a seemingly materialistic account of another aspect of evolution. But an important question remains about the relation of the two, for then some indication of the causal priority of one over the other ought logically to appear. Does intelligence cause not only the unfolding of social institutions but also the cumulative growth of inventions and discoveries? Or, possibly, is the sequence the opposite?

With respect to "mind," "brain," and "intelligence," Morgan was a Lamarckian evolutionist; he clearly believed in the inheritance of brain size and intelligence that were acquired through use, a not unusual idea in his day. He says (1877:38), speaking of the lowest condition of savagery, that "with the production of inventions and discoveries, and with the growth of institutions, the human mind necessarily grew and expanded; and we are led to recognize a gradual enlargement of the brain itself, particularly of the cerebral portion."

The mind, or intelligence, was to Morgan also related to the rise of morality. He says:

> The inferiority of savage man in the mental and moral scale, undeveloped, inexperienced, and held down by his low animal appetites and passions, though reluctantly recognized, is, nevertheless, substantially demonstrated by the remains of ancient art in flint stone and bone implements, by his cave life in certain areas, and by his osteological remains. (1877:42)

In this linking of morality with the brain, Morgan goes on to say:

> In the light of these facts some of the excrescences of modern civilization, such as Mormonism [i.e., polygyny], are seen to be relics of the old savagism not yet eradicated from the human brain. We have the same brain, perpetuated by reproduction, which worked in the skulls of barbarians and savages in by-gone ages; and it has come down to us ladened and saturated with the thoughts, aspirations, and passions with which it was busied through the intermediate periods. It is the same brain grown older and larger with the experience of the ages. (1877:58–59)

Morgan's ideas about the mentalistic or intellectualistic causes of the evolution of institutions was expressed again and again, and in prominent places, such as the final, or summary, paragraphs of his major parts and chapters. And, as in the following example, he never locates the causes in some outside interrelationship:

> Out of a few germs of thought, conceived in the early ages, have been evolved all of the principal institutions of mankind. . . . The evolution of these germs of thought *has been guided by a natural logic which formed an essential attribute of the brain itself.* So unerringly has this principle performed its functions in all conditions of experience, and in all periods of time, that its results are uniform, coherent and traceable in their courses. . . . The mental history of the human race, which is revealed in institutions, inventions, and discoveries, is presumptively the history of a single species. (1877:59; emphasis added)

In Morgan's day, the controversy about the evident differences among the several races of mankind was largely concerned with the question of monogenesis or polygenesis. Was mankind one or several? A strict and literal interpretation of the Bible, especially in America, was the favorite ammunition of the monogenesists. Morgan was so diligent in making his statements so often (and sometimes so irrelevantly) about mankind's being "one in origin" because he obviously felt strongly about this argument—as did his friend and moral preceptor, the Reverend Joshua McIlvaine. It seems plain that this is the reason for those statements rather than an argument favoring unity or racial equality. In fact, Morgan was a Negrophobe, and expressed his sentiments in strong terms (Resek 1960:63).

It seems evident that Morgan was not a materialist, relating the evolution of institutions to the influence of processes of technology or economy outside the institution itself. Nor was he even a functionalist, for he did not relate the evolution of institutions to *anything* outside the human mind. To be sure, he related "systems of consanguinity" to forms of marriage and the family, but the latter arose from "germs of thought," ascending intellectually to greater moral heights: the "systems" were merely the words used to designate the members of the family. They were not two separate processes or institutions but two aspects of the same institution. The more usual case made for Morgan's functionalism and materialism comes from the frequently cited statement that the rise of private property brought about the state and civilization. This is an erroneous interpretation of Morgan. It evidently stems from the statements (cited earlier) by Engels, statements since repeated so frequently that they have achieved the status of received truth.[14]

The rise of the state—political society, *civitas*—was not caused by or even related to the rise of property. All of the above were institutions that were developments out of gentile society, contained in the original germ-idea of government. Morgan said this very clearly in discussing the rise of political society in Rome:

> Mankind owes a debt of gratitude to their savage ancestors for devising an institution [gentile society] able to carry the advancing portion of the human race out of savagery into barbarism, and through the successive stages of the latter into civilization. It also accumulated by experience the intelligence and knowledge necessary to devise political society while the institution yet remained. . . . Out of the ancient council of chiefs came the modern senate; out of the ancient assembly of the people came the modern representative assembly, the two together constituting the modern legislature; out of the ancient general military commander came the modern chief magistrate, whether a feudal or constitutional king, an emperor or a president, the latter being the natural and logical result; and out of the ancient *custos urbis*, by a circuitous derivation, came the Roman praetor and the modern judge. Equal rights and privileges, personal freedom and the cardinal principles of democracy were also inherited from the gentes. (1877:290–291)

The evolution of government was thus a self-contained evolution, onward and upward toward a greater democratic destiny. It was a flowering, or "unfolding," of the potentialities of the human mind, uncaused by outside influences of a materialistic or any other sort.

[14]A modern Marxist, Emmanuel Terray, in a chapter titled "Morgan and Contemporary Anthropology" (1972:9–92), argues that the greatest significance of Morgan's thought is not so much his "Darwinistic evolution [*sic*]," nor his "structuralism" [somehow discerned by Lévi-Strauss], but his "materialist conception of history."

Materialism does enter the picture, but in a manner that can only be called disruptive, or devolutionary. Morgan says, continuing the above discussion:

> When property had become created in masses, and its influence and power began to be felt in society, slavery came in; an institution violative of all these principles, but sustained by the selfish and delusive consideration that the person made a slave was a stranger in blood and a captive enemy. With property also came in gradually the principle of aristocracy, striving for the creation of privileged classes. The element of property, which has controlled society to a great extent during the comparatively short period of civilization, has given mankind despotism, imperialism, monarchy, privileged classes, and finally representative democracy. It has also made the career of the civilized nations essentially a property-making career. But when the intelligence of mankind rises to the height of the great question of the abstract rights of property,— including the relations of property to the state as well as the rights of persons to property,—a modification of the present order of things may be expected. (1877:291)

Morgan's closest approximation to a materialist statement that would relate property and population increases to the origin of the state occurs in his discussion of the arrival of *civitas* in Greece and Rome, replacing the ancient gens, but even this statement is also mentalistic in its suggestion of the locus of the causality:

> The growth of property, now becoming a commanding element, and the increase in numbers gathered in walled cities were slowly demonstrating the necessity for the second great plan of government—the political. The old gentile system was becoming incapable of meeting the requirements of society as it approached civilization. Glimpses of a state, founded upon territory and property, were breaking upon the Grecian and Roman minds before which gentes and tribes were to disappear. To enter upon the second plan of government, it was necessary to supersede the gentes by townships and city wards— the gentile by a territorial system. The going down of the gentes and the uprising of organized townships mark the dividing line, pretty nearly, between the barbarian and the civilized worlds—between ancient and civilized society. (1877:131–132)

The several quotations from Morgan are not offered as proof of any interpretation of Morgan's basic theory of evolution, but they do aptly illustrate ideas that he advanced repeatedly. The proof is not readily at hand; it can be found convincingly only in an attentive reading of the whole body of Morgan's work (instead of a piecemeal searching for odds and ends of statements to support a preconception, dogma, or polemical formula). His simultaneous intellectual debts to the British and French Enlightenment philosophers, however indirectly, and to McIlvaine directly (*Ancient Society* is dedicated to him) are so obvious that it defies belief that there have been debates about Morgan's "materialism" or "functionalism," his "Darwinism," or about his debts (or lack of debts) to McIlvaine.

It now seems fair to say that the greatest intellectual significance of Morgan's "Growth of the Idea of Property"—to Marxists or to anyone—derives from his argument that the dominance of private property in society was only a temporary and discordant phase in moral–social evolution. Certainly he was correct in attributing "communism" to such gentile societies as the Iroquois (though not to all the societies he mentioned). And, of course, Marxists, and others, were pleased to find in *Ancient Society* the denunciations of the evil role of property. John Wesley Powell, a prominent anthropological contemporary of Morgan's, paraphrased the main message of *Ancient Society* as meaning that European-style private property and its associated system of aristocracy and blatant privilege were "pathological conditions of the body political" and that "government by the people reflected the normal condition of mankind."[15]

THE SIGNIFICANCE OF *ANCIENT SOCIETY*

Morgan's work, in its various aspects, did not survive unopposed and unaltered in anthropology, although certain ideas—particularly the brief discussion about the role of private property—were maintained in Marxist philosophy. But *Ancient Society* aroused a remarkable amount of interest in many disparate quarters, and it may justly be stated that it is the most influential work in the history of ethnology—if only for its catalytic effects.

The controversies aroused by *Ancient Society* may be conveniently reviewed under the categories according to which they have already been discussed: (1) *kinship terminology* (the discussion of the classificatory system initiated in Chapter 2 of this volume); (2) *social structure* (or the discussion of the "Growth of the Idea of Government"); (3) *property and the origin of civil society* (or the "Growth of the Idea of Property"); and finally (4) the *general theory of evolution*. The criticism, rebuttals, and new ideas and researches on social organization down through the anthropological generations have tended to conform closely to the above separation of the different aspects of Morgan's thought.

1.   Several related questions and lines of inquiry about kinship terminology have developed out of the problem brought up by Morgan. A

---

[15]Powell 1880:121. Morgan approved of Powell's remarks in a letter to him (n.d.; cited in Resek 1960:Footnote 19).

basic one has been the question: What are kinship terms? Closely related to this are questions like: What is the function or purpose of kinship terms? What are they functionally related to in the society? To social structure? To ideology? To language? Are they systematically interconnected, and do they evolve as systems?

2.   The problems of Morgan's ideas about social structure—in particular, the evolution of the family—also have been reduced to a few related questions: Was the ancient gens of the classical world similar to the Iroquoian clan? Was it matrilineally organized in its earlier manifestations? Was it communistic in organization? These, too, have continued to provide not only fuel for controversy but also productive lines of research.

3.   The role of property in relation to the origin of the state and civil society has not excited anthropology; "Boasian anthropology" in the United States and "social anthropology" in Great Britain and Europe did not address themselves to this matter very directly. Yet it was to become a very important subject of debate between Marxists and anti-Marxists. Its influence in modern cultural anthropology derives from the influence of that controversy.

4.   Similarly, Morgan and anti-Morgan theories of evolution did not engage anthropology on either side of the Atlantic until about the middle of the twentieth century. Outside academic anthropology, however, Marxism and those counterpoised against Marxism preserved the kernel of the argument; they seemingly were the catalytic agents of the few anthropological proponents of cultural evolutionism, such as Childe, Steward, and White. But questions about the nature of cultural evolution inspired by Morgan are the broadest, as well as the most deeply significant, of any of the questions listed above. Yet they are, or at least should be, dependent in some part upon the way all of these above questions are addressed or answered. For these reasons, it seems fitting that the book should close on this topic, better enabling us to see subsumed and somewhat summarized all of the foregoing.

II

KINSHIP TERMINOLOGY

The first major controversy over kinship was concerned with the question of whether kinship terms were biological (genealogical) or social (artificially contrived). Within the latter category controversies subsequently arose over whether different kinds of kinship terminologies were caused by different cultural mentalities (or "social psychologies") or by varying principles of social organization. Still later the question arose as to what specifically these principles were.

The most imposing figures in the burgeoning field of ethnology during the late nineteenth century addressed the question of the nature of the classificatory kinship systems as posed by Morgan. McLennan, Lubbock, Lang, Westermarck, Durkheim, and many others took the puzzling problems of primitive kinship nomenclature very seriously. They are discussed in Chapter 4.

In America, A. L. Kroeber, a foremost student of Franz Boas, introduced a new kind of criticism of Morgan's solution to the classificatory–descriptive problem. In his article "Classificatory Systems of Relationship" (1909), Kroeber maintained, first, that all kinship terminologies, including our own "descriptive" system, are really classificatory—but in different ways; and second, that the source of the distinctiveness of the various kinds lies, not in marriage or social organization, but in the "psychology" of the people in the different societies. In this claim he was challenged by Cambridge University ethnologist W. H. R. Rivers and later by the redoubtable A. R. Radcliffe-Brown, an early student of Rivers. This controversy is titled "Mind versus Society," for Rivers and Radcliffe-Brown believed that the causes of kinship terminological patterns lie outside the people's mentality and are to be found in the social organization (or structure) itself. This is the subject of Chapter 5.

In Chapter 6, the ground has shifted somewhat. Radcliffe-Brown now finds another antagonist, Malinowski, who is even more of a psychological reductionist than Kroeber—and much less conciliatory. These two, so often lumped together as British functionalists, were actually poles apart in every important respect.

Chapter 7 reviews more specific arguments about the influence of social organization on kinship terminologies. "Alliance versus Descent" means that whereas it may be accepted that kinship is somehow social or cultural or artificial or man-made rather than simply biological as Morgan had believed, yet it is still arguable whether the basic organizing principles in the society are due to the marriages made for purposes of alliances among groups or due to the significance of unilineal descent in the formation of the groups. Radcliffe-Brown, again, is the foremost proponent of the latter view, while a newcomer, Claude Lévi-Strauss, and one of his foremost disciples, Louis Dumont, argue the case for alliance (and for the related principle of reciprocity) as the major organizational nexus for kinship.

Chapter 8 concludes Part II by discussing the findings of Fred Eggan and Alexander Spoehr, two American students of Radcliffe-Brown during his brief stay at the University of Chicago. They found that in the southeastern United States several Indian kinship terminologies known from historical sources to have been of the Crow type had gradually changed to a standard Malayan (generational) pattern. Since those changes were found to have fol-

lowed certain adaptations in economic and social organizational matters, Eggan and Spoehr felt they had made a major confirmation of Radcliffe-Brown's essential argument—but with the refinement of greater specificity.

4

Kinship Terms: Biological or Social?

As noted earlier, Morgan was worried by the delay in the publication of *Systems of Consanguinity and Affinity* because of his fear of being anticipated by John McLennan in certain respects.[1] It was for this reason that in 1868 he published his article "A Conjectural Solution to the Origin of the Classificatory System of Relationships." Here he reported his daring reconstruction of family forms and the related kinship systems (terminologies) through 15 stages beginning with the "primitive horde" of complete sexual promiscuity and ending with modern monogamy.

In 1876, McLennan published *Studies in Ancient History*, which contained a reprint of *Primitive Marriage* together with several additional essays. Two of these were attacks on Morgan's *Systems*.[2] Morgan read this while his own *Ancient Society* was in press and he hastened to incorporate a 12-page "Note" in reply to the criticisms. In the paragraphs below we follow the thrust and parry of the arguments only as they refer to the nature of kinship terms; other topics, such as the disagreements about exogamy and endogamy, will be deferred to Part III.

McLennan struck at the very heart of Morgan's theory, although Morgan did not think so. Morgan could not see how he could possibly have gone wrong. Obviously, kin terminologies are "systems of consanguinity"; that is, they *must* be biological systems of "blood-ties."

[1]In 1865 McLennan had published *Primitive Marriage*, postulating, among other things, a primal stage of promiscuity. He also anticipated Morgan's idea that the first descent rule would necessarily be matrilineal, as had Bachofen. (According to Lowie [1917a:91] Bachofen's basic position had been expounded as early as 1856 at a philologists' congress, but Morgan did not learn about Bachofen until much later.)

[2]The two relevant essays were "Mr. Morgan's Conjectural Solution of the Origin of the Classificatory System of Relationship" (1876:249–276) and "The Origin of the Classificatory System of Relationship" (1876:277–301).

There was no question of this to his mind, and the answers elicited by his questionnaire from societies all over the world were, in respect to the same questions, designed in every case to find the words for various "blood-relationships." The relationship of the persons is specialized in the Aryan, Semitic, and Uralian systems and classified in categories among all others. Only distinct forms of marriage can explain those differences (1877:441). There simply was no other explanation, Morgan felt, hence his confidence.

And certainly Morgan was correct: marriage and the family form are so intimately connected that only a change in the former creates a response in the latter. The systems of consanguinity are, he believed, simply the words used by the people for the specific relationships thus created. But Morgan meant words for specific *blood* relationships. His scheme could not be attacked by McLennan on the basis of the accuracy of Morgan's tables; the only argument remaining was that the terms of the classificatory systems were not attempts to denote actual degrees of consanguinity at all. McLennan's argument, it is evident, completely mystified Morgan and thus he failed to reply directly to this main point.

So far as can be told, McLennan's was the first writing to make this kind of criticism directly to Morgan's *Systems*. But hark back to Plato's description of the classificatory system quoted in the epigraph to Chapter 2. The implication there is of the functional significance of such systems in destroying the loyalties of a person to his genealogical (or nuclear) family, thus relegating those loyalties to the community at large—and with no reference at all to marriage and the actual form of the family (parenthood, polygyny, promiscuity, etc.). And then think of the important discussion by Fustel de Coulanges: There were two kinds of fathers in archaic Latin, *genitor*, the consanguineal father, and *pater*, the jural, authoritarian status (and there was a similar distinction between *genitrix* and *mater*). It may be that McLennan, independent of Fustel de Coulanges, had seen the problem of the classificatory system in a very different light from Morgan who perforce had seen the terms of parenthood in the classificatory system solely as analogous to *genitor* and *genitrix*. His schedules, the questionnaires he sent around the world to obtain the systems of consanguinity, were just that: queries about actual blood ties. The question was begged, therefore, in the very beginning, even though the schedules did in fact reveal classificatory tendencies.

McLennan made two major points that were related to each other but which have often become separated in later discussions of his theory. One was that "kin terms" are not kinship in the genealogical sense, the other was that they are not sociologically important, being "terms of address, merely." For example, McLennan notes, accurately and tellingly, that the Iroquois Indians, and many others, have inheritance of office, blood-revenge kin groups, with "all the duties and privileges of blood relationship." These are all calculated through females and comprise a recognized system of blood ties, but the female side of the terminological system remains classificatory, just as does the male side. The classificatory terms "are barren of consequences, except as comprising a code of courtesies and ceremonial addresses in social intercourse" (1886:273). Darwin made the same point in the second edition of *The Descent of Man:* "It seems almost incredible that the relationship of the child to its mother should ever be completely ignored, especially as the women in most savage tribes nurse their infants for a long time" (1871:588).

McLennan left himself open to attack by saying that kin terms were simple "modes of addressing persons." A great many critics since have pointed out that kin terms are also used in reference. This is not a telling point, for it does nothing to McLennan's argument. In fact, it may be doubted that he meant that the terms are not, or cannot, be used in reference. Donald McLennan, his younger brother, pointed out in an editorial note to the second edition of *Studies in Ancient History* (1886:269–273) that Lafitau and other observers of primitive life had noted that classificatory terms were used "to indicate the respect due from the speaker to the age and station of the person spoken of." And this was true whether addressing actual relatives or not! In this note, Donald McLennan also said that the terms denote *social status*—the first time, so far as can be told now, that this particular usage was ever published with respect to the nature of kin terms. It will reappear.

It should be noted that McLennan, being so dismissive of the significance of kinship terminology, did not really follow up the very important implications of his only partly-realized ideas about what the terms really designated. The little time he spent writing about them was mostly to say what they were *not;* that is, they were plainly not systems whose sole purpose was that of designating blood ties.

Readers of McLennan's work often failed, much as did Morgan, to appreciate his argument for still another reason: he was so acidulous and overbearing[3] that a counter-animosity was easily aroused. Sir Henry Maine had received the brunt of McLennan's acrimony far more

[3]In print, that is; he actually had been a gracious host when Morgan called on him (and on Darwin, Lubbock, Maine, Huxley, and others) on his travels abroad in 1870–1871.

than Morgan; he was attacked in various ways, but mostly for his notions about kin ties as the basis of primitive polity and for the related notions that patriarchy, not matriarchy, was characteristic of it and that society was evolved from the extension, through generations, of the nuclear family. McLennan had, in fact, devoted a whole book, *The Patriarchal Theory* (1885), to the overthrow of Maine's theory.

In any event, McLennan's ideas did not obtain much support, at least for very long. He had dealt a hard blow to Morgan, however, in arguing for the lack of genealogical significance of kinship terminology, and in England especially McLennan's view tended to prevail. The result was a kind of negativism and a related inactivity—even a lack of controversy—for many years.

Sir John Lubbock, to be sure, had a few things to say; he had points of both agreement and disagreement with Morgan.[4] In the Letters columns of the journal *Nature* (1875) Lubbock and Morgan had a curious exchange. Lubbock, in the third edition of his 1870 work, had noted that Morgan seemed to hold two incompatible theories about kin terminologies: (1) they *do not* change, being "artificial," "complicated," and distinctive of a people, and therefore can be used to trace historical connections in cases of similarity of the pattern of the terms; and (2) they *do* change and have undergone changes compatible with the evolution of the family. Morgan's reply to this criticism (1875)[5] was not to the point and Lubbock's longer reply seems perfectly reasonable (and not unfriendly), to which Morgan responded by saying that he repudiated the first in favor of the second view.

It seems probable that Morgan's inability to see the justice of Lubbock's criticism stems from the fact that he went through such a change of mind that he failed to realize that the reader of *Systems* might not be aware of the difference. It may be remembered that the first version of the manuscript had sat in the Smithsonian's editorial offices so long that Morgan became very impatient. When finally McIlvaine suggested an evolutionary sequence leading from promiscuity to monogamy that would account for the major varieties of kin terminologies, Morgan quickly tacked it on the manuscript—or so it would seem to the reader. But to Morgan, evidently, this became the major conclusion of his work and undoubtedly the reason for writing *Ancient Society* (1877), which was nearly ready for publication at the time of

[4]Lubbock (1834–1913) was a scientific popularizer whose *The Origin of Civilisation* (1870) was widely read. However, he has had almost no influence on the history of anthropology except for his introduction of the terms *paleolithic* and *neolithic*.

[5]At second hand: his acquaintance with the criticism was through a review of the book in *Nature* (Anon. 1875).

his replies to Lubbock and therefore probably in the forefront of his mind.

Lubbock was a sort of evolutionist, sharing with Morgan the preoccupation of opposing the degradation theory. He also shared with McLennan and Morgan the idea of original promiscuity. His most succinct statement of his feelings about Morgan and McLennan occurred in his review in *Nature* (1876) of McLennan's *Studies in Ancient History* (1876). He summarized and compared the works of Bachofen, Morgan's *Systems*, his own work, and the works of Maine that were criticized by McLennan. It is interesting that in referring to McLennan's criticism of Morgan he states (alluding to his debate in *Nature* with Morgan, mentioned above) that he is not sure that either he or McLennan understands Morgan's thesis.

As for forms of marriages, Lubbock's own view is that "individual marriage rose out of capture." He thus seems to find himself, on this point, accepting some of McLennan and some of Morgan, but he claims little for himself:

> This view, indeed, seems so natural that I wonder it had not been before suggested; and I observe that one or two recent writers have treated it as a recognized and well-known fact, whereas it cannot at present claim to be more than an individual theory which none of the authorities on such a question, such as Mr. Darwin, and Mr. McLennan himself, have as yet accepted. (1876:133)

Ancient Society, in Morgan's final version, carried no reference to Lubbock except to borrow a few ethnological statements. There is no mention of Lubbock's evolutionary view of marriage systems and the related terminologies, nor is there mention of Lubbock's criticism of Morgan's idea expressed in *Systems* that similarity in the kin nomenclatures of two societies suggests historical connections between them. There is nothing to be surely vouchsafed about Morgan's omissions unless it is that he simply must have skipped around in Lubbock's book, hastily looking for data that suited him.

Andrew Lang, like Lubbock an important intellectual figure in British ethnology and folklore studies in his time, made several important points in his *Encyclopaedia Britannica* article, "Family" (1878).[6] Morgan's *Ancient Society* had appeared only the previous year, but Lang seems already to have absorbed its significance better than his contemporaries and, perhaps as a consequence, made a salient critique of Morgan's ideas about the classificatory kinship system and its relation to marriage customs.

---

[6]This article deals mostly with social-structural controversies and is discussed more fully in Part III.

His first criticism is the factual one that there seems to be an enormous number of classificatory kinship systems of the Malayan type but absolutely no case on record of the Consanguine family that is supposed to have created this system. His second is of the mechanics of change from Consanguine to Punaluan families and Malayan to Turanian nomenclatural systems. Morgan saw the change as due to conscious moral reform; that is, to prevent the marriage of brothers and sisters. Lang says: "It is difficult to believe that exogamy was a conscious moral and social reformulation, because *ex hypothesi*, the savages had no moral data, nothing to cause disgust at relations which seem revolting to us. It is as improbable that they discovered the supposed physical evils of breeding in and in" (1878:23).[7]

Lang goes on to discuss Lubbock's criticisms of McLennan, especially his reversing of the idea that marriage-by-capture leads to exogamy (as above) and Spencer's criticism that there must have been "many conspiring causes" (of exogamy), rather than only one. Lang's concluding sentence is: "No hard and fast theory is likely to be accepted as more than provisional in the present state of knowledge, when science has only for a few years been busily occupied on this investigation" (1878:24).

Certainly this is a wise comment by Lang. He did not despair, however, and continued to work on the subject, finally publishing *Social Origins* in 1903. In it, along with many other important matters, he devoted several interesting pages precisely to the theoretical point that McLennan had used to make his rather inconclusive and undeveloped attack on Morgan's *Systems*. That is, what *are* classificatory kinship terms? The flavor of the argument may be revealed by quoting one of his more telling paragraphs:

> An Urabunna calls a crowd of men of his father's status by the same term as he calls his father. This need not point to an age when, by reason of promiscuity, no man knew his father. Were this so, a man of the generation prior to his father might be the actual parent of the speaker, and all men under eighty ought to be called "Father" by him—which they are not. The facts may merely mean that the Urabunna styles his father by the name denoting a status which his father shares with many other men; a status in seniority, "phratry" [which Lang calls our more familiar "moiety"], and totem. We really cannot first argue that our ideas have no relation to the terms employed by savages, and then, when we want to prove a past of communal marriage, turn around and reason as if our terms and the savage terms were practically identical. We cannot say "our word 'son' must not be thought of when we try to understand a native term of relationship which includes sons in our sense," and next argue that

---

[7]This duplication of "in" appeared in the original and seems likely to have been intentional. It is used by horse breeders.

"sons" in our sense, are regarded as real sons of the group, not of the individual—because of a past stage of promiscuity making paternity indiscoverable. (1903:101)

McLennan had had the beginning of this idea, but he was so caught up in criticizing Morgan that he failed to show what positive use could be made of the idea that classificatory kin terms are not genealogical but denote something else altogether—social status. To be sure, one of the purposes of *our* kinship terms may be to pinpoint a genealogical position in a family, although not all of the meanings have such a purpose. One of the virtues of the word *status*, we may note at this point, is that it does not prejudice the case in the way the expressions *kin terms* or *consanguineal system* do. Status, a social position relevant to interpersonal behavior, may be based on any of many different criteria—age, sex, political power, profession, wealth, pedigree, and so forth; these can vary from society to society. Any one of these may be genealogical, as at times they are in English, but to argue that the terms used in primitive society must correspond to our own folk criteria is to be ethnocentric as well as wrong. On the contrary, as Lang argues, "the classificatory names for relationships are, to a great extent, expressive of status, seniority and mutual duties and services in the community—these duties and services themselves being gradually established by power—the power of the seniors" (1903:129). Lang's discussion was the longest and best argument for the perspective on status terms to that date; Fustel de Coulanges's interesting discussion (see Chapter 1, this volume) referring only to the classical Indo–Europeans. Yet Lang was far from taking much credit for his view, and he cited favorably not only McLennan but also Westermarck's *History of Human Marriage* (1891).

E. B. Tylor, in 1888, wrote a classic paper on marriage and descent, using for the first time a formal comparative method of arriving at statistical correlations. Among various acute suggestions and discoveries about several social institutions (to be discussed in Part III), Tylor found such a strange correlation between exogamy and the classificatory system of nomenclature (meaning by this the Turanian–Ganowanian, or Iroquoian, system) that he decided that they were "in fact two sides of one institution" (1888:72–73). This idea came to him as a consequence of finding 22 societies

whose customs as to the marriage of first cousins seemed remarkable; it is that the children of two brothers may not marry, nor the children of two sisters, but the child of the brothers may marry the child of the sister. It seemed obvious that this "cross-cousin marriage," as it may be called, must be the direct result of the simplest form of exogamy, where a population is divided into two classes or sections, with the law that a man who belongs to Class A can only take a wife of Class B." (1888:73)

Tylor goes on to remark that he had previously read this kind of explanation in Fison and Howitt's *Kamilaroi and Kurnai* (1880:76) but had not realized its significance. (It should be noted that the correlation of cross-cousin marriage with classificatory terms and exogamous groups that intermarry does not necessarily specify precisely what kind of exogamous groups. Tylor noted the two exogamous classes, or moieties, Morgan specified the *gens,* others will say *sib,* or *clan,* or *lineage.* Any of these have the same effect so long as they are exogamous and unilineal—cross-cousins will be separated and parallel cousins joined in terminology in all generations.)

Edward A. Westermarck, in his *History of Human Marriage* (1891), used Morgan's comparative method and the techniques of supplementing his library research by sending out questionnaires to missionaries and other Europeans living near primitive peoples to investigate the origins of human marriage and family life. He criticized Morgan's theories of primitive promiscuity and group marriage and also the related, more contemporary, theories of the prohibition of incest (or exogamy). These are discussed in more detail in Part III; here it is relevant to remark only that Morgan's idea that the classificatory kinship system reflected prior marriage customs—that it was a genealogical system—was argued to be wrong.

The sole noteworthy defense of Morgan in the 1890s was by J. Kohler in his 1897 *Zur Urgeschichte der Ehe (On the Early History of Marriage).* It sounds lame today, but Kohler thought he saw justification for Morgan's linking of group marriage with the classificatory kinship system in the recently available data on the Omaha and Choctaw Indians' systems. These are familiar to us as *Omaha* and *Crow* systems—they do indeed warrant intellectual scrutiny—but to Kohler, understandably, they were new and astonishing. The Omaha system is based on patrilineal descent, the Choctaw on matrilineal; the two nomenclatural systems show exact reversals, or mirror images (although there are many minor differences in both from one society to another). In the Omaha system, all of the women of the mother's patrilineal clan (of all generations) are designated by a single term, *inaha,* which also includes the *genitrix.* Among the Choctaw, all the men of the father's matrilineal clan are called by a single term, which is also applied to the *genitor.* Kohler thought that from these facts it followed that there had been a system of group marriages, because whole groups of men were called fathers in the one society and whole groups of women called mothers in the other.

An excellent reason for bringing up Kohler's work is that it permits the discussion of an interesting review of it by the great French sociologist—ethnologist Émile Durkheim in 1898. Durkheim gets to the heart of the matter by questioning whether the above terms should be translated as "fathers" and "mothers." He argues that the extravagant lumping together of several generations of people in a matrilineal clan with own father and in a patrilineal clan with own mother suggests a very different interpretation. Durkheim says that Kohler has not answered the critical question that Darwin put to Morgan: How can the child believe himself to be born of more than one mother? In a system like the Choctaw in which a child calls a whole group of men father, it is assumed that this represents potential descent, and therefore group marriage is postulated. But there is never any doubt about the tie between mother and child, whatever the marriage form may be. Therefore, when a group of women are designated *mother*, this does not reflect the situation with regard to descent; why then, should the application of the term *father* be based on descent? Durkheim concludes, logically, that these so-called kinship terms are not simply a matter of blood ties:

> Kinship, in effect, is essentially constituted of legal and moral obligations which the society imposes on certain individuals. These individuals belong to groups where the members are, in general, of a common origin or consider themselves to be. . . . [But] many considerations, foreign to the idea of descent, may determine the way in which the society divides, among the different members of the family group, the domestic rights and obligations. Some feature of the social system, some religious belief, may cause the child to be more closely linked or farther removed from one parent or the other; accordingly, he will not have the same degree of kinship with the two. In sum, kinship varies with the way in which the family is organized, depending upon whether it has more or less members, the place given to each, etc. Now, this organization depends above all on social necessities, and consequently is only loosely connected with the completely physical fact of descent. (1898a:316–317; my translation)

Durkheim acknowledges the tremendous significance of Morgan's discovery of the classificatory kinship systems but considers their explanation via the hypothesis of collective marriage to be too improbable to be taken seriously. At the same time, Westermarck and his predecessor Starcke, in criticizing Morgan, propose that the classificatory terms correspond to a social as opposed to a natural kinship (this would be something like status versus consanguineality). But, Durkheim asserts,"

> all kinship is social, because it consists essentially in legal and moral relationships, sanctioned by the society. Either it is a social link or it is nothing.

Westermarck makes the above distinction because for him, as in common
usage, true kinship is confounded with consanguinity, and only expresses the
latter. But when this confusion is removed, there can only be one kinship,
which is that which is recognized as such by the society; this is supported by
the tables which we owe to Morgan.[8] (1898a:318–319)

Shortly thereafter, N. W. Thomas (1906) devoted a whole book to
disputing Morgan's assumptions about native Australian society, in
particular arguing (and, really showing) that so-called kin terms denote
statuses other than those of consanguinity. Here the controversy
seems to have ended until the arrival of W. H. R. Rivers, a professional
medical psychologist converted to anthropology while on the Cambridge University Anthropological Expedition to Torres Strait led by
Professor A. C. Haddon in 1898.[9]

[8]It should be of interest that Westermarck's type of distinction between natural
("real," genealogical) and social kinship is still with us in such usages as "fictive" and
"ceremonial" kinship and "blood brothers," implying that ordinary kinship systems are
true—"real," genealogical—while these usages are not as true.

[9]Rivers made three important subsequent ethnological studies; he went to the Todas
in South India in 1902 and back to Melanesia in 1908 and 1914.

5

Kinship Terms:
Mind or Society?

Rivers is best known today for introducing the "genealogical method" (1900) into fieldwork, by which all members of a community are placed in the network of their mutual kinship and marriage connections. Rivers was impressed with L. H. Morgan's evolutionism, particularly that aspect of it that attempted historical reconstruction of marriage and family types from surviving kinship terms. Rivers' best-known attempt at this is in his reconstruction of Melanesian society (1914a) and his two general theoretical works on social organization (1914b and 1924).

Rivers did not succeed in rehabilitating Morgan, but he did stimulate a revival of interest in the study of kinship terminology and social structure. Undoubtedly, he created the beginnings of this interest in his student, A. R. Radcliffe-Brown (then Alfred Brown); and his exchanges with A. L. Kroeber constitute a significant stage in the continuing controversy over the meaning of and function of kinship terms. It should be remarked at this point that Rivers formed a lasting friendship with Sir Grafton Elliot Smith, a medical colleague who was obsessed by the conviction that all of human civilization had diffused from Egypt. Smith converted Rivers to this dogma, and as a consequence Rivers lost much of his influence in ethnology—in particular, he lost Brown.

Rivers' most significant argument about the nature of kin terms is contained in his smallish textbook, *Kinship and Social Organization* (1914b). To a considerable extent this book was the product of his dissatisfaction with a brief article A. L. Kroeber had published in 1909. This article, called "Classificatory Systems of Relationship," completely rejected Morgan' use of kinship terminologies in reconstructing history and, most notably, denied that kinship terminologies were determined by forms of marriage and family or directly by any other kinds of social conditions. We must devote attention to the Kroeber–Rivers controversy because it reveals in its essence the very broad distinctions that have come to be drawn in ethnology between schools of thought called variously "history versus science" or "humanism (or the humanities) versus positivism."

Basically, these dichotomies are reducible to one, but that dichotomy is difficult to name appropriately. Ethnology itself has become a duality, or, at any rate, its practitioners belong to two "cultures" that have not understood one another. At this point, we are going to attempt to experience this basic duality rather than try to explain it. Our experience begins with the first challenge to evolutionism–positivism–functionalism–determinism by something else—which here, for short and with no implications of invidiousness, we call Boasian anthropology.

A. L. Kroeber was one of Franz Boas' earliest and most prominent students, and from Boas he had heard Morgan and other evolutionists discredited. But accompanying the general negativism and scepticism so characteristic of Boas' attitude toward the ethnology of his early days was a productive side that led to the creation of a school of enthusiastic researchers who came to be called, often, the American Historical School—not a particularly evocative name, for the Boasian conception of culture was the main issue. For the moment, let us edge into one of the earliest of the controversies between the two schools by examining the Kroeber–Rivers debate. In order to review this to our own intellectual advantage, let us forswear taking sides.

Kroeber begins by arguing that Morgan's distinction between classificatory and descriptive kinship systems is entirely fallacious. English language kin terms (a descriptive system) actually classify; for example, our single word *cousin* includes 32 different genealogical relationships. Kroeber's main point is that different languages classify relationships differently; to call one classificatory and another descriptive is simply a subjective judgment. (Kroeber here has failed to follow Morgan's own precise and simple distinction between the two kinds of systems. The descriptive system isolates lineal lines of descent from its collaterals; the classificatory system merges collaterals, as, for example, father and father's brothers and male cousin or male parallel cousins.)

Kroeber examined 12 American Indian kinship systems and compared them with English to see exactly what principles or categories of relationship underlie them. He found a total of eight:[1]

[1]For the sake of brevity I have listed these in their brief form, following the order of this table (1909:70) rather than his text.

1. Generation.
2. Blood or marriage.
3. Lineal or Collateral.
4. Sex of relative.
5. Sex of connecting relative. (This mainly refers to the frequent discrimination in American Indian systems between an uncle or aunt who is father's as opposed to mother's brother or sister. This is the distinction more commonly known as cross–parallel.)
6. Sex of speaker.
7. Age within a generation.
8. Condition of connecting relative (e.g., an "uncle" who is father's brother may have a different term after father dies).

With the exception of the word *cousin*, which is foreign, the English language kinship system gives expression only to the first four of the above categories. All of the American Indian languages express from six to eight of them—usually seven (number 8 is the rare one). Kroeber's remarks on this difference form an apt expression of what eventually became known as cultural relativity—a notable characteristic of the Boasian perspective:

> The so-called descriptive systems express a small number of categories of relationship completely; the wrongly-named classificatory systems express a larger number of categories with less regularity. Judged from its own point of view, English is the less classificatory; looked at from the Indian point of view it is the more classificatory, inasmuch as in every one of its terms it fails to recognize certain distinctions often made in other languages; regarded from a general and comparative point of view, neither system is more or less classificatory. (1909:80)

The next point is that the difference between English and American Indian systems is not due to differences in social organization; therefore, anterior forms of marriage and family cannot be inferred from the terminologies. "The causes which determine the formation, choice, and similarities of terms of relationship are primarily linguistic. Whenever it is desired to regard terms of relationship as due to sociological causes and as indicative of social conditions, the burden of proof must be entirely with the propounder of such views" (1909:83).

Kroeber ended his argument with a blunt statement that was eventually to cause considerable misunderstanding: "Terms of relationship reflect psychology, not sociology. They are determined primarily by language and can be utilized for sociological inferences only with extreme caution" (1909:84).

Rivers (1914b) replied directly to Kroeber's article. He admitted that Morgan's explanation of the classificatory system in terms of promiscuity or polyandry might not hold; he maintained, nevertheless, that it can be explained in its general characteristics and its details by forms of social organization. For Kroeber to say that the relationship terms are determined by language is simply to say that elements of language are determined by language—which is not to say anything significant at all. And to say that the terms are reducible to psychology is to take the problem out of the realm of sociological cause and effect.

Rivers was thus preparing the ground for his larger work, *The History of Melanesian Society* (1914a), which would use kinship terminologies in order to postulate extinct systems of marriage and clan–moiety organization. It should be remarked at this point that the one reconstruction of Morgan's that seems worth underlining again is his argument that the exogamous gens organization does indeed correlate with cross-cousin marriage and the related Turanian or Gonowanian (i.e., Iroquois or bifurcate-merging) system.

Many years later, Kroeber commented on his exchange with Rivers, attempting to adjudicate their dispute and above all to clarify his statements about kin terms reflecting psychology. It was in 1952 that he issued a collection of his major essays accompanied by his own editorial commentary on them. With reference to his 1909 article, he admits that the word "psychological" was an unfortunate choice. He says (1952:172): "I should have said that kinship systems are linguistic patterns of logic. . . . It would have been right to say that, as part of language, kin term systems reflect unconscious logic and conceptual patterning *as well as* social institutions." In other words, kinship systems form a semantic domain that can be analyzed in terms of itself and its own internal relationships.

In a prescient aside—and most usefully for us—Kroeber mentions further differences between himself and Rivers. They may stand as perhaps personal and idiosyncratic sets of contrasting traits, but they also in some measure can be related to what may be called the two cultures of ethnology. Kroeber says:

> There usually are deeper personal issues underlying differences of interpretation such as these. Rivers began as a laboratory physiologist who pushed on to psychology and then to ethnology. He was accordingly seeking deterministic proofs as rigorous and definite as in the exact sciences, to use his own words; and he found them in the determination of kinship by social institutions. He wanted to make social science a "true science." I came from humanistic literature, entered anthropology by the gate of linguistics, saw meaning in forms and their relations, but deeply distrusted a determinism that attributed specific, limited, but sufficient causes to cultural phenomena. (1952:172–173)

As we shall see repeatedly as our story unfolds, the antideterminism (or antipositivism) of so many American anthropologists (and Lévi-Strauss) may be basically a manifestation of the fact that Boas and his students built their ideas of culture—and how to analyze it—firmly on the strong foundation of the analogy of culture to language. Kroeber continues:

> But the pioneers like Morgan, the men trained in laboratories like Rivers, the ruck of social scientists hoping somehow to imitate physics, kept and keep trying; and yet they achieve either only bits or constructs that are mainly unreal. It is the pattern rather than precise causation that is the meaningful result by and large achievable in the study of culture—as the history of linguistics should long ago have sufficed to teach us (1952:173)

Rivers is sometimes cited as having argued for the reconstruction of such things as moieties and forms of marriage out of surviving systems of kinship nomenclature, somewhat in the way Morgan argued for group marriage from his perusal of surviving systems. But Rivers was not that simple. With many examples and with numerous statements such as those that follow, he set the program for the study of kinship as successfully pursued by his student, Alfred Brown, and Brown's numerous followers. For example, Rivers says:

> The nomenclature of the classificatory system carries with it a number of clearly defined social practices. One who applies a given term of relationship to another person has to behave towards that person in certain definite ways. He has to perform certain duties toward him, and enjoys certain privileges, and is subject to certain restrictions in his conduct in relation to him. These duties, privileges and restrictions vary greatly in number among different peoples, but wherever they exist, I know of no exception to their importance and to the regard in which they are held by all members of the community. (1914b:11–12)

With respect to Rivers' fame as Morgan's champion and, correspondingly, as McLennan's detractor, we should be aware of certain complications. McLennan, remember, was trying to make a case against Morgan's assumption that primitive kinship terms were genealogical, and he unfortunately left the impression that the terms were "merely" terms of address. Rivers dwells on this, attributing to McLennan the idea that the terms have no functions whatsoever. Thus when Rivers describes rights and duties of such people as mother's brother to Ego and the relationship of cross-cousin marriage to certain kinds of kinship systems, he thinks he is vindicating Morgan by showing that the terms *are* related to social practices. But this can easily be refuted; in fact, Morgan was not relating the systems of nomenclature to any social practices other than those directly related to genealogy (i.e., marriage practices). Rivers is on much firmer ground when he uses his own data on "rights and duties" to refute Kroeber. Ironically, this seems more in line with what McLennan had in mind, not Morgan.

Robert Lowie illustrates Kroeber's point about determinism. Lowie was trained by Boas, but he had come to anthropology from chemistry and appropriately enough he found himself inclined to side with Rivers' argument about the dependent relationship of kin terminology to social behavior and group structure. In particular, Lowie (in 1915) approved of Rivers' (and Tylor's, discussed in Chapter 4) idea that exogamous groupings account for the widespread form of the classificatory systems that separates cross from parallel relatives. (In Morgan's terminology, this is an account of why certain lineal and collateral relatives are merged.) But Lowie also points out that exogamous groupings do not explain why *generations* are separated in terminology. Some societies with exogamous clans, like the Crow and Omaha systems, have ignored the distinction between generations when a strong unilineal organization is present (in father's side for the Crow type, mother's for the Omaha). This exogamy accounts for the merging of some parts of lineal and collateral lines and for an intrusion over the separation of generations. But why, in so many other systems, are lineal and collateral lines merged, but with generations clearly demarked? How, for example, are we to account for the Hawaiian generational system? Rivers had said that the breakdown of exogamous marriage practices accounts for it. Lowie (1915a:70–71), despite his sympathy for Rivers' general perspective, cannot swallow this argument. (This problem, it should be noted here, will reappear from time to time. Its solution, it now seems, will best be discussed later in our section on social structure.)

With respect to the Kroeber–Rivers argument about the social-structural determinants of kin terms, Robert Lowie retreats somewhat a year later (1916) in pointing out additional limitations to the "sociological" view when he argues that distributional studies show that only historical factors (diffusion of traits) account for the presence of certain features of kinship in certain places. In the end, he occupies a middle ground between Rivers and Kroeber, approving of certain features of both men's views. In 1917, Lowie emphasized linguistic factors. In his larger work, *Primitive Society* (1920), however, Lowie again insists on a close correlation of "Dakota" terminology (Morgan's Turanian–Gonowanian system) with unilineal exogamous groups, but this linking is not causal: "the relation between the two is one of identity, not of cause and effect" (1920:162). It should be of interest that in this, his first book-length treatment of social organization, Lowie devotes very little attention to kin terminology—it is as though he had lost interest.

6

Kinship Terms: Structure and Function

The dispute between Rivers and Kroeber, insofar as it caused Rivers to criticize Kroeber for giving psychologistic (more recently, this is often called reductionistic) explanations of social phenomena, had its philosophical counterparts on a greater scale in Europe. With respect to social institutions, Émile Durkheim was the most influential proponent of a positivistic, scientific philosophy that elevates "social facts" to a plane of autonomy that, far from being the sum of individual minds, propensities, and actions, makes them the causes of those characteristics. Put another way, it is profoundly against psychological (and of course biological or racist) reductionistic explanations of human social behavior. Durkheim did not write much about kinship terminologies—the best statement of his view is found in his review of Kohler, discussed in Chapter 4—but he did promote an attitude that was to have a profound effect on later studies of kinship in France and Great Britain.

The flavor of this attitude may be experienced by contrasting the following statements with those made later by Kroeber in 1909. In his first book, *The Division of Labor in Society*, Durkheim says:

> Social facts are not the simple development of psychic facts, but the second are in large part only the prolongation of the first in the interior of consciences. . . . For example, if, as often happens, we see in the organization of the family the logically necessary expression of human sentiments inherent in every conscience, we are reversing the true order of facts. On the contrary, it is the social organization of the relations of kinship which has determined the respective sentiments of parents and children. (1893:349)

In another book, *The Rules of Sociological Method*, Durkheim says:

> If then, we begin with the individual, we shall be able to understand nothing of what takes place in the group. In a word, there is between psychology and sociology the same break in continuity as between biology and the phys-

icochemical sciences. Consequently, every time that a social phenomenon is directly explained by a psychological phenomenon, we may be sure that the explanation is false. (1895:104)

Of all those later anthropologists who found intellectual palatability in the above argument, it was Alfred R. Radcliffe-Brown who had the greatest influence on later studies of social structure and (our major interest at this point) kinship terminology. Radcliffe-Brown, as previously noted, had been a student of Rivers and A. C. Haddon at Cambridge University, and he allied Rivers' kind of positivism in social organization with Durkheim's antireductionism. However, he soon rejected the kind of historical reconstructions attempted by Rivers.

As usual, we find that anthropologists make their most interesting and revealing statements when engaged in direct argument with a particular opponent. In this case, we find Radcliffe-Brown entering the lists on the side of Rivers in his renewal of the argument with Kroeber over the nature of kinship terms. Kroeber's modest article of 1909 had resulted in a kind of overkill by Rivers, who, as we saw, brought out a whole book in rebuttal (1914b). Kroeber replied to this in a 1917 monograph, *California Kinship Systems.*

In this monograph Kroeber admits that he made too sweeping a statement in 1909; he also says that he was misunderstood by Rivers when he used the term *psychological* to describe the locus of the determinants of kinship terms. He never meant that "terms of relationship can be explained directly from the constitution of the human mind"; rather, he was referring to the kind of factor that in language would produce a grammatical dual. Since he cannot find a more appropriate word he must continue to use *psychological,* but with the above caveat (1917a:386–387). In this monograph, Kroeber makes it much plainer than he had in 1909 that he is using the analogy of language and its analysis by linguists. Toward the very end Kroeber repeats what has nearly become a refrain: "If the issue were primarily the narrower one of the preeminence of so-called psychological and so-called social influences on kinship systems, I should still lay more stress on the former influence, because, after all, kinship systems are terminologies, terminologies are classifications, and classifications are reflections of 'psychological' process" (1917a:395).

But Kroeber thinks there is a larger point to be made. The "basic issue" is "whether kinship terminology is determined rigidly by specific social phenomena of only one kind." Yet so many variable factors forbid the discovery of such a sweeping causality. "Two irreconcilable methods of prosecuting ethnology and history here confront each other" (1917a:395). It may be well to recall here that Kroeber had earlier called this dispute a "deeper personal issue" between Rivers and himself; here he depersonalizes it to call it "two irreconcilable methods"—a formulation much to be preferred.

Here it may be useful to point out that in these early years of the blossoming of Boasian anthropology, tremendous strides had been made—particularly by Boas himself and his prize student, Edward Sapir—in the study of primitive (nonliterate) languages. Grammar, phonology, semantics, and "classifications of reality" were being "teased out" of texts and observed speech behavior. As it was discovered that different languages caused people to perceive external reality in distinctly different ways, so it was also discovered that there were deep, unconscious, "non-rational" (in Boas's phrasing) cultural determinants of personality, ethnic psychology, and codes of social behavior ("grammars of behavior") due to the "enculturation" of people growing up in a particular society. It was this kind of view that Kroeber was trying to impart to the world.[1] It was an anthropological perspective on the mentality, or cultural psychology, of societies or groups.

Radcliffe-Brown wrote a criticism of Kroeber in 1935, entitled "Kinship Terminologies in California," to the effect that a correspondence between kinds of terminologies and kinds of social structure had not been found among the California tribes because the studies that would reveal the relationship had not been made. Kroeber's reply was conciliatory and he backed down in a few places; but he continued to make his point that "language cannot be left out" (1936:338). The issue by now was quite muddled and Kroeber never did make his point about language clearly enough for Radcliffe-Brown (and, for that matter, a great many other anthropologists) to understand him.[2]

Radcliffe-Brown's last important remarks in this debate occurred in

---

[1]And he never stopped until he died at a well-advanced age. I had been a student of his at Columbia in the late 1940s and a colleague in the early 1950s. I was much a determinist, materialist, and evolutionist in those days and also youthfully sure of myself, so I tried to convert him. One day it dawned on me that it was like trying to convert a linguist—impossible. I hurried to his office to try out my discovery that he was treating culture like a language and himself as its analyst, discovering its "patterns" and "style" and "configuration" like a linguist discovering its grammar! He looked at me in surprise (I supposed, surprise at my acuteness), but it turned out that he thought everybody understood *that*, that the language analogy was the very essence of Boasism (so it was surprise at my dullness).

[2]E. W. Gifford entered the lists in a 1940 article to reaffirm faith in Kroeber's dictum that kin terminologies are "linguistic phenomena" and only "secondarily social phenomena," with no necessary cause–effect relationship between them.

his Presidential Address to the Royal Anthropological Institute in 1941.[3] Here for the first time he directly confronts Kroeber on the question of kinship nomenclatures as language, and whether, therefore, they are a different kind of reality from social institutions such as marriage customs, clans and lineages, and social practices. Using many ethnographic instances from widely separated geographic and language areas, he shows the relationship between "general structural principles" and general kinds of terminologies. In summary, Radcliffe-Brown argues:

> By the principle of the unity of the sibling group a type relationship is set up between a given person and all the members of a sibling group to which he is related in a certain way. It is by reference to this principle, I hold, that we must interpret the classificatory terminology and such customs as the sororate and levirate. By the principle of the unity of the lineage group a type relationship is set up between a given person and all the members of a lineage group to which he is related in a certain way. It is by reference to this principle, I hold, that we must interpret the terminologies of the Fox, the Hopi and the Yaralde, and other similar systems in many scattered parts of the world.[4] (1941:87)

The foregoing explanations, it may be noted now in anticipation of later discussions, are typical examples of Radcliffe-Brown's brand of scientism. In the classificatory nomenclature, children of siblings of the same sex are given the same term (they are parallel cousins). Why? Because of the "principle of the unity of the sibling group." When the terminology cuts across the generations of a lineage, another "principle" explains this. Since nothing really new, as information, is added to the analasis, but only different words for the same phenomenon, all we have is a tautology affirming Radcliffe-Brown's faith in the social relevance of the terms. We may be inclined to agree with him, but so far no satisfactory proof, or even argumentation, has been adduced. This is typically the case when "principles," "forces," "powers," and the like are brought into the explanation—they are tricky because they sound good.[5]

Bronislaw Malinoswki was a near-contemporary of Radcliffe-Brown's in Great Britain; he too had been influenced by Rivers and

[3]This address, "The Study of Kinship Systems," is most readily available in his collection of reprinted essays of 1952. Much of the address is directed against the Morgan–Rivers uses of terminologies in "conjectural history," as well as against Kroeber.

[4]The Fox, Hopi, and Yaralde were here analyzed as further examples of the Crow (or Choctaw) and Omaha types of terminologies that "violate the generational principle."

[5]I well remember my *Introduction to Chemistry* text. On the very first page it addressed the major question: What holds atoms together in a molecule? The answer did not take long: "Forces of Attraction." (Why does morphine put you to sleep? Its "Dormitive Powers." Why do sheep herd so closely together? The "Gregarious Instinct.")

Durkheim, with the same resulting ambivalence. Malinowski and Radcliffe-Brown are frequently classed together as being cofounders of the functionalist school in Great Britain. They did share a dislike for "conjectural history," and they did wish to put social anthropology on a more scientific basis with explanation focused on synchronic relationships from which generalizations would be made. But their generic similarity is not maintained beyond that. The most significant difference between the two has to do with the ultimate locus of explanation: Malinowski was a psychological reductionist,[6] and Radcliffe-Brown was averse to this. The differences between the two are developed in different contexts subsequently, but for the present purpose we concentrate on kinship terminologies and their meaning and explanation.

Malinowski, it might be said, stands in stark contrast to Radcliffe-Brown in seeing kinship from the inside out. From the inner human procreative need arise outside cultural institutions such as marriage and the family. Malinowski insisted over and over that everything begins in the sentiments of peoples' participation in their own individual family with its need-serving "functions." When relatives other than these are given kinship terms and modes of association, the terms are "metaphors" and the modes of behavior are "extensions" of the feelings of individuals that arise in their own family.[7]

Radcliffe-Brown, on the other hand, was inclined to look more from the outside in, with such institutions as marriage, family, and terminological systems seen as parts of a total organization, or *structure*, that holds the whole society together. The kinship sentiments of individuals, being dependent variables, would be irrelevant to the analysis of the interrelationship of the various social institutions and codes of behavior.

It is of historical interest that both Malinowski and Radcliffe-Brown studied the Australian aborigines. The Australians had figured prominently in L. H. Morgan's evolutionary scheme, particularly because their system of so-called marriage classes seemed to provide a factual basis for Morgan's ideas about group marriage. Both Malinowski and Radcliffe-Brown were introduced to the study of primitive social orga-

---

[6]He once put it: "In one way the whole substance of my theory of culture . . . consists in reducing Durkheimian theory to terms of Behavioristic psychology" (1935a:II:236).

[7]Malinowski states these ideas most clearly in his articles on kinship and marriage in the *Encyclopaedia Britannica* (1929), "Kinship" in *Man* (1930), and "Parenthood, the Basis of Social Structure" in V. J. Calverton and S. D. Schmalhausen, *The New Generation* (1930). Attention also should be called to an excellent article by Meyer Fortes, "Malinowski and the Study of Kinship" (1957:157–188).

nization by Rivers, but both disagreed with Rivers' (and Morgan's) belief in "conjectural history." Malinowski's first full-length book, *The Family Among the Australian Aborigines* (1913), was written (from library sources) mainly to disprove the group marriage hypothesis and to show instead that the individual (nuclear) family, and parenthood especially, was the basis of social structure.

Radcliffe-Brown, meanwhile, was doing fieldwork among the Australian aborigines in 1910–1912. His 1914 review of Malinowski's above-cited book points up the basic differences between them. He reports that Malinowski's orientation toward the family node cannot explain the Australian ideas of kinship, for they are bound up in group relationships—those of kinship systems, classes, and clans. It seems evident that Malinowski's orientation would be useful in understanding aspects of an individual's psychology, but an individual's psychology would not be useful in understanding the overall social system.

Given Malinowski's orientation toward parenthood as the basis of kinship, it is no wonder that he could not give a satisfactory explanation of classificatory kin nomenclatures. If genealogical father–mother and son–daughter are the "true" terms of kinship, then when the terms include other relatives with them either they are simply metaphors, "extended" in meaning from the primary relatives, or they are homonyms of completely different meanings. Thus we have Malinowski sharing Morgan's view that kin terms are genealogical in basic meaning though not sharing with him the idea that prior forms of marriage had caused a person to have many fathers and mothers undiscriminated.

Raymond Firth (1936:272–277), a prominent student of Malinowski's, found that in the Polynesian island of Tikopia the children do *not* learn and use kinship terms in the order specified by Malinowski (parents' terms first, then gradually metaphorically extended outward to other relatives) but in just the opposite order. The first term learned is applied to all grownups, and only later and gradually through tutelage does the child learn to differentiate among the various categories of relatives. Malinowski's preface to Firth's book nevertheless claims that Firth's data vindicate the extensionist theory, a truly grotesque twisting of Firth's findings.

Malinowski's one brief effort to explain Trobriand kinship terminology, in *The Sexual Life of Savages in Northwestern Melanesia* (1929:434–435), illustrates the mess one can get into with the extensionist psychologistic view. The Trobrianders have a terminology of the type we have noted earlier as Choctaw (nowadays, Crow), a system of matrilineal lineages wherein male members of father's matrilineage are called by the same term, regardless of generation—illustrating Radcliffe-Brown's now-famous "unity of lineage principle." To Malinowski, the Melanesian word *tama*, when applied to father, *means* father (*genitor*); when applied to others it must be explained some other way. Meyer Fortes comments on this as follows:

> . . . Malinowski soon arrives at this extraordinary fallacy. "The anomalous extension of the word for father (*tama*) to the father's sister's son is important, for it demonstrates the influence which language has upon customs and ideas . . . " and so on. The whole paragraph deserves study as an example of a beautiful methodological and logical howler due to preconceived ideas; and this is no slip of the pen for the rest of the discussion on Trobriand kinship terminology follows this line. (1957:176)

As Fortes goes on to point out, Malinowski here has revived Kroeber's 1909 view of kinship terminologies as linguistic and psychological phenomena rather than phenomena determined by social conditions and institutions. He has added the notion that classificatory uses recur because of a particular psycholinguistic phenomenon, a metaphorical extension of the primary meaning of, for example, *tama* from own *genitor* to other males (those of his father's matrilineage). This idea of primary meaning has been attacked cogently. Here we should digress somewhat from the chronology of this chapter to mention two of the earliest critics of the extensionist view, J. D. Unwin (1929, 1930) and A. M. Hocart (1937). Unwin's protest was basically against the practice of using English genealogical terms for native categories. Hocart pointed out that the use ethnologists have made of genealogical assumptions about the meaning of "kinship" terms is wrong:

> The effect on theory has been disastrous. The order in which we have learned the uses of *tama* and similar words has been confused with the order of development in actual history. Because we first took it to mean father we slip unwittingly into the assumption that it meant father originally.
> This fallacy has now received official expression in the term "kinship extensions." That expression implies that the meaning father is primary and that all other uses result from extending the term to an ever-widening circle of kinsmen. (1937:346)

Hocart goes on to argue that the meaning of a kinship term should be learned by the ethnologist in the same way as any other word; that is, the full range of uses of a word like *tama* (in this case in Fiji, where he worked) should be discovered—after which it would be found that *tama* can be defined as meaning "males of the previous generation on the father's side." This significance is unexpected to a European because the whole social organization is different; the criteria of classification of kin is distinct from ours. Hocart says:

In short, what we seek most is the next of kin, and so we run up and down the family tree. The Fijians (and the Australian aborigines, and the rest) do not, because there is no point in doing so. All they want is such information as will enable them to place each man on the correct side in the right generation. An inquiry proceeds thus: "How are you related?" "Of the same side and generation." "Why?" "Because our fathers were of the same side and generation." Or else: "We belong to successive generations on opposite sides, because he is of my mother's side and generation." (1937:350)

E. R. Leach discussed Malinowski's data on the social organization of the Trobriand Islanders in such a way as to show that kinship *categories* are primary, not the genealogical meanings: "Kinship categories express differences of locality and of age status rather than genealogical relationship" (1958:131). "Locality" (that is, hamlets or villages) would refer to the places of residence of such kin categories as father's male group (*tama*), own subclan group (*kada*), and so on. Leach actually solved numerous puzzles in Malinowski's account by departing thus from the basic assumption that the primary kin terms are genealogical. It seems curious indeed that Malinowski should insist that the primary meaning of *tama* was own *genitor* when one of the salient facts of Trobriand social organization, as he himself reported it, was the professed ignorance of the role of physical paternity in creating pregnancy! Furthermore, as Leach shows, the Trobrianders actually seemed to have little interest in pedigree altogether (1958:143).[8]

Malinowski's psychologistic functionalism as applied to kinship terminological systems, now known usually as the extensionist hypothesis, is still viable, largely because it has been the basic assumption of G. P. Murdock, who had been an influential teacher at Yale University of several students who themselves have become teachers of anthropology. Although it may be relevant that Malinowski taught at Yale from 1939 until his death in 1942, it is not possible to accurately assess his direct influence on Murdock (but see Murdock's statement below).

Murdock's work, although it includes Malinowski's assumptions, does not lend itself to easy identification with any school. His major work, *Social Structure*, is, he says in the opening sentence, "a synthesis of five distinct products of social science—one research technique and four systems of theory" (1949:vii). Of course, this eclec-

---

[8]As late as 1965 an anthropologist–linguist, Floyd Lounsbury, published an article, "Another View of the Trobriand Kinship Categories," arguing against Leach and in favor of Malinowski's view. This particular debate runs beyond our chronological limits and so is not discussed further, but, as we shall see in other connections, cycles in theory instead of progress often seem to occur.

ticism may have caused Murdock to arrive at contradictory conclusions, but since our present effort is confined to findings about kinship terminology, we shall ignore most of the many criticisms that have been made of the book's methodology, assumptions, and theoretical misconceptions.[9]

In his brief preface to *Social Structure*, Murdock points up his close intellectual accordance with Malinowski and his distaste for Radcliffe-Brown. After acknowledging his direct debt to his teacher (in Yale sociology), Albert G. Keller, particularly for the idea of the importance of the "comparative study of earlier and simpler peoples," Murdock says: "More important even than the above, however, was the discovery that culture is adaptive or 'functional,' subserving the basic needs of its carriers and altering through time by a sort of mass trial-and-error in a process which is truly evolutionary, i.e., characterized by orderly adaptive change" (1949:xii). This view, ascribed usually to Malinowski, should, he avers, also be credited to Keller.

> A decade ago the author might have been inclined to rank functional anthropology among the important influences upon his thinking. Not so today. Personal contact with Bronislaw Malinowski brought intellectual stimulation and some clarification respecting social institutions but no fundamental point of view not previously acquired from Keller. The work of Radcliffe-Brown on social organization appears exceedingly impressive upon superficial acquaintance and was, indeed, the factor which first induced the author to specialize in the field. On closer view, however, its virtues wane, and they fade into insubstantiality with intensive study. In the controversy between Kroeber and Radcliffe-Brown, for example, the expressed views of the latter seemed, and still seem, appreciably sounder, but in the actual analysis and interpretation of data the former has proved right and the latter wrong in nearly every instance. (1949:xv–xvi)

And then, again to fit the parallel to Malinowski, Murdock acknowledges his psychologism: "The third system [Boas was the second "profound influence"] of organized knowledge which has significantly influenced this volume is behaviorist psychology. . . . Of all the systematic approaches to the study of human behavior known to the author, that of Hull [the Yale behaviorist psychologist] exceeds all others in scientific rigor and objectivity, and it is the only one against which he can level no serious criticism" (1949:xvi).[10]

Murdock approves of the Malinowskian idea of classificatory terms

---

[9]The method, that of statistical correlations of data from what was then called the Cross-Cultural Survey files, has been the most frequently criticized.

[10]Recall Malinowski's statement about his career goal of reducing Durkheim to behavioristic psychology.

being extensions of primary terms and adds the Hullian notion of the psychological process involved: that of "stimulus generation" (1949: 132). Murdock also accepts a modified version of the major criteria of classification that had been proposed in Kroeber's "Classificatory Systems of Relationship" (1909). Thus Murdock is clearly allied with the psycholinguistic "inside out" modes of thought.

However, far from accepting what at first may seem like the obvious and necessary logical corollaries of Kroeber's and Malinowski's views—the indeterministic–reductionistic view of kin terminologies—Murdock put the terminologies to a grand cross-cultural statistical test of the influence of certain social institutions on them. He found that descent rules were the most significant determinants of terminology, followed by marriage rules and residence rules. His final sentence in this chapter is strikingly *un*-Kroeberian: "It seems clear that the elements of social organization, in their permutations and combinations, conform to natural laws of their own with an exactitude scarcely less striking than that which characterized the permutations and combinations of atoms in chemistry or of genes in biology" (1949:183).[11]

The Kroeberian view of the determinants of kin categories was taken up again and refined in more modern linguistic terms by one of Murdock's students, Ward Goodenough, in 1956. This view differs from Hocart's argument about how to find the meaning of a kinship term largely in that Hocart offers no method for *discovering* the meaning: he simply asked the informants what *tama* means. Goodenough, on the other hand, wants to find the meaning in the actual speech behavior in varying contexts, after the method employed by a linguist attempting to uncover the phonemic pattern of a strange language. He wants to be able to reorder the data in terms of components that do not necessarily correspond to the informants' ideas about the why of it, but at the same time he wants to use the terms semantically in ways that do not violate the informants' sense of appropriateness.

Thus, to use an English analogy, Goodenough says (1956:95) that the word *cousin* can be tried out in various contexts until it is discovered that the contextual elements in connection with it can be described as

---

[11]A sentence very like this also concludes the whole book (1949:332). There are many critics of Murdock's scientism—the point especially has been made that statistical correlations do not say anything about causal chains and their direction—but no one, so far as I know, has pointed out the grand paradox of an author's holding at the same time (that is, in the same book) such totally contradictory conclusions: that classificatory kin terms are psychologistic extensions of the primary terms and yet are determined by outside social influences, conforming to inexorable "natural laws."

FaBroSon (father's brother's son), FaSiSo, FaBroDa, FaSiDa, and so on. These notations are not likely to be the same as the words the informant would use to define the meaning of cousin, but that does not matter. What the method would do is discriminate synonyms and homonyms from the primary meaning of, say, *tama*. This is precisely what Malinowski failed to do.

An inspection of all the above genealogical kin types included in *cousin* suggests a shorthand way of describing the meaning of cousin: either sex of own generation, collateral lines. The aim is to use the least number of criteria by which all included kin types of a given kin term can be distinguished from all others in the paradigm of related terms. "Meaning," of a certain sort is thus elicited from the informants' usage but not from his or her own ideas of the meaning. The linguist is satisfied if the list or chart of components adequately separates the terms from each other (in further "correct" usage) when the components are few in number. Is this the "true" meaning.[12]

There is another sense in which Goodenough's method cannot answer the original and basic question asked in these chapters: Are kinship terms "systems of consanguinity and affinity" or are they something else (in any given culture)? Goodenough loaded the dice by deciding in advance that in order to get rid of the problems of metaphorical usage he would restrict his universe of kin terms to those in descriptive and referential usage (thus his method cannot assess the problem of McLennan's terms of salutation referring to "age and station"). Murdock had himself restricted the scope of kin terms analyzed in *Social Structure* (1949) to terms of reference exclusively because they are usually more specific (more genealogical) than terms of address (1949:98), and throughout it is evident that he assumes that kin terminology is basically genealogical. In addition, the genealogical method as developed by Rivers (1900) was Murdock's systematic approach in collecting information. This is all right, of course, but then the findings have no relevance to the controversies on the meaning of kin terms.[13]

[12]Burling (1964) points out to those who take componential analysis seriously as a method for finding out some kind of "cognitive reality" in the natives' heads that it is, rather, only "hocus-pocus" because there are usually many alternative verions that can be offered to solve the problem.

[13]The problem of the meaning of kin terms was addressed philosophically by a philosopher–become–ethnologist, Ernest Gellner, in 1957, and his argument was frankly weighted toward an assumption that the terms were supposed to be genealogical. He thought an "ideal language" (that is, without polysemy or any ambiguity) could be made up for kinship systems because of the facts of life—that only two persons, a physiological father and mother, are the source of "descent systems"; thus discrete pigeonholes of

Floyd Lounsbury's articles (1956a,b) are also frankly addressed to genealogical kin terms only: "Metaphoric extensions can be expected for any lexical item. In the structural analysis of a semantic field, however, they are excluded. We have not intended to deal with all of the meanings of the Iroquois kinship terms here, but only with those that fall within the field defined as *genealogical kin*" (1956b:144). Lounsbury is also of Yale University and may be presumed to have acquired this orientation from Murdock.

Romney and Epling (1958) apply certain principles of componential analysis to a classic Australian group, the Kariera, and it is good to return to the early battleground. This article is useful in particular, however, not only because it makes a kinship system so perplexing to others seem actually simple but because it shows that a form of componential analysis does not have to restrict itself to genealogical kin types and terms of reference and so avoid the question of their meaning. Further, the analysis relates the kin terminology directly and simply to meanings related to social behavior: marriage rules, residence rules, and affinal behavior. This is especially surprising because Kroeber's 1909 article, which Romney and Epling regard as the pathfinder, was also a source of fundamental controversy because it asserted a *lack* of congruence between terminologies and social institutions.

Perhaps this seeming paradox can be resolved by considering that Kroeber's article contains two distinct ideas that somehow were fused in his mind—or which, at least, were not segregated by his readers. First, and what so annoyed Rivers and Radcliffe-Brown, is the group of related assertions to the effect that kin terminology is best understood as a form of language–psychology, not related via cause and effect to the forms of social organization. Second, but not necessarily logically related to the first, is a method of analysis of terminologies—not an assertion about what a terminological system *really is*. It is this second idea that has survived better, as an ancestor to what has come to be called componential analysis. This analysis stems from, or was suggested by, the Boasian method of language analysis by which "rules" of

---

genealogy could be named, with one term for each pigeonhole. More or less parenthetically, he averred the British social anthropology paid too little attention to biological genealogy. The controversy that ensued involved several prominent social anthropologists opposed to Gellner's reductionism. Their articles lie outside the temporal limits of the present volume, but I cite them here for the convenience of any interested readers. They are Needham (1960), Gellner again (1960, 1963), Barnes (1961, 1964), Beattie (1964), and Schneider (1964).

grammar, for example, are found (or, anyway, stated) by the linguist on examining a sufficient number of behavioral instances. It seems likely that Kroeber confused the fact that he could use a linguistic type of analysis on kinship terminologies with the subject of terminologies itself—that it was itself like language (and thus basically a mental phenomenon). And since terminologies are language, then their basic characteristics will tend to be relatively unresponsive directly to societal characteristics.

It is this latter aspect of Kroeber's 1909 article that is gainsaid by Romney and Epling's article. But the other aspect, the analytical frame that was such a useful precursor, was not misused by making the unwarranted assumptions about "primary" and "secondary" terms that Murdock and his students added to it. It is for this analytical frame that Kroeber's 1909 article should be given positive credit, and Romney and Epling have rightly supported this.

7

Alliance versus Descent in the Semantics of Kinship Terms

In a 1943 article, "The Social Use of Kinship Terms Among Brazilian Indians," Claude Lévi-Strauss made his first contribution to the solution of the problem we have been addressing in Part II. Also, in a sense, the article presaged his later argument about the significance of *exchange* and *alliance* in the relations of kin groups. This theory has been one side in a controversy with several British social anthropologists indebted to Radcliffe-Brown, whose view has come to be called *descent theory*. This controversy has mostly to do with social structure (marriage rules and kin group composition) and is therefore discussed in more detail in Part III, Social Structure. But to an important extent some of the controversy has bearing on the assumptions about the meaning of kinship terms.

The Nambikuara Indians of Brazil, like many other South American forest dwellers, have a standard system of cross-cousin marriage and the bifurcate-merging system of terminology so usually associated with it. (Parallel cousins of Ego are classed with brother and sister and cross cousins with wife and brother-in-law; similar bifurcations and mergings are made in the adjacent generations above and below Ego's.) It seems plain, however, that the classifications are not simply extensions of primary consanguineous terms, nor metaphors, since the Indians have a difficulty when for some (rare) reason they need to point out, for example, the "real" status of their consanguine children. A roundabout means is used, adding to the status term ordinarily in use a second word used to designate newly born animals—a clear physiological implication. Similarly cumbersome means are used to designate other relatives such as *genitor* or *genitrix*. Plainly, the classificatory *category* contains the primary meaning of the terms.

Of further interest was what happened when early European missionaries introduced the institution of coparenthood (from *compérage*), an institution which, in Catholic Europe, was used to form a ritual extension of the family—an adoption, so to speak. The Brazilian Indians adopted strangers into their tribes by classifying men of appropriate ages as brother-in-law (and thus their sisters were marriageable). It would have been normal for the introduced *compérage* institution to have become assimilated to the native brother-in-law institution but for one thing: the institution of *compérage* at that time placed restrictions on intermarriage of the members. *Compérage* was therefore assimilated into the category of "father." Plainly, again, classificatory terms have to do primarily with the distinctions based on "own–other" marriageable (affinal) groups, not nuclear families.

Lévi-Strauss thus does not make the genealogical assumption that primary kin terms are metaphorically extended outward. But, like Kroeber's, his view is mentalistic: the language-structure imposes the types of classification upon the outside social world. A bifurcate-merging kinship system is related to a rule of cross-cousin marriage but neither causes the other, being but two aspects of the same thing. It is something else, an unconscious mental construct, that imposes both the marriage rule *and* the classificatory terminology. In the very first paragraph of the preface to the first edition of *The Elementary Structures of Kinship* (1949:xxiii), Lévi-Strauss says: "The basic purpose of this book is to show that marriage rules, nomenclature, and the system of rights and prohibitions are indissociable aspects of one and the same reality, viz., the structure of the system under consideration." What *is* this "structure"?

Lévi-Strauss used *structure* rather loosely in his 1949 work and a certain amount of confusion has resulted, especially since Radcliffe-Brown and his partisans used it to designate the actual, visible parts of the society, such as associations, clubs, kinship units, and political institutions, and their interrelationship. When Lévi-Strauss is being careful he uses *structure* to mean something quite different—different especially in the salient characteristic of being invisible. Let us approach this concept in brief historical perspective.

In his famous introduction to *Handbook of American Indian Languages* in 1911, Franz Boas counseled ethnologists to see the parallels between language and culture, especially since manners and customs, just as the grammar of a language, probably have unconscious origins. Boas says:

> It seems necessary to dwell upon the analogy of ethnology and language in this respect, because, if we adopt this point of view, language seems to be one of the

most instructive fields of inquiry in an investigation of the formation of the fundamental ethnic ideas. The great advantage that linguistics offers in this respect is the fact that, on the whole, the categories which are formed always remain unconscious, and that for this reason the processes which lead to their formation can be followed without the misleading and disturbing factors of secondary explanations, which are so common in ethnology, so much so that they generally obscure the real history of the development of ideas entirely. (1911a:66–67)

Boas addressed himself directly to kinship usage in one revealing passage that suggests the possible priority of language as a determinant of social customs. He mentions that our term *uncle* classes together what usually in primitive society are two distinct classes, father's brother and mother's brother. He continues:

Here, also, it is commonly assumed that the linguistic expression is a second-ary reflex of the customs of the people; but the question is quite often in how far the one phenomenon is the primary one and the other the secondary one, and whether the customs of the people have not rather developed from the unconsciously developed terminology. (1911a:69)

Lévi-Strauss (1958:20) rightly tells us that Boas should be fully cred-ited with this important assumption about the nature of culture, which, by the way, antedated by eight years the famous formulation of structural linguistics by Ferdinand de Saussure (*Cours de linguistique général*). Boas never carried this very far in his own ethnological work, although he probably taught it carefully to students. A. L. Kroeber, as we have seen, applied this linguistic view in his 1909 "Classificatory Systems of Relationship" and later in other cultural institutions and patterns further removed from language, particularly the famous study (1919a) of changes in women's fashions.[1] Lévi-Strauss is not a biolog-ical or psychological reductionist in the way Malinowski plainly and frankly was. Nor is he exactly an idealist, holding to the notion of the causal priority of ideas in human action as opposed to outside material events and situations. In a personal communication to David Schneider, he pointed out that he gives no priority to ideas in social life or action; rather, both ideas and action derive from "qualities of mind" (Schneider 1965:79: Footnote 1). In earlier chapters I have called this kind of structuralism *mentalism*, meaning that the locus of explana-tion lies in the mind but not necessarily or primarily as consciously held ideas or ideology. Gender, number, tense, and relational catego-

---

[1] Lévi-Strauss particularly approved of Kroeber's 1919 article because women's fash-ions had predictable changes of a sort that no one was conscious of, yet there were numerous rationalizations, or "secondary" explanations, by nearly everyone (Lévi-Strauss 1958:58). Elsewhere he calls it "a landmark of structural research" (1958:275).

ries in general, it should be remembered, are in some sense in the mind, though not necessarily consciously (or if consciously, they may not be accurate, being "secondary" in Boas' sense). It may be well to quote Lévi-Strauss on this matter:

> In the study of kinship problems (and, no doubt, the study of other problems as well), the anthropologist finds himself in a situation which formally resembles that of the structural linguist. Like phonemes, kinship terms are elements of meaning; like phonemes, they acquire meaning only if they are integrated into systems. "Kinship systems," like "phonemic systems," are built by the mind on the level of unconscious thought. . . . The problem can therefore be formulated as follows: Although they belong to *another order of reality*, kinship phenomena are *of the same type* as linguistic phenomena. (1958:32)

Many linguists do not claim that by their analysis they can discover how the mind of the subject is actually working. All they can do, in effect, is make a shorthand description of linguistic behavior that "predicts"; that is, such things as the grammar and phonology posited are useful in enabling a stranger to consistently make up statements that make sense to the subjects—the analysis need not have anything to do with what is or was in the subjects' heads (see our earlier discussion of Goodenough's 1956 componential analysis). On the other hand, some linguists (normally the structuralists) stress the discovery procedures that would elicit an informant's own unrecognized principles of classification and conceptualization rather than the conceptual models of the analyst. Lévi-Strauss belongs to some extent in this group, but his methodology (to many) lacks the sophistication that would help insure that something is being discovered rather than simply imposed on the data by himself.

Lévi-Strauss borrowed from Durkheim's prize student (and nephew), Marcel Mauss, the very important idea of social solidarity being initiated and maintained by gift exchange, of which the exchange of women by marriage is the most important. Note well, however, that the emphasis is not on *a* gift or *a* particular marriage but on the continued exchange of gifts (however delayed)—that is, of reciprocity. The mentalistic "structural principle" at work here in keeping reciprocity continuous, as in marriage exchanges, is alliance. Related to alliance is dualism, a structural principle that itself points up the give-and-take of reciprocity.

In contrast to the Malinowskian extensionist view of the nuclear family as the basic unit, with its notion that the primary meanings of kinship terms originate there, Lévi-Strauss believes that reciprocity in marriages is basic, reflecting the unconscious structural principle of alliance; hence *affinality*, not parenthood, is basic.

This lies in direct contrast to those British social anthropologists who follow Radcliffe-Brown's emphasis on the consanguineal family and the larger descent systems as the fundamental building blocks of society. Thus, in a society practicing cross-cousin marriage, the kin-term category including mother's brother also includes father-in-law; while male cross-cousin is also brother-in-law. What, then, is the fundamental meaning of the kin terms? Mother's brother is the important figure in mother's lineage and related to Ego by "complementary filiation." Ego is a member (in two different ways) of two different unilineal descent groups, Ego's father's and mother's; mother's brother and own father are thus complementary figures—and Ego's dual relationship, along with others, helps tie the descent groups together in a form or organic solidarity. The meaning of the kin term is an expression of the behavior and attitudes related to this fact, with the contrast of the indulgent adult of mother's lineage with the more authoritarian figure of the father.

But to Lévi-Strauss and his followers, a kin term that simultaneously includes mother's brother and father-in-law has its primary meaning contained in the latter relationship. The universal presence of the incest taboo and the rule of exogamy requires that there be "wife-givers"—that is, fathers-in-law—and in societies with cross-cousin marriage this is the kin category that includes mother's brother. Hence the primary meaning is "father-in-law" and the underlying structural principle is that of alliance, not the Radcliffe-Brownian conception of the structure of unilineal descent groups being allied by consanguineal ties between such persons as a male ego and his mother's brother.

Louis Dumont published a paper in 1953 called "The Dravidian Kinship Terminology as an Expression of Marriage." The Dravidian language group, mostly people of South India, have a bifurcate-merging (Iroquoian) system of the familiar type associated with cross-cousin marriage. (The Tamil are the Dravidian people whose kinship system so excited Morgan, for it was identical with his Seneca Iroquois and the first he found like it in Asia.) Dumont clearly posed the issue of alliance versus descent and criticized the prevalent descent theory of British social anthropology in direct terms. He got an immediate reply from Radcliffe-Brown in the same journal (*Man*), to which he subsequently briefly replied. This was a useful exchange, for the alliance aspect of Lévi-Strauss' message, complicated by immersion in his long, very detailed book, had been misunderstood and garbled by most of those who had noticed it at all. (*Structures élémentaires* had been published only four years earlier and was not translated into English until 1969.)

Dumont takes the simplest aspect of this system (as we have seen in the preceding discussion of Lévi-Strauss) to be that father and father's brother (and others) are given the same term but other males in the same generation on the mother's side are given another term. He emphasizes that these are two classes of people rather than a form of relationship that stresses the membership of father and mother's brother as basic with the meaning extended to others in the class. Likewise, since mother's brother's term includes the class "father-in-law," it has usually been assumed that the latter is secondary in importance. But these assumptions could be ethnocentric, as A. M. Hocart has suggested. Dumont believes that these ideas are based simply on the common notion that one's kinship position necessarily precedes one's marriage. In a sense it is true, of course, that Ego's genealogical position is acquired at birth and the marriage much later—and in our system we do not acquire in-laws until marriage. But also, of course, this view of "in-lawness" is our own and not necessarily like that of the Dravidians.

In our view the relationship of Ego's father to Ego's mother's brother is through their differing relationship to Ego's mother (and thus to Ego). But it can be looked at quite differently. Suppose the basis of the relationship is that of the two classes of men, A's and B's, who have formed what Dumont (after Lévi-Strauss) calls an alliance. *This* may be primary, and then expressed by the marriage of an A to a B's sister. Marriage is thus a function of alliance, not its cause and not prior to it. And affinal groups are created by the continuity of such marriage reciprocities and, in a new sense, the in-laws of Ego are actually created not only before his own marriage but even before his birth.

Alliance relationship thus defines the mother's brother of Ego in terms of his social relationship to the father. However, it must be remembered that these are classes (categories) of people in affinal status to each other—marriage is a relationship between groups. The basic meaning for the "cross" category is thus affinal; my mother's brother is most essentially my father's affine.

Similarly, in the same generation is found the alliance opposition between Ego's mother and father's sister. That is, the two women have an alliance relationship identical to father and mother's brother. Both of these sets in alliance are the basis of the "cross" relationship, and their progeny are cross-cousins. Cross-cousin marriage thus makes alliance an institution that endures through the generations.

How does Dumont know this? What is the evidence, or superiority in logic, that makes his theory of alliance via marriage the basis of, the meaning of, the terminology? How does he know that the brother-in-law relationship of A and B is more the essence of the term than that B is "uncle" to A's son or daughter? Or, from Ego's perspective, is that person, B, more significantly of the class "father-in-law," or of "mother's brother"? And, to put it still another way, is the significance of A's marriage to B's sister an expression of A's and B's alliance, or does it's significance lie in the fact that a child born to the marriage will be a member of two descent groups, uniting them structurally by "complementary filiation"?

Dumont does not prove his case, of course, just because he can explain Dravidian terminology in a way distinct from descent theory. His introductory paragraph states: "Field acquaintance with Dravidian kinship terminology made me feel very strongly its systematic, logical character; I could not help thinking that it centered in marriage, and that it should be possible to express those two features in a simple formula" (1953b:34). This statement is not exactly a claim for his empiricism, but Dumont's strong feeling that his analysis is correct is justified by his close and long personal acquaintance with the Dravidians. It should be noted that in this article he does not apply his analysis to other peoples. Again, in arguing that "my mother's brother is essentially my father's affine," Dumont says: "The only difference from customary views on the subject lies in the way we have taken, not the way through the mother, as suggested by our own vocabulary, but, I believe, *the native way, as imposed by the terminology*" (1953b:37; emphasis added). One may not agree that this analysis is "imposed by the terminology," but one may be disposed to accept Dumont's feeling that this is "the native way" since he is a preeminent student of the Dravidians.

Is Dumont's argument hard to understand? One would think not, yet Radcliffe-Brown's critique in *Man* (1953) began: "Sir,—I cannot claim that I understand the article on Dravidian kinship terminology by Mr. Dumont though I have read it carefully several times. I should like to be enlightened as to its meaning, and I suspect that there are others in the same position as myself." Radcliffe-Brown's familiarity with a system similar to the Dravidian, the Australian Kariera, entitles him (apparently) to argue that while one's mother's brother is surely the brother-in-law of one's father, he is not thought of as being "essentially" a relative by marriage. "In fact the Australian aborigines have no terms to indicate relatives by marriage, 'alliance' relatives or affines. Yet there is clearly a great similarity between Australian and Dravidian systems of kinship terminology" (1953:169).

Dumont had a brief last word, again in *Man* (1953a). This piece poses the issue more clearly. In his earlier article he gave the impression that it was his personal familiarity with the Dravidians that gave him the authority to speak of the preeminence of affinality and marriage over descent in their thought. But now, in response to Radcliffe-Brown's statement that in Australia mother's brother is *not* thought of as a relative by marriage, he argues that he is not talking about how an Ego thinks of a particular relative; rather, he would take the whole terminological system and "try to determine from its structure what the content of each of its categories is."

Dumont is here arguing for a kind of analysis of the system, not the behavior patterns or the attitudes of particular Egos to particular relatives. What is the difference in English between father and uncle, mother and aunt, brother (or sister) and cousin, son (or daughter) and nephew (or niece)? In all these examples the main difference, "the axis of the system," is the distinction between Ego's direct line and the collateral lines. (This, it may be recalled, is essentially the definition of the descriptive system made by L. H. Morgan.) If this is accepted, then how a given Englishman thinks of his own father's sister is an utterly distinct question, to be investigated in an altogether different way.

As for Radcliffe-Brown's assertion that the Australians have no terms for relatives by marriage, Dumont argues that perhaps there are no distinctive terms for a given relative by marriage (that is, to distinguish *wife* from the categorical term which includes all female cross-cousins—the marriageable category). Dumont says that the whole category is "tinged with affinity." In short, Radcliffe-Brown will not widen the concept of affinity to include whole groups of people. But if there are prescribed or preferred mates, then it must be "that affinity in a way precedes the actual marriage." Affinity, in societies such as those of the Dravidian-like systems, *inherit* affinity just as we inherit our "blood" relationships.[2]

Is Dumont's argument a case of psychological or, perhaps, mentalistic, reductionism? Not exactly, and certainly not in the usual meaning of the logical fallacy of explaining in causal terms the actions of phenomena at one level of integration (such as social behavior) by underlying levels (such as psychological or biological characteristics of mind).

This exchange between Dumond and Radcliffe-Brown is the best example of the two different perspectives, alliance versus descent, on the functions of, or nature of, marriage systems with respect to the meaning of kinship terminology. Other, more famous, papers such as those of E. R. Leach (1951), sympathetic to Lévi-Strauss' alliance theo-

---

[2]In 1957, Dumont presented his argument for the inheritance of affinity in more general terms and at greater length in a complete monograph.

ry, and Meyer Fortes' (1953) classic discussion of the structure of descent groups, say little directly to the point of kinship terminology, although from internal evidence one surmises that Leach would side with Dumont and Fortes with Radcliffe-Brown. These papers and others will be featured later in the alliance–descent discussion in the context of social structure itself (Part III).

8

The Meaning of Kinship Terms as Suggested by Historical Changes in Pattern

Lewis H. Morgan took a long time to comprehend the various startling implications of his discovery of classificatory kinship systems. For years he argued that the systems did not change and that therefore similarities in pattern among societies would reveal historical relationships between them long after even the languages had diverged from the parent stock. But finally he adopted McIlvaine's idea of stages of moral progress from promiscuity to monogamy, which were designed to show how different marriage systems accounted for the major kinds of kinship patterns. This was a completely genealogical view of the meaning of kinship terms, and so naive that it was soon attacked in many quarters.

There were two suggestions in *Ancient Society*, finally, that require notice in the present context, for although Morgan did not seem to realize it fully, they stood in direct contrast to the basis of his scheme. One instance was his recognition of the influence of the gentile organization, which, he thought, was made exogamous ostensibly to prevent the intermarriage of brothers and sisters. The other was the influence of the inheritance of private estates in lineal succession.

In the first instance Morgan did not exactly give up his genealogical view, but he was nevertheless aware of the influence of a social institution upon the kin terms. He saw the "Malayan System of Consanguinity and Affinity" (generational or Hawaiian) giving way to the "Turanian–Gonowanian System" (bifurcate-merging or Iroquois). The true kin, "brothers" and "sisters" of the gens (clan), were terminologically separated from the marriageable affines of the other gens.

This remains genealogical in essence, however, because Morgan did not see gens membership as directly giving a status, but instead changing the form of the family (by prohibiting the marriage of brothers and sisters), which in turn alters genealogical relationships.

In the second case, however, we are closer to a functional view of the influence of one institution on others; private property, as it increased in variety and amount, steadily augmented its influence toward monogamy, descriptive kinship terminology, governments, law courts, and slavery. The great Aryan, Semitic, and Uralian systems of kinship, all basically alike (descriptive) were created by the monogamian family.[1] But despite the functional interconnections that result in monogamy, the kinship terminology itself is directly related to the family form. It is not caused by it, for it is part of it; a certain kind of marriage and family is a genealogical form, and the "systems" of terms are simply the verbal aspect of it. So, again we see that the sociological functionalism so often attributed to Morgan is appropriate only if we exclude kinship terminology—kinship terms were to him of genealogical significance only, not social.

It remains a fact that in general the several kinds of classificatory systems are correlated with "primitive" societies that do not have individual estates of economic significance, while descriptive systems are largely related to Western civilization and its archaic precursors. Morgan thought this correlation was due to the moral progress of the West in favoring monogamy, but his briefly made point about the significance of property may have been prescient.[2]

W. H. R. Rivers took up Morgan's arguments about primitive versus modern society and made them more specific and cogent, ignoring the "moral imperative" and decreeing with well-considered ethnological examples, that the classificatory system (in his examples, bifurcate-merging) was directly caused by "exogamous groupings" (clans or moieties). He said:

> If you are dissatisfied with the word "classificatory" as a term for the system of relationship which is found in America, Africa, India, Australia and Oceania, you would be perfectly safe in calling it the "clan" system, and in inferring the ancient presence of a social structure based on the exogamous clan even if this structure were no longer present. (1914c:82)

[1] I have paraphrased Morgan's summation (1877:424–427) for the sake of brevity.
[2] An interesting essay in philological research by A. M. Hocart (1928) argued that the Indo–European system of nomenclature was originally (prior to the classical civilizations) a classificatory system, as might have been expected because of other resemblances of early Indo–European society to normal primitive society. This tends to support Morgan's point.

Similarly, the descriptive system is directly equated with the monogamous family in the same sense of functional dependency (1914c:85).[3] The functionalism, however, is tempered by the idea that terminological systems lag well behind changes in social structure, as is indicated by his statement that past structures can be inferred from present systems of nomenclature.

Since Rivers' time numerous scholars have proposed typologies of nomenclatures that attempt to show their functional correlations with types of social structure or levels of social complexity (all have been mentioned previously). Certain simple correlations seem nowadays to be fairly acceptable: Omaha-type cousin terms with patrilineal descent groups (although many patrilineal groups do not have Omaha terms); Crow-types with matrilineal descent groups (although many matrilineal groups do not have Crow terms); descriptive terms ("Eskimo," "New England Yankee," etc.) with bilateral systems and nuclear family households; and bifurcate-merging (Iroquoian) systems with intermarriage of exogamous groups or cross–parallel distinctions.[4] But such correlations do not tell us about the direction of causality nor what the terms "really mean"; for example, they do not permit an adjudication of the Dumont–Radcliffe-Brown argument about the significance of the mother's brother. Similarly, attempts to correlate kinds of terminologies with evolutionary stages of complexity have been unsuccessful. This is largely because the ego-oriented terminologies are associated with close-knit familial (kinship) forms of social structures, which are, perforce, themselves dependent features of other, larger economic, political, and ideological parts of culture. As these latter grow in complexity from primitive through more modern forms, the kinship structure is changed in various ways but does not itself grow commensurately in size or complexity. In fact—obviously—the kinship organization of modern industrial society, compared to that of a tribe such as the Iroquois, has *de*volved, as new forms of nonfamilial organization and associated statuses and titles (especially the use of personal family names) have arisen to take on many of its social, political, economic, and religious functions.[5]

It would be much more edifying to consider examples of historically known changes in the social structure of particular societies to see in

---

[3]Rivers repeated these statements almost word for word in his article "Kin, Kinship" in *Hastings Encyclopaedia of Religion and Ethics* (1914b:703), thus attesting to his estimate of the significance of this idea.

[4]See Goody (1970) for a convenient summary of these correlations.

[5]See Service (1960) for a fuller discussion of the evolutionary problem and an attempted solution.

what manner (and how soon) changes occurred in the terminological pattern. It has long been noted that discrepancies exist in the nomenclatures reported for societies at different times in their history. But so ingrained has been the assumption that the systems were relatively static that the discrepancies were usually dismissed, at least on the part of earlier writers, as errors in reporting. A salient example of this is Radcliffe-Brown's criticism of E. H. Man's data on the Andaman Islanders collected almost 50 years earlier (even though Radcliffe-Brown was on his first field trip and admitted his inexperience and the difficulties in getting data on kinship terms and marriage rules [1922:60–70]). Inasmuch as the native population had been decimated by disease by this time, it seems incredible that Radcliffe-Brown could have dismissed Man's work so easily. Perhaps it is a case, so often encountered, of the disdain of the "professional," university-trained in ethnology, for the earlier amateur.[6] As in the case of the Andamanese, the typical historical occurrence of modern times has been disruption of the primitive social structure in various ways related to depopulation, amalgamation of scattered groups, territorial removals, and disruption of the aboriginal subsistence economy, all of which have the frequent result of breaking up or at least simplifying marriage rules and the forms of social interaction based on them. (Sometimes, of course, the alteration is due to tutelage, as in a mission, so that the basis of the social structure is considerably altered and new foreign forms of nomenclature are learned and adopted. This form of acculturation is not germane at this point.)

Ideally, a set of related social changes that were evolutionary in their direction and momentum would be the most useful indicators of functionally related changes between structure and nomenclature. The typical changes among primitive peoples in our recorded history, however, have been disruptive and in the main devolutionary; but just as the acquisition, or the strengthening, of a clan–lineage system might be followed by, say, a Crow or Omaha development in nomenclature, which if recorded would be very useful, so, to some extent, would be the loss or weakening of the clan–lineage system, were it to be followed by changes in the Crow or Omaha nomenclature.

---

[6]Yet in a footnote Radcliffe-Brown says of his own attempts to understand Andamanese kinship: "The difficulty of being really sure on these matters is due (1) to the fact that the breaking-up of the old local organization has produced many changes in their customs, and (2) to the difficulty of questioning the natives on matters connected with relationships when they have no words in their language to denote any but the simplest relationships" (1922:82n). As we have seen, Radcliffe-Brown was later to outgrow this naive genealogical view of kinship. The Andamanese *categories* of status were simple, not their genealogical relationships.

Numerous ethnohistorical studies, supplemented sometimes by comparative studies, do show the close functional relationship between exogamic units and the "bifurcation" of cross or parallel relatives. The first well-known finding of this kind was by Rivers (1914a,c) in Melanesia and Polynesia, which has already been mentioned. But Rivers was interested in "extrapolating backwards," using his assumption of the close association of nomenclature to marriage customs along with the assumption that the nomenclatures will persist, in order to reconstruct the past history of Melanesian marriage. He was not, in other words, trying to prove this "meaning" of kinship terms by historical research, for the strict relationship of terminology to marriage was to him a given.

Fred Eggan was the first to directly challenge by ethnohistorical research the assumption of the stability of kinship terminology.[7] In investigating the social organization of Indians of the southeastern part of the United States, beginning with the Choctaw, he found a series of changes that could be historically documented, with the bonus that other southeastern tribes (Chickasaw and Creek) were found to have changed in different degrees but along the same general lines.

These groups (as well as others in the Southeast) had evidently all had a social structure featuring matrilineal exogamous clans and the Crow system of nomenclature typically associated with it. The processes of historical change and adaptation to modern culture featured an increasing emphasis on patrilineal inheritance of land and wealth, and this was associated with a continuing breakdown in the clan system. In particular, the relations of children to father was strengthened at the expense of the mother's brother. In all cases the direction of change was from Crow nomenclature toward a generational system.

In a related study of the Cheyenne and Arapaho kinship system, Eggan found again that the generational type of system of these two tribes may well have been a late result of historical changes in plains life that had been carrying the tribes at different rates away from the

---

[7]H. I. Hallowell anticipated Eggan's work in a 1928 publication, testing for correlated social changes in Abnaki terminology since 1693–1775 (when Jesuit missionary dictionaries were compiled). He concluded that the considerable changes in terminology were due to "contact" with other Indians and Europeans rather than structural social change. It is regrettable, however, that he accepted Frank Speck's (1915) judgment that the "family band" as a nonexogamous landholding unit was the aboriginal Algonkian form of organization. Eleanor Leacock (1954) conclusively showed that this organization was due to participation in the fur trade and not aboriginal at all. The Abnaki might very well have provided an excellent example of the relation of terminology to structure via historical changes had Hallowell not been misled by Speck's work, for these Indians had actually undergone drastic social organizational and economic changes prior to their changes in kin terminology.

bifurcate-merging and Crow–Omaha types of systems. Even the Crow Indians themselves seem to have been in the process of changing toward a generational system. Eggan does not insist on a single cause for this phenomenon, but he would nevertheless argue for a functional rather the simple diffusionist explanation so commonly employed in America.

He notes that in the variations from tribes peripheral to the plains toward the central location of the Cheyenne–Arapaho, there is a variation from cross-cousin systems to systems sanctioning marriage with more distant cousins, to finally, systems that allow marriage completely outside the range of blood relatives. The implication is that the conditions of plains life fostered the desirability of a wider range of familial alliances, and, more specifically, that the change in marriage customs from clan exogamy and cross-cousin marriage toward a more unspecified and wider marriage system created the generational system simply by removing the affinal (or cross–parallel) bifurcation (Eggan 1937a:94–95).

Alexander Spoehr carried on the same kind of historical and comparative research in the Southeast, adding a full study of the Seminole (who are related to the Creek) to further surveys among various communities of Creek, Cherokee, and Choctaw. Spoehr's findings (1947:227–230) bear out Eggan's more tentative conclusions and his general summary remarks are worth noting:

1.   Changes are regular. "Similar kinship systems of tribes under similar conditions of contact can be expected to change in similar ways" (1947:227).

2.   Lineage types (Crow–Omaha) change to generation types under conditions that cause a decline of lineage ties and clan ties and greater independence of the elementary family with its own bilateral extensions. A probable corollary is the strengthening of the conjugal unit. Another suggestion is that disturbances in the aboriginal system of exchange of goods and services and in the distribution of income cause the abandonment of widely extended kin ties.

3.   The change from lineage system to generation system may reveal in its intermediate stages certain divergences or inconsistencies, which in turn may suggest the particular kinds of social changes taking place; this may lead to a better understanding of the dynamics of change.

4.   Terminologies, behavior patterns, and form and function of family, clan, or local group do not change at the same rate under pressure. The Southeastern data show that vocative terminology is more susceptible to change than referential terminology; kinship behavior patterns

change before the terminology; clans or exogamous groups are affected before the terminology changes.

5. More studies of kinship during periods of transition promise frutiful results.

So far we have examined the arguments on historical change in reverse, so to speak. The evidence suggests that modern conditions have caused a sort of devolution by removing or diminishing the role of exogamous groups in regulating marriage and in maintaining aboriginal status arrangements. Yet there is an even more striking devolution and disruption of aboriginal social structures that can happen without any acculturative agencies coming into firsthand contact with the aborigines. This is the disruption caused by European contagious diseases, which have often decimated tremendous areas before many of the natives had even seen the foreigners. A usual consequence of depopulation after such epidemics is the merging of unrelated survivors into communities that therefore no longer have their old exogamous divisions. The realignment of kin relations is usually neolocal, cognatic, and bilateral. The loss of bifurcation representing the exogamous divisions is likely to be found first in Ego's own generation with sibling terms used for all cousins rather than parallels alone. Gertrude Dole (1957:290–358) has documented this devolution from what she calls "formal" to "informal," or fluid, kin groups in three widely separated world areas: the North American plains, Oceania, and tropical South America. The disrupted informal groups typically developed generational kinship terminology.[8]

Does this mean that all cases of societies with generational terminologies are decultured, devolved, or somehow disrupted versions of societies formerly characterized by more formal exogamous groupings such as clans or lineages? Or might there be still other functional reasons for a generational system? In all of the discussion so far, it has appeared that generational terminologies result from simplification of the social structure, as though there were no longer structural necessities, such as exogamous groupings, for distinguishing one kind of relative from another except by age and sex. Morgan himself thought that this system was the earliest and simplest of all. It caused him to place the Hawaiian society, because its generational terminology had been reported to him, as among the most primitive known.[9]

---

[8]See Wagley (1940) for a more specific historical documentation of the social-organizational consequences of depopulation.

[9]It should be noted that Rivers, usually considered such a staunch defender of Morgan, nevertheless argued that Morgan was wrong and that the Malayan (Hawaiian) sys-

Morgan could not have known much about the Hawaiians and other central Polynesians or he would have been greatly perplexed by them. Far from being unable to place "own" father and mother among the generalized and numerous relatives called by the same terms, the Hawaiians seem obsessed with their individual pedigrees and genealogies! Every person holds a precise rank, which is strictly inherited by birth order. Thus, not only are the lines of descent from both parents carefully delineated through many generations but the inherited seniority of each ancestor within his own sibling group can be recounted. Far from being simple, the actual kinship structure is as complex as it could possibly be—it is, so to speak, *total* kinship of the fully genealogical sort.

But the means by which each individual's inherited status is identified is not in terms of an ego-centered pattern of kinship nomenclature, and it was therefore not included in the schedules drawn up by Morgan. Instead, they are sociocentered—that is, objectified—names or titles which are passed on strictly by inheritance. Identification of individuals both in reference and address is by such means. The only information left out of this system is of course the generation of the individual. The generational "kinship" terms are typically used in address in ways that convey polite deference of younger to older (or more distinguished) or friendliness and kindness of elder to younger (or less distinguished).

Despite the extremely generous use of such terms as father and mother, brother and sister, and son and daughter, the Polynesians know the genealogical relationship of everyone, and they can state it with precision. Since most primitive peoples use kinship terms instead of personal names, the Hawaiian system deserves further attention.

Are there reasons other than disruption or depopulation for the obliteration of exogamous groups (or the bifurcation of cousins into cross–parallel terms)? One obvious possibility is that if a society were for some reason to permit parallel-cousin marriage, then the cross–parallel distinction would lose one of its most important features—that of distinguishing actual and potential affines from consanguineals (except for those of the immediate family of the individual after the actual marriage, as in Euro–American society).

The Fijians, as described by Hocart, "sometimes *arrange* marriage of ortho-cousins 'for noble issues'" (1933:264n). This remark is the earliest published that I have found that notes, however briefly, the social

---

tem was late, having become a simplified system, with its exogamous distinctions being "blurred" (1907)—an acute idea in his time.

effect of parallel-cousin marriage in consolidating and perpetuating high status, in opposition to cross-cousin marriage, which tends to broaden the alliance aspect of marriage. To be sure, considerable attention has long been paid to "royal incest," the practice of brother–sister marriage (perhaps classificatory brothers and sisters—that is, parallel-cousins). The Hawaiian major chiefs, Egyptian pharaohs, and Inca emperors seem to be the most famous examples; often the explanation has been that these people are showing their power by flouting the rules against incest that ordinary mortals must strictly observe. Other well-known cases of preferred parallel-cousin marriage are the numerous Arab chiefdoms and later Near Eastern emirates and sultanates.

It seems evident that among aboriginal chiefdoms such as the central Polynesians, as well as among more modern Arabs, a general cultural ideal is the continued maintenance of the hereditary rank positions of all family lines in relation to each other. This would occur, of course, with parallel-cousin marriage; in a society of such patrilineal emphasis as the Arabs', the specific marriage of a boy to father's brother's daughter would be ideal. But, naturally enough, individual families, particularly if they are not very high in status, may prefer to make an advantageous marriage into another family line, thus, frequently, between cross-cousins. One thing seems clear. The higher the rank, the fewer are the marriage choices among equals, and thus there will be more frequent cases of close-in endogamy—endogamy-by-rank, it may be called. The lower the rank of the family, the more widely is it likely to cast in an attempt at an advantageous marriage, and the more likely, therefore, that a cross-cousin marriage will occur.

In any event, it would seem that there are two separate but related reasons for the nullifying of the bifurcating feature of the bifurcate-merging system. Both are related to a strong emphasis on hereditary rank. For one thing, such rank must be specified for individuals, hence the usual substitution of titles and names of descent lines and their seniority in status. A normal primitive bifurcate-merging system would be of no use in such cases. But one feature of all kinship status systems remains, that of generation (and, of course, sex). This does not mean that the generational kinship system is the simplest of all, as Morgan thought. It is simple when it is a residue of a previous ego-centric system, but the *other* kinship system, which objectifies descent lines and birth order on a society-wide basis no matter what Ego is involved, is as complex as can be. Thus it takes up space in the total system of statuses that in other, more primitive, systems (and smaller societies) would be delegated to some kind of ego-centered bifurcate-merging or Crow–Omaha system.

The other feature of hierarchical societies is the just-mentioned tendency toward endogamy-by-rank. Parallel-cousin marriages are the more frequently preferred, but they cannot be obligatory because for various reasons another kind of marriage sometimes might be more desirable; that is, either parallel- or cross-cousin marriage could be advantageous in some particular situation, hence neither is literally proscribed. Meanwhile, the cross–parallel distinction is not made in the egocentric conception of kinship, and the terms for identifying Ego's personal kindred are calculated denotatively by genealogy. The generational system used by Ego, it may be noted, is typically used in address only and is a form of politeness. The denotative system is normally used in reference; that is, in Ego's calculating how closely certain individuals are related to him in order, for example, to claim their mutual action as a vengeance group.

*   *   *

In conclusion, it seems evident that historically described changes in kinship terminology are functionally related to certain changes in the wider social environment. In a general sense, this means that Rivers was correct in arguing for this dependency. But two important things must be kept in mind. First, and most obvious, the dependence of terminology on structure is not always simple and direct. Second, a particular feature of the terminology may change in relation to an outside structural change but leave other features unchanged—kinship terminologies are really not the *systems* that they are usually assumed to be, because changes in one part do not necessarily have any functional effect on others. These two caveats mean that we cannot predict the impact of social change on a particular kind of kin term.

Let us go back to Morgan's two original ideas as presented at the beginning of this chapter. One argument was that membership in the exogamous gens created a special kind of terminology, which we are now calling bifurcate-merging. The other concerned the influence of private property in ending the classificatory system in favor of the descriptive. In both instances he seems to have been correct to an extent, although the mechanics of the process needs much reworking.

In the first case, it was E. B. Tylor (1888) who called the attention of anthropologists to the fact that exogamous groupings create "cross-cousin" marriage (which he first named in this discussion); then Rivers, as we saw, made it firmly a part of the definition of the classificatory (bifurcate-merging) terminology. But a better proof of it had to wait the charting of the historical changes in structure as described by Eggan and Spoehr.

The systems in the southeastern United States and of the Crow Indians had all been originally of the Crow type; that is, they were bifurcate-merging with the added feature that Ego calls all women of his or her father's matrilineal lineage by the term for father's sister regardless of what generation the women are in. It had been presumed by Radcliffe-Brown and his students (and by Lowie much earlier) that this "vertical" grouping was due to the influence of strong exogamous lineages or clans (and the Omaha system similarly, although it is a mirror image of Crow because the lineages or clans are patrilineal). In all the cases studied by Eggan and Spoehr, the changes in the Indians' life that diminished the significance of exogamous lineage and clan (and therefore the marriage customs) all had the effect of gradually reducing the Crow system, and its one-sided bifurcate-merging aspect as well, to the generational terminology.

As for Morgan's other idea, that private property and its inheritance by discrete lines of descent brings about a descriptive system, nothing can be said except for the incomplete association between monogamous households and descriptive terminology. Conceivably, a change in property relations could have an effect in creating or modifying households. As we noted, both Eggan and Spoehr remarked that modern changes from matrilineal societies toward a greater emphasis on patrilineal inheritance of land or private wealth had the effect of strengthening the conjugal unit and probably helping in the continued breakdown of the clan system. But in these cases the direction of change was from Crow nomenclature toward a generational rather than a descriptive system.

Morgan's notion about the influence of private property could possibly be resurrected in another, quite different, way. If private property tends to require that individual descent lines be identified, it seems likely that when these are important they will be named. In European history, precisely this kind of thing happened. Place names and titles (Duke of Burgundy) among one kind of people (landed aristocracy), occupations among another (Baker, Barber, Smith), and many other kinds of criteria all came to take up space as surnames where once kinship terms and baptismal names sufficed. But in all cases, in all societies, a form of denotative kinship always remains—that is, some ability to come close to actual genealogy, at least putatively. One's father's sister's husband's mother, or some such roundabout statement, can be made (even if sometimes inaccurately). This is what we have been calling a denotative process, and it is not a kin terminological system or pattern of the same general universe that we have been discussing. Yet it can have a functional utility, as needed, and in some cases it can be very important—as in the cases of aristocracies the world around, including many chiefdoms in the non-Western world. Such denotative specifics are of the egocentric type, and the more generally useful system of surnames, titles, and occupational status terms (Doctor, Bishop) are sociocentric, but all have uses in interpersonal conduct. These latter are capable of endless proliferation and are extremely variable from one kind of society to another. And also, the kinds of status terms may be very suggestive of certain salient aspects of the society under investigation.

It is at this point that Morgan's suggestion about private property could be fruitfully modified. It seems to be true, for example, that new kinds of property in private hands reduced the significance of clans and lineages in the southeastern United States and correspondingly reduced the Crow type of classificatory nomenclature. But the nomenclature, as we noted, did not become descriptive—it became simpler (*more* classificatory, in a sense).

In some cases known to the author,[10] the aboriginal kin system may have changed under modern acculturation, to be sure, but a more obvious change was that it was not only getting simpler but finally going out of use altogether. It tends to be completely abandoned, of course, to the extent that the aboriginal language and customs are abandoned—a frequent happening. But in cases of lesser acculturation, an egocentric kinship system may fail to survive (that is, fail to be useful) when such sociocentric forms of personal identification as names and titles connoting status differences and occupation, and family names that reflect wealth, providence, and how "old" or aristocratic they are, become useful as status terms. But this is not the "descriptive kinship system" of Morgan, although it is *very* descriptive of a kind of society. It is not kinship in the usual sense of the word (not ego-centered and not necessarily familial) and therefore has not been subjected to an appropriate analysis.

[10]Havasupai Indians of Arizona, Guaraní of Paraguay, Tepehuán and Tarascos of Mexico.

III

SOCIAL STRUCTURE

Social structure is used here in a broad sense to refer to those parts and aspects of society that are basically organizational and institutionalized. It is related to kinship terminology, for example, but it is not the same thing; exogamous lineages influence kinship terms, but they nevertheless demand a separate form of analysis. Similarly, one might think of totemism as having primarily a nomenclatural function in society, but the controversies about totem and taboo have occurred largely with reference to their relevance for the integration of society. The origin of religion, as a controversial topic, also was argued in terms of its relationship to social organization rather than as a belief system.

In the next chapter, controversy is not as direct and personal as it was in earlier chapters; rather, a diffuse misunderstanding related to different theoretical perspectives persisted, with controversy being more implicit than explicit. But Chapter 10, "Totem and Taboo," returns to the more confrontational kind of argument, as does Chapter 11, "The Origin of Religion."

9

What Are Descent Groups?

Two entirely discrepant kinds of theories about the fundamental nature of primitive descent groups appeared early in the history of ethnology and were maintained for well over the 100 years covered by our present survey. On the face of it, it seems amazing that a supposedly unified discipline such as ethnology could have been so divided in theory about such basic institutions. Perhaps the answer is simply that we are not a unified discipline.

Maine and Fustel de Coulanges versus Bachofen and McLennan

In the 1860s the foremost writers on the subject of primitive social organization had, as we saw in Chapter 1, anticipated Morgan in certain respects. One of those had to do with the evolution of the family structure in its broader connections. Since we have already met the writers in question, it will suffice to summarize their differences on this point.

Sir Henry Maine's *Ancient Law* (1861) seems to have been the first important work to call attention to the general evolutionary significance of descent groups. As we noted, Maine insisted on the qualitative difference between the primitive kinship principle of organization and the modern political or civil organization. The kinship principle, he insisted, was patriarchal; in particular, it featured strict patrilineal inheritance of membership and authority. For our present purposes this is significant as recognition of an important aspect of the *unilineality* of the descent groups. Another important aspect of the descent group was that it was an "assemblage of co-proprietors."

But Maine did not develop his ideas about the internal structure of the descent group as fully as did Fustel de Coulanges's *The Ancient*

City in 1864. Maine and Fustel shared the idea that the marriage of single pairs forming a nuclear family was the original basis of society and that patriarchy was the political ingredient of the agnatically organized gens. But Fustel de Coulanges more than Maine analyzed the gens as a theocratic *hierarchical* organization, arranged on the aristocratic principle of primogeniture as well as patrilineality. It should be noted that neither Maine nor Fustel de Coulanges held a conception of unilaterality in the marriage customs of the descent group, despite the presence of unilineal (patrilineal) inheritance.

Here it may be useful to introduce the reader to an important distinction between *unilineality* and *unilaterality*, which will be observed from now on. "Unilineality" will refer only to *inheritance*—of a name, membership, property, status or rank–office, a residential right, and the like—either through fathers only or mothers only. "Unilaterality" will refer only to exogamous *marriage*, whereby one-half of Ego's bilateral relatives—considered as mother's or father's "side"—are excluded from marriage with Ego. Many primitive descent groups are simultaneously unilineal and unilateral, which has led many ethnologists to use the words interchangeably. This has caused great mischief at times, as we shall see, because certain important peoples have descent groups that are unilineal but not unilateral.

Johann J. Bachofen's *Das Mutterrecht*, appearing in the same year as Maine's *Ancient Law* (1861), held strongly to the proposition that matriarchy rather than patriarchy was the earliest organizing principle of primitive society. It was assumed that promiscuity prevailed and that therefore fathers would not be recognized as genitors of particular children. This matrilineality was assumed to have led to matriarchy, the actual sociopolitical dominance of females.

It was John Furgeson McLennan's *Primitive Marriage* (1865) that introduced the concepts *exogamy* and *endogamy* and therefore introduced, at least implicitly, the characteristic of descent groups we are calling unilaterality. From this time on exogamy loomed large in the deliberations and controversies over the basic nature of descent groups (as well as in the related controversies over totemism). Like Bachofen, McLennan assumed that the original stage of human social evolution was promiscuity, with matrilineal descent therefore prior to patrilineal descent. This publication, along with Bachofen's, was an important catalyst to Morgan, whose huge manuscript *Systems of Consanguinity and Affinity* continued to languish in the Smithsonian's editorial offices. Morgan saw that he was being anticipated in these respects and he greatly feared that such men as McLennan would in time render his own studies of kinship useless. This never happened, but McLennan did severely criticize *Systems* when it finally appeared in 1870.

There is one fundamental way in which none of the above men could possibly anticipate Morgan or rival him in any important respect about primitive kinship terminologies or social structure: Morgan had direct personal experience with the Seneca Iroqouis over many years and then with the Michigan Ojibway; finally, he made four ethnological excursions to the Far West. None of the above writers had ever had an iota of firsthand ethnological experience.

Morgan and the Clan–Gens Problem

Morgan's direct contact for many years with the clearly defined organization of the Seneca Iroquois, which featured a matrilocal (and matrilineal) lineage as a residential unit (the longhouse) and the clan, a more dispersed unit of matrilineally related lineages, greatly influenced his perspective. In *League of the Iroquois* (1851) Morgan's main focus was to combat widely held prejudices about the Indian "savages," and one of his important devices was to describe the Iroquoian organization as a wise, intelligent, purposive one comparable to that of the admirable classical Greeks. (It was not until 1867, when he delivered a paper called "A Conjectural Solution to the Origin of the Classificatory System of Relationships" [published in 1868], that he actually posited a connection between kinship terms and forms of marriage.) His interest in demonstrating similarity between the Iroquoian descent groups (which today we usually call clans) and the Greco–Roman gens resulted in his calling the Iroquoian group a gens also. As we shall see, they are so opposite in certain fundamentals that they should not be called by the same name.

The full development of Morgan's ideas about the evolution and significance of the unilineal, unilateral kin groups did not appear until the publication of *Ancient Society* in 1877. By this time he had collected such a mass of data that he could confidently assert that this organization "furnished the nearly universal plan of government of ancient society, Asiatic, European, African, American and Australian." Morgan continued more specifically: "The Grecian gens, phratry and tribe find their analogues in the gens, phratry and tribe of the American aborigines." Additionally, he found the Irish *sept*, the Scottish *clan*, the Albanian *phara*, and the Sanskritic *ganas* to be similarly comparable to the Iroquoian descent group. "Gentile society wherever found is the same in structural organization and in principles of action" (1877:60–61). What are the essential features of this unit of organization, which Morgan claims is the fundamental building block of ancient society?

"A gens . . . is a body of consanguinei descended from the same common ancestor, distinguished by a gentile name, and bound together by affinities of blood." But it includes only half of the descendants, by tracing relationship through only the female line at first or only the male line later, as among the Greeks and Romans (1877:61–61). Morgan was very insistent about the freedom and equality among the members of the gens. Even the sachems and chiefs of the Iroquois claimed no superiority, nor were their posts hereditary. "Liberty, equality, and fraternity, though never formulated, were cardinal principles of the gens" (1877:79). This, he said, was true of all American Indians, and generally, too, they were or had been characterized by matrilineal descent and totemic names for the groups.

Morgan was so convinced of the "democratical" nature of American Indian society that he was bitter toward the historian, H. H. Bancroft, who had accepted the Spanish chroniclers' accounts of the Aztec "monarchy." In 1876 Morgan published a long essay, "Montezuma's Dinner," in the *North American Review*, with the aim of setting the record straight. He argued brilliantly about the ethnocentrism of the Spaniards, as well as their tendency to exaggeration. Rather than empire, Morgan insisted, the Aztec were a "confederacy of equal tribes." Rather than a king or emperor, Montezuma was a successful war chief in a "military democracy." (Much of the material from this article appeared in *Ancient Society* in the chapter, "The Aztec Confederacy.")

Morgan had been aided by a young friend, Adolphe Bandelier, who was beginning a brilliant career as an archaeologist and historian. Bandelier became a sort of correspondence-school disciple of Morgan's and translated from the Spanish many relevant documents. His own later publications agreed with Morgan's interpretation. Although Morgan and Bandelier were largely wrong, their careful scrutiny of the documents was valuable in establishing some new canons in the historiography of primitive peoples.[1]

Ancient Society carried chapters on the Grecian gens, the Roman gens, and an important chapter called "Gentes in other Tribes of the Human Family." In all of these Morgan thought he had found significant parallels with the American Indian form of organization.

It is puzzling that although Morgan cited Fustel de Coulanges's *The Ancient City* (1864) with reference to the theocratic nature of the ancient social institutions, he seemed unaware of the important ways in which Fustel de Coulanges's findings contradicted his own—at any

[1]The Morgan–Bandelier correspondence has been published with a long introduction by the editor, L. A. White, which critically discusses Bandelier's studies of the documents on the Aztec.

rate, he did not mention them. Fustel de Coulanges wrote a full chapter entitled "The Gens at Rome and in Greece." As noted earlier, he did not describe anything like exogamy (or unilaterality) among the ancients nor, above all, were they "democratical" in Morgan's sense. He states categorically at the very beginning of the chapter: "The *gens* had its chief, who was at the same time its judge, its priest, and its military commander" (1864:101). Each group was named for its patrilineal ancestor, and the priest–chief offices of the main line and of the younger ramifying lines were *inherited* by primogeniture (1864:83–85). Morgan must have read the book very selectively.

SOME SUBSEQUENT COMMENTARIES ON MORGAN

The first criticism of Morgan's ideas about the ubiquity of the egalitarian, unilateral form of kin groups was in Andrew Lang's important *Encyclopaedia Britannica* article, "Family," which specifically disagrees with Morgan: "The only gentes we know, the Roman gentes, show scarcely a trace of exogamy" (1878:23). On the other hand, American reviewers were much more receptive to Morgan's ideas (and probably much more ignorant of Greek and Roman scholarship).[2]

John R. Swanton (1905) was the first American to challenge Morgan's argument and also the first to challenge his interpretation of kin groups among American Indians (rather than his interpretation of the Greco–Roman organization). Swanton tellingly called attention to the fact—so obvious today—that Morgan's data on American Indians were much overbalanced on the side of the more settled, richer tribes, of whom the sedentary Iroquois were the most important, but which included others such as the Hopi in the Southwest and remnants of tribes, now moved west, which had formerly been sedentary horticulturalists in the Midwest and Southeast. Swanton also pointed out that less sedentary, nonhorticulturalist groups of the Far West, those who were at a much lower grade—if one thinks of them as representatives of an evolutionary stage—lacked the unilateral organization and, furthermore, were not matrilineal. Swanton was referring to a vast region—northwestern inland Canada, inland Washington, Oregon, California and Idaho, Nevada, Utah—that was populated almost exclusively by small bands of hunter–gatherers whose social structure seemed to emphasize the nuclear family, with nothing else much larger than the occasional extended family.

[2]Howard Becker (1950), a specialist on the sociology of ancient Greece, has made an excellent summary of the opposition to Morgan, as well as a sort of defense of him.

Robert Lowie, whose career seems to have been largely centered around an anti-Morgan pivot, was impressed by Swanton's argument, and finally brought about a fuller confrontation of Morgan's ideas with data representing a more worldwide sample. Lowie's fullest discussion was in the chapter "History of the Sib" (his word at that time for clan) in his *Primitive Society* (1920), the fullest challenge to Morgan's *Ancient Society* to be based on greater ethnographic sophistication.

In brief, his argument is as follows, (stated most succinctly at the beginning of the chapter):

> The bilateral family is an absolutely universal institution; on the other hand, the unilateral sib has only a restricted though wide distribution. It is true that many of the more highly civilized nations of the world, like the Greeks, are known to have passed through a period in which they were organized into sibs. But this may simply indicate that at a certain level the sib system tends to decay, leaving the always coexisting family in possession of the field: it does not by any means prove that the sib is older than the family. A survey of the data clearly shows that the family is omnipresent at every stage of culture; that at a higher level it is frequently coupled with a sib organization; and that at a still higher level the sib disappears. (1920:147)

Lowie then speculated plausibly on how the sib originates. He directly opposes Morgan on this point: Morgan held that it was an intellectual–moral achievment so "abstruse" that it could have happened but once in human history and had thereafter diffused to other areas (1877:320). Lowie, usually the antievolutionist, arch-diffusionist, was much more an evolutionist–functionalist than Morgan here, arguing that the sib can easily come into existence anywhere, given the appropriate circumstances and demography (1920:147 et seq).

In Lowie's opinion, the first question is related to the fact that the sib is a *selected* group of kin. He argues that the principle of "unilateral" descent (unilineal, in our present usage) is closely related to the problems of the transmission of property rights and the mode of residence after marriage. If, for example, a group has a tendency toward patrilocal residence and the males are living in rather close proximity, then the children growing up together are felt to be too closely related to intermarry. As soon as the unit makes this "felt exogamy" a rule and names itself (so that membership is recognized even among the females who are removed at marriage), the group can proliferate and become less a local residential group, but it will remain exogamous and thus truly both unilineal *and* unilateral.

Lowie's argument that the sib grew out of a bilateral type of family was largely designed to lay to rest all of the discussion as to whether Morgan was right in his supposition that a matrilineal order preceded the patrilineal. But Lowie did not touch upon the fundamental problem in Morgan's discussion. As noted earlier, Morgan's equation of the Greek and Roman gens with the organization of such American Indians as the Iroquois was not accepted by some European scholars. This problem involved two major factual issues: (1) Morgan represented all gentes as "democratical" and "communistic," whereas such scholars as Fustel de Coulanges and others later had described the Greek and Roman gentes as hereditary aristocracies with unequal control over landed properties. (2) Morgan thought that all gentes were exogamous, whereas important classical scholars found no exogamy in these groupings. The fundamental social structure is drastically reshaped depending on which of these views is accepted. Lowie seemed unaware of this significance, for logically he could have ignored the Greek and Roman gentes as *not* being sibs, because not exogamous. It seems likely that he would have discussed such an exclusion, for he was thorough in trying to discredit Morgan in every way he could.[3]

Subsequent Contributions: Raymond Firth

Raymond Firth's *We, the Tikopia* (1936) is a landmark in ethnology for its meticulous study of a kind of social structure which in his day had not been subjected to acute analysis but which we find today to be in large supply in the primitive world. This structure contrasts sharply with Morgan's gens and Lowie's sib. Let us examine briefly the core kinship groups of Tikopia, which Firth calls *house* and *clan.*

The island of Tikopia is a small Polynesian outlier, not in the central culture area, but sharing in general Polynesian culture in a rather attenuated way. The social structure and the system of inherited ranks and statuses in Tikopia are generically Polynesian—that is, there are houses that are higher in inherited rank than others. In a general sense, the three-class system of Polynesia is also represented here. The aristocratic theocratic class (*ariki*) is of chiefs' families; a second group of minor nobility (*pure*) consists of families that have a ritual elder as head; and the commoner families (*fakaarofa*) have no ritual privileges of any note. This system of inherited status positions is of importance

---

[3]In the chapters of *Primitive Society* called "Rank" and "Government," Lowie alludes to societies that have hereditary "aristocracies" and "classes," as opposed to those that recognize only achieved ranks and still others that are fiercely egalitarian. But nowhere does he relate these political contrasts to the structure of his sibs or other descent groups. His later book, *Social Organization* (1948), is similar in this respect (but varies in giving up the use of "sib" for the more widely used "clan").

in understanding the alignment of kin in the social structure of house and clan.

The word *paito* is translated "house" by Firth and evidently has the dual meaning we sometimes use in English. The house in the sense of household is thought of as having proliferated and in time became several closely related households, which usually lived near each other. The *paito* in this phase is named for its founder and becomes what we usually call a lineage. "It is not a unified local group, but has strong local affiliations; its members are linked in kinship by ties of descent from a common ancestor; it has a definite social status correlated with the rank of its head, and this in turn is dependent upon his ritual functions" (1936:361).

The clan is a much more dispersed group of a higher order; that is, it is composed of related lineages. The lineage of the chief of the clan gives his house name to the clan as whole. Membership is thus patrilineal in terms of the inherited names, but neither the lineage nor the clan is thoroughly exogamous or endogamous, so in cases of marriages within the clan the children belong to the clan through both father and mother (i.e., here we find a unilineal descent group which is *not* unilateral).

Firth quotes a native saying: "The chief dwells and dwells, then dies. His sons separate off to the rear and dwell as the *kainana* [clan], while the eldest lives as chief" (1936:362). The younger sons become lesser chiefs, eventually founding households, then lineages, of their own, and the system proliferates in this manner. The chiefs of the four Tikopia-wide clans are therefore related, but each chief is in turn inferior to his elder. The chiefs of clans and lineages and the differences in status among them are theocratic ("ritual and political" in Firth's terms) more than economic (1936:358–361).

Other kinship groupings exist, of course, in relationship to the major structures of household, lineage, and clan. Most important, there is— always—what is nowadays in ethnology called the personal kindred, a group of close relatives from the point of view of an individual. This is perforce bilateral, counting relatives on both mother's and father's side; and it is ephemeral, since its composition is only from the mortal individual's perspective. But the main descent groups, lineage and clan, can be seen as corporate structures—corporate because they exist as visible parts of the society without regard to any particular perspective.

Firth, however, wants a change in emphasis from the individual linkages to

> one of the most important factors in such kinship groups, . . . the principle of fission and dispersion in the creation of them. As a rule of historical tradition,

and presumably in actual social process, they have arisen through the branch-
ing and re-branching of the family structure, acquiring greater autonomy and
independence the further they move away from the parent stem. (1936:370–
371)

In the ranking of these branches, great importance is attached to seniority of the line and the chiefly bearer of the name. For this process
Firth suggests the term *ramification*, consistent in metaphor and
etymology with the idea of "genealogical tree." He therefore proposes
the designation *ramage* for such groups as the variously dispersed *paito*
(because it seems undesirable to use native terms if the structure being
described is held to be of broader ethnological significance). In his final
chapter Firth points out social-structural variations throughout Polynesia and concludes that the ramage is generally a basic or characteristic feature (1936:597). (Recall the similar emphasis on ramification by Maine and Fustel de Coulanges for the early Mediterranean
gens.)

In summary, the ramage can be seen as contrasting with Morgan's
gens (Lowie's sib or the modern clan) in few though very basic particulars: (1) The ramage lays emphasis on the genealogical aspect of the
kinship of the members, while Morgan's conception emphasizes the
codification of conduct between unilateral kin; (2) The ramage is not
primarily exogamous, while Morgan's is thoroughly so; (3) The ramage
is composed of parts (families, sublineages, chiefs, and headmen) arranged hierarchically in hereditary rank, while the component families
of Morgan's groups are egalitarian; and (4) The accession to the ranked
positions is patrilineal by seniority, whereas birth order is ignored in
Morgan's description.

SUBSEQUENT CONTRIBUTIONS:
EDMUND R. LEACH

A survey of the important general works on primitive social organization in the years following the publication of *We, the Tikopia* reveals
little or no awareness of the clan–gens problem. Even when the discussion is explicitly devoted to resolving the complex historical and semantic confusion about the meanings of clan, gens, sib, sippe, deme,
moiety, phratry, and so on, little is said that shows the realization that
there are really two basically distinct kinds of descent groups.

G. P. Murdock, in his comprehensive work *Social Structure* (1949),
shows appreciation of the various forms social groups can take but
nowhere does he show interest in the difference between ranked and
egalitarian types, even though his discussion of consanguineal groups

is a thorough mixture of references to societies of both types. This is not said to castigate Murdock, but to call attention to the times—and Murdock was a leader in those times.

Also appearing in 1949 was Claude Lévi-Strauss' *Formes élémentaires de la parenté*. This massive work, dealing largely with marriage systems and associated kin terminology patterns, had an ethnographic emphasis on greater Southeast Asia. The sample ranged from very simple, small societies such as central Australians to much more complex mountain chiefdoms—even petty kingdoms—in the mainland of Southeast Asia. He did not make the social-structural discrimination we are looking for in the present context, but his work did elicit comments by Edmund R. Leach which call attention to the difference between egalitarian societies and hierarchical societies with regard to questions of marriage and structural forms.

Leach directs us to the fact that the Kachin, as he found through actual fieldwork, differ "on the ground" from Lévi-Strauss' model of that type. The "Kachin model" is described by Lévi-Strauss as made up of exogamous patriclans which marry in a "circle" of indirect exchange. So far, this scheme could be found and comprehended in an egalitarian tribe. But Leach points out that Kachin society is typically a three-class society of hereditary lineages of chiefs, lesser aristocracy, and commoners. (These lineages are basically of the type that Firth calls the ramage; that is, rank is based on seniority in the historical budding-off, or ramification, of an original lineage.) Lévi-Strauss sees this type of marriage exchange as a movement of women in one direction, balanced in reciprocity by a countermovement in bride wealth from wife-taker to wife-giver group. Thus a political–economic balance is struck, and alliance is maintained between groups, as though they were equals.

Leach is at pains to show that rank should not be left out of the equation in the Kachin case. What actually happens is that hereditary rank, with its political and economic perquisites, dominates the exchange. Instead of thinking of women moving from A to B to C and back to A in exchange for goods in balanced reciprocity between equals, think of a daughter being given by a member of a chiefly lineage to a man in a lesser status (an aristocrat), who returns a bride-price. Meanwhile a man of the aristocracy gives a daughter to a commoner, again in exchange for a bride-price. In a sense, then, women are not moving in a circle, but down to a lesser family (while men marry up).[4]

What is going on, Leach avers, if one can use the analogy of a feudal manorial system, is as follows:

[4]Chiefs' sons marry outside the domain.

(1) From a *political* aspect, chief is to headman as feudal Lord of the Manor is to customary freeholder.

(2) From a *kinship* aspect, chief is to headman . . . as father-in-law to son-in-law.

(3) From a *territorial* aspect, the kinship status of the headman's lineage in respect to that of the chief is held to validate the tenure of land.

(4) From an *economic* aspect, the effect of this matrilateral cross-cousin marriage is that, in balance, the headman's lineage constantly pays wealth to the chief's lineage in the form of bridewealth. . . . The most important part of this payment is in the form of consumer goods—namely cattle. The chief converts this perishable wealth into imperishable prestige through the medium of spectacular feasting. The ultimate consumers of the goods are in this way the original producers, namely, the commoners who attend the feast.[5] (1951:69)

As Leach has pointed out (1951:89–90), Lévi-Strauss made a great advance over earlier theorists by not considering kinship and marriage solely as a system in itself. That is, he brought into the system an element, reciprocity in gift giving, that had been left out in the previous schemes. But he converted this reciprocity from economic factors into symbols of relationship. Leach, in dealing with a society whose social structure is hierarchical rather than egalitarian in rank, economics, and authority, shows how those factors have not only changed the character of the groups but the function of marriage itself.

Leach describes the Kachin more fully in his later book, *Political Systems of Highland Burma* (1954). Here are found both egalitarian and hierarchical lineages. These polar types (which he calls in native Kachin terms *Gumlao* and *Gumsa* respectively) are analyzed and contrasted in far greater depth than Firth's brief contrast between the ramage and the egalitarian clan. In this book one of Leach's major purposes is to challenge British social anthropology's equilibrium assumptions by showing how, under certain conditions, the two contrasting types of society can change from one to the other. From the present point of view, this idea is fully acceptable, but of much more interest here is Leach's recognition of these types and his degree of emphasis on it.

Leach mentions (1954:159) the lack of precedent for his analysis.[6] Fortes and Evans-Pritchard's (1940) typology of African political sys-

---

[5]This redistribution of consumable goods is a very prominent feature of the validation of status and authority in hierarchical kin groups generally.

[6]He does mention Morgan's *societas–civitas* distinction (from *Ancient Society*) as a sort of precedent, but most curiously, he seems to be unaware of Morgan's clan–gens problem and the arguments about it—which would have been remarkably germane to his point.

tems ("cephalous" and "acephalous") "would not cover Kachin *Gumsa* society," he says, and as for Firth's (1936) discussion of the Tikopia, Leach remarks:

> The Tikopia . . . have indeed what may be considered a "pure" lineage system associated with notions of a class hierarchy but here the whole scale of social activities is on such a minute scale that analogy is not very useful. I think that there are plenty of societies in the world of the Kachin *Gumsa* type, but it so happens that social anthropologists have not yet got around to looking at them. That makes it all the more difficult for me to achieve lucidity. (1954:159)

Discussion of many of Leach's important findings is omitted here in order to concentrate on the present question, the failure not only of American ethnology but even of many British social anthropologists, more completely dedicated than the Americans to the study of social structure, to pay appropriate attention to this startling dichotomy in types of descent groups.

Several British social anthropologists working in Africa have described hierarchical political systems and even focused on the aristocratic rankings within the clan (as in Hilda Kuper's *An African Aristocracy* [1947]), but nowhere do we find any recognition of the broader significance of this kind of organization or of its significant contrasts with other clans. It may be that the British social anthropologists' individual concentration on one area was at fault, since a recognition of the clan–gens dichotomy could come only from field experience with both. And relatedly, there seems to have been little, if any, comparative analysis done, except by Fortes and Evans-Pritchard (1940).

Firth himself wrote the foreword to Leach's book and reserved most of his praise for the introduction of "dynamic" theory made at a "higher level of abstraction" than in other social anthropological works, which remain merely descriptive. He did not refer to the possible great significance of the *Gumsa–Gumlao* dichotomy, or even mention its kinship to his own brief suggestion of a similar dichotomy between ramage and the unilateral clan. Possibly Firth was too modest to call attention to his own work. But no other social anthropologist seems to have remarked this point, so perhaps Firth himself was unaware of what seems today to have been an exciting ethnographical discovery.

Meyer Fortes' "The Structure of Unilineal Descent Groups" (1953) should be mentioned here because it is appropriately regarded as an important critical summary of the state of the art of social anthropology at mid-century by one of the acknowledged masters. It particularly emphasizes the British studies of descent groups, but nowhere does it directly allude to the fundamental difference between the two kinds noted briefly by Firth (although Fortes does cite the Tikopia study in another context). This is a significant omission in such a general article, for it reveals what must have been a truly widespread lack of awareness in British social anthropology of Firth's important analytical distinction, one that on the face of it would seem to be easy for a science of ethnology to correct.

Leach's 1954 book was too late for Fortes' article, but I have found no subsequent books or general articles in British social anthropology that recognize this particular significance of Leach's contribution. Even S. F. Nadel, in his last general book, *The Theory of Social Structure* (1957) shows no sign of appreciating Leach's major analytical points; instead he takes him to task for his criticisms of the British "equilibrium assumptions," which seem untoward to Nadel.

Why such a widespread lack of awareness of this problem? Two circumstances suggest themselves. As nineteenth-century evolutionist perspectives were superseded, two quite different brands of academic ethnology took over: (1) In America, with some influences from Germany, a new set of interests and problems became prominent under the leadership of Franz Boas. (2) In Britain and its dominions, a new kind of ethnology became dominant in the universities, best characterized by the work of Radcliffe-Brown and some of his followers. The first of these, operating mostly in America, the home of the original clan, simply was not very interested in matters of social structure.[7] Since the problem was not being directly addressed, and since the ideas of Morgan and other earlier American evolutionists were either ignored or discredited, it is not surprising that nothing was accomplished. But the second group, the so-called British social anthropologists, was supposed to be particularly interested in descent groups, and, therefore, this is where one would suppose Morgan's error would have been corrected. Finally it was, in a quiet sort of way, by Firth's and Leach's ethnological discoveries, but it is still surprising that so little notice of it was taken. It may be relevant that the clan–gens problem arose in an evolutionary climate, and neither of these twentieth-century ethnological schools was evolutionary minded.

SUBSEQUENT CONTRIBUTIONS:
KALERVO OBERG, PAUL KIRCHHOFF, AND MORTON FRIED

In 1955, Kalervo Oberg described a type of lowland tribe in South America having what he called "politically organized chiefdoms." He

[7]With the exception of Robert Lowie.

distinguished these from what he called "homogeneous" and "segmented" tribes of the lowlands.

> The distinguishing features of this type . . . [are] that the chiefs have judicial powers to settle disputes and to punish offenders even by death, . . . and to requisition men and supplies for war purposes. . . . Chiefs have large numbers of wives, are carried in litters, live in large houses, are addressed by a string of titles, and often speak to the commoners through an intermediary. (1955:484)

Oberg contrasted this kind of inequality with the preceding (the segmented) type, which has a structure of named unilineal kinship groups, such as sibs and moieties, and, often, named associations of age-grades. Nothing more is made of the difference between this (implicit) equality and the inequality of the chiefdoms, however. The point of the paper is that increasing production of food leads from "monogeneous" (bilateral) marginal hunter–gatherer societies to segmented tribes with greater size and social concentration. Finally, a food surplus makes for chiefdoms succeeded by "states" and "theocratic empires." But the distinctions are useful for us, as we shall see, despite Oberg's insistence on food surplus alone as the prime mover.

Oberg's article, concerned only with lowland South America, seems not to have attracted any attention as a theoretical contribution. The word *chiefdom*, however, has achieved some currency. It calls attention to an important feature, centralized leadership, which in the context of classification of types of political organization is a distinct virtue.

Paul Kirchhoff's "The Principle of Clanship in Human Society" was the first work to fully conceptualize the clan–gens problem and address it to a broad spectrum of aboriginal societies. But just as British social anthropology paid little heed to Firth's and Leach's findings, so in America did Kirchhoff's contribution languish. It was rejected by journal editors from the year 1935, when it was first submitted, until 1955, when it was finally "published" in a mimeographed version in *The Davidson Journal of Anthropology* (a publication by anthropology students at the University of Washington, where Kirchhoff was then teaching).[8] This long-standing situation must reflect, not perversity on the part of an editor or two, but widespread lack of interest in a problem that is essentially related to an evolutionary perspective.

Kirchhoff sees an early stage of society preceding the arrival of the clan as one of relatively small communities with no bonds tying them together except sentiment and propinquity. The important fact is that

---

[8]Fried's *Readings in Anthropology* (1959) reprinted the article, thus giving it an appropriately wider audience.

"the concept of descent is still completely absent" (1955:261). This does not mean that ties and obligations of kinship and marriage, cutting across such common entities, are not present, but these are horizontal, not vertical, as in true descent reckoning. Such societies are most common among food-gatherers and hunters, although some in rich environments such as the Northwest Pacific Coast of North America are exceptions in having full genealogical conceptions of descent. Clanship, based on the concept of descent, marks off new and larger types of segments, which are useful in creating greater stability among economically cooperating groups. "It takes a number of different forms, but its essence appears to be the same everywhere: to group together in one permanent unit all those persons, living or dead, who can claim common descent" (1955:263).

There are two major types of social units based on descent. One type is that of unilateral exogamous clans. It is of great significance that everywhere the above features exist the membership is on an "absolutely equal footing with the rest: the nearness of relation to each other or to some ancestor being of no consequence for a person's place in the clan" (1955:264). The high degree of cooperation among these clans also features "rigidity," and the equalitarianism among them makes it difficult to create differentiation and specialization, which would require new forms of cooperation; these clans are thus an obstacle to further development, according to Kirchhoff.

The second type of clan, strikingly different, is found among the early Indo–European and Semitic tribes, the Polynesians, most Indonesians including the Philippines, and others scattered throughout the world. Contrary to the first kind, which emphasizes equal and common membership, this clan has membership in differing degrees of importance depending upon the genealogical nearness to the direct line of descent from the founding ancestor. Thus genealogies that would include distant ancestors, unknown or at least unnecessary in the first kind of clan, are very important in the second type, particularly among the *aristoi* and the closely related "nobles."

As a corollary of the above feature, according to Kirchhoff, there is no rule of clan exogamy. In fact, close *en*dogamy is frequent among the *aristoi* to insure the continuity of status among the offspring. Exogamy divides the first kind of society into two or more blocks with clear-cut boundary lines, equal to each other and homogeneous within. The second type

> may be likened to a cone, the whole tribe being one such cone, with the
> legendary ancestor at its top,—but within it are . . . a number of similar cones,
> the top of each coinciding with or being connected with the top of the whole

cone. The bases of these cones, representing the circles of living members of
the various clans at a given moment, overlap here and there. (1955:267)

This "conical clan" reserves all leadership functions in economic,
social, and religious matters to those of high descent—those closest to
the ancestor of the clan–tribe, who typically is regarded as a god. The
spectrum of rank is very broad, from the holy priest–chief to the
lowliest commoners (and sometimes drudge–slaves). But all of these
people are relatives of greater or lesser degree. This is in great contrast
to the egalitarian, unilateral–exogamous principle of clanship, and is
capable of advancing to even higher degrees of size and complexity, for
it is extraordinarily flexible and adaptable. "However, this contrast
should not induce us to overlook the fact that both of these principles
of clanship and the form of the clan to which they lead, belong essentially to the same phase of the evolution of society" (1955:270). It is
difficult to understand why Kirchhoff insisted on this. Early in his
article he pointed out (1955:265) that the equalitarian clan was "typical of small tribes with only migratory, small-scale horticulture or
primitive forms of animal breeding." We could add that the archae-
ological strata in areas where sequences reach high development, in
both New and Old Worlds, typically exhibit strata in sequence from
"early agriculture" or "village culture" to "formative" (or "theocratic"); clearly these sequences are from egalitarian clan-like society
to conical chiefdoms, in that order everywhere.

Morton Fried, in 1957, wrote the only article prior to the 1960s that
addressed itself directly to the point of Kirchhoff's distinction between
equalitarian descent groups and the conical groups distinguished by
internal hereditary ranking. He showed, however, contrary to
Kirchhoff, that the two kinds were undoubtedly an evolutionary sequence, pertaining to vastly different levels of cultural complexity and
with very distinct corporate functions. He also emphasized the theoretical significance of Firth's (1936) description of the ramage and
Leach's (1951, 1954) discussions of Kachin social organization. I find no
evidence, however, that this important article had any influence on
subsequent studies of kinship.[9]

NONUNILINEAR DESCENT GROUPS

In 1955 Ward Goodenough published an interesting article, "A Problem in Malayo–Polynesian Social Organization." He had realized from

[9]Two important general articles in the *International Encyclopedia of the Social Sciences* (1968) are "Kinship" by Fred Eggan and "Descent Groups" by Jack Goody. Neither
mentions Kirchhoff's or Fried's articles.

working in Oceania that the traditional Americanist conception of social groupings, based on a longstanding preoccupation with unilateral, exogamous groups, was misleading when applied to the widespread Malayo–Polynesian kin groups that were not based on such principles. His article was mainly directed toward showing what the original and normal form of organization had been—with modern types as modifications of it due to changes in the nature of landholding groups, and with these changes due, in turn, to differences in the degree of restriction (or scarcity) in lands belonging to the group. This focus, however interesting, is not directly relevant to the present point of the relation of hereditary rank to social structure and marriage forms, but it did, evidently, stimulate considerable interest in the study of nonunilinear types of social organization, which thus include our hierarchical, nonexogamous ramage type (without specifying it).

In 1959, the *American Anthropologist* carried three adjacent articles on nonunilinear descent groups. William Davenport's "Nonunilinear Descent and Descent Groups," stimulated by Goodenough's article, made a broad comparison and classification of types in this category. Melvin Ember's article described "The Nonunilinear Descent Groups of Samoa," while Nancie Solien described those of the Caribbean and Central America. These cases are not directly related to the matter being addressed in this chapter, but they do represent a significant change in perspective. Unlike Firth's and Kirchhoff's contributions, they do not oppose a single type (such as ramage or conical clan) to the unilateral–exogamous clan, but present a sort of grab bag, a residual category, that includes all types that are not unilinear.

Since World War II, and particularly during the 1950s, a great deal of ethnology was suddenly being done in areas that were more modern peasant villages than aboriginal tribes, and this was responsible for the new interest in nonunilinear types of "composite" (endogamous or "agamous") villages, 'matrifocal extended families," "cognatic" kinship, and the like. Firth, Leach, Kirchhoff, Oberg, and Fried, by contrast, had been concerned with aboriginal types of organization in the older anthropological tradition.

SUMMARY REMARKS

The first task must be to reduce the terminological confusion to some kind of order that will do justice to the important facets of the problem as they have appeared historically.

First of all, it seems clear that Morgan made a serious mistake in his insistence that an Iroquois-like organization was found in parts of the world wherever a descent group was reported. (He should be pardoned, of course, given the magnitude of his task and the state of ethnology in his time, but he must nevertheless stand trial.) Fustel de Coulanges's *The Ancient City* (1864), however, had described the Indo–European, Semitic, and later Greco–Roman gens as almost precisely like Firth's ramage and Kirchhoff's conical clan (although neither of them noted it). But Morgan decided to call the American Indian exogamous group a gens, Firth called his largest units (of related ramages) clans, while Kirchhoff decided to call both the egalitarian exogamous groups and the classical gens clans.

Since then confusion reigned widely, but there seems finally to have been a gradual leaning toward *clan* as the word for the unilaterally exogamous, egalitarian descent group. If we accept that usage, then we have *gens* as a logical choice, just as Fustel de Coulanges originally had it, for the kind of descent group described by Kirchhoff as the conical clan and by Firth as ramage. Because of such a proliferation of names for these groups (each undoubtedly submitted in order to reduce confusion), it may be useful to collate these usages categorically under the clan–gens dichotomy.

Clan	Gens
A named descent group that is *unilineal, unilateral, exogamous, egalitarian* by heredity, thus with *only ephemeral* (or "charismatic") *leadership*, with *little or no emphasis on genealogy* for ranking purposes.	A named descent group that is *unilineal* (in only certain respects), *bilateral, agamous, hierarchical* by heredity, thus *with permanent leadership offices*, with *much emphasis on genealogy* for ranking purposes.
Morgan's *gens* (1877)	Fustel de Coulanges's Greco–Roman *gens* (1864)
Lowie's *sib* (1920)	Firth's *ramage* (1936)
Lowie's *clan* (1948)	Leach's *Gumsa* groups (1954)
Leach's *Gumlao* (1954)	Oberg's *chiefdom* (1955)
Kirchhoff's equalitarian *clan* (1955)	Kirchhoff's *conical clan* (1955)

To dichotomize primitive descent groups in this way does not square with Morgan's idea of a *societas* (primitive society), characterized by egalitarian exogamous descent groups (his gens), as opposed to a *civitas* (political society). It is true that Morgan did not see the *societas* stage as a simple homogeneous one, but rather as six ascending "ethnical periods": *savagery*, with lower, middle, and upper epochs, and *barbarism*, also with lower, middle, and upper epochs. These were demarked mostly by "materialistic" criteria, such as the various "arts of subsistence," and technology generally. But there is no corresponding demarking of stages in political or social development from his egalitarian "gentile" (or clan) society toward greater centralization, inequality (hereditary rank), new forms of property, and so on. The political transformation from *societas* to *civitas* was in his view relatively abrupt.

But if we now consider the hierarchical gens as distinct from and later than egalitarian clan society, and intermediate between clan society and political civilization, many problems are resolved that had remained since Morgan's time to plague modern evolutionists like Childe, Steward, and White, and probably all Marxists. In order to maintain Morgan's dichotomy they were forced to explain away the highly controversial class (rank) systems of some of the primitive societies of the Pacific Northwest Coast, the southeast (U.S.), Polynesia, and the circum-Caribbean area as being either figments of the Europeans' ethnologists imaginations (as Morgan and Bandelier argued with respect to the Spanish chronicles on the Aztec) or misinterpretations by modern ethnologists of societies acculturated (contaminated) by the influence of Western civilization's money economy, colonialism, missions, and so on. There certainly have been numerous occasions of ethnocentrism and contamination, but the record is too complete now to doubt that there really was a stage of hierarchical gens-like organization later than clans and antecedent to the archaic civilizations, and surviving elsewhere into historical times.

If this is accepted, then we must begin to rethink the whole matter of cultural evolution, especially political evolution, and reconsider the question of the qualitative leap from primitive society to the early civilizations. What used to be seen as the crucial *societas–civitas* distinctions—classless society versus propertied classes, lack of government versus the state, the rule of custom versus the rule of repressive law, and so on—no longer seems to hold. The gentile society that lies between the stage of egalitarian clans and full-fledged governments, such as the six archaic civilizations, is found in all major continents, irrespective of language family, culture area, or race. Its size, density, and complexity of population and society is greater than that of the egalitarian-clan type of tribe and less than that of the archaic civilizations. The question naturally arises: Does the gentile society become larger, denser, and more complex than clan society because of the sociopolitical inventions that made its growth possible, or is it that the demographic changes came first and brought the sociopolitical changes about in their wake as a kind of automatic functional result? This topic is discussed in Part IV.

10

Totem and Taboo: Society or Mind?

In the history of ethnology the two quintessentially human inventions, totem and taboo, have sometimes been treated as separate problems in explanation, sometimes together (for they frequently appear as twin aspects of the same social form). Also, they appear as quintessentially ethnological scientific dilemmas, posing the methodological problem of whether to treat them as psychological–mentalistic phenomena or as positivistic and deterministic aspects of an organismically conceived social order—functionally causing the mental, ideological aspects to occur rather than being caused by them.

These two subjects, perhaps more than any others, have also provoked the nature–nurture controversy so prevalent in ethnology since its mid-nineteenth-century origin. This old problem is also a new one in that much scientific progress has been made in human genetics, social psychology, ethnology, and ethnological descriptive data, making it possible to rethink the relationship of human biology to culture. Possibly some borderline sciences—or interdisciplinary research, at least—will become increasingly relevant. At any rate, the original old questions were good ones in that they have not been easily or conclusively solved.

HISTORY OF THE CONCEPT "TOTEMISM"

There are, historically, a few incidental notes on the widespread phenomenon whereby social groups have been given (or have taken) the names of plants or animals, and less often other natural phenomena, as their own, with a mystical or magical rapport established between them. Andrew Lang (1905:vii) says that Garcilaso de la Vega, an Inca on the maternal side, notes this feature in his *History of the Incas* (not further cited). The first more general ethnological account of

133

Indians in North America was by the American statesman and ethnologist, Albert Gallatin (founder of the American Ethnological Society of New York in 1842), who gave currency to the Ojibway term
totam in his huge *Archaeologica Americana* in 1836.

Sir George Grey (1841) was able to make detailed comparisons of
Gallatin's report with his own ethnological findings in Australia, finding evidence of the same kind of unusual cult existing in areas as widely
separated as North America and Australia and among such widely
disparate races and kinds of societies and environments. Grey did not
venture any theory as to the origins of the totemic institutions, though
he did observe them carefully. He was evidently the first to note that
these plant and animal names not only functioned as family names, but
that a man could not marry a woman of his own family name. He had
noticed the association of marriage taboos with totemism, which was
ever after to make this a double-barreled problem in explanation.

Not much happened in the years immediately following the appearance of Grey's work. According to Tax's review of the history of
social organization and kinship, a great amount of information on
primitive society was accumulating, but nothing that took intellectual
account of it occurred until the 1860s (1955:448–449).

It was with the publication of John F. McLennan's *Primitive Marriage* in 1865 that the word *exogamy* was first put to use. In his view,
as we saw at greater length in Chapter 1, the practice of female infanticide resulted in marriage-by-capture and finally led to the rule of
exogamy: wives *must* be acquired from other tribes (whether by capture or exchange). It should be of interest that exogamy as a concept
had not become either equated or allied with another phenomenon, the
incest taboo, or "horror of incest," that was later to become a favorite
way of arguing about the origin of human society and the psychological
makeup of human beings. The following discussion will continue the
emphasis on totemism; to the extent that the inquiry on the incest
taboo becomes independent of totemism, it will become the subject of
a subsequent subdivision.

It was McLennan's view that exogamy became related to totemism
in the following way: the totem was simply a nomenclatural means of
identifying people of the same stock when as time went on they became dispersed. It was regarded as a sacred obligation not to steal
women from your own stock. This is largely an argument about the
rise of exogamy, with little being adduced about totemism as such.

However, McLennan eventually began a long-lasting interest in
totemism as a more purely religious set of traits, as is evidenced by the
title of his sequence of three articles in the *Fortnightly Review* (1869–

70), "The Worship of Animals and Plants." Names of animals and vegetables were affixed to the exogamous stocks because they were already an important part of the preceding, and earliest, form of human thought and worship. There was, in effect, a prehistoric "totem stage" when plants, animals, and such things as heavenly bodies were considered to be "gods" (we would say "spirits" today) before the anthropomorphic gods appeared. In this new approach, McLennan does not forget or give up his earlier appreciation of totemism as allied with exogamous tribal divisions, closely related to rules of marriage, protection of the species, mystical respect, and so on. He simply says that these are the residue of an earlier, more pervasive conception of men's relation to nature, as viewed by early man. There are, of course, a great many religious uses of plants and animals in primitive society, including "worship" of such in the form of personal tutelary and guardian spirits, as well as spirits of places such as villages, mountains, and lakes. Furthermore, many of the cases cited by McLennan were of *incarnations*; that is, of priests' saying that such and such a god would, or did, appear at such and such a time in the form of a particular bird or fish. McLennan uses all of these far-fetched indications of plant–animal myths and "worship" to argue that this once was the *only* religion, that man–gods were late developments.

But when exogamy became a rule of marriage, with matrilineal descent only (fatherhood being unknown), the further linkage of particular plant and animal species as ancestor spirits was made. Thus the specified institution called totemism—that is, the belief in a biological species as ancestral to a human clan—is only one form of a much wider and more various set of plant–animal fetishisms of primordial man.

E. B. Tylor was personally well-acquainted with McLennan and had "much conversation" with him when McLennan was working on "The Worship of Animals and Plants." Tylor had his own opinions, however, though in the hopes that new ethnographical data would reduce the complexity of the subject, he postponed publishing until 1899, when his "Remarks on Totemism" appeared. His criticism of McLennan was direct and based on fuller and more accurate data, data dealing with tribes with true "clan-totemism," which he contrasts with the many cases of plant–animal worship that are not associated with social groups. He showed that the data cannot be arranged to suggest that the latter are prior to the former, nor can those groups with anthropomorphic gods be seen as later and superior to all. Tylor preferred to reduce the disorder by considering the problem of true totemism as the relation of exogamic groups to plant–animal species with associated religious rites. He offers no explanation but affirms the significance of this unity in his final sentences:

> "Exogamy can and does exist without totemism, and for all we know was originally independent of it, but the frequency of their close combination over three-quarters of the earth points to the ancient and powerful action of the totems at once in consolidating clans and allying them together within the larger circle of the tribe. This may well have been among the most effective processes in the early social growth of the human race. (1899:148)

James G. Frazer published a small manual of totemism in 1887, in which he pursued the same reasoning as McLennan, connecting totemism with the origin of deities. But it is preferable to discuss his later four-volume *Totemism and Exogamy* (1910) in the context of other works written after Tylor's remonstrance.

In 1898 Émile Durkheim published his famous "La prohibition de l'inceste et ses origines." He and Tylor evidently were unaware of one another's work, but it was almost as though Durkheim intended to put into practice the suggestions made by Tylor. Durkheim phrases the problem somewhat differently from Tylor, however, placing more emphasis on explaining the incest taboo than on investigating the totemic features with which it is linked. In Durkheim's usage, it should be noted, exogamy and the incest taboo are synonymous. Marriage, implying conjugal relations (sexual union), was prohibited among members of the same totemic group, and so, too, was any "illicit" sex.

"Exogamy is the binding force of the clan," emphasizes Durkheim, and the clan is universal in the sense that "all societies have either passed through this organizational form, or were born from other societies which had previously passed through it" (1898b:25). Since the exogamy of the clan is primordial, clan exogamy is the actual origin of the incest taboo. But there is a more broadly based form of inquiry that can be made, placing exogamy as a *taboo* in the class of religious ritualistic prohibitions that are universal and lie presumably at the very basis of religion. Taboos, in this general sense,

> have as their objective to avert the dangerous effects of a magical contagion by preventing all contact between a thing or a category of things, in which a supernatural principle is believed to reside, and others who do not have this same characteristic, or do not have it to the same degree. The first one is said to be tabooed in relationship to the second. (1898b:70)

The totemic being flows in the clan and the two member sexes must avoid sexual contact with each other just as the profane avoids the sacred. Durkheim goes on to show how widespread are the taboos against association of the two sexes in many other domestic respects and social occasions, particularly the drastic taboos on the occasions of menstruation, which is "the spilling of the sacred blood of the totem."

"Once the prejudices relating to blood had led man to forbid all union between relatives, the sexual feeling was obliged to find a milieu outside of the familial circle (where it could not be satisfied); and that is what made it differentiate itself very early from the sentiments of kinship" (1898b:108–109). Thus ritual exogamy is eventually presented to the social mind, after long experiencing it, as an incest taboo that engenders strong emotions, even horror, at the idea of violating it— even now in modern societies with no memory of the religious origins of exogamy. (This is an important aspect of Durkheim's subsequent sociology: the reasons for the origin of a "collective representation" may have little to do with the ongoing consequences of its presence.)

Durkheim later presented his mature thoughts on totemism, after long research, in his *Les formes élémentaires de la vie religieuse* (1912). Discussion of this will be postponed briefly because an important segment of the book critically discusses some prominent theorists whose work appeared after his articles on incest. Also in the interim, a great harvest of ethnological facts relevant to totemism had been made in Australia and North America.

Tylor's idea (in "Remarks on Totemism") that totemism is only a particular case of the general worship of animals, not the "foundation of religion," appealed to many because it appeared to simplify what had seemed at first enormously complex. It led, in fact, to an even further simplification in the hands of leading North American ethnologists. This group, of which Boas (1910), Fletcher (1897), and Hill-Tout (1901–1902) were most representative, succumbed to what seems in other questions to have been a sort of antisociological tendency, preferring usually to see the ultimate answer to such problems as totemism as lying in the psychology of individuals. In this case, the totems of individuals (in North America they were prominent as what these anthropologists called "guardian spirits") were held to provide the basis for the totemism of a group. As the founder of a descent group, a prominent individual's fame would be aggrandized with the passage of time; as a result, his personal totem would become that of the group, transcending the individual totems of the other members.

It was Hill-Tout, ethnographer of various tribes in British Columbia, who argued this at greater length and with more cogency than the others; consequently he was the most beleaguered by the Europeans whom he criticized. Andrew Lang, in his last work on the subject, *The Secret of the Totem* (1905), and Émile Durkheim, in his final word, *Les formes élémentaires* (1912), were the two who attacked him most directly. Lang's was the first, but Durkheim's certainly attracted the greater attention.

Lang pointed out (1905:203–204) that his original theory in *Social Origins* (1903) had been based largely on data from the Australian aborigines, chosen because they are in the lowest state of savagery known. (This theory, so briefly presented then, is unchanged in the present version, and is presented now more fully.) Hill-Tout, particularly, and most of the other Americans, especially Boas, used material gathered on the Northwest Coast of North America from tribes in a much more developed state of culture; these tribes were in a much more mixed-up state as well, due to their many dislocations, migrations, intermixtures, and diffusions. The American ethnologists concluded from this material that there were many kinds of totems, some pertaining to individuals, others to families, exogamous groups, and endogamous groups. Thus the association of the totems with exogamy (*true* totemism, according to Lang) seemed to the Americans to be "accidental rather than essential."

Here again, in some degree at least, is demonstrated the typical Boasian dislike of any sociological determinism and of a predilection for the individualistic, psychologistic perspective. Lang and Hill-Tout actually had a considerable correspondence (as related in the "Appendix" of Lang's *The Secret of the Totem*), and although many of the arguments turned on minor details, it was apparent that a main difficulty was something that neither seemed aware of: the American Boasians were not evolutionists in their thinking, whereas Lang was thoroughly so. His argument that the more primitive Australians take us much closer to primordial conditions than the developed Northwest Indians went right past Hill-Tout—and neither Lang nor Hill-Tout seemed to understand why.

Lang, it may already be evident, held to a much more sociological theory of totemism. That is, as primordial social groups formed, they needed to be differentiated by names that could be represented in pictographs and gesture language. What would better lend themselves to such graphics than the familiar plant and animal species of their habitat? Eventually, myths arose to make still more striking the mystic rapport between the species and the human groups that bore their names. Incest taboos (or exogamy) are among the various superstitions arising from this situation. The powerful significance of *names*, which Lang insisted upon, was one of the central elements of his theory that his critics belabored. *The Secret of the Totem* was an answer to his critics, and it particularly emphasizes this matter.

Lang's new phrasing is as follows:

> The problem has been to account for the world-wide development of kinships, usually named after animals, plants, and other objects, and for the rule that the members of these kins may never marry within the kinship as limited by the name, Crow, Wolf, or whatever it may be. Why, again, are there kinships regimented, in each tribe, into two "phratries" [moieties], exogamous, which also frequently bear animal names? (1905:111)

Lang begins by postulating not a primal, promiscuous, undivided horde, but rather a series of small groups of females, each group dominated by a lone male who had driven the weaker males away. This postulates a condition of necessary exogamy, or partial incest taboo, in that the weaker males would have to find sexual mates elsewhere. Such a circumstantial organization could become rationalized in time, with the development of intellect, to be formulated as a *conscious* rule: "No marriage within this group of hearth-mates." Exogamy, in such a case, would result in the theft of wives from other groups.

But this question, so far, belongs in the section on taboo, for the matter at issue remains: Why are plant and animal species mystically (or ritually) associated with groups? Lang argued that the various superstitions, myths, and taboos associated with totemism must necessarily have arisen *subsequently* to a group's actually bearing the name of the totem. If a group bore such a name, *"and if its origin were unknown,* [it] would come to be taken by the groups as implying a mystic connection between all who bore it, men or beasts" (1905:116). Lang goes on to cite the truly worldwide prevalence (in the primitive world especially) of the belief that the name is a part of the person, the soul of the bearer.

Why are plants and animals chosen as names for groups of people? Because, as was mentioned earlier, such names are not abstractions and are familiar in the environment, thus lending themselves to graphic representation. The practical social need of distinguishing social groups by naming only gave rise later to mystic, ritual, or religious embellishments. That is, the *origin* of totemism lies not in some religious stirrings, as in the individual's fears which lead to a belief in a "guardian spirit," but in social organization itself. Possibly the names, as sobriquets, were given to particular groups by others—even enemies. But the point is that it was much later, long after the origin of the names was forgotten, that over generations the mystical feeling of kinly association and protection arose. This by definition is not rational; that is, it matters not if the animal is lion or mouse (or flea or grub), the association is of the spirit or soul of mice with our souls.

Souls of *anything* can be magically efficacious. The flavor and power of Lang's argument cannot be conveyed in brief nor his erudition communicated; his numerous and well-chosen examples from around the world must be read before one can comprehend the power and significance of names to the primitive mind.

The germ of totemism is thus the naming of groups. The fact that the name is typically that of a plant or animal is not the problem, for that choice is simply an expectable one given the primordial circumstances of man's being so closely connected to nature. That this relationship of particular groups with particular kinds of plants or animals should become religious (mystical, ritual, sacred) is also perfectly expectable, given primitive man's disposition to endow everything significant with such qualities. Totemic exogamy, in many person's thoughts a primary quality of totemism, was to Lang's mind the least important characteristic, arising only long after the others, and again perfectly expectable because of the "savage modes of thinking" which are much given to taboos.

One further point was stressed by Lang in opposition to the Americans' view that group totemism began with individual guardian spirits. An individual man could not give his name to a group because early society was *matrilineal.* (Most of the English and French evolutionists had accepted Morgan's view on this, as had the primary ethnographers of the Australian aborigines, Fison and Howitt, Spencer and Gillen. It is relevant here that the Boas group in America had not.)

Émile Durkheim and Marcel Mauss had brought out a long essay in 1903, which involved the question of totemism as an aspect of the broader language–thought, or social–psychological, aspects of "primitive classification." This essay argued that the primordial forms of the society impose on the people a classification that they are subsequently to impose on the rest of nature, including plant and animal groups. For some reason this essay attracted no attention that survives as either controversy or approval outside the Durkheim circle. However, it is not in the spirit of dismissal that it is, at this point, not discussed; it is because Durkheim's later writing on the subject in 1912, *Les formes élémentaire de la vie religieuse,* is undoubtedly the climax of his career and thus deserves fuller attention. Certainly his argument by 1912 had benefited from further thought, although it was not markedly altered from the earlier and briefer exposition.

Basically, Durkheim is taking a side exactly opposite to that of Frazer and the allied one of Boas and his followers in America. Given that there are two kinds of totemism, totems of individuals and totems of the clan, which is historically prior to the other? Which is derivative? As we saw, Boas and the Americans derive clan totems from individual totems. Durkheim says:

> The desire for an undue simplicity, with which ethnologists and sociologists are too frequently inspired, has naturally led many scholars to explain, here as elsewhere, the complex by the simple, the totem of the group by that of the individual. Such, in fact, is the theory sustained by Frazer in his *Golden Bough*, by Hill-Tout, by Miss Fletcher, by Boas, and by Swanton. (1912:200)

Durkheim takes the opposite view, that the clan totemism is prior, and he posits several logical flaws in the idea of the priority of the individual totem. The most telling case against that idea and for his own, however, involves an evolutionary–historical, factual argument. Durkheim says:

> If individual totemism were the initial fact, it should be more developed and apparent, the more primitive the societies are, and inversely, it should lose ground and disappear before the other among the more advanced peoples. Now it is the contrary which is true. The Australian tribes are far behind those of North America; yet Australia is the classic land of collective totemism. *In the great majority of the tribes, it alone is found, while we do not know a single one where individual totemism alone is practiced....* In America, on the contrary, the collective totem is in full decadence; in most of the societies of the North-west especially, its religious character is almost gone. Inversely, the individual totem plays a considerable role among these same peoples. (1912:206–207)

Durkheim here has arrived at his reason for devoting a major work to the Australian aborigines and for labeling their religion *elementary forms*. To him the Australians represent the earliest and most primitive surviving types of primordial men. Both Frazer and Andrew Lang had ascribed this same significance to the Australian data. Although Lang had his differences with Frazer's latest work, *Totemism and Exogamy* (1910), they shared the basic idea that, in Durkheim's phrase, totemism is a "belief in a sort of consubstantiality of the man and animal." But, counters Durkheim (1912:213), what about the religious character of the totemic beliefs and practices? Why does a man who considers himself an animal of a certain species also attribute marvelous powers to this species, and especially why does he make a cult of the images symbolizing it? Both Frazer and Lang denied that totemism was basically or originally religious. When religious-like taboos are associated with totemism, it is because, according to Lang, ideas of spiritual power, like the Siouxan *wakan* or Polynesian *mana*, tend to suffuse their ideas of the relationship of totemic beings. But to Durkheim this is precisely the question, not the answer.

Mana, used in a generic sense to include not only the Oceanic concept but also such other well-known manifestations as Siouxan *wakan*, Iroquoian *orenda*, and Algonkian *manitou*, is, according to Durkheim, the spiritual principle or force that inhabits the totemic relationship in its very origin. It is like a vital principle which gives life and spiritual qualities but which is impersonal and abstract, so that although individuals die the spirit maintains its continuity. It is the elementary force which is the basis of all religious thought in general (1912:227). In effect, Durkheim argues against the nearly universal European−modern idea that religion is to be defined in terms of mythical personalities, gods, or spirits.[1]

Much of the effort in Durkheim's *Formes élémentaires* consists of attempting to explain the social psychology of symbolism, concepts of society, distinctions between the *sacred* and *profane* realms of action, and the relation of group conceptualizations of society and reality as *représentations collectives*. This is required by his idea that society itself is the most significant reality, with its own categories suggesting (or imposing) categories on the external world—especially of plants and animals.

The American ethnologists referred to in Durkheim's work did not include A. A. Goldenweiser, who had recently (1910) published his analytical critique of the studies of totemism (presumably too late to come to Durkheim's attention). Goldenweiser's contribution was of that quintessentially Boasian sort of negativism so prevalent (and, it may be added, so necessary) in the early decades of the twentieth century in America. This long critique, called "Totemism: An Analytic Study," seems to have had the unhappy result of reducing the interest in the subject in America, for his argument led American ethnologists to conclude that there was no unitary, definable category of totemic practices that could be fruitfully studied. Rather, the characteristics assumed to be associated were absent or combined in highly various ways, with no necessary connections among them. Such unity as adheres to the phenomena usually grouped as totemic is really only psychological, "a specific socialization of emotional values" (1910:275). Even the main feature of totemism, the taboos against killing and eating the totem, only overlaps with the presence of the naming of social groups by natural phenomena. So far as "origins" are concerned, they must have been in highly diverse disarray, with the later greater congruence due to "convergent evolution" by which distinctly different phenomena come to resemble one another when they share a psychological basis.

[1]Henri Hubert and Marcel Mauss, students and colleagues of Durkheim, wrote a notable work on this point in 1904, "Esquisse d'une théorie générale de la magie."

At this point we may let Boas speak for himself. In 1916 he published "The Origin of Totemism" with the express purpose of countering Frazer and Durkheim and making his own views more explicit. On this latter point he begins with a characteristic example of his brand of particularism and relativism.

Both Frazer and Durkheim had attributed to Boas the view that the origin of totemism lay in the priority of the individual *manitou* or guardian spirit, which only later was extended to a kinship group. Boas says (1916:316) that among the Kwakiutl there is an analogy between the legends of the totem and the guardian spirit tale, suggesting "that *among this tribe* there is a likelihood that under the pressure of totemistic ideas the guardian-spirit concept has taken this particular line of development" Boas' methodological principles do not allow generalization from one culture to others via the old evolutionistic comparative method.

> First of all it must be borne in mind that ethnic phenomena which we compare are seldom really alike. The fact that we designate certain tales as myths, that we group certain activities together as rituals, or that we consider certain forms of industrial products from an esthetic point of view, does not prove that these phenomena, wherever they occur, have the same history or spring from the same mental activities. . . . On the contrary, wherever an analysis has been attempted we are led to the conclusion that we are dealing with heterogeneous material. (1916:317)

Totemism is a problem of this kind; the concept has a unity that is only subjective, not objective. It is "artificial, not natural." (Boas seems to mean that it is *our own* analytical category, not a unity found in nature.)

The stress Durkheim and others placed on the aspect of totemism that identifies man and animal would be reversed by Boas. He feels that this is one kind of problem and occurs much more widely than in the context of totemism—in magic, art, and so forth. But the other aspect of totemism has to do with the (also very widespread) recognition of exogamic kinship groups. This is a universal social phenomenon, but totemism is not. Thus exogamy may be assumed to be very old, certainly much older than the totemic exogamic groups. "We may, therefore, consider exogamy as the condition on which totemism arose" (1916:320).

Ethnological data seem to show the lines of development. Once there were relatively independent family groups that had rules against incest—these are well represented by Eskimo (who have no totemism). Greater population and other factors, mainly economic, led to the separation of husbands, or wives, from their parental groups and thus favored the growth of unilateral families. The dispersed unilateral grouping, maintaining its exogamic feature, must be identified, hence "the elements of totemic organization are given wherever a unilateral family is designated by some characteristic feature" (1916:322).

If this is correct, there should be a great variety of devices used in naming the unilateral groups. But a given cultural type (cultural area, or tribe?) will tend to give names to its groups from within a certain "domain of thought." That is, the classificatory principles will tend to be similar in a given culture type. "We may conclude . . . that the homology of distinguishing marks of social divisions of a tribe is a proof that they are due to a classificatory tendency" (1916:323).

In a brief article in 1910 and again at greater length in a 1918 article, "Form and Content in Totemism", which was much aided by Boas' above article, Goldenweiser wrestled with the problem posed by Durkheim. He says, in the second article, that totemism can be dichotomized into the essential elements of form and content for purposes of understanding it.

The *content* of totemism is the actual beliefs, practices, and attitudes involved; the *form* consists of the social units themselves. The content is highly diverse in the primitive world, but the form is always of social units (usually clans), equivalent subdivisions of the society and functionally homologous from one "totemic complex" to another. The problem had been that earlier writers, beginning with McLennan and culminating with Durkheim, all had content uppermost in mind. Even when they recognized the significance of such an important social feature as exogamy, they treated it as a religious belief, a *taboo*, rather than as related to the formal aspect of the complex. Boas had made a very similar point.

But Goldenweiser reversed Boas in one respect. He agreed that the content of totemism derives from man's experiences in and with nature, which are allied with religious, mystical attitudes: "Religious attitudes toward things in nature are as universal as religion itself" (1918:293). Thus the content was available, as a set of beliefs and rituals, before designations were needed for newly appeared hereditary, exogamous clans. Goldenweiser also reversed Durkheim's idea that the forms—exogamous groups—were very early and functioned in creating the content.

To Sigmund Freud, in his famous *Totem and Taboo* (1913), the most interesting aspect of totemism is that the totemic groups prohibit sexual relations (and marriage) among the members of the same group. Totemism itself as a socioreligious institution has long been abandoned, but taboo is still with us—and therefore it begs for explanation.

And, judging from the extremely severe punishments (usually death) meted out to the man who commits incest with a woman of his totemic clan, it is not only a broadly conceived but an intensely dreaded act. (Further discussion of Freud's theory of taboo will be renewed in the next section, *"Taboo."*)

As for totemism itself, Freud considers tribal (or clan) totemism to be the important kind, to the exclusion of individual and sex totems. He emphasizes that it is a religious as well as a social system. This is particularly evident in the similar taboos associated with it: killing (or eating) the totem animal is forbidden; sexual intercourse is forbidden between the humans of the group (1913:186). It is, of course, highly suggestive that the animal (or plant) identification as ancestor—thus primal *father*—is made, for father–child problems lie at the very basis of Freudian theories of neurosis.

> If the totem animal is the father, then the two main commandments of totemism, the two taboo rules which constitute its nucleus,—not to kill the totem animal and not to use a woman belonging to the same totem for sexual purposes,—agree in content with the two crimes of Oedipus, who slew his father and took his mother to wife, and also with the child's two primal wishes whose insufficient repression or whose re-awakening forms the nucleus of perhaps all neuroses. If this similarity is more than a deceptive play of accident it would perforce make it possible for us to shed light upon the origin of totemism in prehistoric times. (1913:230)

Freud now proposes to discuss totemism as a religion, a set of beliefs and ceremonies, rather than as a social system as such. First, as briefly noted above, Freud states that the totem animal is a substitute for the father, hence the killing (sacrifice) of the totem and the ritual eating of it results in a holiday in which it is also mourned: "The ambivalent emotional attitude which today still marks the father complex in our children and so often continues into adult life also extended to the father substitute of the totem animal" (1913:246).

The origin of the Oedipus complex lies in the Darwinian conception of the primal horde, whereby a male father dominates the horde and sexually monopolizes the females. When eventually the sons overcome the father and free themselves by killing him, Freud argues that a fundamental ambivalence arises that characterizes, more or less, all subsequent parent–child relationships—but particularly the mixed jealousy–hatred and love–guilt feelings of adult males toward the aging or dying father. The totemic "ancestor–father" and the feasts and taboos associated with its celebration are chiefly forms of expiation of what was judged a sin.

They undid their deed by declaring that the killing of the father substitute, the totem, was not allowed, and renounced the fruits of their deed by denying themselves the liberated women. Thus they created two fundamental taboos of totemism out of the *sense of guilt of the son,* and for this very reason these had to correspond with the two repressed wishes of the Oedipus complex. (1913:250)

Following the publication of *Totem and Taboo* in English in 1918, A. L. Kroeber wrote a critique of it in the *American Anthropologist* (1920), "Totem and Taboo: An Ethnologic Psychoanalysis." As an ethnologist–historian, Kroeber finds fault with the factual basis of Freud's assumptions; they are all extremely doubtful, yet the final argument is a pyramiding of all of them. Worse yet, Kroeber says, Freud rests his conclusions not on judgments about historical fact but on an assumption about or a definition of totemism which is fundamental to his theory but which is not accepted by any modern ethnologists writing about totemism. This is that exogamy and "totem abstinence" are the two fundamental prohibitions of totemism. Furthermore, the argument that these two taboos are the oldest, and that therefore other taboos derive from them, is nothing but assertion, whereas Goldenweiser's contrary argument was based in a careful examination of worldwide ethnographic data.

This is one side of Kroeber, that of Boasian particularism—above all, critical about the misuse of data. But there is another side that approves of many aspects of Freud's psychoanalytic theory, such as compulsion neuroses, displacement, and above all likelihood of there being unconscious mental (psychological) aspects underlying many human cultural institutions: Freud brings to anthropology "keen insight, a fecund imagination, and above all a point of view which henceforth can never be ignored without stultification" (1920:305).[2]

At this point a few lines may be devoted to Malinowski's functionalist theory. Malinowski's simple explanation of totemism is the very essence of his more general psychobiological, utilitarian, individualistic perspective. Totemism as a complex is separated into three components, each to be explained separately: (1) It is concerned with plants and animals; (2) There is a cultish or ritualized relation between the biological species and man, symbolizing a sort of affinity between them; and (3) There is a merging of social groups and their practice of ritual–magic.

To explain the first is easy. The great concern with plants and animals is due to the fact that they supply mankind with food, and it is

---

[2]Kroeber practiced psychoanalysis in San Francisco from 1920–1923. Later, however, he was to become quite critical and "disillusioned" with the "culture–and–personality" school in anthropology (1952:300).

food which is primary in the mind of the primitive. As for the second question, the affinity is caused by the fact that animals, in particular, are alive, expressive, and thus similar to man in obvious ways. This is less true of plants and inanimate objects, but they are "secondary," not the "substance of totemism." With the third component we are reminded again of Boas in the focus on the individual. Ritual in totemic practice becomes magic and magic necessarily leads to individual specialization. As the specialist's family proliferates in time and becomes a clan, we have the common conjunction of individual clans having the name of a plant or animal species and practicing the rites and taboos associated with its cult (1948:27–28).

In his article "The Sociological Theory of Totemism" (1929), Radcliffe-Brown defines the subject very generally as "apply[ing] wherever a society is divided into groups and there is a special relationship between each group and one or more classes of objects that are usually natural species of animals or plants but may occasionally be artificial objects or parts of an animal" (1929:117). The narrower definition so often used, which applies only when the groups are exogamous and unilineal, (Radcliffe-Brown calls this "clan-totemism"), is considered as only a variety of totemism in general.

In a rapid survey of native Australia, Radcliffe-Brown finds several strikingly different kinds of groups with a totemic association with plant or animal species. There is "sex-totemism" (men associated with one biological species, women with another), exogamous moieties totemically defined, "section-totemism" (the four-class system), "clan-totemism" in several different versions, "individual" (or personal) totemism, and with all these coexist great variations in kinds of ceremonials and rituals (such as rites of increase and taboos against eating the totemic species).

Such diversity means that the earlier quests for the origin of totemism were fruitless, since such diversity must mean that the origins themselves would have to be diverse (1929:122). Such speculation has no place in an inductive science.

> "[The task] of a science of culture is to reduce the complex data with which it deals to a limited number of general laws or principles. Approaching totemism in this way we may formulate the problem that it presents in the form of the question, "Can we show that totemism is a special form of a phenomenon which is universal in human society and is therefore present in different forms in all cultures?" (1929:123)

Radcliffe-Brown begins his explication by substituting the term *ritual* relationship and attitude for Durkheim's word *sacred*. All societies adopt or impose on their members a ritual attitude of respect toward certain objects. Thus a flag of a nation, in Durkheim's discussion, is sacred for the national group, or the object of a ritual relationship to Radcliffe-Brown. "And the function of the ritual attitude towards the totem is to express and so to maintain in existence the solidarity of the social group" (1929:125). Radcliffe-Brown thus agrees with Durkheim in this respect, but he would argue that this view is incomplete. It does not as yet explain why what we usually call totemism has selected biological species instead of other things. Durkheim had argued that these species were capable of being represented graphically,[3] but Radcliffe-Brown points out that the totemic graphic designs that so impressed Durkheim were characteristic of only a part of Australia.

Radcliffe-Brown prefers to begin with what seems to be a general fact, that societies dependent on wild food will make the important plants and animals objects of the ritual attitude, whether they have totemism or not. The nontotemic Eskimos and Andaman Islanders, as examples, have a veneration of certain animals that is society-wide. Totemism, suggests Radcliffe-Brown, is a special development of this general relationship between society and a natural species. When a society becomes segmented into components like clans, "a process of ritual specialization takes place by which each segment acquires a special and particular relation to some one or more of the *sacra* of the community" (1929:127).

As a familiar example of the process of such segmentation, Radcliffe-Brown discusses the ritualism of the Roman Catholic Church. The saints of this church are sacred to all members of the religion. But the church also is segmented into local congregations, with each one placed into a special relationship to its patron saint. Also, an individual can have a patron saint; this is analogous to the personal totem or guardian spirit found in Australia and America. In contrast to Durkheim's theory, which emphasizes the clan and the role of the totem in promoting clan solidarity, Radcliffe-Brown sees the clan as a segment in relation to other segments, with totemic beings having a relationship to each other that reflects the differentiation and the connection of the parts to the whole. Also in contrast to Durkheim, natural species do not become sacred because they are selected as representatives of social groups; rather, such species are selected as representatives of social groups because they already are objects of the ritual attitude. They are already sacred in obedience to the "general law" formulated by Radcliffe-Brown: "Any object or event which has important effects upon the well-being (material or spiritual) of a society, or

[3]Andrew Lang, not Durkheim, was the first to say this.

anything which stands for or represents any such object or event, tends to become an object of the ritual attitude" (1929:129). Totemism, therefore, is part of a larger whole which provides a representation of the universe and incorporates both the social (or cultural) order and the natural order as one entity. Totemism is not the social (or moral) order projected into nature, nor vice versa. Environment and society, or religion and nature, are not differentiated in the "primitive mentality" (1929:130).

There is, in this article, a notable contrast to the Boasian view. Radcliffe-Brown sees the process of society building as segmentation and differentiation, proceeding from the general to the particular. Boas, and other Americans we have noted, begin with individuals as the basic building blocks of society.[4]

We must depart slightly from our arbitrary cutoff date of 1960 to consider a 1962 book by Lévi-Strauss, *Le totémisme aujourd'hui*, simply because it is widely considered to be the definitive work on this subject. It also reveals Lévi-Strauss' distinctive mode of theoretical thought. Lévi-Strauss has been heavily dependent on several aspects of Boasian ethnological thought. His work on totemism is also much informed by the critical remarks of Boas alluded to earlier. In fact, there is a sense in which it could be argued that he has exaggerated some of Boas' attitudes, that he is a super-Boas in certain respects.

First of all, Lévi-Strauss agrees with Boas that totemism is an "artificial entity" existing solely in the mind of the anthropologist, conforming to nothing in reality. But since totemism has in fact been considered as a reality, Lévi-Strauss decides to discuss it in that way first. A useful way to begin might be to consider briefly his criticisms of Radcliffe-Brown's structuralism–functionalism and his approval of a limited idea that Radcliffe-Brown later offered.

Lévi-Strauss says of Radcliffe-Brown: "To say that anthropology is amenable to the method of natural science is, for him, to maintain that anthropology is a natural science" (1962:61). Thus, Radcliffe-Brown "naturalizes" the thought of Durkheim, incorporating the social and natural orders rather than establishing the social on a separate plane. Like Malinowski, he thinks an animal becomes a totemic object because it is first of all "good to eat." (This is what Lévi-Strauss calls the "obstinate taste for utilitarian interpretations" [1962:63].)

But Lévi-Strauss finds that later in his career Radcliffe-Brown took a

---

[4]Radcliffe-Brown devotes his discussion nearly entirely to Durkheim, however, rather than to Boas. He is evidently not interested in explicitly criticizing the Boas group, nor even (surprisingly) Malinowski.

rather different view of ritual; but this was in a context different from totemism. The context was Radcliffe-Brown's opposition to Malinowski's utilitarian–psychologistic theory of magic. Mainly, the origin and function of magical rites was to reduce or abolish the anxieties people feel about risky enterprises. Radcliffe-Brown (1939:149) argues that it is just as plausible to turn the argument around: magic and religion themselves can create fears and anxieties in men. Lévi-Strauss correctly points out that this same argument could be used against Radcliffe-Borwn's own earlier theory of totemism, that men adopt a ritual attitude toward these plant and animal species which arouse their interest. "Could it not just as well be maintained that (as the bizarre nature of the lists of totems suggests) it is rather because of the ritual attitudes which they observe toward certain species that men are led to find an interest in them?" (1962:68).

Lévi-Strauss ends Chapter 3, a discussion of functionalist theories of totemism, with this statement:

> Actually, impulses and emotions explain nothing: they are always *results*, either of the power of the body or of the impotence of the mind. In both cases they are consequences, never causes. The latter can be sought only in the organism, which is the exclusive concern of biology, or in the intellect, which is the sole way offered to psychology, and to anthropology as well. (1962:71)

We are now prepared to consider more fully Lévi-Strauss' reasons for approving of what he calls Radcliffe-Brown's "second theory," which appeared 22 years after the first (1929) theory. This was in the Huxley Memorial Lecture for 1951, prominently displayed as an example of "The Comparative Method in Social Anthropology" (the title of the lecture), but without emphasis on its novelty.

The demonstration of this theory pursued Radcliffe-Brown's usual "natural science" method of explaining a particular phenomenon in terms of a much more general process. For example, typical instances of totemism in Australia involve moieties as the exogamous social grouping; their totemic species thus are twofold. If we begin, then, with the question of why the Darling River peoples in Australia have a moiety social division with Eaglehawk and Crow as the totems, we must look far afield. In this and other cases, Radcliffe-Brown first searched for similarities in the paired totems, noting that Eaglehawk and Crow, for example, are both meat eaters and can be compared with the people of the moieties in this respect. But Radcliffe-Brown's second thoughts told him that along with similarities there were always differences. Eaglehawk is a hunter, Crow is a thief and carrion eater (and both, as animals, can be distinguished from the humans of the moieties). This can be seen as a kind of very general structural principle, the union of opposites. Thus this case and the other, numerous examples of moiety totemism are no more than special cases of correlations and oppositions named in other ways: sky—earth, war—peace, upstream—downstream, red—white, and so forth. To Lévi-Strauss these are particular fashions of "formulating a general problem, viz., how to make opposition, instead of being an obstacle to integration, serve rather to produce it" (1962:89).

Since some of the paired oppositions listed above are not natural species, neither are they, strictly speaking, totems. One of the original questions, therefore, still remains: Why are plants and animals so frequently chosen to play this mnemonic role? Lévi-Strauss provides a memorable phrase here to remind us of the basic divergence in Radcliffe-Brown's two different theories: "Natural species are chosen not because they are 'good to eat' but because they are 'good to think'" (1962:89).

Radcliffe-Brown does not explain this important change in his theory (as Lévi-Strauss put it, "he was not the man to admit with good grace that he might change his mind, or to recognize possible influences" [1962:89]). Lévi-Strauss suggests, however, that the 10 years preceding his 1951 lecture saw a coming together of anthropology and structural linguistics, and that perhaps at least an "echo" of this might have found its way to Radcliffe-Brown's mind.

> The ideas of opposition and correlation, and that of a pair of opposites, have a long history; but it is structural linguistics and subsequently structural anthropology which rehabilitated them in the vocabulary of the humane sciences. It is striking to meet them, with all their implications, in the writings of Radcliffe-Brown, who, as we have seen, was led by them to abandon his earlier positions, which were still stamped with the mark of naturalism and empiricism. (1962:90)

Lévi-Strauss is rightly hesitant to attribute to Radcliffe-Brown a realization of the revolutionary implications of his ideas were they to be rigorously and logically extended beyond the question of Australian totemic moieties to the whole realm of methodological analysis of human culture. He gave no sign of doing so, and in fact it would seem too much to expect anyone to cast aside a lifetime's consistent, polemical, almost messianic, organismic approach to ethnology. It is safer to believe that for just once in his life Radcliffe-Brown was as other people are most of their lives, inconsistent. One cannot believe it possible for such a man to go the whole way with Lévi-Strauss, to actually *substitute* for the thoroughgoing organismic analogy the strange and limited analogy of structural linguistics.[5]

---

[5]Lévi-Strauss says in his final chapter: "Radcliffe-Brown would probably have rejected the conclusions which we have just drawn from his analysis, for until the end of his life,

THE INCEST TABOO

As noted in the previous section, the early history of taboo was closely linked with totemism. That is, the taboo on marriage within the totemic group (later called totemic *exogamy*) and the frequently allied taboos on eating (except sometimes ritually) and killing or injuring one's totem were only later to be considered with other prohibitions as a general class called *taboo*. Of these, eventually, the exogamic rule, finally called the incest taboo, was not only deemed to be universal (and thus well outside the more limited occurrence of totemic exogamy), but it also became a favorite way of arguing about the very origin of humanity. Food taboos, as well as many other kinds of similar restrictions on behavior, are so ubiquitous, but also so various, that they have not been subject to analysis or controversy, although much descriptive material has been published about them.

It was, then, exogamy and the incest taboo of all the taboos that specifically aroused the most interest and consequently the most controversy in the history of ethnological theory. It is also, like totemism, an institution that has obvious social-organizational aspects and at the same time poignant subjective psychological and emotional features—the legalistic, social-organizational phrase "prohibition of incest" is also frequently called the "horror of incest."

Lewis H. Morgan (1877), in facing the grand problem of what he considered the evolution of monogamy by stages out of promiscuity, was in a sense concerned with the origin of exogamy, of course. But he saw this progression as a moral one involving the trends toward the ideals of monogamous marriage and sexual fidelity. He also thought that inbreeding was deleterious and said so several times (1877:65, 70, 321, 389), but he did not cite it as a mechanism or cause for outmarriage, although it did "increase the vigor of the stock." But Morgan was talking about marriage systems rather than trying to explain why there was an incest taboo.

Westermarck's huge *The History of Human Marriage* (1891) was, at least in part, an attempt to counter Morgan's theories about the evolution of marriage; he particularly combatted the ideas of original promiscuity and group marriage. The major way in which these were denied was by arguing that human society had *always* had exogamy and the prohibition of incest was to be attributed to an instinctual aversion.

This theme of natural aversion to sex among close relatives (or

---

and as is proved by a correspondence with him, he held fast to an empiricist conception of structure" (1962:92).

hearth-mates) indeed does seem "natural," viewed introspectively. A great many anthropologists have held to this view and have therefore found no need to examine it further. Others have accepted it but have embellished it with attempted explanations of why the aversion should exist. These have been mainly of two kinds: (1) The "aversion" is a cultural, subjective consequence of a rule of exogamy (or related taboo against sexual relations of close relatives) which served sociological, integrative functions *between* or *among* discrete families; or (2) The original rule and subsequent aversion has a sociological function *within* discrete families.

Probably the best-known explanation of the first kind, if not the original, must be that of E. B. Tylor in 1888.[6] His much-quoted statement can stand repeating for its historical significance. He said:

> Exogamy, enabling a growing tribe to keep itself compact by constant unions between its spreading clans, enables it to overmatch any number of small intermarrying groups, isolated and helpless. Again and again in the world's history, savage tribes must have had plainly before their minds the simple practical alternative between marrying-out and being killed out. (1888:267)

Many anthropologists of structural–functional or evolutionary leanings seem to have accepted this kind of explanation, particularly since its vigorous prosecution by Leslie White (1949:303–329). His main point is as follows:

> The struggle for existence is as vigorous in the human species as elsewhere. Life is made more secure, for groups as well as individuals, by cooperation. Articulate speech makes cooperation possible, extensive, and varied in human society. Incest was defined and exogamous rules were formulated in order to make co-operation compulsory and extensive, to the end that life be made more secure. These institutions were created by *social* systems, not by *neurosensory–muscular–glandular* systems. (1949:328–329)

Of the second theory, Sigmund Freud was the first to popularize the idea of the psychological–sexual strains in the nuclear family between parents and children. His "Just-so" story about the sons killing the father need not detain us here, but he did dramatize the psychological content of what today are often called *role strains* in the nuclear family.

Malinowski belongs among those who are concerned with the social–psychological aspects of the internal constitution of the nuclear family, although he was one of the most effective destroyers of Freudi-

---

[6]McLennan's marriage-by-capture theory (see chapter 1, pp. 7–8) could be stretched to be included here, and would of course be the first (1865), but he had no followers of his theory and it remains as a mere historical curiosity.

an theory (in favor of behaviorism). His Trobriand Islanders, being matrilineal, have the mother's brother as the authoritarian disciplinarian of a couple's children, while the father of the children is the meekly affectionate husband of the mother. Whatever psychological strains there are here are mostly between Ego and his mother's brother, who, perforce, has no sexual access to Ego's mother. Rules against incest pertain, however, just as they do in a patrilineal society. So much for the sexual competition aspect of Freud's account.

But Freud's theory aside, Malinowski remains in the forefront of those who maintain the inside-out view of the individual and his nuclear family, with parenthood in particular as the keystone of society—just as he did in his theory about kin terminology. He says, in brief (1927:252), that if incest were permitted "the fundamental pattern of all social bonds, the normal relation of the child to the mother and father, would be destroyed." This does not explain, of course, why it is that the incest taboo also applies to brother–sister relations, nor above all why it is applied so frequently in the primitive world to parallel-cousins but not to cross-cousins, since neither kind of cousin has anything to do with parenthood (and, in rebuttal to those who fancy the anti-inbreeding theory, both kinds of cousins are equally close genetically).

The answer to the question of why the fundamental incest taboo of parent–child relations always affects the other close relatives is that Ego tends to "extend" such feelings. It was G. P. Murdock's *Social Structure* (1949) which elaborated Malinowski's theory to its most general dimensions. This was by means of the extensionist theory, which we encountered before in the discussion of kinship terminology (which also begins in the parent–child relationship). The explanation of why the taboos exist first in the nuclear family is basically Malinowski's: the resolution of intrafamily conflicts over paternal authority, jealousy, and so on. The extension of this taboo to outside relatives is via "stimulus generalization" (a tautology borrowed from Yale behaviorist—Hullian—psychology). This means, for example, that because a mother's sister seems to resemble the mother, the taboo is extended to her.

Murdock "tested" this proposition with cross-cultural statistics, but his test used marriage rules, not incest taboos, and these may not be the same thing. They may (or may not) be related historically; it would seem that Murdock and others see outmarriage as prior, occurring because inmarriage would create strains, and outmarriage would be easier if the individual were *propelled out* by the incest taboo (otherwise the person might not want to marry out).

There is a gross factual error here in the assumption that marriage is a matter of the individual's "sexual choice" (Murdock's concluding chapter is called "The Social Law of Sexual Choice"). In most (or all, so far as I can ascertain) primitive societies such an important matter as a marriage is not primarily a matter of sex and certainly not a matter of the individual's sexual choice. In fact, it is very common for marriage partners to have been betrothed as infants (promised by the affinal parents or kin groups) or even before they were born.

Reo Fortune, in his *Encyclopaedia of the Social Sciences* article, "Incest," has the following telling point to make: Since there is a tremendous range of extension of the taboo to large unilateral clans, moieties, and many degrees of removal of consanguinity,

> the inference is that neither jealousies nor aversions are the prime determinants of the social forms concerned in the regulation of incest. The founding of a theory of incest upon the supposed effects of the practise upon the internal sturcture of the procreating group is a theoretical overelaboration of the restricted range of incest which is found in modern society. In practically all societies, however, penalties upon incest are not motivated by the damage done within the incestuous group by the incest. The penalties are imposed upon the offenders by the wider society as a protest against the offense of disturbing social cooperation; there are no such penalties imposed on other analogous provocations to jealousy in families. (1932:621)

It is fitting to end this section with a discussion of the theory of Lévi-Strauss, for he applies the same reasoning that we encountered in the section on totemism. He remains firmly on the mentalistic ground suggested by the model of structural linguistics.

First of all, he reasonably argues that theories like McLennan's, Lubbock's, Spencer's, and Durkheim's all mistakenly postulate specific historical sequences to account for a general phenomenon. At the same time, sociological explanations cannot account for a human universal like the incest taboo. But it *is* human; no other animal species has it: "The prohibition of incest is where nature transcends itself. It brings about and is itself the advent of a new order" (1949:25).

To Lévi-Strauss the cornerstone of kinship is marriage systems, which universally are based on and reflect the *opposition* of consanguinity and affinity. Closely related to this is the fact that marriage systems are exchanges; they involve *reciprocity*. The incest taboo is simply another aspect of marriage systems and can be seen therefore as itself an act of creating reciprocity. "The woman whom one does not take . . . is, for that very reason, offered up" (1949:51).

11

The Origin and Nature of Religion

Since most ethnologists were evolutionists of sorts, they believed that contemporary primitive peoples represented to some degree surviving ancestral stages of human culture. From this perspective it was also felt that a study of the most primitive peoples would tend to reveal the origin of such parts of culture as religion, and that this would be tantamount to revealing its true, or basic, nature. Later ethnologists, mainly structural functionalists, ignore the problem of origins and argue that the true nature of religion lies in its role in maintaining social order—in origin and later as well. The Boasians say that none of the above tells the true story, which is found in the endless variety of unique forms.

But there was also a basic controversy that to some extent cut across the evolutionist–functionalist–Boasian theoretical differences. This controversy was whether the basic locus of religion is to be found in the *mind*—as beliefs, thoughts, superstitions, rationalizations, and philosophies—or in *society* in the active form of cults, ceremonies, and rites that promote social solidarity.

The most prominent of evolutionists who located religion in the minds of individuals were Spencer, Tylor, Marett, Lang, and Frazer. The unique Malinowski also argued for mental processes and emotions as the source of religion, but he was nonevolutionist. On the other hand, evolutionist but functionalist too, were Robertson Smith and Durkheim, who emphasized not beliefs but actions. Nonevolutionist Radcliffe-Brown, in opposition to Malinowski, rephrased the basic position of Robertson Smith and Durkheim. Finally, the Boasians behaved predictably and we need examine only two, Goldenweiser and Benedict, as the most prominent examples of critics of both the evolutionists and Durkheim's sociological functionalism.

The Evolution of Religious Thought

E. B. Tylor stated the widely held evolutionary view of origins several times. The following is representative: "The inquirer who seeks . . . the beginnings of man's civilization must deduce general principles by reasoning downwards from the civilized European to the savage, and then descend to still lower levels of human existence" (1863:21).

We begin with Tylor, not because he was the first to write about the origin of religion, but because he was the first ethnologist to attract widespread and important attention to his theory. It also attracted disputation, of course, even from Herbert Spencer, a contemporary evolutionist. (This is one of the few times Spencer deigned to notice Tylor, while Tylor, for his part, made it very plain in his preface to the second edition of *Primitive Culture* that he owed no intellectual debt whatever to Spencer, which is why there was no mention of Spencer among the acknowledgments in the first edition.)

In order to do a comparative study of the religions of the "lower races," Tylor found it necessary to make a minimum, or rudimentary, definition of religion so that the religions of *all* societies could come under observation, rather than just those which worshipped a supreme deity or practiced a codified ethical program. This definition identifies an element common to all societies, the belief in spiritual beings. He named this phenomenon *Animism*, and the word became widely used to describe early or primitive religions that worshipped spirits generally but which had no "high gods." However, this is a misunderstanding of Tylor, for to him even monotheistic modern religions were animistic; that is, they sponsor the belief in spirits or souls. Furthermore, it was McLennan (1869–1870), as noted in Chapter 10, who argued that the worship of plant–animal spirits had preceded the worship of anthropomorphic gods. That is, it was he, rather than Tylor, who more fully approximated the misunderstood meaning of animism.

The matter of precedence is crucial. To Tylor the origin of general animistic beliefs lay in the earliest human's speculations concerning two groups of biological problems. First, what is the difference between a living body and a dead one, and what are the transient states of waking, sleep, trance, disease, and death? Second, what are those human-like beings which appear in dreams and visions? Tylor speculates that the "ancient savage philosophers" used each problem to account for the other by combining them in a conception of "ghost–soul." The ghost–soul animates a living being, and death is caused by its absence; it is also able to flash from place to place and appear to men in a trance or asleep as a phantasm separate from the body to which it bears the likeness; and it is able to enter into ("possess") the bodies of other men, animals, and even of inanimate things. The order of precedence is this:

> Among races within the limits of savagery, the general doctrine of souls is found worked out with remarkable breadth and consistency. The souls of animals are recognized by a natural extension from the theory of human souls: the souls of trees and plants follow in some vague partial way; and the souls of inanimate objects expand the general category to its extremest boundary. (1871:452)

Tylor averred that more recent times had seen a breaking down of the general primitive theory. First to fall before the coming of materialistic pragmatism and then modern science was the belief that inanimate objects have souls. Later, in our own day (and country), the notion of the souls of beasts seems to be dying out. "Animism, indeed, seems to be drawing in its outposts, and concentrating itself on its first and main position, the doctrine of the human soul" (1871:452). The conception of the human soul, separable from its body by death, has remained a constant in human history, from savage thought to the modern theologian.

> The theory of the soul is one principal part of a system of religious philosophy, which unites, in an unbroken line of mental connexion, the savage fetish-worshiper and the civilized Christian. The divisions which have separated the great religions of the world into intolerant and hostile sects are for the most part superficial, in comparison with the deepest of all religious schisms, that which divides Animism from Materialism. (1871:453)

Tylor's ideas were very influential in his time, but they encountered some opposition. The most acrimonious critic of Tylor, as noted above, was Herbert Spencer, but this dispute was almost entirely a personal one having to do with precedence and influence with respect to the theory of souls. It is an interesting episode in the history of anthropology because it involved two of its giants, but it will receive only bare mention here because it was not really a controversy on the same intellectual order as the others we shall witness.

In a review of Spencer's *Principles of Sociology*, Tylor said (1877:141) that Spencer, in discussing the origins of religion, had "followed lines already traced" by himself in *Primitive Culture* and in earlier papers. This of course angered Spencer and an exchange of letters followed in the journals *Mind* and *The Academy*. It seems evident that Spencer misunderstood Tylor. Spencer supported the idea that the first supernatural beliefs held by earliest man would be of the human soul (the "ghost theory"), later extended to animals, plants, and then to objects. This is virtually identical to Tylor's own theory as outlined above, but Spencer did not think so.

Spencer also misunderstood Tylor's animism while disavowing it. He believed that Tylor meant that savages confuse animate beings with inanimate objects and that that was the essence of animism. But Tylor was not speaking of a confusion of beings and things; rather, he meant that in time the idea of human *souls* became extended generally to a belief in the *spirits* of animals and finally to the attribution of spirits to inanimate things (which perforce remain inanimate.)[1] As so often in arguments, terminology alone is really the issue. Tylor and Spencer are saying the same thing but using two different words— "animism" and "ghost theory"—to describe it. But Spencer continued to have the impression that they held two different theories.

Robert R. Marett, a friend of Tylor's and much influenced by him, nevertheless felt that primordial man would have been much less a "philosopher" than Tylor believed, that primitive religion would have been much more a matter of emotion (especially "awe") than reason. The Polynesian concepts of *mana* and the negative aspect of it, *taboo*, were used as examples of impersonal, diffuse, supernatural forces permeating the universe. He coined the word *animatism* ("the attribution of life and personality to things") in order to distinguish the idea from Tylor's animism (1900:15), which featured souls. Animatism, Marett thought, would predate the idea of separate souls, being a more general form of supernaturalism.

Andrew Lang's two basic works on religion (1887, 1909) disagreed in part with Tylor, but on a rather different basis from Spencer or Marett. Lang found the theory of animism congenial but also felt that among savages one might find a conception of all-pervading spirit, like the *mana* of the Polynesians. Lang thought that some manifestations of this might resemble true anthropomorphic "gods," which Tylor thought arose only late in human history. This makes Lang seem less a linear evolutionist than Tylor, since he denied the stages of progression from simple animism to ancestor worship to monotheism. Ancestor worship could have been early, and if the ancestor was a very important person, his ghost would also tend to be more god-like or "All-Father" than others, Lang felt.

A similar idea occurred much later to Father Wilhelm Schmidt (1931) and he found reputable support in Lang's work, although he exaggerated and simplified much of it. More strongly than Lang,

[1]See Robert Carneiro (1967:xxx–xxxi) for a fuller discussion of the above material. I am grateful to him also for additional communications on the subject.

Schmidt insisted that the primordial religion of savages was straightforward monotheism. This worship of a "High God" was true monotheism, but it eventually became confused and degenerated in various ways. He felt (paradoxically, for such an antievolutionist) that resemblances of High Gods among the world's most primitive people would be good evidence for the primordial existence of monotheism. A number of Catholic missionaries trained by Schmidt worked among hunter–gatherers and reported evidence supporting the theory. The peoples reported on were African Pygmies, the Yahgan of Tierra del Fuego, African Bushmen, several Australian bands, Arctic peoples, and the Indians of North America. In many other cases, Schmidt argues that later on myths, especially solar and lunar myths, had intruded upon the monotheism.

There is no need to pursue this, for Schmidt's "evidence" has not been convincing to modern ethnology. For example, Schmidt felt that if a spirit or ghost is propitiated or feared, it is a God being "worshipped." If one such "god" is felt to be superior to others, it is a High God, and if a spirit is said to have "created" something, or if another is called "father," all these are evidence, as survivals, of primordial monotheism.

Sir James Frazer also disagreed with Tylor. In his massive work, *The Golden Bough* (1890), he argued for an evolutionary progression of human thought from magic to religion and then to science. The primordial magic was like scientific thought in that it assumed the existence of impersonal and unchanging laws in the universe, but it was unlike scientific thought because it was derived from faulty reasoning by analogy and superficial associations. Magic finally became discredited as its failures became apparent. Religion tended to replace magic by populating the universe with superhuman gods, whose help mankind gains by rituals of supplication and propitiation. Eventually, some of mankind realized the limits of its power and began to apply scientific logic and experimental methods to gain a superior understanding of nature.

In his famous essay "Magic, Science and Religion" (1925), Bronislaw Malinowski begins by not differing too much from Frazer. Malinowski divides primitive thought between *science* (empirical and rational knowledge) and the *sacred* (religion and magic). He maintains that the Trobriand Islanders are representative of other savages in their clear-cut distinction—a distinction observed in everyday activities, including gardening, fishing, fighting—between their scientific knowledge of how to do these things and the sacred region of cult and belief, religious and magical creeds and rites.

The realm of the sacred appears to us in two different kinds of activities. Malinowski asks us to compare a childbirth ritual designed to prevent the death of the fetus with a ceremony carried out in celebration of the birth. The first is different from the second in that it is a means to an end; it has a practical purpose understood by everyone. The other, a ceremony of rejoicing and presentation of the newborn, has no practical purpose; it is an end in itself rather than a means to an end. This is the difference between magic and religion. The native informant can always state the purpose of a magical rite, but for a religious ceremony all he can do is to say that it is customary or give an explanatory myth. Any aim, or function, of the latter can only be established by an interpretive sociologist, not by the native (1925:37–38).

It is magic, then, more than religion, which is (in some respects) akin to science. Both magic and science have definite practical aims associated with human needs, instincts, and pursuits. Magic could be appropriately called, as Sir James Frazer put it, a pseudoscience. Magic and religion are alike, on the other hand, because they both arise and function in a situation of emotional stress, and both are to be placed in the category of the miraculous, being based on mythology (1925:87).

Malinowski faults theories, such as Durkheim's, of the significance of society.

> First of all, in primitive societies religion arises to a great extent from purely individual sources. Secondly, society as a crowd is by no means always given to the production of religious beliefs or religious states of mind, while collective effervescence is often of an entirely secular nature. . . . Finally, the personification of society, the conception of a "Collective Soul," is without any foundation in fact, and is against the sound methods of social science. (1925:59–60)

As so often, Malinowski sounds very Boasian in his argument for the *individual* as the source of cultural institutions. And like the Boasians, he ignores the fact that Durkheim was talking about the *origins* of religion, not its manifestations in a relatively complex, advanced culture like that of the Trobriands. Malinowski does not address the matter of origins at all, except as emanations from the mentality or psychology of individual persons.

RELIGION IS WHAT MEN DO, NOT WHAT THEY THINK

The first important critique of Tylor, Spencer, Lang, Marett, Frazer, and their sympathizers was by W. Robertson Smith, who faulted them all for maintaining that religion begins as some kind of individual thought or philosophizing. Smith's first influential work was the article "Sacrifice" in the ninth edition of the *Encyclopaedia Britannica* (1886), followed soon by his great classic, *Lectures on the Religion of the Semites* (1889).

Early religion, Smith held, had little to do with beliefs but rather with ceremonial and ritual practice. Further, he argued, the dogmas that people did believe were not acquired by individual effort, they were not a matter of individual choice based on reasoning but a part of general society into which the individual was born. Thus gods and the ceremonies associated with them were taken for granted, just as any other social beliefs and practices were accepted unquestioningly. Just as political institutions are older than political theories, so religious institutions are older than religious theories. Beliefs are subsequent to rites; practice precedes rationalization.

It is public social acts of piety that make it possible to judge a religion, not the individual's private thoughts. In ancient times public ritual conformity was the testimonial of a person's social being; nonconformity would reveal a person at odds with his society. More specifically, religious allegiance and political allegiance were the same thing, "for a man's religion is part of his political connection" (1889:36).

Ancient religion was social and political because of two functions, the regulative and the stimulative. It regulated conduct in favor of the general welfare of society, just as political institutions do today. Religion was stimulative in the sense that rituals performed by a community reinforced the sense of community in the participants. "Religion did not exist for the saving of souls but for the preservation and welfare of society" (1889:29).

In the early history of religion, therefore, the important relationship was not that of the individual person to a supernatural power but that of all of the community to a power serving the community. The idea of God was rooted in the community and its development equaled the elaboration of political organization. This was manifested in ritual *behavior:* Robertson Smith believed that our analytical attention should be on what men do rather than on what men think.

As we saw in Chapter 10, Émile Durkheim believed that totemism was an essential key to the understanding of primordial religion. But his crowning achievement, *Les formes élémentaires de la vie religieuse* (1912), went much further and has been one of the most provocative and seminal works of theory on both religion and society ever written. Naturally enough, its importance can be gauged in good measure by the quality of both its supporters and opponents.

Durkheim had studied under Fustel de Coulanges at the *Ecole Nor-*

male in Paris, and he was much impressed with the argument that archaic religion operated as a political as well as an ideological institution—that is, as a theocracy.[2] In simpler societies—those without institutionalized political rule—Durkheim reasoned that society would perforce have been unified with religion even though not in such a visibly political context. Durkheim accordingly chose to study the most primitive and simple religion known, that of the natives of the central Australian desert.

Early in the book Durkheim defines religion: "A religion is a unified system of beliefs and practices relative to sacred things, that is to say, things set apart and forbidden—beliefs and practices which unite into one single moral community called a Church, all those who adhere to them." (1912:62). Immediately following his definition, Durkheim remarks on the significance of its second element, that religion is inseparable from Church, thus making it clear that "religion should be an eminently collective thing."

How does religion originate? Durkheim chose to discuss the leading theories by reducing them to two types: animism and naturism. All religions have these two aspects. The animistic aspect is devoted to supernatural beings such as spirits, souls, genii, demons, and divinities, all of which are invisible to human eyes; the naturistic aspect is concerned with natural phenomena like winds, rivers, and stars, and with objects such as plants and animals, and rocks. One theory would make animism preeminent and derive natural phenomena from it; the other would reverse the order (1912:64–65). But it is animism which is the more difficult to refute and which attracts ethnologists and anthropologists.

Tylor first, and Spencer following, are to Durkheim the two principal proponents of the animistic theory, diverging from each other only slightly. For them the idea of spirit or soul was suggested to primordial man by the double life he leads, one when awake, the other when asleep. Dreaming is regarded as the same as being awake, so after a man visits another locality in his dream, but awakens to find himself in the place where he went to sleep, he can (from many such experiences) conclude that he must be composed of two beings, one of which has the power of leaving the body to roam abroad. Other manifestations serve to confirm this, among them fainting, apoplexy, catalepsy, and ecstasy. This other being is the "soul."

A "spirit" differs from a soul in that it is a soul which has been

---

[2]Fustel de Coulanges stands as the first important scholar to make this very modern functionalist argument about religion.

completely freed from the body. The puzzle over the fact of death was resolved in this way: the soul has permanently departed the body and is now a spirit. Funeral rites are undertaken once this separation is final. The subsequent apparatus of religious observances—offerings, prayers, sacrifices—comes about in order to appease or conciliate the spirits of the dead. Presumably, then, the first religious rites were funeral rites and the first altars were tombs (1912:69).

According to Tylor (as we have seen), spiritism became gradually extended to other animate parts of nature, animals first, then plants, and finally inanimate things. Thus the animism of man is extended to all of nature.

Spencer disagreed with Tylor really on only this one point: man could not have confused animate and inanimate nature. Nature, according to Spencer, was included in the animistic religion because of the mental tendency of primitives for "the literal interpretation of metaphorical names." That is, to give a common example, if a clan, family, or individual is given a totemic name of a bird, flower, stream, or mountain, then all of these—animate and inanimate alike—will tend to move in time from a metaphorical usage to a literal belief in their reality as soul-bearing bodies.

Durkheim gives Spencer's modification of the animistic theory short shrift: "it is too inadequate for the facts, and too universally abandoned today to demand that we stop any longer for it" (1912:71). Tylor's original scheme, however, especially the origin of the soul in dreams, seemed to Durkheim much more difficult to dispose of. In essence, says Durkheim, the theory holds that primordial man, because of his dreams, came to believe that he was a double entity, one corporeal and the other incorporeal. But this "essence" is not yet the crux of the matter, for it is only after death, when this incorporeal double becomes a free spirit, that it is somehow truly a *sacred* thing, to be revered, feared, and propitiated. How did it so completely change its nature by the mere fact of becoming detached from the organism? In short, how did a profane thing, the wandering vital principle, so suddenly become sacred, the object of religious sentiments (1912:77)? A sort of cult of the dead has come to the fore, in this view, as the primordial basis of religion.

But if this were true, argues Durkheim, the ancestral cult would be most developed among the most primitive peoples, whereas in actuality it is presented in its characteristic form only in advanced societies such as China, Egypt, and the Greek and Latin cities. It is completely absent in Australian societies, the most simple we know. Since the cult of the dead is not primitive, animism lacks a factual basis (1912:80–82).

The final refutation of the animistic theory lies in the consequences of its implications. That is, if religion begins and continues because of dreams, illusions, and hallucinations, then it has no foundation in reality. "How could a vain fantasy have been able to fashion the human consciousness so strongly and so durably?" (1912:87).

In Chapter 10 we discussed Durkheim's theory of totemism in relation to other theories. In the present chapter we have to recapitulate the theory, albeit more succinctly, in order to see it in relation to the origin of religion, for he believed that the totemism exemplified by the Australians lay at the very foundation of primitive religion. Australian totemism, Durkheim concludes (1912:462), contains all of the great ideas and principal religious attitudes that form the foundations of even the most advanced religions, including

> the division of things into sacred and profane, the notions of the soul, of spirits, of mythical personalities, and of a national and even an international divinity, a negative cult with ascetic practices which are its exaggerated form, rites of oblation and communion, imitative rites, commemorative rites and expiatory rites; nothing essential is lacking. (1912:462)

Unlike those who uphold the animistic theory of the origin of religion, Durkheim believes that there is a true reality, represented in religious mythologies in widely differing forms; this reality is the universal objective cause of religious sensations out of which religious experience is made. This reality is society.[3] "For that which makes a man is the totality of the intellectual property which constitutes civilization, and civilization is the work of society" (1912:465).

This interlocking of society and religion is best exemplified in its earliest, most primitive form, the clan-totemism of central Australia, where the clan is seen by the natives as the single most significant part of society.

We now come to a statement (among many with much the same import) that not only lies at the basis of his theory but which became the most frequently criticized, namely, his description of the preponderating significance of the *cult* in all religions, everywhere.

> This is because society cannot make its influence felt unless it is in action, and it is not in action unless the individuals who compose it are assembled together and act in common. It is by common action that it takes consciousness of itself and realizes its position; it is before all else an active co-operation. . . . Then it is action which dominates the religious life, because of the mere fact that it is society which is its source. (1912:465–466)

---

[3]It seems that Durkheim would be better understood today had he possessed the modern concept of *culture* to use here (and elsewhere) instead of *society*.

The "profane" world is the real world as experienced; the "sacred" world is above the direct sensate world, idealized, and it exists in thought—but it is surreal, in a sense, and to it is attributed a higher sort of dignity.

> This ideal world is not outside of the real society; it is a part of it. . . . For a society is not made up merely of the mass of the individuals who compose it, the ground which they occupy, the things which they use and the movements which they perform, but above all is the idea which it forms of itself. . . . Thus the collective ideal which religion expresses is far from being due to a vague innate power of the individual, but it is rather at the school of collective life that the individual has learned to idealize. (1912:470)

Another closely related idea of Durkheim's had also attracted attention, his attitude toward myth and ritual. Religion is not a *simple* rephrasing of the material world in ideal terms. "The life thus brought in being even enjoys so great an independence that it sometimes indulges in manifestations with no purpose or utility of any sort, for the mere pleasure of affirming itself" (1912:471).[4]

A. R. Radcliffe-Brown is allied closely in theory with the "sociological" school associated with Durkheim and Robertson Smith. He was not, to be sure, explicitly concerned with origins as much as they and the earlier evolutionists were, but he was basically like them in repudiating the role of the primitive individual "philosopher" in creating religion. And like them, he was trying to talk about the basic nature, the wellspring, of the supernatural realm, no matter when— early or late in human history.

Radcliffe-Brown exhibited his basic theory in two articles, "Taboo" (1939) and "Religion and Society" (1945). In the first, he straightforwardly says:

> The theory is not concerned with the historical origin of ritual, nor is it another attempt to explain ritual in terms of human psychology; it is a hypothesis as to the relation of ritual and ritual values to the essential constitution of human society, i.e., to those invariant general characters which belong to all human societies, past, present and future. (1939:150)

Radcliffe-Brown says that his theory of taboo, which is a ritual, should be placed in the context of ritual in general, and that ritual itself depends on the human capacity to use symbols of many different kinds. "The primary basis of ritual . . . is the attribution of ritual value to objects and occasions which are either themselves objects of impor-

---

[4]It may have been this statement and others like it that caused certain critics (to be discussed later) to attribute to Durkheim the idea of "crowd psychology."

tant common interests linking together the persons of a community or are symbolically representative of such objects" (1939:151).

Radcliffe-Brown explicitly cited his differences from the ideas of Sir James Frazer. Frazer, he says,

> accounted for taboos of savage tribes as the application in practice of beliefs arrived at by erroneous processes of reasoning, and he seems to have thought of the effects of these beliefs in creating or maintaining a stable orderly society as being accidental. My own view is that the negative and positive rites of savages exist and persist because they are part of the mechanism by which an orderly society maintains itself in existence, serving as they do to establish certain fundamental social values. The beliefs by which the rites themselves are justified and given some sort of consistency are the rationalizations of symbolic actions and of the sentiments associated with them. . . . what Sir James Frazer seems to regard as the accidental results of magical and religious beliefs really constitute their essential function and the ultimate reason for their existence. (1939:152)

In his 1945 essay, "Religion and Society," Radcliffe-Brown again affirmed his opinion that the problem of how religious beliefs first came to be formulated and accepted—the question of origins—will probably not lead to a real understanding of the nature of religions. It would be better to deal with the social functions of religions, the ways in which they contribute to the formation and maintenance of a social order. This view of religion is independent of the truth or falsity of the beliefs; those we might think of as absurd or repulsive can still be very important to the social mechanism, "for without these 'false' religions social evolution and the development of modern civilisation would have been impossible."

In discussing the nature of religion, Radcliffe-Brown found it useful to distinguish the two major aspects of any religion, beliefs and rites. There has been a tendency in European countries since the Reformation to think of religion as primarily a matter of belief. (As we saw in his earlier article, "Taboo," he was at pains to disassociate himself from Tylor, Frazer, and others who tried to explain the nature of religion in terms of hypotheses about the origin of religious beliefs.) To his mind, the understanding of religions should concentrate on rites rather than beliefs.[5]

MODERN CRITICS OF EVOLUTIONISM

Boas and his students have frequently criticized the evolutionists' preoccupation with the speculative search for the origins of various

---

[5]He does not claim originality here, citing among others, the earliest proponent of this idea, Robertson Smith, whose *Lectures on the Religion of the Semites* (1889) was discussed earlier.

aspects of culture, especially for their faith that certain contemporary primitive peoples represent primordial cultures. Inasmuch as Durkheim, even more directly and consistently than Tylor, Spencer, or Frazer, used the Australians as his data on primordial life, it is to be expected that he would be denounced frequently and thoroughly for this method. Probably Lowie's *Primitive Religion* (1948) contained the most influential criticism of Durkheim's theory of origins. But this criticism is now too familiar to detain us further.

Alexander Goldenweiser (1917b), however, does more than rebuke Durkheim for his evolutionism; he subjects every aspect of Durkheim's argument to stern adverse scrutiny. He does this by summarizing Durkheim's position in several fundamental propositions, which he proceeds to attack one by one.

After detailed criticisms of the propositions summarizing Durkheim's position, Goldenweiser makes a final summing up in terms of three kinds of arguments advanced against the "totemic principle" of Durkheim, ethnological, sociological, and psychological.

First, Durkheim's theory is concerned with totemic clans and ceremonial situations, which the Australian societies exhibit. But what are we to think of culture areas that lack totemism and ceremonialism en masse? In North America, societies such as the Eskimo, the Basin–Plateau people of Nevada and California, and other isolated groups are the *simplest* in social organization—yet they lack totemism and elaborate ceremonialism. On the other hand, the most *complex* social systems are those of the Northwest Coast, the Southwest (Pueblo, presumably), the Southeast (U.S.), some of the Plains tribes, and the Iroquois, all of which have elaborate ceremonialism and most of which are totemic. These data suggest the opposite from Durkheim's assumption that simple (i.e., early) social systems would have totemism and clan ceremonialism. (This is a semantic argument, misconstruing completely Durkheim's idea of "clan," which to him meant simply a kinship group.)

Second, Durkheim's conception of society is "strangely narrow":

> Society, for Durkheim is but a sublimated crowd, while the social setting is the crowd-psychological situation. Society as a cultural, historical, complex, society as the carrier of tradition, as the legislator, judge, as the standard of action, as public opinion; society in all of these varied and significant manifestations, which surely are of prime concern to the individual, does not figure in Durkheim's theory.[6] (1917:71)

---

[6]Durkheim *did* say all these things, and in many places. Again, as so often, had he used the word *culture* instead of *society*, he might have forestalled much misunderstanding. ("Culture" in French, in his day, referred simply to cultivation.)

Goldenweiser goes on to make nonsense out of "crowd psychology" as the cause of anything. (We should remember here that Durkheim did not use this expression, nor did he say that social ceremonies were the *cause* of religion, nor that the "religious thrill" was the cause of religion.) Social participation intensifies emotions, which Goldenweiser admits, but this is really all that Durkheim meant by it. (Goldenweiser is at his worst—rock bottom—in this segment of his argument.)

Third, Goldenweiser finds that Durkheim's psychological argument is deficient. Here is that quintessential Boasian statement: "The author [Durkheim] . . . fails to do justice to the contribution of the individual" (1917:72). There are two kinds of individuals who make spiritual contributions to religious experience, Goldenweiser says. One is the average individual who was placed in unusual circumstances, as in the case of the Plains Indians' vision quest undergone by each young male in the society to find his personal guardian spirit in that of an animal or object. This is a uniquely idiosyncratic religious experience, not social at all. The other is the group of exceptional persons who have extraordinary capabilities for religion. These are the religious reformers and teachers, fanatics and miracle workers, prophets, saints, and founders of religious cults.

> Now, it is emphatically characteristic of both of these categories of men (and women) that, temporarily or permanently, they shun the crowd, they flee from the world, they live in solitude, they are proof against religious settings except those of their own making; in their psychic constitution lie infinite potentialities of religious experience and ecstasy. Their god is within them. The lives of such as they constitute a glaring refutation of Durkheim's theory. (1917:72)

Goldenweiser, as noted earlier, does not accept (or, rather, does not understand) Durkheim's idea that the primitive societies of Australia could give us some inkling of primordial religion. So, rather than confining the criticism to Durkheim's chosen ground of central Australia, where there are, of course, no messianic religious leaders such as Jesus or Mahomet, he moves around the modern civilized world, which features such individualistic founders of cults. He does not, significantly, adduce any data from Australia or any other truly primitive society, to show Durkheim wrong about his basic argument, that individual beliefs are sublimated in society's rituals.

The kindest thing that can be said about Goldenweiser's critique is that he did not understand Durkheim, even in the most elementary postulates of the theory. In addition, it is likely that Goldenweiser, like so many critics, simply *argued*, like a debater or lawyer, to put the worst possible interpretation on his antagonist's argument—to win, no matter that academia and, for that matter, science, should demand as much fairness and objectivity as possible. Goldenweiser claims that he has won.

> Thus Durkheim does not succeed in furnishing a satisfactory solution of either of the two problems which stand in the center of his interest: the relation of individual to social experience and the interpretation of the nature and origin of the religious sentiment. Sharp as is the author's wit and brilliant as is his argumentation, one closes the book with a melancholy assurance that Durkheim has left these two perennial problems where he found them. (1917:72)

I have found this essay of Goldenweiser's exasperating on two grounds. One, it is a grotesque misrendering of Durkheim's thought; two, it is a specious argument, purporting to rest its conclusions on actual data—all of which are irrelevant to Durkheim's argument.

Ruth Benedict (1938) also criticized Durkheim's (and Spencer's and Tylor's) emphasis on origins, and described Durkheim's theory as holding that religion was "the outcome of crowd excitement." Benedict thought he believed that over against the unexciting daily routine which he regarded as typically pursued by the individual in solitude or in small groups, he saw in group ritual, especially that connected with totemism, the original basis on which all religions have been elaborated. Religion, therefore, he says, "is ultimately nothing more than society" (1938:627–628).

Benedict avers that no ethnologist, no traveler, no stranger visiting a primitive people ever has difficulty in identifying religious behavior from other, everyday behavior. Thus there must be some core attribute of religion which is universal. This is the *supernatural,* whether it is personified in a god or holy men or exists as an impersonal force, like *mana*, that can inhabit trees, stones, or a mountain. The supernatural is a "wonderful power, a voltage with which the universe is believed to be charged. This voltage is present in the whole world in so far as it is considered supernatural, whether it is regarded as animate or inanimate" (1938:630).

But except for this universal core, and the two universal techniques for dealing with it—compulsion and rapport—primitive religions exhibit a bewildering diversity. The sacred dairy ritual of the Todas and the vision quest of the American Indians have almost nothing in common except for being invested with supernaturalism. That religions can be so unlike is due to the fact that "religion is quite impartial as to what arc of cultural life it shall supernaturalize" (1938:648).

Benedict devotes the bulk of her article to describing the vastly contrasting religious foci of the primitive peoples of Siberia, the American Pueblo Indians, the American Plains Indians, and the Dobuans of

Melanesia. These last three were, along with the Kwakiutl, the cultures contrasted in her *Patterns of Culture*. The outcome is the same for religion as for culture in general: different peoples elaborate and focus on some particular aspects of life and there seems to be no reason for it— it just *is* the way it is, and no cause or explanatory matrix is adduced.

Thus the diversity (particularity or singularity) of cultures is stressed, and here lies the essential negativism of Boasian anthropology, especially in its aversion to classification or generalization. In this, plus the inability to explain—or a conviction of the undesirability of explaining—lies one of the distinctive aspects of the Boasian approach to culture, as we have seen and shall see again.

IV

THE ORIGINS OF GOVERNMENT

For more than 99% of human history, as calculated by archaeologists and primatologists, people lived in small, simple, egalitarian (segmental) bands or tribes. The great watershed in history, which witnessed the rise of institutionalized, centrally directed governmental systems, evidently occurred only 5000 or 6000 years ago. Exactly when is difficult to determine, in large part because the problem is definitional. In part, also, the varying definitions are often related to particular theories of the causes of the origin of the state, and these causes are thought to reveal that which is basic—the true nature of the state.

To begin, we must agree on a very general definition of government which will include the more special polemical definitions of statehood. It seems that fewer people would disagree with the use of the concept government *in place of* state *or* empire *if in our definition of government we include these general features: it is a form of* instituted *social control which is relatively permanent (i.e., not simply the ephemeral rule of a charismatic leader); it is* suprafamilial *(i.e., it exists over and above the rules and etiquettes of the kinship order); it is an* organized structure *of specialized parts arranged in hierarchical order (i.e., it is a sort of bureaucracy); finally, among the many and varying tasks it undertakes or provides, its primary function is an* integrative *one (i.e., by providing benefits to the subjects, especially to the local subparts, as well as by making repressive public laws, it attempts to overcome the fissioning tendencies characteristic of the earlier segmental kinds of societies). Note that this laundry list type of definition implies nothing about causes or origins.*

So far as ethnological history of theories of the origin and basic nature of government is concerned, we begin as usual with the 1860s. There had, of course, been numerous philosophers who offered theories of the nature of human nature, society, and government, from Plato and Aristotle to the Stoics and Epicureans to the revival of Aristotelean and Stoic thought in the fifteenth century in a theological context. These philosophers thought of government as coterminous with society itself; in the fifteenth century it was a God-given entity and the theory thus was not subject to scientific critiques. Others, notably Ibn Khaldun, Niccolò Machiavelli, and Jean Bodin, broke from the theological view to propose completely secular ideas, importantly involving conflict theory, and in particular a theory involving conquest.

The Enlightenment in Great Britain in roughly the sixteenth and seventeenth centuries, and somewhat later in France, featured the social contract theories of Hobbes, Locke, and Rousseau. These theories were of tremendous influence in political and historical philosophy, but again they were basically arguments about human nature and the kinds of governmental restraints needed to control individual human beings. The origins of government posited by these thinkers is the social contract drawn up by individuals in order to end strife. Vico, Montesquieu, and later Adam Ferguson and Adam Smith were also important precursors of the ethnologists, and these four, at least, differed from all the others in paying much more attention to actual data about the primitive cultures which were coming to attention due to the published accounts of missionaries, traders, and natural science collectors. These laid the groundwork for the more specifically ethnological interests of the 1860s.

The controversies from the 1860s to 1960 can be

divided into conflict theories and integrational the-ories. They appear here as two separate chapters because direct personal confrontation between two theorists was rare. The argument was much more diffuse than that, and requires more intervention on my part, particularly since there was actually no school of ethnologists calling themselves integra-tionists—that is my term for those who held vari-ous nonconflict theories. Conflict theorists con-stituted a somewhat more coherent ideology but, nevertheless, they do not lend themselves easily to summary treatment. These two chapters will, re-grettably, be presented in rather disjointed fashion. Perhaps **Conflict** *and* **integration** *are not very satis-factory labels for the two kinds of theories of state formation. I chose them because they seem to have been the most often used, and it is usually wise to stick to common usage rather than to resort to neologisms.*

Nevertheless, some worrisome misunderstand-ings have arisen among some of my students after hearing me propound the gist of these chapters. It is too late to change the labels, and in any event I cannot think of any better ones. All I can do now is to try to explain away the difficulties as best I can. First, to oppose the word conflict *to* integration *seems to suggest to some that the state originated either in warfare or in peaceful circumstances. Therefore, it seems to require only a demonstration of how frequent and severe and nearly ubiquitous was some kind of conflict in the evolution of society to show integration theories incorrect or inaccurate. There are many kinds of conflicts—feud, "class struggle," raids, all-out conquest, preventive strikes, and so on—and some appeared with great frequency during the human career. To say that conflict was probably present at the point of origin of the state, and even to stress its importance as a selective factor, as Spencer did, is not necessarily to state that conflict* caused *the state to come about. If conflict, in actuality or potentiality, existed throughout the several million years of human his-tory, its presence 5000 or 6000 years ago (when the first states were formed)—a comparative moment ago—does not explain the specific origin of the state.*

And to stress integration theories is not to assert that the transition to statehood was peaceful—it could have been, and probably was, stormy. Furthermore, punitive laws can be instituted in order to foster political integration, as when controlled violence is used to suppress uncontrolled violence. But this could be a feature of an integrative theory, despite the use of force.

At issue is this question: How did leadership change from its charismatic, sporadic, and personal form to become centralized, institutionalized, and permanent? Both Maine and Morgan saw the creation of law, and especially of codified legal structures (depending on the invention of writing), as the basis of civilization. To both of them, the propelling mechanism was simply mentality; it was the growth of the idea of government. This view, as such, does not depend on either conflict or peace, but on the idea that law has its main purpose in creating and maintaining peace. Lowie's argument about the rise of the principle of sovereignty also is irrelevant to the presence or absence of conflict, as are the theories of Hocart, Fortes and Evans-Pritchard, and Wittfogel.

It seems evident that integration theories, taken together, conform better to ethnological reality than conquest theories. But there is one form of conflict theory, Herbert Spencer's, which indeed seems sophisticated enough to conform to modern ethnology. Spencer's is not a simple monocausal approach, as is conquest theory, and he also uses an adaptive or "natural selection" matrix for the process of sociopolitical development. Spencer's theory, being so complex, does not lend itself readily to classification in either the conflict or integration schools. The fact that successful warfare over time subjects the populace to "imperative command," preparing it for its role as an obedient citizenry, could as well be called an integrative consequence of one aspect of conflict.

12

Conflict Theory

There are two basic kinds of conflicts that have been posited as causes of the origin of the state. One is—and it was the first, historically—*inter*societal conflict, normally warfare. The other is *intra*societal conflict; its dynamic and locus is internal in the form of class struggle.

Herbert Spencer was the most prominent of the intersocietal conflict theorists of the latter half of the nineteenth century and by far the most sophisticated. There had been, as mentioned earlier, many prominent philosophers, historians, and sociologists who argued for a particular and simple variant of intersocietal conflict, the conquest theory. They were swayed by the cases, first provided by Ibn Khaldun, of warlike pastoral nomads who placed themselves as rulers over sedentary village agriculturists. Of ethnologists, however, only two, Nadel and Oberg, have been particularly insistent on this idea; they are described below, following the discussion of Spencer.

The other form of conflict theory—intrasocietal—is based on the idea that an economically favored group or segment of society becomes an elite power and forms a government to maintain order, and by so doing protects, or perhaps increases, the privileges of its own class. This view stems from Friedrich Engels' *The Origin of the Family, Private Property, and the State* (1884), a work inspired by Morgan's *Ancient Society* (1877). Engels, of course, was not an ethnologist, but since his book derived from Morgan, and greatly influenced subsequent ethnology, we are justified in considering it here.

HERBERT SPENCER

A major thrust of Spencer's whole intellectual career was an attempt to counter the notion that social evolution is in some sense a matter of conscious intellectualism, a course of self-improvement. He held that it is instead a grand universal movement from simple to complex structures, as is evidenced so clearly in biological evolution; this movement actually is due to the fundamental material laws of matter and motion, so that every part of the universe is subject to the same principles.

But so far, this kind of statement is tautological and metaphysical—no causal mechanism is vouchsafed except a "principle" which merely summarily describes the thing to be accounted for. But many modern ethnologists would feel that this is an advance over the conscious rationalism so commonly ventured as the cause of social (cultural) change in Spencer's day.

Spencer is usually thought of as the advocate of social Darwinism, and this is an important aspect of his theory, for he does in fact see persons, firms, and societies as likely to be in a condition of competition as a normal state of affairs. But this competition is not the *cause* of the origin of the state so much as it is an environmental condition that selects for certain governmental characteristics of some societies over others. What are these characteristics of "fitness"? Walter Bagehot, a contemporary of Spencer's (who, incidentally, was the first avowed social Darwinist), put it nicely in his brief book *Physics and Politics* (1872). He argued that warlike competition among societies in early times would favor those with the best leadership and most obedient populace ("the tamest are the strongest"). A major problem in the evolution of a politically directed society would be that of perpetuating the leadership, of making an "official" out of a hero, which means the creation of a system of inheritance of the leading positions.

It is because of the rubric "social Darwinism" that Spencer and Bagehot are often considered to be significant contributors to the conflict theory of the origin of the state. But their ideas of conflict did not really account for the *origin* of government but merely tried to explain why good government, achieved by whatever means, would be likely to prevail in an environment of less able governments. That is, the original governments were not originated out of internal conflict or external conquest; they only found themselves favored in the intersocietal conflict if they possessed certain useful characteristics of governance.

The intersocietal conflict has as its basic result the compounding of smaller communities into larger ones—an evolutionary development toward complexity. Spencer says:

> Here we see that in the struggle for existence among societies, the survival of the fittest is the survival of those in which the power of military cooperation is the greatest, the military cooperation is that primary kind of cooperation which prepares the way for other kinds. So that this formation of larger so-

cieties by the union of smaller ones in war, and this destruction or absorption
of the smaller ununited by the united larger ones, is an inevitable process
through which the varieties of men most adapted for social life supplant the
less adapted varieties. (1876:78)

Spencer's basic theory about the origin of government involves mili-
tarism, but not in the sense of conquest by contending societies, of
which certain ones prevail over others and set up their ruling machinery over them. It is rather (in brief) that the successful conduct of war
leads the members of a society to cooperate and to learn "subjugation
to imperative command." If successful war is frequent enough, it tends
to lead to "permanence of chieftainship." It is, in Spencer's view, a
universal aspect of the evolutionary process that growth of a society is
accomplished by "development," a differentiation of parts in the structure. One of the most significant of the differentiated parts is the military, which naturally increases its power depending upon the prevalence of successes in warfare.

To repeat, despite the emphasis on the military specialization made
by Spencer, his theory is not that conquest, either internal or external,
caused the state to come about; warfare or competition was a part of
the environment to which adaptive responses were made, and certain
aspects of leadership were thus selected in this context—and as such
tended to survive.

But conflict and competition do not accomplish this by themselves.
Conflict, in some relative sense, must have existed, at least frequently
and in threat, throughout the evolution of society—taking various
forms and being resolved (or unresolved) in various ways. But these
resolutions would have depended importantly on adaptive circumstances and the prevalent state of political evolution. And how that
stage came about, not how well it survived, is still the relevant question.

Spencer sees the "regulating agency," or political organization, as
having gone through states of complication (1876:35–36) rather than
as having a sudden origin. The critical state occurs with the "compounding" of formerly separate social aggregates. This compounding
typically takes place when the separate groups are brought together to
face a common enemy, so that the local centers of regulation became
dependent under command of the general center. So long as this per-
sists, one witnesses the beginnings of true government.

This development is accompanied by the increased size and complexity of the dominant center. That is, the predominant political
agency creates additional parts for additional functions. Thus simple
personal government tends to progress to government through agents
of many kinds: prime ministers, head priests, economic executors,

judiciary agents, information-gathering agencies, military leaders, and so on. Generally, such a variety of functions and structures are of two kinds, one kind consisting of *regulatory* functions, which cope with the environment and rival societies, the other consisting of *sustaining* agencies, which are the inner economic or industrial rulers. In time, naturally enough, appears a third system, the *distributing* system. However finally indispensable to the society, it necessarily arises after the appearance of the first two, hence its role in the origin of government is a dependent one. But in the end it takes all three agencies, intertwined, to foment, augment, and organize the division of labor in society. (Here, somewhat irrelevantly for our present discussion, we may note that Spencer warns us of the dire consequences when the controlling aspect of the regulatory government becomes overweening in power and organization: "An established organization is an obstacle to reorganization" [1876:71].)

In sum, though we see in Spencer a stress on conflict, he does not use conflict alone, or the more usual and specific conquest theory, to account for the origin of political institutions. Conflict is omnipresent, at least in potentiality, and thus does not provide the specific variable that would account for the rise of a state. A state deals with conflict, to be sure, but so too does it deal with countless other problems. The explanation, instead, is that political progress, resulting in greater size and differentiation, occurs because it serves many kinds of functions, and those societies well-served by a government will obviously tend to prevail.

A succinct summation of Spencer's main perspective is contained in the following passage near the end of his book:

> Unlike the sustaining system, evolved by converse with the organic and inorganic environments, the regulating system is evolved by converse, offensive and defensive, with environing societies. In primitive headless groups temporary chieftainship results from temporary war; chronic hostilities generate permanent chieftainship; and gradually from the military control results the civil control. Habitual war, requiring prompt combination in the action of parts, necessitates subordination. Societies in which there is little subordination disappear, and leave outstanding those in which subordination is great, and so there are produced societies in which the habit fostered by war and surviving in peace brings about permanent submission to government. (1876:215)

S. F. NADEL AND KALERVO OBERG

Nadel and Oberg each presented conquest theories in the context of an ethnological analysis of a particular society. Nadel's *A Black Byzantium* (1942) described the Nupe kingdom in the northern part of West

Africa, and Oberg's (1940) article discusses the kingdom of Ankole in Uganda, eastern Central Africa.

According to Nadel, a state has the following characteristics:

(1) The state is a political unit based on territorial sovereignty. Membership of the state, i.e., citizenship or nationality, is determined by residence or birth-right in a territory. The state is thus inter-tribal or inter-racial, and distinguishes nationality from tribal or racial extraction.

(2) A centralized machinery of government assumes the maintenance of law and order, to the exclusion of all independent action.

(3) The state involves the existence of a specialized privileged ruling group or class separated in training, status, and organization from the main body of the population. (1942:69)

Nadel concludes that "historically, an inter-tribal sovereignty of this nature can only have arisen from the ascendancy of one ethnic group over others" (1942:69). In other words, the "inter-tribal" aspect of the society results from the conquest of one group by another and it is maintained by force. "The structure of the Nupe state as it exists today, with its ruling class of Fulani conquerors, and also its growth so far as we can with any claim to accuracy trace it back in history, indeed support this [conquest] theory of the origin of the state" (1942:70).

Oberg's case is not such a clear-cut historical case of conquest, and he has to buttress his theory with legends and with data concerning the ethnographic distribution of languages and tribal customs in Uganda.

The kingdom of Ankole, like the many others in the corridor of grasslands along the western border of Uganda, consisted of two distinct castes of people, the ruling pastoralists and the subservient agriculturalists. The legends and songs of the pastoralists all tell the same heroic story of how populations grew in the long closed corridor, and the pastoralists and agriculturalists were then brought into ever closer juxtaposition. The pastoralists, although heavily outnumbered, were accustomed to raiding, and their habits of military cooperation became the basis for a new political order—a graded military aristocracy of pastoralists over the mass of peasant agriculturalists. As in European feudalism, only the aristocracy could bear arms, and, as in caste societies everywhere, intermarriage between the castes was forbidden.

The conclusions of both Nadel and Oberg have their dubious aspects. The most important problem is that these states (and others of the two regions) were not *primary*—that is, they were not self-generated. Beginning perhaps as early as the thirteenth century, military and commercial–political hegemonies of the Arabs extended from the East African highlands all the way across the savannah to the Atlantic coast and at least by the fifteenth century, to the Congo River and beyond.

The original, or "pristine," developments which influenced North

Africa were those of Egypt and Mesopotamia. Subsequent refinements and permutations were contingent on the spread of later empires. One important development was the rise of huge commercial city–states, which dominated the western Sudan by 800 A.D. For example, gold was transported from its source in the southern forest belt by caravans across the Sahara, from whence it appeared in the Mediterranean world and finally northern Europe. Until the fantastic yields of precious metals arrived in Europe from Mexico and Peru, the western Sudan was the principal provider of these metals. From commerce first, and then from the presence of the Islamic theocratic religion, spread powerful centralizing administrative institutions. As Basil Davidson (1959) points out at length, the European world tends to think of Africa's civilization and its history as beginning only with Europe's late knowledge of it.

The "conquest state" reported by Nadel was only a late reappearance of a long series of Moslem-inspired states. The Nupe state, furthermore, was not even independent after it was established, for it was only one of numerous emirates tributary to a much grander sultanate. But even these conquest states were only remnants of much more powerful indigenous Sudanese empires that long antedated them.

Oberg's kingdom of Ankole likewise participated long ago in widespread diffusions and movements of political significance. In other words, both Nupe and Ankole were part of a long-standing historical continuum of military states and empires. We still do not know of a single case of the conquest of one society by another that resulted in the *creation* of governmental institutions which incorporated the conquerors and conquered. Whenever a conquest was successfully consolidated, it was because such institutions already existed among one or both of the societies.

The other kind of conflict theory, that of internal diversification of a society into favored and unfavored classes, thereby inducing "class struggle," has had much more influence in modern ethnology and archaeology. It begins with Engels' misunderstanding of Morgan's *Ancient Society*. As we shall see in later pages, Morgan held an idealistic, or mentalistic, theory of the development of governmental institutions. But for now let us discuss Engels on his own terms.

FRIEDRICH ENGELS

The threshold of civilization, according to Engels (1884:150), was reached when a new advance in the division of labor occurred. At the lowest stage of barbarism men produced goods only for their own needs; exchanges were isolated and due to some fortuitous surplus. In

the middle stage of barbarism, pastoral peoples more generally produced a surplus of cattle, which led to a division of labor between them
and tribes without herds and so promoted regular exchange. The upper
stage of barbarism brought about a further division of labor between
agriculture and handicrafts.

> Civilization consolidates and intensifies all these existing divisions of labor,
> particularly by sharpening the opposition between town and country, . . . and
> it adds a third division of labor, peculiar to itself and of decisive importance: it
> creates a class which no longer concerns itself with production, but only with
> the exchange of the products—the *merchants*. (1884:151).

The merchant class comes to be an "indispensable middleman between any two producers and exploits them both." Along with the
development of this role comes metallic money, the "commodity of
commodities." As commodities were bought and sold with money, so
could loans be made at interest, and lands mortgaged. By these means
the concentration of wealth increased in concert with an increasing
impoverishment of the masses. The older institutions of primitive
society, the gens, phratry, and tribe, could not cope with the new
demands, antagonisms, and contradictions of such an economy. The
previous institutions had no means of settling disputes except public
opinion.

> But here was a society which by all its economic conditions of life had been
> forced to split itself into freeman and slaves, into the exploiting rich and the
> exploited poor; a society which not only could never again reconcile these
> contradictions, but was compelled always to intensify them. Such a society
> could only exist either in the continuous open fight of these classes against one
> another, or else under the rule of a third power, which apparently standing
> above the warring classes, suppressed their open conflict and allowed the class
> struggle to be fought out at most in the economic field, in so-called legal form.
> The gentile constitution was finished. It had been shattered by the division of
> labour and its result, the cleavage of the society into classes. It was replaced by
> the *state*. (1884:154)

This state stands in contrast to the old gentile organization by grouping its members on a *territorial* basis, as opposed to the kinship order.
A second distinction is the institution of a *public force*, which is not
identical with a people's own organization of armed power. This is a
police force of armed men together with other appurtenances, such as
prisons and coercive institutions of all kinds.

Since civilization is based on the exploitation of one class by another, its development is a constant contradiction. "Every step forward
in production is at the same time a step backwards in the position of
the oppressed class, that is, of the great majority" (1884:161). Curi-

ously, Engels leaves it like this without making the logical conclusion one might expect, that the contradictions would proceed to the point at which the oppressed rebel to form a new kind of society, one without propertied classes (as he had argued elsewhere so frequently). But he does end his book by quoting Morgan's famous passage about the role of property in civilization, of which the following are the critical sentences:

> "A mere property career is not the final destiny of mankind, if progress is to be the law of the future as it has been of the past. The time which has passed away since civilization began is but a fragment of the past duration of men's existence; and but a fragment of the ages to come. The dissolution of society bids fair to become the termination of a career of which property is the end and aim; because such a career contains the elements of self-destruction. Democracy in government, brotherhood in society, equality in rights and privileges, and universal education, foreshadow the next higher plane of society to which experience, intelligence and knowledge are steadily tending. *It will be a revival, in a higher form, of the liberty, equality and fraternity of the ancient gentes.*" (1884:162–163; emphasis is Engels')

V. GORDON CHILDE

Although Childe was an archaeologist working mostly in European areas and (to an extent) the "classical" areas of the ancient Near East, his theoretical statements were important to ethnology. His ideas relating to the Near East were particularly pathfinding, for most if not all of classical archaeology had been within the genre of art history rather than analytical science. Childe was the first to have attempted broad-gauged, comparative, evolutionary–functional methods on the archaic materials, and a whole generation of modern anthropological archaeologists are indebted to him.

Childe described the origin of the state (and civilization) as an "urban revolution." Urbanism was seen as the hallmark of civilization, the feature which attended the birth of the original civilizations. Many anthropologists have assumed that he meant that urbanism was not only the salient feature but also the *cause* of civilization. In one of his last statements on the subject (1950), Childe indicated that he merely meant it as a useful rubric suggestive of, and summarizing, several features that seem to have arrived together to create the city–state. Of these, the most important were the progressive techno-economic changes affecting the demography and social organization of communities, mainly by increasing food production. Such greater production not only can support a larger and denser population but in addition create a "social surplus" of food to support the rising class of non-producing military and political bureaucrats, craftsmen, priests, and entrepreneurs. The repressive aspects of governmental organization arise to preserve this increasingly exploitative class structure (hence the "contradictions" that Engels wrote about).

Childe's "urban" conception has been largely superseded, for we now know that some archaic civilizations, like the Maya and Egypt, lacked large population centers prior to their classic phase, and others, like the Harappan (Indus Valley) built their planned cities long after the state had appeared. In fact, many would argue that in other areas as well the state was probably a necessary precursor to true urban agglomerations, rather than vice versa. Many would also argue against the Engels-like attribution of entrepreneurial trade to the origin of the state, since there is no evidence for it but, rather, much evidence for long-distance trade sponsored by government.

Leslie A. White and Julian H. Steward

Two ethnologists, White and Steward, stood almost alone (but separately) in the 1940s and 1950s as evolutionists, along with the archaeologist Childe. White's *The Evolution of Culture* (1959b) contains his only theoretical statement on the origin of the state, however, and it is very brief. It is essentially the same as that provided by Engels: as economy and technology evolve, entrepreneurs and money create the class system and the repressive state arises to maintain that status quo. It is not argued for and is scarcely discussed; it is as though an unarguable historical fact had been presented, without even the necessity of any illustration.

To White, as to Childe and Engels, the mainspring of cultural evolution is technological and economic, and with respect to the rise of civil society, it was specifically the Agricultural Revolution which made societies larger and more complex and divided them into socioeconomic classes. The "state–church" functions to preserve this class system. Here is White's most succinct statement of the class-conflict function:

> The struggle between dominant and subordinate classes has been chronic and perennial in civil society. The lower classes—the slaves, serfs, industrial proletariat—periodically try to better their lot by revolt and insurrection. If the social system is to be kept intact, if it is not to explode in violence and subside in anarchy, the relationship of subordination and superordination between the classes must be maintained; in other words, the subordinate class must be in a condition of subjection and exploitation. It is the business of the state–church to see that this is done. (1959b:313–314)

If White did little in his book to substantiate this theory, we have, on the other hand, Julian Steward's "multilineal evolutionary theory," born out of his feeling that not enough testing had gone on. But Steward's "theory" was not a theory at all, but a methodology. It was a proposal for comparing appropriate independent regional changes in order to find regularities which might be stated as scientific laws. His best-known and most ambitious attempt was his "Cultural Causality and Law: A Trial Formulation of the Development of Early Civilizations" (1949). Five developments were compared—Mesopotamia, Egypt, north China, north Peru, and Meso-America—in order to chart the regularities among them. Those relevant in our present context are the descriptions of happenings during the eras Steward labeled Formative, Regional Florescent, and Initial Empire. The comparisons are quite detailed, with a surprising number of similarities, but it is difficult to find in Steward's account any clear-cut, simple theory of the cause of the origin of the state other than a vague notion of the significance of irrigation. The implications of his discussion are presented here from his "Summary and Conclusions."

Salient is the fact that all of these regions were arid, requiring floodplain and irrigation farming, so that "in proportion as irrigation works develop, population will increase until the limits of water are reached. Social or political controls become necessary to manage irrigation and other communal projects" (1949:206).

This is evidently because competition affected the basic population, who were increasingly subjected to exploitation. In time these empire—state civilizations crumble due to revolutions and "dark ages" appear, until some other group rises to ascendancy and begins the process again (1949:207).

Competition and "classes" are clearly involved because of population growth in areas limited in size because of the necessity of staying within the area of the water control systems. Although Steward does not say directly what the "cause" of the origin of government is, his implications sound like a modest version of Childe. I think he belongs in the conflict school, therefore, even though he does not strongly argue it. Perhaps he did not believe that it needed to be argued, as theory. He did not like theory as much as data, and he was much more impressed with Childe's work than with White's, because the former seemed to be referring to hard facts, dug up by laborious pick and shovel.[1]

---

[1] I knew Steward well, and he indicated this preference to me several times.

13

Integration Theory

The nonconflict theories of the origin of government are so various that to lump them together means that the category "integrative theories" is necessarily a very broad and loose one. Mainly these theories stress one or another of several factors that have the effect of countering the centrifugal, or fissioning, forces which continually threaten any society. These may be legal devices, directly and consciously instituted to foster the integration of the groups, or they may be organizational benefits such as successful military forces, economic specialization, redistribution and long-distance trade, and public works such as irrigation systems and temple construction.

Sir Henry Maine

Maine's *Ancient Law* (1861) was a pathfinder in ethnology in many ways, and equally as relevant to students of history and jurisprudence. For ethnologists, it is one of the earliest and most successful demonstrations of the comparative method, the means by which historical fact-finding is turned into a new form of social science. As in so many other cases noted earlier, and as he remarked many times, it was the success of comparative philology that stimulated Maine's interest in the comparative method in ethnology. It is important to be aware of this influence; all too often Boas and his students in America have related the cultural evolutionary impetus in Europe, and in Britain particularly, to the influence of Darwin.

But it was Maine's inductive, comparative historical method rather than any theory of evolution (though these are of course related) that gained him the greatest respect. His inductive method caused him to scorn the empty theorizing of philosophers of the social contract schools as well as any broad, "systematic" theory of evolution, such as Spencer's was to become. It is probably for these reasons that Maine, of all the Victorians, is treated so charitably by Lowie in his *History of Ethnological Theory* (1937a:49–53).

Maine was interested in the great gulf between primitive ("savage") society and civilized society; that is, he emphasized only two grand stages of progress, not several. This resulted in his technique of contrasting polar opposites. At the historical point where it could be said that civil government originated, Maine spoke of a change in social relationships from *status* (personal and conventional) to *contract* (enforced by legal structures). Thus, it was implicit in Maine's thought that the creation of political law, particularly codified law (after the invention of writing), was the basis, the stuff, of civilization.

This is an argument for the basic nature of government, for its legal structure. But what, we might ask, were the causes—the mechanisms—which created a civil society out of a savage society? Here, as was standard in Enlightenment and later Utilitarian thought, Maine's mechanism was simply mentality. The philological discovery of the cultural affinity of the Aryan-speaking peoples impressed Maine as it did Morgan, and it led both of them often to speak about cultural progress in mentalistic terms and thus to sound racist. It seemed to them that mental superiority was characteristic of the Aryans and accounted for the "progressive" developments which characterized civilization. And progress is due to a rationality whose opposite consists largely of superstition (1861:16).

Lewis H. Morgan

Morgan has often been regarded as an important conflict theorist. This is not an accurate characterization, however, although he did vouchsafe some denunciations of property and the tendency of governments to protect the aristocratic class who held landed estates. Morgan's undeserved reputation as a conflict theorist derives from Friedrich Engels' misunderstanding of *Ancient Society* (1877). In praising this book for its "materialism" and its denunciations of the role of private property and the state, Engels enshrined Morgan as a kind of Marxist theorist on the role of property in creating "class struggle." Of course, many more people have read Engels' small *Origin of the Family, Private Property, and the State* (1884) than Morgan's bulky, complicated *Ancient Society*, and so have not discovered this error for themselves.

According to Morgan, the rise of political society (*civitas*) was not caused by or even related to the rise of property. Political institutions were developments out of the ancient, worldwide gens, which contained the germ-like idea of government. Morgan put it clearly in discussing the rise of political society in Rome:

Mankind owes a debt of gratitude to their savage ancestors for devising an institution (the *gens*) able to carry the advancing portion of the human race out of savagery into barbarism, and through the successive stage of the latter into civilization. It also accumulated by experience the intelligence and knowledge necessary to devise political society while the institution yet remained. . . . As a plan of government, the gentile organization was unequal to the wants of civilized men; but it is something to be said in its remembrance that it developed from the germ the principal governmental institutions of modern civilized states. Among others . . . out of the ancient council of chiefs came the modern senate; out of the ancient assembly of the people came the modern representative assembly . . . ; out of the ancient general military commander came the modern chief magistrate . . . ; and out of the ancient *custos urbis* . . . came the Roman praetor and the modern judge. Equal rights and privileges, personal freedom and the cardinal principles of democracy were also inherited from the gentes. (1877:290–291)

As for property—and by property Morgan clearly was thinking of the landed estates of the old European aristocracy—its power and influence in society played a role in encouraging slavery, the principle of aristocracy and privileged classes, and despotism and monarchy. But the intelligence of mankind should in time modify such excrescences so that democracy is destined to become again universal and supreme (1877:291).

So private property (in land) had an important role in creating certain unwholesome characteristics in society and government, but it was not implicated in the origin of the state. Morgan's view, in fact, did not attribute any deterministic connection between the rise of institutions such as government and materialistic "inventions and discoveries." These had separate careers. The very organization of *Ancient Society* reveals this, and Morgan states it prominently in his preface to the book: "Inventions and discoveries stand in serial relations along the lines of human progress, and register its successive stages; while social and civil institutions, in virtue of their connection with perpetual human wants, have been developed from a few primary germs of thought" (1877:5).

Ancient Society is organized as follows: Part I, titled "Growth of Intelligence through Inventions and Discoveries," deals mainly with the "Arts of Subsistence" and related technological inventions and comprises relatively few pages of the book (1877:11–45). Part II, "Growth of the Idea of Government," is much longer (1877:49–324) and, I think, should therefore be considered the major focus of the book. Part III, "Growth of the Idea of the Family," is brief (1877:325–429); it incorporates several late interpolations in reply to McLennan's critique of Morgan's earlier *Systems of Consanguinity*. Part IV, "Growth of the

Idea of Property," is only 23 pages, but it contains the famous denunciation of private property, which so misled Engels that he was willing to
believe that Morgan had "discovered afresh in America the materialist
conception of history" (1884:50). It seems plain that Morgan did not see
private property as sharing in the beginnings of government or the state,
for that took place as self-determined "unfolding relations" of a few
"primary germs of thought" (quoted above). In summary, Morgan says:

> Out of a few germs of thought, conceived in the early ages, have been evolved
> all the principal institutions of mankind. Beginning their growth in the period
> of savagery, fermenting through the period of barbarism, they have continued
> their advancement through the period of civilization. The evolution of these
> germs of thought has been guided by a natural logic which formed an essential
> attribute of the brain itself. . . . Among the original germs of thought, which
> have exercised the most powerful influence upon the human mind, and upon
> human destiny, are these which relate to government, to the family, to lan-
> guage, to religion, and to property. (1877:59)

ROBERT H. LOWIE

Lowie's *The Origin of the State* (1927) was, so far as I know, the only
important attempt by any of the students of Franz Boas to address this
age-old question. But Lowie was something of a maverick Boasian in
other ways as well, and more than almost any American ethnologist he
remained his own man in his pursuit of important objectives.

In one respect, however, Lowie's acceptance of Boas' antievolu-
tionism and his disrespect for Morgan in particular led him to make a
peculiar mishmash out of his book. The very title, *The Origin of the
State*, was chosen, evidently, because it was a common phrase among
evolutionists and he wanted to rebut them and their very intent. Very
Boasian this, as an example of what has become known as negative
anthropology.

Lowie had first addressed the question of the state in 1920 in his
widely respected *Primitive Society* in a chapter titled "Government"
(Chapter 8). Accepting Maine's (1861) and Morgan's (1877) dichotomization of primitive society as based primarily on kinship, and
state government on territory, Lowie explores the intermediate ground
to try to find out what mechanisms, or institutions, had stimulated this
movement from kin ties to territorial ties. He later wrote an article
expressly devoted to the issue, called "The Origin of the State" (1922).

In these two works, Lowie claimed to have found the intermediate
types of institution in what he called "Associations." He noted that
Morgan's scheme of social organization so emphasized the "sib" (Morgan's *gens*) that he never accounted for an enormously important kind

of organization *not* based on kinship. Age-graded organizations, men's clubs, secret societies, differences of sex and matrimonial status, ritual cult groups, and the like may affect an individual's life far more than sib membership. Such organizations are potential agencies for the formation of a state because they unite people within a circumscribed area into an aggregate that functions as a unit without regard to kinship affiliations.

> Concomitantly with the family and the sib there have existed for untold centuries such associations as the men's clubs, age classes, and secret organizations, all of them independent of kinship, moving as it were in a quite different sphere from the kindred groups, and all of them capable of readily acquiring political character if not invested with it from their inception. (1920:396)

But in his major book, *The Origin of the State*, published five years after the article of the same name, Lowie qualifies his earlier arguments and adds greater sophistication. First of all, he uses a much greater number and variety of examples, and contrary to his earlier antievolutionist view, he now sees the primitive world not as a flat landscape but rather as inhabited by peoples more and less advanced in complexity. Furthermore, he avers (1927:3) that the gap between primitive and civilized societies can be bridged by applying the "principle of continuity and psychic unity" as a methodological aid in describing the intermediate steps. A primeval "state" can be reconstructed, and not merely by a priori speculation. "Though it is a commonplace of ethnology that peoples may advance very unevenly in different phases of civilization, features shared without exception by all unequivocally rudest tribes may be reasonably accepted as not only primitive but *primeval*" (1927:3). This, for a prominent student of Boas, verges on heresy.

If the principle of continuity is truly applicable, then the processes that convert tiny primeval communities of the simplest cultures (such as the Tasmanians, Australians, Pygmies, Fuegians, Shoshoneans, and various other hunter–gatherer societies) to larger, more complex societies ought to be discoverable. Lowie's subsequent chapters test the various possibilities under the rubrics "Size of the State," "Castes," "Sovereignty," "The Territorial Ties," and "Associations."

With respect to the size of the state, there is no clear parallel between size and political organization at the ruder levels, where small, particularistic units coexist with much more numerous populations which are otherwise similar in culture. In general outline, an increased capacity for organization, military or peaceful, was evidently an initial stepping-stone in the development of increased size (1927:29).

As for castes, Lowie directly counters the conquest theory of the origin of the state, particularly as described by sociologist Franz Oppenheimer (1907). Oppenheimer had contended that all states known to history were coterminous with the presence of castes. His data were mostly from the Old World, with particularly striking examples from Africa. In general, and put simply, Oppenheimer held that the state came into being when pastoral nomads raided and pillaged sedentary peasant societies, sparing the victims and eventually coming to settle among them and dominate them permanently as a ruling endogamous caste. There is, as Lowie agrees, abundant evidence of just such conquests, lending considerable plausibility to Oppenheimer's thesis.

But Lowie here cites a very important work rebutting Oppenheimer, William Christie MacLeod's *The Origin of the State, Reconsidered in the Light of the Data of Aboriginal North America* (1924). MacLeod was the first, so far as I know, to argue that caste stratification by conquest would not occur unless an aristocratic ethos and structure were already in existence among the conquerors. Such an argument, of course, does not answer the main questions of how such an ethos or structure came about in the first place, but it does render a significant service in showing the inadequacies of the simple conquest theory. MacLeod's contention is supported by Lowie, who shows the many obvious instances wherein hereditary classes and ranks arose from internal conditions rather than conquest.

As for the principle of sovereignty, Lowie states that it is the badge of the modern state (1927:43). But this concept, involving subordination of a population to a supreme will, is stated by Lowie in an extreme form. Certainly there must have been less extreme forms of sovereignty; "the *germs* of sovereignty may and must be present even on so lowly a level as the Andamanese, where indeed the attitude of each group in excluding trespassers may be taken as foreshadowing territorial sovereignty" (1927:50). Most of Lowie's chapters were devoted to showing that sovereignty (and thus the state) was omnipresent in all of human society—surely a useless way of investigating the specific *origin* of the state.

The territorial tie, largely the construct of Sir Henry Maine, distinguished state or civilized society from primitive society, which was dependent on the kin tie alone as an organizing principle. But both Maine and L. H. Morgan relied too much on logic and not enough on ethnology and history, Lowie says, in discriminating these two antithetical principles. "Why should the peoples of the world, often contentedly living for millennia under a government based on the blood tie, engage in that startling revolution described by Maine, of substituting the totally novel alignment of persons by locality? Neither author provides an adequate solution" (1927:53). The "notion of continuous evolution" (continuity) suggests that the break was not necessarily abrupt, for older and simpler communities must have had some kind of local bond concomitantly with the blood tie. "The two principles, in other words, however antithetical, are not of necessity mutually exclusive" (1927:53). Thus is the postulate of continuity satisfied: no longer must we worry about the miracle of "spontaneous generation" but instead must confront the scientific question of how an originally weak sentiment of territoriality intensifies itself toward dominance.

After numerous ethnological examples are discussed, Lowie sums up the argument so far:

> The traditional distinction established by Maine and Morgan retains its validity in so far as conceptually a union of neighbors is different from a union of kinsmen. It must even be conceded that the blood tie is frequently the overshadowing element in the governmental activities of primitive peoples. Yet, though it often dwarfs the territorial factor, it never succeeds in eliminating it. Nay, if we inquire into the bond of consanguinity itself, we find lurking in the background a spatial determinant of the sentiments underlying it. Abstractly separated by a chasm, the two types of union are in reality intertwined. The basic problem of the state is thus not that of explaining the somersault by which ancient peoples achieved the step from a government by personal relations to one by territorial contiguity only. The question is rather to show what processes strengthened the local tie which must be recognized as not less ancient than the rival principle. (1927:72–73)

But whereas associations are important agencies for countering the blood tie by favoring locality as a unifying principle, Lowie now feels that associations are frequently "separatistic" in their influence. They do not, in short, weld a people into a national whole all alone. Some other unifying factor seems a necessary supplement, and this seems to be the principle of sovereignty.

> A coercive force, then, whether vested in a person or a group, seems the short cut to intensifying and bringing into consciousness the incipient feeling of neighborliness that has been found a universal trait of human society. Once established and sanctified, the sentiment may well flourish without compulsion, glorified as loyalty to a sovereign king or to a national flag. (1927:116–117).

A. M. HOCART

In his *Kings and Councillors* (1936), Hocart was less intent on promulgating a particular theory of the origin of government than on discovering and demonstrating the causal chain via the comparative method. The comparative method that he proposed was not a collection and cut-and-paste assembly of disembodied, unrelated traits, but was rather a comparison among a limited but representative sample of whole cultures which had been well described. His models or analogies for this procedure were comparative anatomy and comparative philology.

The cultures at issue, which he calls "Chief Witnesses," are from seven widely separated areas of the world. They are (1936:29)

1. South Seas   (Fijians)
2. Australia   (Arandas)
3. North America   (Winnebagos)
4. Asia, North East   (Koryaks)
5. Asia, South   (Vedic Indians, Hindus, Sinhalese, Tamils)
6. Africa, West   (Jukuns)
7. Europe, West   (English)

For each of these areas, numerous "Secondary Witnesses" are listed from among neighbors of the Chief Witnesses, in order to eke out, or confirm, data which are scarce or unclear among the Chief Witnesses.

Hocart's method relied on a further principle. Just as in comparative anatomy it had been found that nervous reflexes occurred in simple animals before there were any differentiated (or specialized) nervous tissues, so also in culture with respect to the origin of government (the nervous system of the social organism) did "function precede form"— the form evolves to facilitate the function. "Government is the result of activities already carried out before differentiation of men" (1936:30).

In many of the simpler societies the only consistent social activities that require the regulation by a headman are the performance of rites for the increase of such things as food, wealth, and immunity. "There is then no government, in our sense of the word, among people like the Fijians, because there is no need for any" (1936:31). There is, in other words, a potential leadership, such as the ritual leader, or master of ceremonies, who can take on other duties as the need arises—a nascent governing body is present before there is any governing to do.

But if a machinery was present before it was needed, if it had anticipated the growth of the state, what was it doing? Here it would seem, at first glance, as though Hocart had found a violation of his edict that function precedes form—in terms of the analogy, form was already there, awaiting its new functions. But no, the form that was there was performing another function, a ritual ceremonial leadership; but it was a form which could transfer itself to other functions, as needed. The changing aspects of this original ritual leadership would be in response to the new functional needs.

> This ritual organization is vastly older than government, for it exists where there is no government and where none is needed. When however society increases so much in complexity that a coordinating agency, a kind of central nervous system, is required, that ritual organization will gradually take over this task. (1936:35)

The idea of an evolution from ritual organization to government is difficult for many modern intellectuals to grasp, for we are so accustomed to seeing the eminent practicality of modern administration in its relation to secular economic institutions that it is difficult to see how it could have developed out of the "hocus-pocus" of mere ritual. But the process of forming a regulatory body does not demand that the leader be other than the extant leader, the leader of the life-sustaining rituals.

> If there is to be government, that is, coordination of actions, there must be some to command and a majority to obey. Gradually, then, as the regulation of conduct becomes the main interest rather than the control of nature, we see the leader become the regulator; groups once equal acknowledge the supremacy of one; a vertical arrangement takes the place of a horizontal one. He who begins by leading ends by directing. (1936:37)

One of Hocart's main arguments was that even long after ritualistic leaders had come to be truly instituted governments, able to wage war and peace and to regulate seemingly mundane economic matters, their societies did not separate the sacred or ritualistic aspects of life from the secular or practical. In speaking of the ritualistic religious means of seeking after "wordly and public prosperity," the kings were also responsible for crops, rains, irrigation canals, and so on. Here Hocart makes a very important statement:

> It would be an error to put such works [of irrigation] in a category by themselves as "utilitarian" in opposition to "religious" works such as temples. Temples are just as utilitarian as dams and canals, since they are necessary to prosperity; dams and canals are as ritual as temples, since they are part of the same social system of seeking welfare. If *we* call reservoirs "utilitarian" it is because *we* believe in their efficacy; *we* do not call temples so because *we* do not believe in their efficacy for crops. What *we* think has nothing to do with the matter, but only what the people we are studying think. (1936:217)

Insofar as we, in modern times, are inclined to separate the sacred from the profane, to distinguish religious actions from secular actions, we often are wrongly led to think that the ancient, original theocracies had somehow later "entangled" things like religion and agriculture.

But they were never separated earlier. "Agriculture and ritual were like the fresh milk before it has been separated into cream and skim" (1936:218). Ritual permeated daily life inseparably from practical aims; all aims were practical, but accomplished by ritual means.

Similarly treated was what we often call the separation of church and state, as though they were—as though they ought to be—separate forms with separate functions. "Render therefore unto Caesar the things that are Caesar's; and unto God the things that are God's." Even in societies such as the Winnebago, Yuma, Fijian, and Polynesian, which seem to have dual chiefs, one as the ritual head, the other (often the younger brother of the chief) as the war leader, it is misleading, Hocart says (1936:163), to distinguish these as sacred and secular or spiritual and temporal chiefs. The Fijians, for example, make no such distinction. "Society is an organization for prosperity, and that prosperity is to be achieved by the due observance of certain rules, and various functions in that tasks are assigned to various dignitaries" (1936:163).

Government in precivilized eras thus was theocratic—that is, simultaneously religious and political. And its basic shape, as distinguished from the pre-state societies, was simply centralization. Why did the need for centralization arise? What new functions created this form? The answer is increased specialization, which requires a central coordinating body. Whence specialization? *Not* because of individuals of differing abilities. Form still follows function, and it was new functions that created new types of persons. "Special abilities are the consequence of special tasks and not the other way around" (1936:40).

From Hocart's "Summing Up" (his final chapter), we would do well to quote in full the last paragraph:

> The facts reviewed in this book have suggested that conscious purpose precedes the adaptation of behavior, and the adaptation of behavior is followed by adaptation of structure. A community wants something; it shapes its actions so as to achieve that something, and the result of its action is to alter its organization. It is not indeed government that man wants, for how can he conceive of a government except by experience of it? It is life he wants, and in the effort to live he does one thing after another till he eventually finds himself governed, that is specialized into producers and into regulators of those producers. He does not want a priesthood or a civil service to control him; he wants to control nature for his own benefit; but in the pursuit of this aim he places some members of his community into new functions which in turn produce a new type of men, no longer the all-round handy man, but the men who live largely by thinking. The conscious purpose is the impulse that sets the whole machinery in motion with results that are not foreseen (1936:299)

M. Fortes and E. E. Evans-Pritchard

M. Fortes and E. E. Evans-Pritchard edited a seminal book, *African Political Systems* (1940), which within the British social anthropological school was for its time the most empirical and analytical of the ethnological attempts to foster new understandings of the origin and nature of the state or government. This book contains a representative sample of well-described African societies falling into two main categories, which are called Group A and Group B.

The societies of Group A are characterized by centralized authority and administration and judicial institutions—that is, government—with distinctions in wealth, privilege, and status correlating with power and authority. These are the Zulu, Ngwato, Bemba, Banyankole, and the Kedi. Group B societies lack these centralized governmental institutions and have no sharp division of rank, status, or wealth. These are the Logoli, Tallensi, and Nuer.

Fortes and Evans-Pritchard's comparison of the two groups yields two conclusions of particular relevance to two of the oldest and most prominent theories of the origins of government, conquest and territoriality. With respect to the former, they find that Group A societies often are composed of heterogeneous ethnic groups, some more than others, although there are prominent examples of Group A societies, such as the Zulu and Bemba, which are remarkably homogeneous. It would seem, then, that governmental institutions are useful or necessary when the society *is* composed of diverse ethnic elements, even though these institutions can exist without having to play a unifying role. The fact that caste-like ethnic relations suggest conquest, therefore, does not present itself as necessary to the origin of government—government, as we know, often precedes and implements conquest. Furthermore, centralized government is not necessary to amalgamation in another sense. The stateless (Group B) Nuer have conquered and absorbed large numbers of the neighboring Dinka, but this amalgamation resulted in neither a caste or class structure nor a centralized government.

The other important conclusion concerns the factor of territoriality as promulgated by Maine, Morgan, and many others. Fortes and Evans-Pritchard find that *all* of the societies in their book, A's and B's alike, have a territorial framework. But their significant finding is that territoriality has a different function in the two types of political organization. Among the A's, the administrative unit is a territorial unit, and political power is territorially delimited. In Group B societies, the boundaries are not defined in terms of an administrative system but rather through lineage ties and obligations of cooperation. Thus Maine's "kin tie" is allied to a sort of "territorial tie."

Fortes and Evans-Pritchard summarize: "Political relations are not simply a reflexion of territorial relations. The political system, in its own right, incorporates territorial relations and invests them with the particular kind of political significance they have."[1]

KARL WITTFOGEL

Wittfogel's *Oriental Despotism* (1957) is an attempt to account for one of the salient characteristics of the archaic states, their high degree of centralization and total political power. Wittfogel's solution is his hydraulic (water-control) theory. This is not so much a theory of the origin—or nature, or function—of the state as an attempt to understand why the early states were so repressive. His emphasis is on the Near East and Asia (hence "Oriental" despotism), all of whose archaic states had extensive irrigation systems.

The creation and maintenance of such hydraulic systems presupposes a central authority, and since this amounts to almost total control over agricultural production, the state is enabled to wield an equivalent amount of power over its people. A presumption here is that if circumstances, like control over water, enable a state to be despotic or repressive, then it will be.[2] Water control could, of course, discourage the fissioning tendency of societies by making it more beneficial for potentially dissident groups to remain in the society than to secede.

Perhaps the real significance of water control for the development of civilization is that the agriculture is intensified. Many more people can be supported on the same amount of land than under rainfall agriculture, and thus there is a profound demographic effect.

There are many contrary cases not discussed by Wittfogel. The extensive irrigation system of the Hohokam Indians seems to have been built entirely by accretion, gradually and over a long time, with no

---

[1](1940:9–11). The foregoing conclusions are found in the introduction to the book— there is no concluding chapter. Another conclusion of interest, but not germane to the present discussion, is the influence of demography: in particular, that greater density of population does not correlate very closely with political centralization. This point has been disputed cogently by Stevenson (1968).

[2]A stray thought: A state is known to be despotic when it forcibly represses its people, but if it needs to resort to force, is that not a sign of its weakness? Wittfogel's argument ought to mean that a large, intricate hydraulic system would encourage a state to be centralized and have a large bureaucracy—which is not necessarily the same thing as "despotism."

evidence of any class sytem, despotic or otherwise. The Maya Indians developed, or at least maintained, a civilization in Yucatán, Mexico, without any irrigation, although there is evidence in the Petén area of drainage systems. The soil was very fertile, however, which points up the factor of intensification in relation to demography. The dense populations of the nearby Oaxacan civilization also were maintained by intensification of agriculture, though by "pot irrigation," a means of hand watering from shallow wells, rather than by a central system of canals.

But it can plausibly be argued that, where a hydraulic system is possible, a state may aid powerfully in the *integration* of the society by virtue of the visible and important benefits it confers on groups which are a part of it.

V

ECONOMIC LIFE OF PRIMITIVE PEOPLES

The history of ethnological controversies within the general realm of economics can be readily separated into two distinct issues. The first of these to surface was concerned with ownership of capital goods, especially forms of property such as land: Were they essentially privately or communally owned among primitive peoples? The other question had to do with the nature of exchange systems, with the way primitive peoples or societies moved goods: Was exchange "economic trade" (market pricing, maximizing returns) or was it something "embedded in social relations," maximizing not monetary reward but social status based on generosity and services, on giving rather than acquiring? These have been the main problems in the beginning of the economic controversies, although they have been phrased in several different ways. They will be discussed in two separate chapters, although of course the questions are closely related.

14

Property in
Primitive Society

It now probably seems inevitable, or natural, that expectations held
before the 1860s were ethnocentrically standard and involved the assumption that productive property in primitive society was held in fee
simple by individuals (or households).

The first important statements contrary to the usual opinion seem
to have been made by Sir Henry Maine in his *Ancient Law* (1861) and
Village Communities in the East and West (1871). We have already
noted this in Chapter 1 and need not dwell on it here because Maine
did not theorize very much about it. He was not really an evolutionist
generalizing about the characteristics of stages; he was more a historian talking about the classical Mediterraneans or, later, about Hindu
India. No important ethnological controversy seems to have been elicited by Maine's views on property.[1] It was not until Morgan's day that
any really extended discussion took place.

Lewis H. Morgan

As we saw in Chapter 3, Morgan thought that primitive society
(*societas*) and civilized society (*civitas*) differed greatly not only in
their governmental institutions but also in their property relations.
The increase in amount and kinds of property was proportionate to the
progress of inventions and discoveries. "The multiplicity of the forms
of property would be accompanied by the growth of certain regulations
with respect to its possession and inheritance. . . . [These] are determined and modified by the condition and progress of the social organization" (1877:445).

---

[1]Burrow (1966:162–165) shows this. Burrow also shows that Maine connected the
Hindus with the people of the classical past of Europe as fellow Aryans, historically
separated from the rest of the primitive world.

The long period of what Morgan calls savagery saw a very slow accretion of new forms of property: from clubs and spears to the bow and arrow; from flint knife and chisel to stone axe and hammer; from baskets to pottery; from nakedness to tanned skin garments; from tents to rude houses. By the end of the period the germs of the next ethnical status, barbarism, were created, particularly the beginning of the gentile form of social organization, which within itself contained the rudiments of new forms of government. But still the property of savages was inconsiderable. "Their ideas concerning its value, its desirability, and its inheritance were feeble. . . . Lands, as yet hardly a subject of property, were owned by the tribes in common, while tenement houses were owned jointly by their occupants" (1877:447).

Within the status of barbarism, a period, Morgan says, that must have been more brief than that of savagery, the most distinguishing progress lay in the development of institutions (1877:447). This, above all, was the gens, the unilineal (originally matrilineal) group of relatives. The "first great rule of inheritance" coincided with this development, that of distributing the effects of a deceased person among his gentiles. With the more intensive cultivation of plants, there came about a new species of property, family gardens. Lands were owned in common by the tribe, but a "possessory right" to cultivate land was now recognized in the individual or family group, and it became a subject of inheritance.

In the "Upper Status of Barbarism" (a status never achieved by the American Indians) property became so various and numerous that many new forms of ownership came about. The old tenure of lands held in common continued, but because of more settled agriculture, manufactures, and local and foreign commerce, new forms of individual ownership occurred. Finally, especially with the advent of field agriculture, "it was found that [as] the head of the family became the natural center of accumulation, the new property career of mankind was inaugurated" (1877:461).

As we noted in Chapter 3, Morgan's description of primitive communism and the denunciation of the "career of property," which in civil society became the foundation of aristocracy, attracted the attention and admiration of Marx and Engels, and with the publication of Engels' *The Origin of the Family, Private Property, and the State* (1884), *Ancient Society* became enshrined in Marxist ideology and thus became anathema to many of those of an anti-Marxist persuasion, eventually including many ethnologists. It was Robert Lowie, more than any other, who undertook to answer Morgan in detail, ostensibly in the context of scientific discourse rather than partisan politics.

ROBERT LOWIE

As the title suggests, Lowie's *Primitive Society* (1920) was written with Morgan's *Ancient Society* in mind: "Since Lewis H. Morgan's *Ancient Society* (1877) systematically embodied the older unilineal evolutionism that postulated laws of development, my book inevitably grew into a persistent critique of Morgan" (1920:v). Lowie's argument was well received, particularly in America, and may be judged a good example of the prevalent Boasian attitudes toward evolutionism in general and Morgan in particular.

Chapter 9 of *Primitive Society* is devoted entirely to property, with particular emphasis on the question of "primitive communism." Lowie begins by stating in plain and unequivocal terms that he opposes the evolutionary dogma which states that every characteristic of civilization must have evolved through transitional stages from an original condition far removed from it. An example of this kind of thinking would find our modern, highly developed sense of property to be absent from primitive society, which must have had "communism in goods of every kind" (1920:205–206). Although Lowie does not mention any evolutionist by name, he certainly must have had Morgan in mind (but as we have noted, Morgan did not refer to "goods of every kind").

Lowie rather approves of Sir Henry Maine, who is judged a profound, historically-minded thinker rather than an evolutionist. Maine is cited as having thought that "joint-ownership and not separate ownership is the really archaic institution" (quoted by Lowie 1920:206). Lowie then argues that there are many kinds of joint ownerships, some involving only a pair of partners, others a household or a club, with sometimes a whole village consisting of one father–sib being the landowning corporation. The last would resemble a case of village–communism.

Lowie also argues that a *legal* state of communism is often simulated when, for example, rules of hospitality require that a host share out his food unstintingly with a visitor. But such generosity "is a far cry from a communistic theory that would permit the guest to appropriate food unbidden" (1920:207). This is the difference between ethics and law. Meanwhile ethnographic examples of the widespread sharing of food in conjunction with the recognition of certain individual rights are so abundant that "we cannot content ourselves with a blunt alternative: communism versus individualism" (1920:210).

Tenure of land, for example, generally varies greatly among hunters, stock raisers, and tillers, Lowie says. Among hunters, communal ownership holds for the North American plains, but just the opposite for the Northeastern Algonkian Indian groups. Professor Frank Speck

has established the fact that hunting grounds were divided into individual family property, family in this case being the proprietorship of a
male head and his male descendants (hunting being exclusively a male
occupation). Speck uses data from old travelers' accounts to indicate a
widespread recognition of individual hunting privileges among the Indians of Eastern and central Canada and coastal British Columbia.
(Speck's interpretations, first made in 1915, have become important
buttresses to the theories of other ethnologists who have wished to
discredit evolutionism. Shortly after World War II, however, his work
was subjected to ethnohistorical scrutiny by Eleanor Leacock, who
established that the vaunted "family hunting-ground" was a product of
professional employment of the Indians by white men as fur trappers.
This important controversy is discussed more fully in a subsequent
section of this chapter.)

Among pastoral peoples, Lowie finds that there is usually a highly
developed sense of private ownership of livestock, but land is held
communally. Again there is great variation: some, like the Kirgis, ap-
portion the more valuable winter pasturage among families, with summer pasturage free to the whole kinship group, the *aul*. "Here is once
more a striking illustration of the futility of tossing about convenient
but meaningless catchwords. The Kirgiz are neither communists nor
individualists in an absolute sense." (1920:216).

As for tillers of the soil, data are very confusing. Lowie sees two
reasons for this, especially in North America. One is that primitive
usage has been extinguished over large areas. The second is that even
with regard to peoples who have not been removed from their ancient
holdings and seem to retain their aboriginal ideas of land tenure, such
as the Pueblo of the American Southwest, there has been confusion by
ethnologists as to whether the "sib" (clan) really owns the land and
allows the individual family what Morgan had called a "possessory
right" to cultivate appropriate parts of it. Lowie says flatly that neither
the Hopi nor the Zuñi have any sib- (clan-) held lands. Occupation and
utilization of vacant land allows it to become the property of the users
and to be inherited by their descendants (females, in these cases).

In Africa are found many agricultural kingdoms (with herding as
well) in which, legally, the king owns the land; he apportions it among
his chiefs, who in turn allot it to the peasants in exchange for taxes or
tribute. This, Lowie avers, is akin to the feudal system. In Oceania and
the Philippines there are many varieties of such feudal-like systems;
there are other systems as well, ranging from caste societies to societies with highly aristocratic classes to societies with despotic rulers.
All have an effect on the usual forms of land tenure.

Lowie's argument is based on disorderly *variety*. He argues that one simply cannot generalize about primitive societies; therefore, one cannot use such data to postulate a primordial stage of communism—or presumably of anything else. There is no doubt about the reality of the joint ownership that so impressed Maine, "but it is by no means a fact that the co-proprietors always constitute a social unit of the same type. . . . The burden of proof surely rests with those who believe in a universal stage of communal ownership antecedent to individual tenure of land" (1920:231).

The remainder of Lowie's chapter deals with chattels (movable property as opposed to real estate), incorporeal property, and inheritance. These may be discussed quickly in turn.

Chattels, according to Lowie, are much more likely to be purely personal than land. This is in part because much of this kind of property is a result of individual skill and effort. Many chattels are tools, weapons, canoes, and the like, which are used by individuals alone and adapted to the users' particular preferences. Livestock (as chattels) are often a conspicuous form of wealth and status, and hence are subject to both individual and family property rights.

Incorporeal property perhaps is most familiar to us as patents and copyrights. In some primitive societies, a song composed by a person for an occasion is not to be sung by anyone else. Magical formulas and incantations used by shamans are cherished as trade secrets, though they sometimes are bought and sold, with the seller giving up his right to them. On the Northwest Coast of North America there has been a historical proliferation of individual inherited prerogatives: rights to certain songs and dances, names and titles, carving designs, masks, and so on. Lowie gives numerous examples of the same proliferation elsewhere in the primitive world. His chief aim, of course, is to underscore the tremendous variety of kinds of incorporeal property. "Its very existence among the simpler peoples is of the highest interest; and not less remarkable are the protean forms it assumes under favorable conditions" (1920:243).

The various ways certain kinds of property are inherited reveal the basic feelings in the society about the property. If certain properties are not inherited, something is revealed there, too. Many societies destroy or bury some of the most important possessions of a dead person rather than allow them to be passed on to descendants. These are articles normally in daily and important use by the person. Often, if not always, there is the feeling that these necessities will be used by the spirit in the afterworld, hence they are "killed."

Lowie jumps about the world, noting different forms of inheritance:

primogeniture; the avunculate; inheritance of different items specifically by sex (in the same society); and above all changes in forms of inheritance in the same society (to show that changes are *not* due to change from matrilineal to patrilineal forms of descent in evolutionary sequence). Variety again is the keynote of Lowie's argument against evolutionism. In this regard, it should be noted that to an evolutionist such as Morgan there are gradations in primitive society, such as savagery, barbarism, and civilization, and further gradations within each of these. Lowie, on the contrary, sees only different kinds of peoples; they are called primitive in contrast to civilized. The considerable variety he finds for each kind of property is achieved by failing to note any sort of classification that might be made except geographic (African, North American, etc.) and, sometimes, "occupational" (hunting versus herding and tilling—distinctions he observed only in the case of his discussion of land tenure). This mode of address to the primitive world—leaving it undifferentiated in terms of levels or stages—serves his main argument, which seems to be how truly *differentiated* it really is when looked at in the temporally flat way, the nonevolutionary way. There is no evidence in the text that Lowie was aware of the logical and methodological distinction between evolutionism and what he calls "historicism" in its effect on the appearance of endless variety in the "historical primitive" world. Further, the general impression he gives is that these varieties of customs have little relationship to anything else within a given society—a perspective characterized by others as the "shreds-and-patches" view of cultural integration.

This characterization annoyed Lowie. It *was* inaccurate, from a strictly scholarly perspective. In the final paragraph of his most widely read work, *Primitive Society,* he said (1920:441): "To that planless hodgepodge, that thing of shreds and patches called civilization, its historian can no longer yield superstitious reverence." In the 1947 reissue of the work, Lowie comments on this in a new preface:

> The final paragraph . . . has been rather generally misinterpreted. The sentence in which civilization is called "that thing of shreds and patches" has no bearing on anthropological theory. It was written in a period of disillusionment after World War I. . . . I was casting about for something to say about *our* civilization, and as an admirer of Gilbert and Sullivan naturally bethought myself of the phrase in question. It is true that I did not believe, nor do I now, that *all* elements of a culture are necessarily related by some organic bond; on the other hand, ever since 1915 my treatment of kinship ought to have absolved me from the charge of viewing culture as *only* a fabric of shreds and patches." (1947:ix–x)

It is true, as we saw in an earlier chapter, that Lowie was evidently the first, except for Tylor (1888) in his percipient but too-brief remarks on the subject, to see the functional—evolutionary connection between patterns of classificatory relationship terms and some aspects of social structure. But that was exceptional for Lowie and unprecedented for students of Boas; so much of the rest of the time he treated culture largely in terms of isolated, diffusable traits and patterns that the handy epithet "shreds and patches" seems to fit and is likely to continue to be used.

RAYMOND FIRTH

Firth also opposed many of the important Morgan—Marxist theories, but his opposition was quite different from Lowie's. He was first of all one of the earliest and most prominent of Malinowski's "functionalist" students; he was therefore concerned with the functional and structural interrelationship between such elements as property customs with the technology, social organization, and ideology of a particular society. Firth's kind of ethnographic reality, so to speak, was very different from Lowie's. He addressed the basic questions of this reality in depth as an ethnographer in a living, functioning society—the Tikopia.[2] His reporting of this has a different flavor from Lowie's polemic.

The greatest value of Firth's work is the depth of ethnographic data presented to us, particularly those descriptive of Tikopia. He does not waste much time in generalizing, as Malinowski did, about the primitive world in order to justify or discredit any popular theory. He was above all interested in the workings of this particular society. In contrast to Lowie's arguments based on the endless variety of particular cultural shreds and patches in the primitive world, arguments meant to counter evolutionists' generalizations, Firth merely objects to the lack of scientific methodology of the evolutionists. He states this objection only briefly near the end of his concluding chapter of *Primitive Polynesian Economy*:

> This is not the place to enter into a discussion of the evolutionary theory originally formulated by Morgan, used polemically by Engels, and more recently adopted as the official *credo* of the leading ethnologists of the USSR. But

[2]Here we refer primarily to his *Primitive Polynesian Economy* (1939). He had earlier written *Primitive Economics of the New Zealand Maori* (1929), but that book was written from documentary sources, often fragmentary, whereas the 1939 work was based on firsthand observation of the Tikopia when they were still functioning as a nearly autonomous economic entity.

it is clear that such a theory can be of little use to the anthropologist who is interested in the dynamic, present-day significance of the facts of native life [here Firth gives examples]. . . . Admittedly chronological interpretations, both for the past and future, may follow from a detailed empirical investigation of the observable phenomena of the present, but this investigation is merely stultified when it proceeds from initial *a priori* assumptions as to what human society was like in the past and what it is likely to develop into in the future.

This objection to the historical or evolutionary approach is more concerned with the methodology actually employed in anthropological science than with abstract epistemology. The suggestion is not that such evolutionary speculations are from their very nature scientifically impossible or undesirable. But in the actual history of anthropology reconstructions have been founded upon inadequate evidence, tenuous hypotheses have been regarded as established laws, and above all the stress upon the past has largely prevented the study of present-day reality. (1939:362)

Firth goes on to describe the old contrast between individualism and communism. He believes it is wrong to consider this an antithesis, since both forms of organization, and motives, can coexist. Firth had found, as had Malinowski before him, that individual greed, or acquisitiveness, probably exists everywhere in some measure, but it is always bound by strong mechanisms that control it in the interests of the welfare of the whole community (1939:364).

One could dispute one of the implications of Firth's argument here. It is far too often the case that discussions about property turn into arguments about human motives, or human nature, rather than the actual social controls that exist in one kind of society as contrasted with another. This seems, for that matter, to have been the main trouble with Morgan's view of evolution, for he saw it as essentially a growth in human morality rather than as social–structural, or cultural, evolution. Firth has come a long way beyond Morgan, but still, as do so many, he moves from individuals' motives (acquisitiveness or selfishness) to the society as a whole, and *its* rules. These are not comparable.

T. Cliffe Leslie long before had framed this problem in an acute statement:

> Property has not its root in the love of possession. All living beings like and desire certain things, and if nature has armed them with any weapons are prone to use them in order to get and keep what they want. What requires explanation is not the want or desire of certain things on the part of the individuals, but the fact that other individuals, with similar wants and desires, should leave them in undisturbed possession, or allot them a share, of such things. It is the conduct of a community, not the inclination of individuals, that needs investigation. (Laveleye 1878:xi)

The Ownership of Algonkian Hunting Territories: Frank Speck versus Eleanor Leacock

According to Herskovits' general review of the status of theories of primitive communism (1952:335), it was the ethnographic fieldwork of Frank Speck that provided the initial challenge to the doctrine of primitive communism among hunting–gathering peoples. Speck had found (1915) that among the Canadian Algonkians the main bond of the family was the patrilineal inheritance of relatively permanent and bounded hunting territories that forbade trespass by others. Even if a person wished simply to cross the territory when traveling, permission to do so had to be obtained.

So well established was this family territoriality that even as late as the turn of the century the people still could demark the hunting territories belonging to each family. Even the Penobscot of Maine were able to do this, long after the land had been lost to the dominant white population. This was evidently felt to be a remarkable case of cultural persistence, since it was assumed that this family territoriality was pre-Columbian. If such an institution resisted the very considerable stresses of acculturation over so long a time, it must be a sign that it was of grave significance to these Indians, a kind of cultural mind-set—at least this is the implication.

Hallowell (1949) accepted the view that the family hunting territory was aboriginal, but he very nearly modified Speck's view out of existence, apparently without realizing it. Hallowell studied several Algonkian peoples in Quebec and Manitoba and found that the population density, the ratio of active hunters to nonhunters, and the size of the territories were closely correlated. He was making a rather momentous discovery, for at that time in ethnological history little was known of what might be called functional ecology. Speck had not given an indication of the relationship of factors involved in the ecological adjustment of the numbers of fur-bearing animals in relation to the numbers of active hunters in a given territory, with the actual boundaries demarking the territories being a function of these variables. (It would, indeed, be hard to imagine a formerly numerous family of several adult male hunters, later reduced to one old male, "owning" the original large territory they had all occupied. That is, it is reasonable to expect that in one way or another able-bodied hunters would, in maturity, end up with places in which to hunt—which seems to be what actually happened.) At any rate, adjustments in territory *did* occur, which means that the meaning attached to Speck's ethnographic finding—that there was a "culture trait" among the Algonkian hunters that was strongly concerned with family ownership of territory "over time immemorial"— simply needed considerable modification. It is possible that Speck's findings were carried too far and oversimplified by others, however, because they lent so much seemingly factual authenticity to the argument against the early evolutionary proponents of primitive communism.

The best example of the uses to which Speck's work was put is probably to be found in Lowie, as might be expected because of his long crusade against Morgan. The flavor is suggested in the following example:

> It is often assumed that when peoples support themselves by the chase there is of necessity communal ownership of the hunting grounds. This proposition, however, has been not only seriously shaken but invalidated by testimony from a number of distinct regions. . . . Thanks to Professor Speck's capital investigation of northeastern Algonkian groups, it must now be regarded as an established fact that in parts of North America not only such improvements [like a fishing station or deer fence] but the hunting-grounds themselves were the property of individual families.[3] (Lowie 1920:211–212)

In 1954 Eleanor Leacock published a thoroughly researched rebuttal of the widely accepted opinion of Speck's that the Algonkian family "hunting" territories were aboriginal. Her argument brought together her field data from the area originally researched by Speck and a careful perusal of early historical documents of the European-initiated trade with the Indians.

After the adaptation of many of the Labrador Indians to the fur trade, there came to be established two distinct modes of subsistence there, often mixed and in varying proportions in different regions and historical epochs. One mode involved a major dependence on wild food, particularly deer and caribou, hunted with bow and arrow and later with European firearms; this was supplemented by fishing in summer. The other was trapping for valuable fur-bearing animals such as marten, beaver, otter, and lynx. Though all of these may be eaten, the primary aim was to acquire furs to be traded or sold at the trading post. The Indians acquired in return steel traps, firearms and ammunition, clothes, utensils, and provisions.

Leacock discovered in both the historical epochs and certain areas in

---

[3]Speck and Eiseley (1939, 1942) and Cooper (1939) have also assessed the historical data and concluded that these customs were aboriginal, not a product of modern acculturation.

modern times that, when the economy is largely based on the hunting of big game for food, the basic social unit is a "band" of several families, varying in size depending on the time of year and the amount and kind of game. The band was thus rather fluid and informal. "Individual family territories were obviously incompatible, aside from being unnecessary, with such hunting patterns" (Leacock 1954:25). But among the Montagnais in the "last four or five decades" (before about 1950) flour replaced meat as the staple, canvas replaced skin tents, cloth was used for clothing, and so on. Although the Montagnais augmented their food when possible with fresh meat and fish, hunting was not allowed to compete with trapping in their allocation of time and effort (1954:25–26). The "family hunting territory" was found in the areas where beaver trapping, particularly, was important (1954:27). Such areas should better be called family *trapping* territories (or perhaps trap lines) than "hunting territories," for it seems that the individual trapper (perhaps with the help of a son or two) was more effective in his efforts than a group. And of course the white trader dealt with the Indians as individuals, keeping accounts and subsidizing their traps and other equipment.

Leacock has detailed the varying presence and mixtures of the two kinds of subsistence. It seems very convincingly functional that what was "owned" and individualized, when the family territory was present, were traps and other equipment, not land. The beaver and other sedentary animals living in the territory of the trap line represented *usufruct* rather than territories owned.

Leacock augments her conclusions with studies of other arctic hunters; these studies support the contention that the coming of Europeans, and particularly the development of the fur trade, tended to individualize the division of labor and to break up the earlier communal forms of territoriality (1954:42–43), just as in Labrador. Further, there have been historical researches that show how the coming of Europeans with their trade, new weapons, and territorial pressure intensified Iroquoian political organization and warfare, distorted the Northwest Coast Indians' potlatching, and drastically altered the Plains Indian culture. The relatively more isolated Algonkians of Labrador are nevertheless no exceptions to this kind of adaptation. "One must work from an understanding that fundamental socioeconomic changes have been taking place in some parts of their area for over three hundred years, one aspect of which is the development of the family hunting territory" (1954:43).

15

Economic Exchange and Allocation: Maximization of What?

Of late in ethnology, psychology, sociology, and, expectably, economics, there has been a great deal of theoretical speculation as well as experimentation and field description on the subject of "transactions," "exchanges," "altruism," "pure gift," and "love-as-a-form-of-exchange"—much of it as support to the Wall Street adage that "there is no such thing as a free lunch." Let it be hastily stated that despite the considerable interest these studies arouse, they are recent (which ought to be surprising) and pertain mostly to modern society. So, let it be understood that we are to be examining only the controversies about the movement of valuable goods within, and among, *primitive* societies.

L. H. Morgan's ideas about primitive property, as we saw, advanced the concept of "primitive communism," of which Engels (1884) was to make so much political use. Associated with that notion of property was the relatively unexamined assumption that goods were moved freely, generously, and without a profit motive—that is, that it was only in late barbarism and early civilization that the division of labor in production led to exchanges and finally to "commodity production" for market exchanges.

Engels' rendering of this idea was far more influential than Morgan's, particularly since he put it in the context of a revolutionary call to arms. The continuing division of labor, and the resulting necessity of exchanges, "adds a third division of labor, peculiar to itself and of decisive importance: it creates a class which no longer concerns itself with production, but only with the exchange of the products—the *merchants*" (1884:151).[1]

---

[1]Morgan said much about (and against) private property in *Ancient Society* but little against merchants or capitalism—to which he was, perforce, allied. His feelings against

So, evidently, Morgan cum Engels saw the earlier exchange of goods among primitives as altruistic, a simple giving of "some fortuitous surplus" as "isolated occurrences," because men were producing "only directly for their own needs" (1884:150). This primitive exchange thus resembled a simple gift giving at no real cost to the producer. Morgan, it should be emphasized, was the very first, if not the only, nineteenth-century ethnologist actually to have *observed* among primitive peoples what he described as communism in property, with the associated altruism ("fraternity and equality") of the ancient gens.

Morgan and Engels aside for now, the prevailing point of view at the turn of the century with respect to primitive man, and modern man as well, sought to explain economics as *economics*, an Adam Smithian meaning of the word quite widely accepted as referring to the allocation of scarce resources among unlimited and competing uses or needs. This has to do with rational decisions on the part of society and its institutions and rulers as well as decisions of individuals administering their own fortunes. Rational choice—maximizing gain over loss (whether of money, energy, or the wearing out of tools), considerations of alternative wants, individual self-interest particularly, as a natural human "economic man"—was a conception, however oversimplified, that Bronislaw Malinowski sought to destroy in his redoubtable *Argonauts of the Western Pacific* (1922).

Bronislaw Malinowski and the Kula Ring

Malinowski's was one of the most successful of the many uses of ethnological fieldwork that were destined to lay to rest popular conceptions of human nature, racial characteristics, and religious and philosophical dogmas. He did this first (significantly perhaps because most strikingly and easily) by destroying the myth of *homo economicus*, although he continued the task eventually with respect to popular generalizations about law, magic, religion, and sex.

The most important message in Malinowski's work is the general point that the exchange of "goods" in the important *Kula* ring can be dominated by social and ritual considerations that are *uneconomic* in the usual meaning of the word. Malinowski, as always, is wont to address the motives of individuals as the key problem; in this case, he repeatedly emphasizes that the *Kula* traders were motivated not by the desires of personal gain in wordly goods but by the social esteem ac-

---

property seem to have been devoted to *inherited* property in land; he was, so to speak, pro-democracy and anti-aristocracy.

quired by observing the code of rule and rituals that the society deemed important. Here is a representative passage:

> This social code . . . is, however, far from weakening the natural desirability of possession; on the contrary, it lays down that to possess is to be great, and that wealth is the indispensable appanage of social rank and attribute of personal virtue. But the important point is that with them to possess is to give—and here the natives differ from us notably. A man who owns a thing is naturally expected to share it, to distribute it, to be its trustee and dispenser. And the higher the rank the greater the obligation. . . . Thus the main symptom of being powerful is to be wealthy, and of wealth is to be generous. Meanness, indeed, is the most despised vice, and the only thing about which the natives have strong moral views, while generosity is the essence of goodness. (1922:156)

We have noted that Morgan and Engels, in discussing primitive property, assumed that savages were engaged in "production-for-use" rather than commodity production and that the exchange of goods, or trade, did not arise until the specialization of labor required it. But Malinowski very forcefully describes the exchange of goods among Trobriand Islanders as *not* being required by "economic" needs or by specialization. He reports that

> *the whole tribal life is permeated by a constant give and take;* that every ceremony, every legal and customary act is done to the accompaniment of material gift and counter gift; that wealth, given and taken, is one of the main instruments of social organization, of the power of the chief, of the bonds of kinship, and of relationship in law. (1922:156)

Finally, Malinowski emphasizes the generality of this kind of exchange: "Apart from any consideration as to whether the gifts are necessary or even useful, giving for the sake of giving is one of the most important features of Trobriand sociology, and, from its very general and fundamental nature, I submit that it is a universal feature of all primitive societies" (1922:165).

MARCEL MAUSS: THE GIFT

Mauss' original title in French is *Essai sur le don, forme archaïque de l'echange* (1923–1924). He notes at the outset that in "primitive" or "archaic" societies, exchanges of goods are made as though each act of payment (*prestation*) were voluntary and the repayment like another voluntary prestation (when in fact it is an obligation). The purpose of his detailed study is this: "*In primitive or archaic types of society what is the principle whereby the gift received has to be repaid? What force is there in the thing given which compels the recipient to make a return?"* (1923–1924:1).

Mauss wants to get away from our own ethnocentric views based on modern merchants' use of currency, sale, contract, and capital. His method of "careful comparison" includes Polynesia, Melanesia, and Northwest American Indians. Above all, he wants to get away from the way Western civilization has compartmentalized social phenomena into separate spheres of economic, juridical, moral, aesthetic, and religious matters. He, like Durkheim (his uncle and teacher), wants to look at a social act such as a gift as a total phenomenon; he wants to see it in all its complexity, not abstracted from its reality into an "economic" or "religious" act.

In Samoa and New Zealand the natives have a belief that gifts, particularly of forest game, contain a power or spirit like the *mana* of humans, which is called *hau*. This *hau*, the "spirit" of the gift, is the Maori explanation of "why a gift received has to be repaid." It is their answer to the query: "What force is there in the thing given which compels the recipient to make a return?"

Whatever this force is, it works. Mauss considers carefully all the forms of primitive exchange that are well documented and finds that gift-and-return (reciprocity) is the prime archaic (primitive) form of contract; nowhere is there a natural economy of a simple exchange of goods, wealth, and produce through markets established by the actions of the individuals.

He states categorically:

> For it is groups, and not individuals, which carry on exchange, make contracts, and are bound by obligations; the persons represented in the contracts are moral persons—clans, tribes, and families. . . . Further, what they exchange is not exclusively goods and wealth, real and personal property, and things of economic value. They exchange rather courtesies, entertainments, ritual, military assistance, women, children, dances, and feasts; and fairs in which the market is but one element and the circulation of wealth but one part of a wider and enduring contract. (1923–1924:3)

This system is that of *total prestation*. Total prestation implies that there are three obligations: the obligation to give, to receive, and to repay the gifts received (1923–1924:11).

Mauss makes some of his most trenchant and subtle comments in his "Conclusions" while commenting on Malinowski's Trobriand material. One of his basic conclusions concerns the difficulty in describing the archaic exchange activities in terms familiar to us. Our "present" and "gift" are, for instance, not quite right. "Concepts which we like to put in opposition—freedom and obligation; generosity, liberality, luxury on the one hand and saving, interest, austerity on the other—are not exact and it would be well to put them to the test" (1923–1924:70). He would prefer to be able to describe the *Kula* ring as "neither of purely free and gratuitous prestations, nor of purely interested and utilitarian production and exchange; it is kind of hybrid."

Malinowski had tried to classify the various transactions in the Trobriands according to the degree of interest or disinterest on the part of the individuals, ranging from "pure gift" to "barter with bargaining." Mauss finds this an untenable procedure; there is no such thing as a "free gift" of total disinterestedness. All involve some kind of reciprocity, even if long delayed or immaterial (as in terms of some service, such as protection). Even when a Tsimshian chief, giving a potlatch, destroys or gives extravagantly, this is not disinterested; it is the way hierarchy is maintained or desecrated.

But the opposite of the pure gift, the individual's pursuit of utility (the motive of "economic man"), is equally false to the archaic mode of transaction. Even in our Western societies, where the more purely economic animal was recently created, there are still a large number of transactions and motives involved that are not calculated solely or purely in terms of utility or gain.

And just as Mauss does not wish to disentangle utility (or economics) from other significances of a transaction, so he argues that the prestations should be seen as "total" (or "general") in the sense that many institutions may be simultaneously involved in a *Kula* or potlatch, for they "are at once legal, economic, religious, aesthetic, morphological, and so on" (1923–1924:76). Why is this desirable? Because the only way to answer the question asked at the outset is to understand a gift in its "morphological" context, as well as any other.

The archaic societies Mauss reviewed were all "segmental" in their morphology. They were all societies based on the clan, or "great families," much less divided internally than modern Western nations. The individuals were "less serious, avaricious and selfish than we are" (1923–1924:79). The forms of "contract," making peace, exchanging goods and hospitality, and providing mutual aid were all undertaken by the groups or by individuals representing groups. And there was either complete trust or complete mistrust, no middle ground. Groups could either run away from each other, resort to arms, or "come to terms." Festival and warfare lie close together. The successful primitive and archaic societies substituted "alliance, gift and commerce for war, isolation and stagnation" (1923–1924:80).[2]

---

[2]Raymond Firth (1957b:222) says that Mauss misread some of Malinowski's *Kula* data, but the mistakes he notes seem trivial. Aside from data, Firth says that Mauss tried to read in the *Kula* exchange his own "mystical notion" about the spirit of a gift attempt-

When Malinowski and Mauss inveigh against the holders of a view of "economic man," they are doing so in a strongly empirical, inductive sense.[3] That is, they present actual data on the behavior and institutions *as found* among certain primitive peoples. In interpreting these findings about property and exchange they also present their negative findings: the assumptions of formal, market-oriented economists about human beings simply do not apply usefully to these primitive societies. This kind of negativism has long been an important aspect of ethnological theory, particularly when based on fieldwork.

KARL POLANYI

An economic historian (or historical economist), Polanyi wrote a book, *The Great Transformation* (1944), that further attempted to correct the assumptions of formal economists about their notions of the age and ubiquity of the free market system. In preparing this book he made good use of such ethnologists as Firth, Malinowski, and numerous others, and for the first time he defined and used the two important concepts, *reciprocity* and *redistribution*, in the context of exchange.

Reciprocity is exemplified by the *Kula* in large scale and in small scale by the sexual division of labor in a family, but as Mauss argued, it is broadly characteristic of all social dealings. And there is no "free gift": the principle of *symmetry* in institutional patterning facilitates reciprocity. Redistribution, on the other hand, is mainly carried out under a chief; the principle of *centricity* characterizes its pattern.[4]

---

ing to return to its original possessor. It may be disputed, but it seems possible that Mauss was making a figurative use of the Maori *hau* without making it an explanation, since the explanation discussed above seems structurally and functionally adequate and not mystical.

[3]We should note at this point that when ethnologists like Malinowski and Mauss criticize economists and economic theory it is really only one brand of economist—though a prominent one. The economists themselves have long been divided into two main camps, a traditional one deriving from Adam Smith—like laissez-faire, free market assumptions of price and monetary theory, with individual consumers, producers, and firms making rational, conscious, "economizing" choices of scarce alternative means in relation to particular ends. This is "formal" economics, earlier called "microeconomics." It is this kind of economic theory that is opposed by Malinowski and Mauss.

Opposed to this have been such "macroeconomists" as Lord Keynes, who was interested in national economic *systems* as wholes, and earlier, Veblen and his followers, who were concerned with "institutional" aspects of economic systems. Those opposed to microeconomics also argue that it is far too deductive to apply to most empirically *real* economic systems.

[4]Polanyi (1944:48–49). His fourth chapter, "Societies and Economic Systems," presents nicely the idea that the economic system is embedded in the social system as "a mere function of it."

Following World War II, Polanyi chaired a seminar of volunteers (Columbia University faculty and graduate students) which included several ethnologists and out of which came the very influential *Trade and Market in the Early Empires* (1957). This book was the major catalyst in the formation of what became the "substantivist" position, which raised a critical challenge to microeconomists.

Polanyi's 1953 essay "Semantics of General Economic History" did not receive much more than local notice at Columbia, but when it was reprinted as "Anthropology and Economic Theory" in Fried's *Readings in Anthropology* (1959), it reached a much wider audience in general ethnological theory and provided the basis and definitions for the two meanings of economics now known as "formal" and "substantive."

According to Polanyi, the concept *economic* has, in common usage, become a compound of two meanings that have independent roots. "The substantive meaning of economic derives from man's dependence for his livelihood upon nature and his fellows" (1953:162). It has to do with the means by which a society's material wants are satisfied. The formal meaning, on the other hand, is a set of assumptions deriving from the logical character of the rational action of individuals confronted by a choice of scarce means to be employed for achieving given ends. These two meanings have nothing in common: the former is factual, the latter a form of logic. They are different as the laws of nature differ from the laws of mind (1953:163).

The confusion seems to have had its origin in the applicability of formal economics to the relatively modern operations of the "free market" in the Western world, involving money payments for goods and services. These became quantifiable as prices, much of the material provisioning of people also can be seen as involving their rational choices in allocating their scarce means (money, tools, and effort). The considerable success of economic analyses in modern markets secured the bond between substantive fact and formal logic. (The considerable *lack* of success in many questions also led, as noted above, to the rise of rival theories of "institutionalism" and other macroeconomic arguments).

The question, as put by Polanyi, is not to be answered in terms of the rightness or wrongness of a formal meaning over a substantive one. The formal is based on a set of assumptions that make an analysis of, say, prices more or less useful in a given society. And, as in any set of scientific hypotheses about the relations of different phenomena, such as supply and demand, temperature and pressure (of a gas), or mass and distance (in a gravitational field), it is understood that that formula includes the limiting proviso, *all other factors held constant*. Formalist assumptions as such, therefore, are not empirically right or wrong. The substantive position, on the other hand, simply asserts the right to investigate empirically how a given society goes about provisioning itself and thus to use, discard, or modify any of the formalist assumptions or to invent new ones in order to render the economy being investigated as intelligible as possible. In other words, the substantivist regards the formalist assumptions as culture-bound and possibly ethnocentric when applied to a primitive or archaic society. What must be done first is an empirical investigation of the ways the provisioning aspect of the primitive society in question is *instituted*.

> The human economy, then, is embedded and enmeshed in institutions, economic and non-economic. The inclusion of the latter is vital. For religion or government may be as important for the structure and functioning of the economy as are monetary institutions or the improvement of tools that lighten the toil of labor. (1953:168)

Polanyi makes a further very important point of clarification about the institution of an economic process and the way it is embedded in the society. A society is culturally and socially *integrated* in various ways and by various means, and such things as production, land, and labor are involved in it.

> Empirically, we find the major forms of integration to be reciprocity, redistribution and exchange. Reciprocity denotes movements between correlative points of symmetrical groupings in society; redistribution designates movements toward an allocative center and out of it again; exchange refers to vice-versus movements taking place as between "hands" under a market system. Reciprocity, then, requires as its background, symmetrically arranged groupings; redistribution is dependent upon some measure of centricity in the group; exchange, in order to produce integration requires the presence of a system of price-making markets. It is apparent that the different forms of integration involve the presence of definite institutional supports. (1953:169)

The emphasis on institutions helps to signify that these forms of integration are not simply societal aggregates of persons behaving as individuals; the personal behavior of individuals does not add up to symmetrically arranged groupings, a redistributive chieftancy, or a market system. The formalist microeconomists, by contrast, take the production, exchange, and prices of land, goods, and labor to be the statistical outcome of individuals' (and firms') decisions, no matter what kind of culture.

Similarly, Polanyi points out that by using a substantive meaning of *trade*, the procurement of goods can be investigated in primitive and archaic systems when it is not a part of a money and market network. There are three kinds of trade, not just our familiar market trade; the other two are gift trade and administered trade. In the last two forms of exchange, prices are traditional, customary, subject to treaty negotiations, and so on, but only in market trade is price closely related to supply and demand considerations. Again, as noted above, gift and administered trade is "not so much an individual as a group activity" (1953:175). The value attached to a good is not a statistical outcome of numerous decisions made in production and purchase, as in market trade. How value is achieved and understood is a complex problem to be empirically ascertained by investigation.

It should be emphasized again that Polanyi is not saying that "capitalist" trade, as functioning within a money and market context, does not exist, but that there are other forms of exchange as well and we should devise means to analyze any of them in terms of their own characteristics.

VI

SOCIETY AND CULTURE

That there is a "something" distinctive of the be-
havior of humankind alone among all animals has
been recognized and argued about for millennia.
This something also has been seen as changeable
through time, so that general stages of its evolution
from primitive to civilized manifestations were
noted. More specifically, and of consuming interest
to all ethnologists (and to many people long before
the birth of ethnology), was the tendency of this
something to speciate itself along ethnic lines, so
that one observes a something not only distinguish-
ing humans from apes and primitive peoples from
modern but also region from region, tribe from
tribe, and one modern nation from another.

After centuries of debate in Western civilization,
this something has come to be called culture rather
widely in ethnology and some other intellectual cir-
cles, although the tendency has been combatted by
Radcliffe-Brown's and British social anthropology's
version of the social and social structure. Fairly
closely related to this dichotomy is the controversy
over how this general characteristic of human so-
cial behavior is to be studied and explained: Does it
yield to the positivistic, deterministic discovery of
its own laws, or is it really only an aspect of indeter-
minant mentality?

At the outset of our discussion of the major con-
troversies set off by attempts to define and study
this something, it is useful to try to avoid some of

the difficulties with a few logical strictures. Ethnologists have long studied primitive societies and described them in ways that show a considerable, if only implicit, agreement as to what their subject matter is. This may be called ethnology's predefinitional phase. Yet attempts to define the subject matter of ethnology lead to much less than expectable agreement. This suggests that certain distinct and ultimate aims of the definers are at issue rather than the nature of the subject matter. The disagreements are exacerbated when the definitions are actually attempts to identify what the definer feels theoretically to be the most important or essential attribute or the most distinguishing feature—what the subject matter basically is. *Sometimes what the subject basically is suggests an appropriate methodology for its study, and we then become mixed up in individual methodological preferences and hypotheses rather than useful definitions of the subject matter.*

As a corollary to the above, it may be stated that there seem to be two very different conceptions of a definition. One kind begins with a concept—the name of something—that is somehow received from the cultural milieu and is then explored—we try to define it properly. The other conception of definition begins by first observing things and then classifying them—we give them names only after observation. The two conceptions are usually called real *and* nominal *in the philosophy of science.*

Real definitions are involved with concepts which we have already received from history or the culture and language, so that they are part of our vocabulary. Ideally we should try to define them when we encounter misunderstandings and vagueness in usages. A real definition can be tested by a study of the usages of the concept and attempts can be made to define it accurately—to sharpen it or to draw careful boundaries—meanwhile attempting to remain within the most usual predefinitional meaning. There is an a priori–ness about it, but one finds its relative truth can be test-

ed. There is a grave danger, of course, that because any substantive concept can be meaningful in its connotation *and definable in those terms, it will be thought of as* denoting *some aspect of reality ("werewolf," "mermaid," "abominable snowman" become phenomenalistic entities). The non-philosophical man-in-the-street tends to feel that if a definition of a concept adequately defines it by its connotations, then it is true. But what a thing is, by its definition, is not the same thing, logically, as what it is* like—*that is, what its important properties are, what it denotes. This confusion has been a source of mischief in ethnology. But the major trouble has been in failing to distinguish real from nominal definitions.*

Nominal definitions are made arbitrarily, in order to classify and distinguish one order of phenomena usefully from others—they are not discovered (or thought to be), but invented. Because such definitions are arbitrary they can be various, each serving different intellectual purposes. The something that is the agreed-upon predefinitional subject matter of ethnology can be called culture, *as it has been, and nominally defined in one way if the purpose is to distinguish the peculiar humanness of our behavior from primate behavior in general. It can be defined in a very different way if its processes and developments are at issue; and in still another if the structure and function of particular ethnic social identities are to be compared. A very general—a long and thus not very useful—definition can be made to include all of the above.*

The source of most of our controversies about culture and society is related to the confusion engendered by the use (or misuse) of the real type of definition, especially the failure to distinguish arguments about essential properties of the subject (and often a methodology) from a received predefinitional meaning. As we saw in earlier chapters, for example, the definition of kinship terms implied in the use of the term kinship *confused Morgan (but not McLennan) as to what the terms really were.*

The confusion over totemism *is also a notable case in point, and Boas seemed to have a glimmering of the difficulty when he said (correctly, but awkwardly) that totemism was an "artificial" (i.e., nominal) construct of our own, not corresponding closely enough to the great variety of forms called by that name (a test of a real definition). A* logical *question about totemism is whether the concept seems useful when defined and used in a certain specified way (nominally); from there we may go on to explore its properties. It may be suggested at this point that we have received the words* society *and* culture *from the past and treated them as though they refer to different kinds of things. But they should not be treated as different entities but as different forms of abstract classifications; how they may be redefined should depend on the aims and methods of research. If they contain, however implicitly,* hypotheses *about the phenomena, then they should be recognized as such, otherwise the dice are loaded—as in the study of status terms when they are called* kinship systems, *implying in that way that their properties include genealogical descent (kinship) as well as important functional interrelationships (systems).*

16

The Superorganic

The conception of a science of the "social" is usually attributed to Auguste Comte, who wrote an expository book about the new science, for which he coined the word *sociology*. Most of Comte's attitudes and ideas came from his teacher, Saint-Simon. In turn, Saint-Simon was a true child of the French Enlightenment, a positivistic current which ran through the Encyclopaedists and back to Montesquieu. These are merely mentioned here, but it is desirable to point out that in the fuller discussion we give below of Émile Durkheim and the French Academic School we find a long national history of positivistic, rationalistic, anticlerical attitudes toward the study of society.

In Great Britain a rather similar eighteenth-century phenomenon occurred, particularly in the persons of the "moral philosophers" David Hume, Adam Smith, and Adam Ferguson. In their case, as with the French sociologists, the discussion of social institutions involved a large amount of data of the kind that later ethnologists would call culture. But the concept of "the social" or "society," defined in such a way that it tended, as a structure, to oppose in aims and methods the concept of *culture*, had not been broached, for the latter notion was not yet in consistent usage. The controversy had to wait for the transfer of one variety of the concept from Germany to the English-speaking world.

The verb *to culture* in the sense of "to cultivate" (originally the soil, eventually the person) is very old, and the modern humanistic sense of it as enlightenment and refinement of taste is as old as the conception of "civilized." We need not concern ourselves with culture and civilization in these senses. *Custom, moeurs, l'esprit des nations*, the *superorganic*, and *social heritage* are all terms quite close to some of the notions involved in the later Tylorian conception of culture and (in part) to the still later Boasian conception. A more essential ingredient in the latter general sense seems to have had its birth in Germany, but we must take note of two divergent purposes and trends which took place there (aside from the usual use of *culture* and *civilization* to connote refinement).

The French and British Enlightenment epochs, as was just noted, contained many strands of thought which were finally to lead to a view of human behavior, particularly to the history of nations and the evolution of civilizations, which involved a positivistic, naturalistic, and rationalistic attitude, and, more importantly for our present sketch, a sense of the systemic, organismic interrelationship of the institutions and other parts of society. This heritage was an important intellectual base for such evolutionists as Herbert Spencer in England and Émile Durkheim in France, helping to create respectability for their scientific efforts. In Germany matters were different, for there remained two opposing views about the study of human society. There was a strong positivistic, natural history tradition, especially as manifested by the wide-ranging German geographers, the stern, positivistic materialism of Marx and Engels, and the somewhat related but later "neo-positivism" of Max Weber. Equally powerful were the historical–philosophical schools sometimes labeled neo-Kantian, the Baden School, and Southwest German philosophy.

It became commonplace in Germany to see the opposed sides as represented by the labels *Naturwissenschaften* (natural sciences) and *Geisteswissenschaften* (spiritual sciences). In the former, the methods of science, comparison, induction, and the formulation of laws were felt to be appropriate to the study of human society; in the latter, Dilthey's *Verstehen* (intuitive, subjective understanding) was felt to be the appropriate method. These have also been called the *nomothetic* and *idiographic* methods, respectively.

The *Geisteswissenschaften* attitude lay at the very basis of the attitude toward culture held by such of Boas' immediate predecessors as Wilhelm Windelband, Heinrich Rickert, and above all Wilhelm Dilthey. When this (and possibly the work of Theodor Waitz [1858]) was reworked in Boas' mind by his field experiences, there emerged in the United States a sense of "cultural psychology" that Radcliffe-Brown was impelled to oppose directly.[1]

Geisteswissenschaften has been translated variously, but we must note that the context of its use was in opposition to *Naturwissenschaften*. *Geist* is "spectre," "spirit," "soul," sometimes "ge-

---

[1]"Cultural psychology" is a useful concept, used often by A. L. Kroeber after he had stopped using "social" for "superorganic," finally changing it to "culture." See particularly his article "The Possibility of a Social Psychology" (1918) as reprinted with comment in his collected essays (1952). A whole chapter (Chapter 15) in his text *Anthropology* (1923) is titled "Cultural Psychology."

nius," but as Rickert argued (see Kroeber 1949:123–124), this was an attempt to talk about culture without using that word (which in Germany in usual parlance meant refinement). Culture in this sense was a mental phenomenon: socially shared attitudes, values, habits of mind—the "folkways," "spirit," or "genius" of a people.

There had also been at least one explicit usage of the concept "culture" in Germany that approximated the modern meaning Tylor was to give it in his pathfinding work *Primitive Culture* (1871). This appeared in the works of Gustav Klemm, who between 1843 and 1852 published his ten volumes of the *Allgemeine Culturgeschichte der Menschheit* and in 1854 and 1855 his two-volume *Allgemeine Cultur-wissenschaft*. Klemm sometimes uses the word in the sense of cultivation, but mostly he uses it in the sense of the superorganic possessed by all human societies (as distinct from all animal societies) and as distinguished into specific, qualitatively different kinds. In Volume I (1843:I:21) he "defines" culture with a list of examples of cultural activities that includes customs, arts and skills, domestic and public life in peace or war, religion, science, and art. In one place Klemm makes a statement that is startling in its modernity: "It was Voltaire who first put aside dynasties, king lists, and battles, and sought what is essential in history, namely culture, as it is manifest in customs, in beliefs and in forms of government" (1843:I:18).

E. B. Tylor acknowledges his indebtedness to Klemm,[2] but since Tylor entitles his most famous book *Primitive Culture* and begins the book with a definition of culture, he is thought of as the most significant innovator of this concept, at least in English-speaking ethnology. Tylor said: "Culture, or civilization . . . is that complex whole which includes knowledge, belief, art, law, morals, custom, and any other capabilities and habits acquired by man as a member of society" (1871:1). (This laundry list type of definition suffers from not offering a characteristic which can tell us what culture is *not*—other animals acquire habits as members of a society.)

As we shall see, many ethnologists have conducted their research using *superorganic, society, civilization,* or *social structure* instead of *culture* without doing any damage. At this point it would seem that any of these might be used interchangeably and, conversely, that any of them might have a very different meaning and theory attached to it.

For these reasons, and to stay above the struggle for a while, we

[2]In *Researches into the Early History of Mankind* (1865:13) and *Primitive Culture* (1871:1, 64). Most of the information and references noted above may be found in Kroeber and Kluckhohn (1952:Part I).

hereafter use the relatively uncontroversial (perhaps because now lit-tle-used) word *superorganic*. Spencer was the first to use the word, but as we shall see, he was inconsistent in his use of it, and he held some assumptions about the nature of society which we may not want to hold today. But since his usage has gone out of style, we may now freely redefine and use the word. Kroeber, in his important essay "The Superorganic" (1917), used the word much more aptly than Spencer to distinguish the methods and subject matter of ethnology and what he calls "history" (to be discussed later) from the biological sciences in general. Without now going into the various aspects of Kroeber's essay that aroused such controversy, let us note at this initial point that there has been widespread agreement among proponents of both the concepts "culture" and (human) "social structure" that these concepts refer to things and events peculiar to human society. The general roots of human behavior are to be found in our biological nature, to be sure, but manners, customs, technologies, laws, religions, governments, arts, and kinship systems are vastly different in historical time and geographical space, and the methods, techniques, and assumptions of the biological sciences (including psychology) are incapable of explain-ing these differences. For example, biology studies only general things such as the physiology of the human need to eat; it will not explain the existence of food taboos or the differences between French and Can-tonese cuisine. So, all we need to know for our next purpose is that *superorganic* remains a purposely vague term synonymous with that in human behavior and its various products and institutions which is not explicable in its variable manifestations as biological (or "racial"). When it is necessary to be more specific, we can use a qualifying adjective or advert to Tylor's definition of culture. This is purposely not a formal definition, but most readers should know now what in general is being referred to; anyone who does not will understand soon by the context of its usage.

HERBERT SPENCER–ÉMILE DURKHEIM

Durkheim's attack on Spencer brings up a major problem about the relationship of motivation, rationality, and purposes of human beings as individuals with respect to the growth, development, function, and structure of the solidary society. Although Durkheim singled out Spencer for special critical treatment, particularly in his first impor-tant book, *The Division of Labor in Society* (1893), he could as well have included Tylor and Walter Bagehot and the many British intellec-tual descendants of Adam Smith, James Mill, and Jeremy Bentham, all of whom saw the superorganic as the result of individuals' interests, and all of whom emphasized rationality.[3]

Spencer's major preoccupations in his theoretical arguments for a science of society involved: (1) the analogy of a society to a biological *organism*, featuring functional interdependence of specialized parts; (2) *evolutionism*, featuring an increase in specialization of function and differentiation of structures; (3) the idea of society as *super-organic* (he always hyphenated the word), something "beyond" the purely biological; and (4) cause-and-effect *determinism* of an impersonal sort.[4] His emphasis on individualism and competition and the survival of the fittest—in short, his social Darwinism (which, since his ideas about competition anticipated Darwin's, should more properly be called "social Spencerism")—do not figure in Durkheim's rebuttals. Let us examine these main currents in Spencer's sociology at greater length, following them with Durkheim's critiques.

1.   *The organismic analogy.* A society is more than an aggregation of individual persons, Spencer argues, and must be regarded as an "entity," because the relationships ("arrangements") among them have a general persistence—thus the whole is an individuality as distinguished from the individuality of its parts. The life of the aggregate is a matter separate from the lives of the units of both an organism and a society. The cells of the living tissues of an organism are born, live, die, and are replaced countless times over, but the life span of the organism is far longer. Similarly with a society, the integrity of the whole and of its specialized functional divisions is maintained in spite of the deaths of its component citizens (barring some huge catastrophe).

Spencer was frequently attacked for this simple analogy, usually by attributing to him more than he had intended. In the revised edition of *Principles of Sociology* (1885:I:592) he stated, in answer:

> Here let it once more be distinctly asserted that there exist no analogies between the body politic and a living body, save those necessitated by that mutual dependence of parts which they display in common. Though, in foregoing chapters, sundry comparisons of social structures and functions in the human body, have been made, they have been made only because structures and functions in the human body furnish familiar illustrations of structures and functions in general. (1885:I:592)

[3]Durkheim often points up his basic disagreement with "the economists" and "utilitarians," and these men were intellectual forebears of most economists not only in Britain but in France.

[4]In this section I have mostly used Robert Carneiro's excellently edited abridgement of the third edition of Spencer's unwieldy three-volume *Principles of Sociology* (1876). Any other sources used will be noted.

2. *Evolution.* The organic analogy is further pursued by Spencer in his conception of societal evolution. First, it should be noted that Spencer applied his formulation to the whole cosmos, with successive stages arising as inorganic, organic, and finally superorganic phenomena. This differentiation of matter is a movement from homogeneity to heterogeneity, from simple to complex, with increased differentiation of structure. This scheme of cosmic evolution is also applicable separately to the evolution of both living bodies and societies. Growth in the size of both kinds of bodies is matched by an increase in development, that is, by more functionally discrete parts united in the larger structure. This development is not an inevitably linear form of progress but is "divergent and redivergent." As Carneiro says:

> "He saw evolution as a process of successive branchings in which increased heterogeneity goes hand in hand with increased adaptation. This view of evolution stands in direct contrast to that which sees evolution as a simple series of stages. Indeed, the more one reads of *Principles of Sociology* the clearer it becomes that Spencer was far more concerned with *process* than with *stages.* (1967:xlii–xliii)

Spencer did sometimes speak of stages of development; that is, he classified societies in terms of the complexity of their sociopolitical development as simple, compound, doubly compound, and trebly compound. Nothing much came of this, however, and the scheme not only was not used by others, but evidently was not even noticed enough to be criticized.

3. *Society as super-organic.* Spencer meant by this term that societies were to be understood as entities that were more than, and different from, the sum of their individual parts. He did not use this concept to distinguish the societies of human beings, however, from those of other animals. Tylor had done this with his famous definition of the concept of "culture" precisely to make this point in 1871. It is evident, however, that although Spencer did not explicitly speak of the distinctiveness of human social behavior, much of what he wrote exhibited this point.[5] It is interesting, and probably important, that Spencer was interested in causation, and thus in social structure, rather than mentality, and he evidently did not find a use for Tylor's

---

[5]For example, early in *Principles of Sociology* (1876:7–8) he is at pains to point out that a human society bears an "extreme unlikeness" to an individual organism in an important respect. An organism is a "concrete whole," while the parts of a society are "discrete," "dispersed," "not in contact, they nevertheless affect one another through intervening spaces, both by emotional language and by the language, oral and written, of the intellect."—in other words, by culture.

conception of culture. Tylor, on the other hand, was expressly interested in rational human thought. Spencer seems not to have spoken of this difference in perspective (between himself and Tylor), but he did make an interesting comment on his differences with Comte. In a letter to George H. Lewes, an admirer of Comte, Spencer said:

> What is Comte's professed aim? To give a coherent account of the progress of *human conceptions*. What is my aim? To give a coherent account of the progress of the *external world*. Comte proposes to describe the necessary, and the actual, filiation of *ideas*. I propose to describe the necessary, and the actual, filiation of *things*. Comte professes to interpret the genesis of our *knowledge of nature*. My aim is to interpret, as far as it is possible, the genesis of the phenomena *which constitute nature*. The one end is *subjective*. The other is *objective*. How then can the one be the originator of the other? (Carneiro 1967:xxii)

Carneiro (1967:Footnote 129) suggests that Spencer failed to state plainly a distinction between societies of humans and the other social animals, not because he was unaware of it, but because his evolutionism led him to emphasize the continuity of nature, to include humans, rather than discontinuity. (After all, in those days of Darwinian controversy, the man-in-the-street as well as many intellectuals did not see mankind as a part of nature but as a special creation.) The evolutionary idea of the emergence of distinct levels of phenomena did not play much of a role in the thinking of his time.

4. *Determinism*. Carneiro's point has undoubted merit, but perhaps it ought to be supplemented by another. It would seem from some of our earlier chapters that even certain ethnologists of later days are more concerned than Spencer with *humanness*, with its discontinuity with the rest of nature, when they focus on thought, mind, mentality, or, in Kroeber's term, "cultural psychology." As with some of the earlier Germans and E. B. Tylor, the concern with mentality logically required a conception of something like Tylor's "culture" and Kroeber's later "superorganic." But Spencer's main interest, as he said, was in interpreting nature, not knowledge, and he saw society as an entity conforming to mechanistic laws. He evidently decided, therefore, to ignore mentality, or thought, as a creative or deterministic aspect of man's social life, except in the simplest way.[6] This probably is what was

---

[6]Spencer published his single volume *The Study of Sociology* in 1873, antedating the first volume of *Principles of Sociology* by three years. This was a methodological and hortatory treatise arguing for the great value of a true science of sociology. Here, more explicitly than in *Principles of Sociology*, he laid bare his opposition to the doctrines of theological thought, free will, and the "great men" theories of history.

to bother Durkheim the most. Durkheim, equally positivistic, felt that a sort of mental construct ("conscience collective") should necessarily be included in the scientific sociological endeavor—but not merely in the intellectualistic sense.

Émile Durkheim, it seems readily apparent, was much indebted to Spencer for the idea of a true science of comparative sociology, the organismic analogy, conceptions of specialization of function, differentiation of structures, the relationship of all these to societal integrations, and much more. Durkheim's criticisms of Spencer should be thought of as supplemental; in a sense, Durkheim used Spencer as a springboard for important further flights (Carneiro 1967:1; Parsons 1961:x).

1. *The organismic analogy.* Spencer had been at pains to show the organizational similarity of an individual organism to a society. To his mind, as to others before him (especially Adam Smith), the key aspect of this analogy was *function*, the specialization of parts "doing something" ever more efficiently as they became more particularized toward the ongoing process and progress of the whole arrangement—"the need which it supplies." Why do individuals and groups become specialized? Do they perceive the social needs and decide to be of aid? Or do they find that in so doing they can serve themselves better? If social solidarity is in fact achieved by furthering the division of labor, what is the position of the individual minds in the furthering of this solidarity?

Durkheim's whole book, *The Division of Labor in Society* (1893), is not exactly a sustained attack on Spencer (although it is sometimes taken as such), but Spencer seems to be criticized by name far more often than others. Yet the book has a positive side in its attempt to make clear, in the context of the relation of the organismic division of labor to social solidarity, that there is another sort of superorganic entity fostering both social solidarity and the division of labor—and this is not "a simple resultant of individual natures," as Durkheim maintains Spencer believed (1893:349). These "individual natures" of Spencer's thought would increasingly tend to perceive how their welfare and happiness (or reduction of misery) could be related to increasing, or maintaining, the division of labor, for specialization clearly increases productivity.

Durkheim calls into question the organismic analogy in terms of its function in promoting civilization and higher social solidarity. First, he argues that there are two distinct kinds of "positive solidarity":

mechanical solidarity, derived from similitudes; and *organic* solidarity, which is related to the division of labor. The *segmental* type of society is of small "hordes" (bands) associated on the basis of equality and resemblance. Even the individuals in segmental societies resemble one another more than in the "organized societies" that have organic solidarity. It is in centralized organization that we find the beginnings of individuation; therefore it is not the desires of individuals that formed the division of labor.

Thus Spencer has it all backwards. "Society is itself, not the secondary condition, but the determining factor in progress. It is a reality which is no more our work than the external world, and to which, consequently, we must submit in order to exist. It is because it changes that we must change" (Durkheim 1893:344).

2. *Evolution.* Durkheim shows how the more primitive segmental societies have been displaced or changed by the development of organized structures. Is this development the cause of the disappearances, or vice versa? Neither, for there is yet another factor in this evolution. *"The division of labor varies in direct ratio with the volume and density of societies, and, if it progresses in a continuous manner in the course of social development, it is because societies become regularly denser and generally more voluminous"* (1893:262). This is reminiscent of Spencer's discussion of growth accompanied by development, but Spencer's emphasis was on development (specialized differentiated parts) suggested by varied environments. Durkheim has it the other way: "If work becomes divided more as societies become more voluminous and denser, it is not because external circumstances are more varied, but because the struggle for existence is more acute" (1893:266). But specialization is accompanied by competition only at first; "it is a mellowed *dénouement*," as interdependence increases.

3. *Society as superorganic.* Spencer coined the word *super-organic,* but as we have seen, it was related to his analogy between society and an individual organism; hence *supra-* or *hyper-organismic* would have been less confusing. But for most of his life and in most of his work, Durkheim endeavored to demonstrate that there was a subject matter to be studied that really was an entity *sui generis,* a subject matter that should not be thought of as analogous to an organism or studied by methods related to the biological or psychological sciences: it was *supra*individual, an aspect of social life, but not merely people in association, either.

Social solidarity, according to Durkheim, is not a product of the division of labor, of individual self-interest, or of reason but of a system of beliefs and sentiments, the collective conscience,[7] which constrains the individual's biological–psychological urges. This system does not express the individual's interests and operations but regulates them— indeed, in some respects it *creates* them. Thus, it is not the sentiments and emotions of individual parents and children that create a particular form of a family but the opposite; it is the society's collective conscience about appropriate family life which is responsible for the usual sentiments and emotions held by the family members. This is, of course, quickly suggested by anthropological data, which attest to the widely varying forms of family life found in different societies around the world.

Durkheim's main objection to Spencer's view of the superorganic was that he did not consistently treat social institutions as truly *sui generis*. This argument is put on a broad theoretical basis in his book *The Rules of Sociological Method* (1895). His principal charge against sociologists, including Spencer, was that they were reductionists, not treating the phenomena of human society as "social facts" on their own terms but in terms of the psychology, or wills, purposes, and rationality of individual persons, who (normally) are supposed to have utilitarian ends in mind.

Durkheim felt that human social life, its "social facts," had two distinct aspects: (1) the social substratum, or the associational morphology of society; and (2) the *collective representations* with which the collective conscience somehow creates the symbols, emotions, and values that the people share. These two may be thought of as the "objective" and "subjective" aspects of society: that is, the behavior and mentality of a people in the social context have two aspects from the point of view of an observer. One is the actual physical association of the people in, say, a clan in central Australia; the other is the beliefs, values, and emotions associated with the totemic rites of the clan. Which causes which? Better, which provides the environment that constrains the others? Perhaps they are simply two aspects of the same thing.

The increased division of labor in societal evolution, Durkheim said,

---

[7]*Conscience collective* was Durkheim's usual concept. *Conscience* in French means both "consciousness" and "conscience." I think that the latter should be the translation, most of the time at least, since many of the habits, sentiments, and emotions alluded to are not necessarily at a conscious level. But they do provide "moral" constraints, close to our sense of "conscience." Remember, Durkheim used this conception often in the context of opposing Spencer's and the "economists'" idea of *conscious* rational choices being the cause of solidarity. Beware of the English translations of Durkheim that use "collective *consciousness*," for it woefully distorts his message.

was due not to its perceived utility—though we now perceive its utility once it is accomplished—but to the increased volume and density of the social substratum. Thus the objective society has some priority over the subjective in this particular explanation. But what about totemism? *Les formes élémentaires* (1912) was a product of Durkheim's later life and reflects his more developed interest in the subjective, the power of collective representations. Here the objective clans are, to be sure, closely related to the subjective aspects of the totemic symbols, but if anything it was the subjective that gave shape to the objective—and if, in the rituals, the participants were "celebrating society," no straightforward utility, need, or purpose was evident. Durkheim's notions of causality need further examination.

4. *Determinism.* The main motivating theme in Durkheim's scientific view of society was his antireductionism. Unlike Spencer, he argued that there was a profound gulf between the organic nature of man and the social, and never can the specifics and varieties of social life be explained in terms of the general organic characteristics of man. Similarly, the methods and assumptions of the organic sciences, including psychology and all studies of the individual, are inappropriate to the study of social phenomena. There is a body of social data to be studied as real *things*, even when—especially when—they seem to be spiritual or symbolic phenomena. Even when these things and their interrelationships, their functions and the laws of their behavior, seem to be truly mental, if they are shared socially they must be studied in their own terms, not in terms of the wills, intentions, or processes of thought of individuals, for that is psychological reductionism. "Every time that a social phenomenon is directly explained by a psychological phenomenon, we may be sure that the explanation is false" (1895:104).

"We arrive, therefore, at the following principle: *The determining cause of a social fact should be sought among the social facts preceding it and not among the states of the individual consciousness*" (1895:110). The causes, functions, and results of social facts are to be found in some social end whose point is not primarily or immediately to serve individuals—although, of course, it does happen sometimes to serve the individual, for individual life is closely related to the collectivity. (For example, a public official or a man of technological genius may serve his individual nature at the same time that social gains are a happy consequence of his activity.)

Where does one look to find the causes of social change, progress, or evolution? Certainly not to some inherent tendency to improve ourselves or acquire greater happiness, for such are not causal laws which must be established between kinds of *social* facts. The causes of social

phenomena are internal to society. *"The first origins of all social processes of any importance should be sought in the internal constitution
of the social group"* (1895:113).

Durkheim often calls this internal constitution "the social milieu."
This consists of two kinds of elements, things and persons. Things are
material objects and other products of previous social activity, such as
laws, customs, literature, and art. These possess no motivating power,
although "they bear a certain weight on social evolution." The active
factor must be the persons, the human milieu itself. Of this there are
two main aspects: the size of the society and the "dynamic density," or
degree of concentration, of the group—the degree of interaction and
amount of social relationships.

Such could be said to be the substratum or associational basis of
social life. What holds it together—organizes it, constrains the natural
self-seeking propensities of human beings—are the beliefs, traditions,
and sentiments of the collectivity: the collective representations of the
collective conscience, a "moral milieu" in close relationship to the
social milieu, but not quite the same thing. Why do people feel con-
strained by these representations to serve the needs of the collectivity?
If it is indeed not founded on rational self-interest, what is the motivating impulse?

Durkheim says that the collective conscience is autonomous, that it
is above the will of individuals. But "will" is not the same thing as
emotions, sentiments, and feelings, and Durkheim's argument for the
autonomy of the social was grounded in some general conception of a
social psychology in which people saw or felt positive symbolic meanings related to the integrity of their society in such things as totems,
flags, rituals, and negative threats and fears, also symbolically represented in breaches of normal conduct or criminality. The collective
conscience was in some sense a collective worry about threats to the
well-being of the society, often only felt rather than intellectually con-
ceptualized—hence the importance of symbolic representations and
the coercive conceptions of good and duty allied with them (1895:liv,
Footnote 5).

> There is in every society a certain group of phenomena which may be differ-
> entiated from those studied by the other natural sciences. When I fulfill my
> obligations as brother, husband, or citizen, when I execute my contracts, I
> perform duties which are defined, externally to myself and my acts, in law and
> in custom. Even if they conform to my own sentiments and I feel their reality
> subjectively, such reality is still objective, for I did not create them; I merely
> inherited them through my education. (1895:1)

In sum, that which Durkheim thought was needed to supplement the positivism of Spencer's superorganic was something like a *Geisteswissenschaft* and the later Boasian conception of culture. It was *not* like Tylor's usage, however (never mind Tylor's actual definition of culture at the moment). Tylor used the concept as though reasoning minds were at work in a society, with culture a kind of precipitate. At times the reasoning was mistaken, as in his theories about the origin of religion being due to attempts to explain the inexplicable. But mainly Tylor was like Spencer, heritor of utilitarianism and rational positivism. Durkheim never really confronted Tylor's kind of positivism, and we are the poorer for this particular absence of controversy.

But Durkheim, in talking about what Boasians were finally to call culture, remains distinctive in his positivism, in his antireductionism, and in his insistence on the scientific causality and functions to be found among collective representations. These must be treated as real things, not "spirit"—as though they were something inexplicable. This brings us directly to the controversies among Boasians about the nature of culture, the relations of the individual to it, and the methods to be employed in its study.

A. L. KROEBER–EDWARD SAPIR

In 1917 A. L. Kroeber published his article "The Superorganic" in the *American Anthropologist*. By *superorganic*, in contrast to Spencer, he meant "culture," although often at that early date he used *the social* and *civilization* synonymously with *culture*. Kroeber begins with a discussion of the obvious distinction between biologically inherited physical traits, such as whales' flippers, birds' wings, and bears' fur, and the human ability to build boats and airplanes and make clothing.

It is a commonplace to attribute such obvious differences to man's superior intelligence. Kroeber grants that the intelligence of man is undoubtedly superior to that of other animals but maintains that that is not the most significant point of difference. The difference in intelligence is one of degree, but the difference between the organic and the "social" (cultural) is one of kind. "The beast has mentality, and we have bodies; but in civilization man has something that no animal has" (1917b:27). As a species, an animal "has no society [culture], and therefore no history. Man, however, comprises two aspects: he is an organic substance, that can be viewed as a substance, and he is also a tablet that is written upon" (1917b:32).

Much of "The Superorganic" is given over to separating the organic from the cultural in terms of the more specific racial versus cultural inheritance. Another common view that Kroeber singles out is that of the eugenics movement as being similarly mistaken for confounding the organic with the social (cultural) aspects of human behavior. Although he does not cite Durkheim, Kroeber seems equally intent on destroying reductionism. And, like Durkheim, he sees the cultural level as not only irreducible to the organic level but also not explicable in terms of individuals.[8]

Several pages of "The Superorganic" are devoted to antiindividualism and, strikingly, to laying to rest the myth of the "great man" in history.

> Mentality relates to the individual. The social or cultural, on the other hand, is in its essence non-individual. Civilization, as such, begins only where the individual ends; and whoever does not in some measure perceive this fact, even though only as a brute and ruthless one, can find no meaning in civilization, and history for him must be only a wearing jumble, or an opportunity for the exercise of art. (1917b:40)

In "The Superorganic," Kroeber was for the first time to present his argument (oft-repeated) about the significance of simultaneous inventions: Darwin and Wallace; Mendel's fortuitous discovery of the law of heredity and its simultaneous rediscovery by De Vries, Correns, and Tschermak, and several others. The consequences of this for theory should be noted. Here is a typical statement:

> If, therefore, anyone's interpretation of mentality is disturbed by some of the particular equivalences that have been suggested, he can easily find others that seem more just, without dissenting from the underlying principle that the march of history, or as it is the current custom to name it, the progress of civilization, is independent of the birth of particular personalities; since these apparently averaging substantially alike, both as regards genius and normality, at all times and places, furnish the same substratum for the social. (1917b:46)

A further but closely related aspect of Kroeber's idea of the superorganic is that it is discontinuous with biological evolution—there is no "missing link."

> The dawn of the social thus is not a link in a chain, not a step in a path, but a leap to another plane. It may be likened to the first occurrence of life in the hitherto lifeless universe, the hour when that one of infinite chemical combinations took place which put the organic into existence, and made it that from this moment on there should be two worlds in place of one. Atomic qualities and movements were not interfered with when that seemingly slight event took place; the majesty of the mechanical laws of the cosmos was not diminished;

---

[8]Clark Wissler (1916:200–201) said much the same thing a year earlier than Kroeber. I have not discussed Wissler's work because it did not attract any controversy.

but something new was inextinguishably added to the history of this planet. (1917b:49–50)

Kroeber ends with a related note that was characteristic of his whole life's work: whereas the preceding characterizations of culture sound much like Durkheim's, he remains consistently *anti*positivistic, idiographic rather than nomothetic. Hear him in the final sentences of "The Superorganic":

> The processes of civilizational activity are almost unknown to us. . . . The forces and principles of mechanistic science can indeed analyze our civilization; but in so doing they destroy its essence, and leave us without understanding of the very thing which we seek. The historian as yet can do little but picture. He traces and he connects what seems far removed; he balances; he interprets; but he does not really explain, nor does he transmute phenomena into something else. . . . What we all are able to do is to realize this gap, to be impressed by it with humility, and to go our paths on its respective sides without self-deluding boasts that the chasm has been bridged. (1917b:51)

Edward Sapir, in a six-page commentary on "The Superorganic" in the *American Anthropologist* ("Do We Need a Superorganic?" [1917]), begins by commending Kroeber's article, though with two interesting caveats. Mostly they have to do with overkill, or as Sapir puts it, "a too-rigidly classificationist or abstractionist tendency."

First, although the content of the individual's character is "overwhelmingly moulded by social traditions, . . . yet it is always the individual that really thinks and acts and dreams and revolts" (1917:442). And some individuals, of course, have indeed had the ability, the luck, and the right circumstances to impress themselves on civilization. To be sure, the average historian is apt to grossly exaggerate the influence of specific personalities, but depreciating this tendency should not lead us to eliminate completely the individual as a culture factor. "One has only to think seriously of what such personalities as Aristotle, Jesus, Mahomet, Shakespeare, Goethe, Beethoven mean in the history of culture to hesitate to commit oneself to a completely non-individualistic interpretation of history" (1917:443).[9]

---

[9]It may be of interest that several times in later years Sapir seems to contradict this. In his famous article, "Culture, Genuine and Spurious" (1924), he says that *culture* in the anthropological sense is something like the spirit or genius of a people but is not psychological or "pseudo-psychological" in the way these terms are often used. The culture is "historical" in origin, not psychological, biological, or racial (1924:84). Much later (1937), in his *Encyclopaedia of the Social Sciences* article "Custom" (a major aspect of, or near-synonym for, culture), he says: "The word custom is used to apply to the totality of behavior patterns which are carried by tradition and lodged in the group, as contrasted with the more random personal activities of the individual" (1937:658).

In his second caveat, Sapir objects to Kroeber's argument that just as in evolution life or organic nature transcended the inorganic, so does the social (cultural) constitute a similar "leap to another plane." "If I understand him rightly, he predicts a certain social 'force' whose gradual unfolding is manifested in the sequence of socially significant phenomena we call history." What Sapir finds objectionable is the idea that this is a distinct order of actual phenomena. Rather, it seems that Kroeber has not seized upon "the true nature of the opposition between history and non-historical science" (1917:443).

Sapir held that there is a mass of phenomena that are "ideally resolvable into inorganic, organic, and psychic processes." The social is not a distinct kind of thing, but only those reactions that depend on "social inheritance." This does not depend on any specifically new "force," but is merely "a heightening of psychic factors." "No doubt the growth of self-consciousness is largely involved in the gradual building up of this technique of social transference." But the study of the social is not the study of a new kind of irreducible subject, it is simply a *different kind of science*. "Social science is not psychology, not because it studies the resultants of a superpsychic or superorganic force, but because its terms are differently demarcated." Sapir argues that there are two kinds of sciences, "conceptual" and "historical" (or descriptive).[10] He feels that Kroeber has mixed up perspective and methodology with subject matter (this is like confusing real and nominal definitions). But the methods and perspectives that are essential to *history* can be applied not only to the social but even to the inorganic realm, as in geology. So, Sapir concludes, he and Kroeber do not differ fundamentally on what they mean in their conception of history and of the uniqueness of historical phenomena, but certainly this view needs no aid from a "superorganic," nor is it necessary to insist on eliminating the individual (1917:447).

FRANZ BOAS–A. L. KROEBER

About a year after the publication of "The Superorganic," Kroeber published "The Possibility of a Social Psychology" (1918), in which he reiterates an important aspect of his view of culture which we have already seen demonstrated more specifically in his 1909 article, "Classificatory Systems of Relationship." By asserting that cultural patterns (such as kinship terminologies) are psychological, he made himself

---

[10]This is evidently close to the *nomothetic* and *idiographic* distinction. Appropriately, Sapir's only footnote recommends to the readers the "penetrating analysis of the fundamental distinction between historical and natural science" by H. Rickert, one of the philosophers of the Southwest German school mentioned earlier.

widely misunderstood in 1909, but now he is beginning to clear up the confusion (though as recently as 1952 (1952:52, 173), in his commentary on his articles, he was still having to explain that he did not mean *psychology* in our usual usage, but the mental aspect of culture, or "conceptual patterning"). In addition, he is trying to straighten out a fundamental Boasian problem in cultural anthropology, a confusion between subject matter and methodology (once again, a confusion of real and nominal definitions).

Boas had much earlier made assertions that anthropology as science is really biology and psychology. He says: "Thus an examination of our problems suggests that the whole group of anthropological phenomena may be evanescent, that they may be at bottom biological and psychological problems, and that the whole field of anthropology belongs either to the one or to the other of these sciences" (1908:7). Boas ends a few pages later by forecasting that "anthropology will become more and more a method that may be applied by a great number of sciences, rather than a science by itself" (1908:10). Note the use of the word *science*; Boas thought of ethnology (cultural anthropology) as a "method" (Kroeber's "history"), not as a distinct kind of science.

Kroeber evidently had absorbed this view from Boas and elaborates (and clarifies) it in the following way (1918:53–54). There are four kinds of "equal reality" of natural phenomena: "matter and force as such, those of life as such, those of consciousness, and those of social life or culture. These four varieties of facts or experience may also be denominated as the inorganic, the directly organic or vital, the mentally organic or psychic, and the civilizational or superorganic or, better, superpsychic." There are four basic kinds of sciences corresponding to these levels of phenomena: "physical and chemical, in the realm of the inorganic; biological, in the domain of the organic as such; psychological, concerned with the psychic aspects of the organic or the mental as such; and social, operating with superorganic phenomena."

But there is another kind of division. "Data may be viewed directly as they present themselves; or we can seek to pass through them to the processes involved. On this basis the sciences are either historical and only incidentally concerned with mechanisms, or unhistorical and wholly devoted to the determination of mechanisms." This results in eight kinds of disciplines.

1. Superorganic phenomena: social psychology; cultural history.
2. Mental organic phenomena: psychology; biographic history.
3. Vital organic phenomena: physiology; natural history.
4. Inorganic phenomena: physics, chemistry; astronomy, geology.

It is evident in Kroeber's discussion of the above scheme that the term *social psychology* means a "processual science"—positivistic, deterministic, and dealing with the superorganic (cultural) phenomena. Why does such a science not exist, at least in terms of some successes? Comte and Spencer tried, but without great success. The reason seems to be reductionism. Comte's prescription was an old materialistic monism: "The very term 'sociology' carries the fatal defect of the overshadowing of the cultural by the subcultural." As for Spencer, even though he qualified his organic analogy by claiming that he was not identifying the social with the organic, he nevertheless used examples which were treated as though they were on a level with the organic. In short, Kroeber finds the same defects in Comte and Spencer that Durkheim went to great lengths to combat; furthermore, Durkheim wanted to establish a positivistic science of just what Kroeber miscalled social psychology—a processual science of culture. It is curious that Kroeber seems to be unaware of Durkheim's priority in this—or even of his existence.[11]

Here it seems evident that Kroeber had inherited from Boas the idea that the subject matter (culture) required "historical" (idiographic) *methods*, and he wanted to disentangle the two, which had been confused as one by the *Naturwissenshaften–Geisteswissenschaften* dichotomy.

In several other articles Kroeber tried to make it clear that an interest in "processes" can be distinguished from an interest in "events," just as "physiology" can be distinguished from "natural history." In 1935 he attempted to clarify his conception in the article, "History and Science in Anthropology." History, in his view, is not primarily or necessarily concerned with time sequences or documents, as in the public view of it, but with "descriptive integration." This means that the description, or re-creation, of a culture involves the attempt to preserve the whole context of phenomena—they are to be depicted in their patterns, or interrelationships. Science, on the other hand, "decomposes" phenomena in the attempt to discern processes, to analyze (1935:63).

These two approaches are applicable to any of the basic levels of phenomena, Kroeber feels, but clearly the inorganic level has been the main domain of processual science, whereas the historical approach was first used with human societies and still seems most productive at that, the superorganic, level. The historical approach began with a

[11]True, Durkheim's works had not been translated into English in 1918, but they were by 1952 when Kroeber was commenting at some length on the above essays—and of course Ph.D.'s in 1918 were supposed to read French as well as German.

concern with temporal sequences and the attempted reconstruction of the past in terms of documentary evidence. Anthropology is as likely to be concerned with space relations, however, but this does not invalidate an interest in the past. "If this is correct, the point often made, not only by Boas and his followers but by sociologists and functionalists, that history is legitimate and proper, but historical reconstruction unsound and sterile, loses much if not all validity" (1935:64). (This remark was to get Kroeber into hot water.)[12] Kroeber's main point here, something he emphasized all his life, was that *culture*, more than the organic or inorganic subjects, seems uniquely amenable to "descriptive integration" (idiographic) methods, which he calls history. He never did relinquish his conviction that the "patterns" (sometimes referred to as "configurations" or "styles") should be the main focus of interest. Although he did not deny causality ("science"), he certainly did not expect much of it in the realm of culture.[13]

With Sapir, Franz Boas shared a dislike for Kroeber's negation of the role of the individual. It is difficult to see why, but it was there, despite Boas' (and Sapir's) sharing of Kroeber's conviction that ethnology (or cultural anthropology) requires the historical method, which depicts mental patterns of a society (a "culture"). A letter to L. A. White from Clark Wissler (an associate of Boas' on the staff of the American Museum of Natural History for some years) may give a clue as to why Boas so persistently opposed Kroeber, and of course all determinists, on the issue of the role of the individual. It is a curious intellectual mix-up, for Kroeber carried many of Boas' ideas of the nature of culture to

[12]Boas (1936) objected to much of the way Kroeber had characterized him, particularly as one who was opposed to "historical reconstruction." He meant, he said, that reconstruction of "low probability" should be abjured. Also, for much of the article he misunderstood Kroeber's use of the word *history* (as "descriptive integration"), thinking of temporal sequences in the usual meaning.

[13]I do not burden this passage with the tens of citations that would bolster this contention far beyond the need. The first 150 pages of Kroeber's collection of his own essays, *The Nature of Culture* (1952), include 18 essays, all more or less directly on this point. I cannot refrain from mentioning a conversation I had with Kroeber when we were colleagues at Columbia University about 1951–1952. I had asked him how, among all the burdens of administration—chairman of the Department of Anthropology at Berkeley, editing the monographs of the *University of California Publications in American Archaeology and Ethnology*, holding office in the American Anthropological Association, and fieldwork—he had managed to write so much. His answer was, "I am very fortunate in that I do not need to revise my writings." Well, evidently he did not revise his manuscripts, but his published articles (see Part I of *The Nature of Culture*) were a continuous 18-fold printed revision of his idea about the superorganic patterning of culture and the "descriptive integration" of it. And see also elsewhere at greater length his *Configurations of Culture Growth* (1944) and *Style and Civilizations* (1957).

almost super-Boasian lengths of clarity and refinement. Wissler is evidently in some wonderment about Boas' disinclination to consider causation. He thoroughly rejected racism and biologistic explanation of cultural differences, but to Wissler it was not plain what Boas thought *was* the causal element. He says:

> The followers of Boas were fond of saying that the environment caused cultural differences, and so would Boas at times, but if pressed on the subject he would deny that too by asserting historical causes. What he meant was never clear. When Goldenweiser spoke of "fortuitous" causes, Boas would reject that too.
>
> I suspect that Boas had an unswerving belief in something like the freedom of the will, a feeling that man could do what he liked at any time, that he respected no limitations and so there were no laws of culture and no basis for prediction. His favorite expression was, "I am interested to observe what each tribe did at any given time."[14]

How Boasian, really, was Kroeber except for the matter of the role of the individual! Kroeber said much the same (as Boas' above-quoted statement) many times. For example, in describing his differences with Rivers on the subject of kinship systems, he says: "If I understand him correctly, he is interested in why things are, I primarily in how they are. His steadfast motive is to explain social phenomena, whereas I deliberately limit my purpose to characterizing them" (1917:387).

Boas said it again and again. For example, he said (quite neatly for him) in 1932:

> In short, the material of anthropology is such that it must needs be a historical science, one of the sciences the interest of which centers in the attempt to understand the individual phenomena rather than in the establishment of general laws which, on account of the complexity of the material, will be necessarily vague and, we might also say, so self-evident that they are of little help to a real understanding. (1932:258)

(Boas frequently used "understanding" in contexts like this—which suggests that he is thinking of historical *Verstehen* as propounded by Dilthey.)

But, against Kroeber's "The Superorganic," Boas says: "It seems hardly necessary to consider culture a mystic entity that exists outside the society of its individual carriers and that moves by its own force" (1928:245).

But cultures change and a dynamic lies somewhere; why cannot we "find" the laws of its behavior? Because "the forces that bring about the

---

[14]New York, March 31, 1943. Wissler, as noted above, regarded culture much as had Kroeber, as superorganic, suprapsychological (Wissler 1916, 1923).

changes are active in the individuals composing the social groups, not in the abstract culture" (1928:246). Or again: "The morphological classification of societies may call to our attention many problems. It will not solve them. In every case it is reducible to the same source, namely, the interaction between the individual and society" (1928:246). (Boas is apparently the source of Sapir's much quoted dictum, responding to Kroeber's "The Superorganic": "It is always the individual that really thinks and acts and dreams and revolts.")

Again, Boas says:

> The problems of the relation of the individual to his culture, to the society in which he lives have received too little attention. The standardized anthropological data that inform us of customary behavior, give no clue to the reaction of the individual to his culture, nor to an understanding of his influence upon it. Still, here lie the sources of a true interpretation of human behavior. (1932:258)

Finally: "An error of modern anthropology, as I see it, lies in the overemphasis on historical reconstruction, the importance of which should not be minimized, as against a penetrating study of the individual under the stress of the culture in which he lives (1932:269).

Ruth Benedict—A. L. Kroeber

Somehow, it seems, Boas impressed his concern for the individual on his important students, particularly Edward Sapir and Ruth Benedict—but not, as we saw, on Kroeber.[15] As late as 1934, we find the culture–individual problem at its most paradoxical in Benedict's famous *Patterns of Culture*. Here we find a very well-written exercise in Kroeber-style "descriptive integration," one which uses the language analogy for the depiction of cultures, as Kroeber recommended. Boas was evidently pleased with the book, for he wrote an introduction full of praise for it. Race and biology are distinguished from culture; a culture itself tends to be integrated around its values or themes—its "genius" (which Benedict calls its "configuration"); and he must have approved of Benedict's (1934:47–48) discussion of the significance of Wilhelm Dilthey (in particular, his "Typen der Weltanschauung") and Oswald Spengler. But, says Boas in his "Introduction," "The desire to grasp the meaning of a culture as a whole compels us to consider descriptions of

[15]It may be relevant that Kroeber was an early student of Boas—he was awarded the Ph.D. in 1902—and at that time Boas was in his diffusionistic stage. Boas' conversion to the emphasis on the dynamics of the individual and culture dates from 1910 (Boas 1940:311).

standardized behavior merely as a stepping-stone leading to other problems. We must understand the individual as living in his culture; and the culture as lived by individuals" (Benedict 1934).

As for an "understanding" of the relationship between culture and the individual: "This requires a deep pentration into the genius of the culture, a knowledge of the attitudes controlling individual and group behavior." It is not the so-called functional approach, but it "is concerned rather with the discovery of fundamental attitudes than with the functional relations of every cultural item."

Benedict's concluding chapter, titled "The Individual and Culture," is devoted mostly to the question of how normal and abnormal behavior would be defined differently in cultures of different configurations. Fine, but this chapter begins with the ritual Boasian statement that she logically believes that "the large corporate behavior we have discussed is nevertheless the behavior of individuals" (1934:232). "Society in its full sense as we have discussed it in this volume is never an entity separable from the individuals who compose it" (1934:233–234). Since she did in fact separate (that is, discuss separately) cultural configurations from race, biology, *and* individuals, one wonders why such a truism needed to be repeated—a society is *of course* composed of individuals—when in the context of her book she rendered the individual so utterly irrelevant.

17

Cultural Anthropology versus Social Anthropology

During their early years in the discipline of ethnology Malinowski and Radcliffe-Brown had amiable relations, and while they were together in Australia in 1914, they "had many lengthy discussions on anthropology and the aims and methods of field research, and we reached fairly complete agreement" (Radcliffe-Brown 1946:38). But by about 1930 Malinowski began making use of the concept "culture" and of a "functional" view of it in ways that thoroughly distressed Radcliffe-Brown, so much indeed that he was to take pains to speak only of *social* anthropology rather than cultural anthropology and *structural*–functional analysis rather than *functionalism.*

BRONISLAW MALINOWSKI

"What is the deepest essence of my investigations [of Trobriand man]? To discover what are his main passions, the motives for his conduct, his aims. . . . His essential, deepest way of thinking. At this point we are confronted with our own problems: What is essential in ourselves?" (1967:119). This kind of Dilthey-cum-Boas *Verstehen* was to be accomplished by Malinowski's pitching his tent in the middle of a Trobriand village, learning the local vernacular, and participating in the daily life of the native as fully and empathetically as possible.

Malinowski defines culture thus: "It obviously is the integral whole consisting of implements and consumers' goods, of constitutional charters for the various social groupings, of human ideas and crafts, beliefs and customs" (1944:36). This is not too different from Tylor's or the usual Boasian definition, except for his additional idea of "constitutional charters." Elsewhere he emphasized that culture was a "social heritage" (1931:621), which could have been usefully included in the above definition.

How does culture work, and why? Here Malinowski sounds like an unregenerate British economistic utilitarian of the type so scorned by Durkheim. (Could there be any relevance to this in the fact that Malinowski was trained at the London School of Economics and taught there in the early part of his career?) Culture functions basically to gratify physiological needs and "derived" secondary psychological needs. The basic needs give rise to cultural institutions which function at several levels or layers. In Malinowski's words:

> Man like any animal must receive nourishment, and he has to propagate if he is to continue individually and racially. He must also have permanent safeguards against dangers coming from the physical environment, from animals or from other human beings. A whole range of necessary bodily comforts must be provided—shelter, warmth, a dry lair and means of cleanliness. The effective satisfaction of these primary bodily needs imposes or dictates to every culture a number of fundamental aspects; institutions for nutrition, or the commissariat; institutions for mating and propagation; and organizations for defense and comfort. The organic needs of man form the basic imperatives leading to the development of culture in that they compel every community to carry on a number of organized activities. Religion or magic, the maintenance of law or systems of knowledge and mythology occur with such persistent regularity in every culture that it must be assumed that they also are the result of some deep needs or imperatives. (1931:627)

Thus the deep biological needs are satisfied by cultural modes, which in turn create new needs—"derived imperatives." The forms of organized cooperation, the ideology, habits, and customs are themselves as indispensable to the production of food or procreation or defense as the raw materials and sexual drives which nature provides—they are "instrumental."

Such was Malinowski's reductionistic functional theory. This reductionism took several forms. In one, the cultural aspects of social solidarity are seen as related to the psychology of individuals having a moral force which grows out of personal attachments.

> These are primarily formed in the processes of parenthood and kinship but become inevitably widened and enriched. The love of parents for children and of children for their parents, that between husband and wife and between brothers and sisters, serve as prototypes and also as a nucleus for the loyalties of clanship, of neighborly feeling and of tribal citizenship. (1931:641)

Similarly, Malinowski related the classificatory kinship system to the extension of sentiments and meanings originally experienced by individuals in the primary groups, the nuclear family. We have discussed this in Chapter 6, so there is no need to do more at this point than to show its relevance to his overall reductionistic theory about culture.

Further examples may be briefly cited. Even art is "organically founded. The artistic imperative is a primary need; it is the chief function of art to satisfy this craving of the human organism for combinations of blended sense impressions" (1931:644). Similarly, systems of magic exist to help mankind by psychologically bolstering him in the face of frustration due to his ignorance and lack of physical, practical control over all events (1931:637–638). And myth in general has a function which is neither explanatory nor symbolic: "It is a statement of primeval reality which lives in the institutions and pursuits of a community. It justifies by precedent the existing order and it supplies a retrospective pattern of moral values" (1931:640). Thus:

> Culture is then essentially an instrumental reality which has come into existence to satisfy the needs of man in a manner far surpassing any direct adaptation to the environment. . . . The source of all this consists in the cumulative character of individual achievements and in the power to share in common work. (1931:645)

The above descriptions of function and culture actually came rather late to Malinowski; they are most completely expressed in his article "Culture" in the *Encyclopaedia of the Social Sciences*, evidently written about 1930.

Malinowski's final discussion of function and culture is in his posthumously published *A Scientific Theory of Culture* (1944). His views are not much altered from those just discussed, except for a more consistent use of the word *culture* and the substitution of "individual culture" for what he had formerly (sometimes) called a "society." Culture consists at bottom of institutions that satisfy basic biological needs, as we saw. Thus a *science* of culture needs "a theory of culture, of its processes and products, of its specific determinism, of its relation to basic facts of human psychology and the organic happenings within the human body, and of the dependence of society upon this environment" (1944:12). Malinowski's "minimum definition" of science "implied that the first task of each science is to recognize its legitimate subject matter" (1944:14). The subject matter *culture*, however, in his view of its function, is basically biological, for it is the biological needs that define the cultural institutions and provide the explanations of them. The laws to be discovered which "explain" culture are thus biological and the "derived institutions" are psychological.

It is difficult to conceive of a more thoroughgoing reductionism than Malinowski's. In this late phase of his life he made it very explicit, general, and theoretical; but even in his field methods, much earlier, he made it plain that the aim was to understand the biological–psychological *individual*, and that such things as kinship terminologies were due to the "extension" of the individual's feelings and emotions outward from their source, namely, the relations of the individual child to its parents. To reduce social–cultural matters to the individual, as we recall Durkheim's (and Kroeber's) warnings, is to reduce it to the biological–psychological realm.

RADCLIFFE-BROWN IN REPLY

Radcliffe-Brown was a confirmed antireductionist; in particular, he was one who analyzed *societies* rather than *cultures*. Let us see, in his words, why he preferred to call himself a "social" anthropologist rather than a "cultural" anthropologist, and why, later, he preferred to distinguish himself from Malinowski's brand of functionalism. In his earlier and middle years he did not eschew the use of the word *culture*, yet it is evident that he used it as equivalent to *a society*, and certainly not in Malinowskian terms.

By 1940, Radcliffe-Brown was consistently referring to the bedrock subject matter of social anthropology as "social structure":

> Let us consider what are the concrete, observable facts with which the social anthropologist is concerned. If we set out to study, for example, the aboriginal inhabitants of a part of Australia, we find a certain number of individual human beings in a certain natural environment. We can observe the acts of behavior of these individuals, including, of course, their acts of speech, and the material products of past actions. We do not observe a "culture," since that word denotes, not any concrete reality, but an abstraction, and as it is commonly used, a vague abstraction. But direct observation does reveal to us that these human beings are connected by a complex network of social relations. I used the term "social structure" to denote their network of actually existing relations. It is this that I regard it as my business to study if I am working, not as an ethnologist or psychologist, but as a social anthropologist. I do not mean that the study of social structure is the whole of social anthropology, but I do regard it as being in a very important sense the most fundamental part of the science. (1940:2)

In one of his most programmatic essays, Radcliffe-Brown thoroughly belittled the concept of culture. A *science* of culture is not possible, he avers (1957:106) because "you can study culture only as a characteristic of a social system. Therefore, if you are going to have a science, it must be a science of social systems." What, then, is culture? It is "a certain standardization of modes of behavior, inner and outer" (1957:95).

His stern antireductionist position was plainly manifested as early as 1923: "I wish most emphatically to insist that social anthropology is a science just as independent of psychology as psychology itself is independent of physiology, or as chemistry is independent of physics; just as much and no more. This position is by no means novel, Durkheim and the important school of the Année Sociologique have insisted upon it since 1895" (1923:133).

In a straightforward blast at Malinowski, in a paper called "Functionalism: A Protest," Radcliffe-Brown says:

> Malinowski has explained that he is the inventor of functionalism, to which he gave its name. His definition of it is clear; it is the theory or doctrine that every feature of culture of any people past or present is to be explained by reference to seven biological needs of individual human beings. I cannot speak for the other writers to whom the label functionalist is applied by the authors, though I very much doubt if Redfield or Linton accept this doctrine. As for myself I reject it entirely, regarding it as useless and worse. As a consistent opponent of Malinowski's functionalism I may be called an anti-functionalist. (1949:320–321)

Radcliffe-Brown's own view of function, when he does use the term (and he disdains "functionalism"), is that it is the concept

> that enables us to study the interrelations of a structure and an associated process. . . . The function of an institution, custom, or belief, or of some regular social activity, such as a funeral ceremony, or the trial and punishment of a criminal, lies in the effects it has in the complex whole of social structure and the process of social life. (1949:322)

The foregoing remark appeared in the *American Anthropologist*. Evidently Radcliffe-Brown wanted his views on functionalism to be plainly heard on both sides of the Atlantic, for in the British journal *Man* he wrote "A Note on Functional Anthropology," a longer, more thorough critique of Malinowski. Among several criticisms he makes one important point about reductionism, that even if a "true" reductionist explanation is made it can only refer to a general similarity, not the particular dissimilarities that are the normal questions at issue:

> But the basic biological needs of human individuals, whether we accept Malinowski's catalog of seven or not, are the same in all societies. It is difficult to see how reference to these needs can enable us to understand the manifold diversity that characterizes the forms of association amongst human beings. Yet this is the fundamental axiom of functional anthropology. Religion can be shown to be intrinsically though indirectly connected with man's fundamental, that is, biological needs. But does any demonstration of this provide an explanation for the diversities found amongst religions? Malinowski has not tried to show how this can be done. (1946:40)

E. E. EVANS-PRITCHARD

Evans-Pritchard and Raymond Firth were Malinowski's first two students in ethnology. Evans-Pritchard clearly was heavily indebted to the charismatic influence of Malinowski, and despite some very real differences that developed during his career, he continued to resemble Malinowski in his idiographic interest in fieldwork and his desire to penetrate the subjective peculiarities of the individuals in a given society. Also, to put this another way, he felt that "the humanities" provide the best model for ethnology, eschewing the nomothetic or "natural science" approach of Radcliffe-Brown.

Evans-Pritchard evidently was intellectually wooed away from Malinowski for a time and seems temporarily to have embraced a social structural–functional approach suggestive of Radcliffe-Brown. In a paper called "Anthropology and the Social Sciences," he stated quite categorically in his conclusion:

> I am assuming that there are functional interdependencies in culture. If there are not, then Social Anthropology will have a position as an art, like History, in humanistic studies. In this case, much of what I have written in this paper will be irrelevant. Some social anthropologists indeed, would be willing to accept this position, and I admit that those who, like myself, believe that social interdependencies exist and can be established, base their beliefs on faith rather than achievement. (1937:73)

In the Marett Lecture of 1950, however, Evans-Pritchard was to completely reverse his field and claim that social anthropology is indeed a form of historiography or art, that it studies societies as "moral systems" rather than as "natural systems," seeking "patterns" rather than "scientific laws" (1950:152). It is supposed by many that this about-face was probably due in some measure to his conversion to Roman Catholicism during World War II, with its commitment to a belief in individual free will and a kind of metaphysical idealism.

Radcliffe-Brown wrote a long letter to the Editor of *Man* to criticize the above Marett lecture on its reappearance in Evans-Pritchard's collection of his essays, *Social Anthropology*. A few excerpts from the letter follow:

> What is the precise nature of the disagreement between Professor Evans-Pritchard and some other anthropologists? Briefly, it is that some anthropologists speak of social anthropology as being a scientific discipline, meaning by that it uses the inductive method of observation, comparison, classification and generalization . . . in order to arrive at a theory based on and tested by empirical data. Professor Evans-Pritchard says, that, on the contrary, social anthropology is a historical discipline making use of the same methods as those ordinarily adopted by historians.

> We shall land ourselves in utter confusion unless we distinguish two differ-
> ent kinds of investigations with which social anthropologists do or may con-
> cern themselves. One is the systematic comparison of a number of diverse
> societies. The other is the ethnographic study of a particular society in which
> there is some theoretical analysis; an example of an excellent study of this
> kind is Professor Evans-Pritchard's book on the Nuer. (1951:13)

Radcliffe-Brown goes on to describe the endless discussion and controversy about the similarity and difference between science and history (1951:13). Here he distinguishes nomothetic and idiographic inquiries. History, he says, is idiographic (particularizing), while "theoretical
sociology" is a nomothetic, theoretical, generalizing study. Social anthropology includes both theoretical sociology *and* ethnography that
studies particular societies—hence both nomothetic aims and idiographic aims are to be included in the single discipline of social
anthropology.

18

The Locus of Cultural Reality: Is It in the Mind or Is It an Entity *sui generis?*

Closely related to the controversy over the *Naturwissenschaften* and *Geisteswissenschaften* views of human social behavior—is that behavior governed by deterministic laws of nature or not?—is the question as to whether culture, as the main ingredient in that behavior, is a *sui generis* level of reality, to be investigated and explained on its own terms, or whether it is only as an aspect of mind, or psychology. Frequently, as we have seen, the arguments take the form of reductionism and antireductionism. In this chapter we consider those arguments when they take the form of defining or describing culture in terms of its locus. Does culture consist of real things and events, observable directly or indirectly in the actual world, or is it an "abstraction" from behavior, with its real locus in the minds of the people being studied (or, as in a few definitions, is it really only in the mind of the ethnologist)?

E. B. Tylor's famous definition does not take sides on this issue: "Culture, or civilization, taken in its wide ethnographic sense, is that complex whole which includes knowledge, belief, art, morals, law, custom, and any other capabilities and habits acquired by man as a member of society" (1871:1). In his opening chapter, "The Science of Culture," Tylor does make a ringing declaration of positivistic faith against the doctrine of human free will (1871:2–4), and he also excludes from a consideration of the evolution of culture the question of "hereditary varieties or races of man," regarding mankind as "homogeneous in nature" (1871:6). At the same time, in the corpus of his work the main direction of his interests is toward an understanding of mind and thought—in short, an intellectualistic theory of culture. This interest does not in itself, however, constitute an explicit enough argument about the locus of cultural reality for us to consider it at length in the present chapter.

This intellectualistic, or rationalistic, bias held by Spencer, Tylor, and others in Britain in the last century had an important catalytic effect. As we saw earlier, Durkheim's theory of "the social" (culture) as a nonrational, often unconscious determinant of human social behavior was directed at Spencer; as we shall see in this chapter, the very important Boasian view was stimulated in answer to such theories as Tylor's. Such important theorists as Lowie, Kroeber, Sapir, and Benedict were in turn stimulated by Boas to make their own (somewhat variant) conclusions about the locus of culture.

Closely related to the question of the whereabouts of culture is the matter of what it basically is, and what it is should reveal (some say) which of the sciences should be expected to explain it. If its locus is mind, then it must be basically mental, and its appropriate discipline would be psychology (social or cultural psychology); if culture is an entity *sui generis*, a reality "outside of individuals," then its explanations should be undertaken by disciplines like "culture history" or "culturology."

In the following pages we pit the two sides against each other in terms of the following protagonists. On the "mind" side appear, in this (roughly temporal) order, Boas, Sapir, Benedict, Malinowski, and Lévi-Strauss. On the other side are found the arguments of Durkheim, Lowie, Kroeber, and White (again, in temporal order).

CULTURE IN THE MIND

FRANZ BOAS

In all of his pronouncements about culture and how to study it, Boas always referred to cultures in the specific sense. Tylor's definition, it may be noted, refers to culture in the general sense. Additionally, we note that, although Boas shared with Tylor the notion that culture should be reduced to individual mental processes, he was to insist that the main difficulty in the "intelligent understanding" (*Verstehen*) of particular cultures was due to the preeminence, in the mental processes of the people, of a nonrational, largely unconscious mode of thinking, experiencing, valuing, and interpreting the external world. Robert Lowie reports (1947:317) Boas as stating in seminars that ethnographic detail was of concern "only as a way to understand human mentality." Further: "He once told me [Lowie] how hard he had had to struggle against early rationalistic influences; and the burden of all his ethnological teaching, paralleling his linguistic position, was that every philosophy and form of behavior must be apprehended from the insider's point of view."

Boas' first straightforward explication in print of this subjectivism was his espousal of the language–linguistics analogy as a model for ethnography (1911). Just as, say, a Kwakiutl Indian cannot describe his language in such a way that a stranger may use it to speak Kwakiutl, so the habits, customs, modes of thought, and values of his culture cannot be readily explained by a native informant. Just as a linguist learns to speak Kwakiutl by immersion in it, so he attempts understanding of the Kwakiutl mind–culture by participating in their daily lives. This view, it may be reiterated, was a direct lineal descendant from the earlier Germanic preoccupation with ethnic diversity and attempts to characterize the "genius of a people" in nonracial terms. And just as folk tales and myths make good texts to record for linguistic analysis, so they manifest well this genius, the individuality in its values.

This idea, that rationality and conscious thought are secondary and often only rationalizations of behavior, was characteristic of Boas' theory. Habit and emotion were far more important in any individual's adaptation to society than sweet reason. This means that the field-worker's job, as Boas said so often, was to get "behind the veil" of a people, to understand sympathetically the subjective and mental rather than the manifest, or phenomenal, aspects of culture.

The reintegration of culture, the modification that new traits undergo in order to fit the integration already achieved, was to Boas a subjective matter, a fitness as felt by the people, rather than a functional or structural integration of the culture traits themselves. But, as we shall see more directly in Benedict's realization of this idea, each culture is unique in the form that integration takes, and the general direction of its modifications—its "drift"—can be accidental, setting each culture off on its own particular path. Historical accidents, environmental changes, outside contingencies of various kinds are influential, but the effects are always modified by the subjective culture that already exists: "We must remember that, no matter how great an influence we may ascribe to environment, that influence can become active only by being exerted on the mind; so that the characteristics of the mind must enter into the resultant forms of social activity" (Boas 1911a:163).

Inasmuch as the locus of the most important and interesting aspects of culture to Boas was the mind of the individual, so that culture is basically mental, the appropriate *science* of culture would be some variant of psychology. Sure enough, this is what Boas said many times (especially in his 1940 collection of earlier essays, *Race, Language, and Culture*): the "laws" of human behavior are psychological, and the motive force of change lies in the individual in his relation to society (1940:257, 269).[1] "It seems hardly necessary to consider culture a mystic entity that exists outside the society of its individual carriers, and that moves by its own force" (1928:235).

Edward Sapir

Sapir is thought of primarily as a linguist; certainly he was the most prominent of Boas' students to contribute to the burgeoning new science of anthropological linguistics. But Sapir was also respected for his contributions to culture theory and to the culture-and-personality school when they were in their formative periods. Both because of his intellectual powers and prestige and (more important) because he was present at the right time, Sapir has been a powerful force in the development of theory in ethnology as well as linguistics. Here is a representative statement by him about the locus of culture:

> The so-called culture of a group of human beings, as it is ordinarily treated by the cultural anthropologist, is essentially a systematic list of all the socially inherited patterns of behavior which may be illustrated in the actual behavior of all or most of the individuals of the group. The true locus, however, of these processes which, when abstracted into a totality, constitute culture is not in a theoretical community of human beings known as society, for the term "society" is itself a cultural construct. . . . *The true locus of culture is in the interactions of specific individuals and, on the subjective side, in the world of meanings which each one of these individuals may unconsciously abstract for himself from his participation in these interactions.* Every individual is, then, in a very real sense, a representative of at least one sub-culture which may be abstracted from the generalized culture of the group of which he is a member. (1932:151–152; emphasis added)

Sapir evidently believes he is being "realistic" and therefor places the locus of cultural reality where it *really is*, in the minds of individuals—for what could be more obvious than that? Sapir continues in this vein to wonder whether culture, when its locus is thought to be elsewhere than in individual minds, is not only an abstraction (a word he frequently uses in this discussion) but even metaphysical:

[1]M. J. Herskovits, in his biography of Boas, said: "The psychological approach to culture was fundamental in Boas' thinking. From the first, he insisted that it be taken into full account, and often referred to cultural, as against physical, anthropology as the 'mental' side of the science" (1953:70).

> The concept of culture, as it is handled by the cultural anthropologist, is necessarily something of a statistical fiction and it is easy to see that the social psychologist and the psychiatrist must eventually induce him to reconsider carefully his terms. It is not the concept of culture which is subtly misleading but the metaphysical locus to which culture is generally assigned. (1932:153–154)

(The "metaphysical locus" is "society," as indicated earlier in a long passage.)

Sapir is saying something which is to be repeated in many guises by subsequent commentators in ethnology. Culture is a "statistical fiction"; it is an "abstraction from behavior"; it is not coterminous with "society," which is itself an abstraction; and its real locus is in the minds of individual *people*. It may be well to note again Sapir's emphasis on "reality." He puts it this way:

> That culture is a superorganic, impersonal whole is a useful enough methodological principle to begin with but becomes a serious deterrent in the long run to the more dynamic study of the genesis and development of cultural patterns because these cannot be *realistically* disconnected from those organizations of ideas and feelings which constitute the individual. (1932:146–147); emphasis added)

This, of course, brings up but does not solve the question so often asked of science: Is science basically an investigation of everything real, or is it about logical problems and conceptual constructs addressed to *selected aspects* of reality, abstracted from their real matrix? Sapir, like so many, seems to feel that science deals with reality in all its complexity, whereas anything "abstracted" from that matrix becomes "metaphysical" and therefore somehow wrong or misdirected. It is a most curious paradox that he was able to discuss languages in terms of grammars and phonemic patterns, completely abstracted— that is, separated—from the minds, emotions, age, sex, and speech organs of his informants. But where does one find the real, the true, locus of language but in the minds and speech organs of the individual speakers? Should a psychologist and physiologist therefore be the only appropriate students of language?

When we locate culture in the mind and above all when we emphasize that it is the minds of *individuals*—and what other minds are there?—we must be suggesting that the true science of culture is some form of psychology. It is no great wonder, therefore, that Sapir became a founder, perhaps *the* founder, of the culture-and-personality school. Implicit (and in later years explicit) in this interest is a feeling that culture is somehow unreal, or as Aberle says of Sapir at this point in his development (the early 1930s): "It [culture] is only a convenient and fallacious way of talking about the sum of individual behavior. Its causes are to be sought in socialization patterns" (1960:21). A still later work of Sapir's succinctly nails it down:

> It will be the future task of the psychiatrist to read cause and effect in human history. He cannot do it now because his theory of personality is too weak and because he tends to accept with two little criticism the impersonal mode of social and cultural analysis which anthropology has made fashionable. (1966:576–577).

RUTH BENEDICT

Benedict was not so straightforwardly reductionistic as Sapir (especially in his later years), but like Sapir and Boas, her own contributions—as in her famous *Patterns of Culture* (1934)—did not really feature the role of individuals and individual psychology. But in her programmatic statements she, like Sapir and Boas, states that the true locus of cultural patterns lies in the psyche, although modified by "history."

> The difficulty with naive interpretations of culture in terms of individual behavior is not that these interpretations are those of psychology, but that they ignore history and the historical process of acceptance or rejection of traits. Any configurational interpretation of cultures also is an exposition in terms of individual psychology, but it depends upon history as well as upon psychology. It holds that Dionysian behavior is stressed in the institutions of certain cultures because it is a permanent possibility in individual psychology, but that it is stressed in certain cultures and not in others because of historical events that have in one place fostered its development and in others have ruled it out. (1934:214–215)

This dictum was repeated many times by Benedict, but her own work, particularly *Patterns of Culture*, did not attempt any "history" at all: she concentrated intently, and only, on the psyche, the personality writ large, of the culture. This is again reminiscent of the linguist; as Aberle put it, "she observes the pattern and its power to rework materials over time, but does not attempt to account for differences of pattern between cultures" (1960:24).

In fact, the closest she ever comes to any actual interest in change (which would be historical in her very broad sense) is to note that cultural changes—normally borrowings of culture traits—will involve a process analogous to language "drift," whereby the unconscious human minds of the society strive to maintain the general form of the culture and its general direction. As she says in her "Configurations of Culture in North America":

> It is, however, the reality of such configurations that is in question. I do not see
> that the development of these configurations in different societies is more
> mystic or difficult to understand than, for example, the development of an art
> style. Many cultures have never achieved this thoroughgoing harmony. There
> are peoples who seem to shift back and forth between different types of behav-
> ior. . . . But the fact that certain people have not . . . [achieved harmony], no
> more makes it unnecessary to study culture from this angle than the fact that
> some languages shift back and forth between different fundamental gram-
> matical devices in forming the plural or in designating tense, makes it unnec-
> essary to study grammatical forms. (1932:26–27)

Nowhere does Benedict indicate that it is possible to ask why a
fundamental pattern moves in a certain direction. It simply does, just
as drift in a language is an autonomous process. But where is the locus
of the cultural configuration, and therefore of its changes? The answer
sounds easy and obvious:

> Society in its full sense as we have discussed it in this volume is never an
> entity separable from the individuals who compose it. No individual can arrive
> even at the threshold of his potentialities without a culture in which he par-
> ticipates. Conversely, no civilization has in it any element which in the last
> analysis is not the contribution of an individual. Where else could any trait
> come from except from the behavior of a man or a woman or a child?
> (1934:233–234)

Could it then be that she believes, as did Boas, that ethnology is only
a method or technique of description rather than a science? This seems
to be the case. She described herself as a humanist and urged, in her
address as American Anthropological Association president (1948),
that ethnologists should more explicitly recognize this mode of looking at culture, which certainly suggests that the subject matter of
ethnology—culture—is not amenable to scientific analysis. And if it is
not, then some kind of cultural psychology or a "comparative psychiatry" utilizing the ethnologist's descriptive monographs would be the
closest approximation to a science of culture. The final chapter of
Patterns of Culture develops this thesis.

BRONISLAW MALINOWSKI

Inasmuch as we have treated much of Malinowski's theory of
culture in Chapter 17, in his opposition to Radcliffe-Brown, we need do
little more here than call attention to his reductionism. He has, in fact,
answered our questions about the locus of culture with succinctness
and clarity. With respect to society of the Durkheimian or Kroeberian
sort, he says: "A social group consists always of individuals"
(1931:622). Therefore, it is obvious that "the psychological nature of

social reality is . . . due to the fact that its ultimate medium is always the individual mind or nervous system" (1931:623).

Culture, insisted Malinowski, is a "social heritage" (1931:621), which would seem to suggest that it is something more than a totality of individual needs, minds, motives, and emotions. This much is certain, that his famous monographs on the Trobriand Islands did indeed wonderfully evoke, descriptively, the *culture* of the society in its complexity and reality, and he did not, in those books, make very many programmatic claims for scientific theory. But, significantly, he did feel that the main aim of the description was to make culture come alive in the "flesh-and-blood organism," which is the individual. This focus logically led him to his later theoretical formulations, which insisted that the purposes and functions of cultural institutions were to serve biological needs, with those cultural modes in turn creating new psychological needs, or "imperatives."

The locus of culture is thus in mind and body. Its reality is biological and psychological. He says, in his posthumously published *A Scientific Theory of Culture,* that "the first task of each science is to recognize its legitimate subject matter" (1944:14). But this subject matter, culture, turns out to be basically biological and derivatively psychological, and that is where its "laws" will be discovered.

Throughout Malinowski's work there was revealed a strong tendency to explain customs and institutions in terms of individual motivations. The basic needs are biological, to be sure; but much less obvious and thus, perhaps, of more interest to him—judging by the far greater number of examples he gives—are the individual motivations. These seem to have been of two kinds, inborn and acquired. Of these two, the inborn, or natural, motives figure far more frequently in his writings. Of these, ambition or self-interest seem the most prominent and result in "calculating man" eternally weighing alternative choices in behavior. This is the essential Malinowski, psychologizing his cultures.

CLAUDE LÉVI-STRAUSS

We have seen Lévi-Strauss' method and theory at work on the problems of kinship and marriage and totemism (Chapters 7 and 10). In the context of this chapter we shall try to see whether those illustrations can be combined with some of his (confusingly many) programmatic statements to summarize his position in terms of the locus of cultural reality. It is helpful that he eschews the word *sociology* in favor of *ethnography* and *ethnology* (sometimes *anthropology*), which saves us from the problems we encountered with Durkheim, and he also uses the word *culture,* which rescues us from the wide confusion resulting from Radcliffe-Brown's recalcitrance over both "culture" and "ethnology."

In Chapter 1 ("Introduction: History and Anthropology") of his wide-ranging volume of collected essays (1958), Lévi-Strauss early acknowledges his debt to Boas. He does it by contrasting history and ethnology:

> They share the same subject, which is social life; the same goal, which is a better understanding of man; and, in fact, the same method, in which only a proportion of research technique varies. They differ in their choice of complementary perspectives: history organizes its data in relation to conscious expressions of social life, while anthropology[2] proceeds by examining its unconscious foundations. (1958:18–19)

Lévi-Strauss then describes "the principle that anthropology draws its originality from the unconscious nature of collective phenomena." It is exactly what Boas decreed in 1911 (in the famous "Introduction" to *Handbook of American Indian Languages*): Just as in the study of a primitive language, the analyst does not expect the informant to correctly describe the structure of the language, so in investigating other aspects of culture, the analyst must distinguish "secondary [conscious] rationalizations" of the natives from the real origins and real function of the observed habits and customs. "Boas must be given credit for defining the unconscious nature of cultural phenomena with admirable lucidity." Lévi-Strauss then quotes the key paragraph in Boas, linking ethnology to linguistics:

> "The great advantage that linguistics offers . . . is the fact that, on the whole, the categories which are formed always remain unconscious, and for this reason the processes which lead to their formation can be followed without misleading and disturbing factors of secondary explanations, which are so common in ethnology, so much so that they generally obscure the real history of the development of ideas entirely." (1958:20)

Although, as Lévi-Strauss remarks, Boas said this 8 years before Ferdinand de Saussure's *Cours de linguistique générale,* which is usually credited with the innovation of structural linguistics, and although Boas founded American linguistics, "yet with respect to anthropology he displayed a timidity that still restrains his followers" (1958:20–21).

One is at a loss, at first, to understand how followers of Boas, among whom Benedict, Kroeber, and Sapir were preeminent, could be said to be restrained. They carried out Boas' 1911 dictum (quoted above) about

---

[2]Lévi-Strauss began the paragraph using *ethnology* in this position. He often uses the two words as synonyms.

"history and psyche" in as enthusiastic a fashion as can be imagined for mere mortals. One wonders what Lévi-Strauss has in mind for a freer, or fuller, treatment of the unconscious mental structure underlying cultural institutions. Perhaps he means that the analyst could, or ought to, range more *widely*—to get beyond the "geist" of a single culture?

The answer is an unqualified yes, as stated in the "Introduction: History and Anthropology," written as a general statement of his position for the collection of his theoretical essays (1958). One must take this essay more seriously than some of the earlier, more fumbling ones. He cites the language analogy, whereby the structural linguist has discovered, by comparative methods, certain language uniformities such as "distinctive features" or "pairs of oppositions" which go beyond "empirically different entities" (one guesses he means beyond the specific individual languages). So: "The transition from conscious to unconscious is associated with progression from the specific toward the general" (1958:21).

> In anthropology as in linguistics, therefore, it is not comparison that supports generalization, but the other way around. If, as we believe to be the case, the unconscious activity of the mind consists in imposing forms upon content, and if these forms are fundamentally the same for all minds—ancient and modern, primitive and civilized (as the study of the symbolic function, expressed in language, so strikingly indicates)—it is necessary and sufficient to grasp the unconscious structure underlying each institution and each custom, in order to obtain a principle of interpretation valid for other institutions and other customs, provided of course that the analysis is carried far enough. (1958:21–22)

The locus of the most basic aspect of culture is therefore mind or mentality, with emphasis on the unconscious—no different so far from the ideas of Boas, Sapir, and Benedict. The one large difference lies in the degree of generality that Lévi-Strauss wishes to achieve compared to the particularistic specificity of cultures which restrained the others. This difference, however formidable, is not germane to the subject of the present chapter.

This form of reductionism has confused many people, since the more expected and usual kinds—such as those inveighed against by Durkheim and later by Kroeber—have explained cultural institutions in terms of individuals ("great men" or just men thinking rationally) or in terms of individual psychology. Lévi-Strauss eschews the psychology of emotions, sentiments, or "needs" and of individuals' rational thinking in favor of "the unconscious activity of the human mind." It is not the minds of varying individuals and therefore it is not some kind of psychology that is invoked, but something else pertaining to all of humanity. Nevertheless, Durkheim would still certainly denounce it as reductionism, as may become clear in the next section.

CULTURE *SUI GENERIS*

ÉMILE DURKHEIM

As we have seen in his criticism of Spencer (Chapter 16), Durkheim was a strenuous antireductionist. He eventually put this theoretical argument into one volume, *The Rules of Sociological Method* (1895). There is, however, one constant difficulty with Durkheim: he does not use the word *culture* (which in French means cultivation, improvement, tillage) but only various other locutions—"social facts," "collective representations," and "collective conscience." Still, as noted earlier, he is clearly alluding to the hold that culture, in Tylor's usage, exerts over the social behavior of individuals.

Durkheim's war against psychological reductionism was total, and he waged it during his whole productive life. His first book, *The Division of Labor in Society*, argued that Spencer's view of the superorganic as a simple product of individuals' rational calculations was badly mistaken. In *Suicide* (1897) he undertook to demonstrate that such a poignant, utterly emotional, antisocial, irrational deed as killing oneself can be explored in a nonpsychological way, in terms of scientific sociology. Finally, *Les formes élémentaires de la vie religieuse* (*The Elementary Forms of the Religious Life*), published in 1912, was similarly devoted to a subject normally deemed nonrational, emotional, subjective, and psychological, but which could be better explained by a sociologist (ethnologist) than a psychologist.

Where, then, is the locus of culture (the social)? Durkheim wisely does not address the question quite this way, but rather addresses this question: Where is the locus of the *explanation* of social data? This locus is not in individual minds, to be discovered by psychological analysis, but outside them—in the society. And social facts should be treated as "things" (*choses*) having an objective existence in the external world and being capable of examination in the manner of science. This does not mean that they have to be material things, but they "are things by the same right as material things, although they differ from them in type."

> What, precisely, is a "thing"? A thing differs from an idea in the same way as that which we know from without differs from that which we know from

within. Things include all objects of knowledge that cannot be conceived by purely mental activity, those that require for their conception data from outside the mind, from observations and experiments, those which are built up from the more external and immediately accessible characteristics to the less visible and more profound. To treat the facts of a certain order as things is not, then, to place them in a certain category of reality but to assume a certain mental attitude toward them on the principle that when approaching their study we are absolutely ignorant of their nature, and that their characteristic properties, like the unknown causes on which they depend, cannot be discovered by even the most careful introspection. (1895:xliii)

The above was written in Durkheim's "Author's Preface to the Second Edition" of *The Rules of Sociological Method* in answer to mistaken criticisms of the first edition; it may therefore be taken as a carefully considered statement. Further on in the same preface, he reconsiders the criticisms of his antireductionism: "Practically all sociologists now demand a separate existence for their science; but because society is composed only of individuals, the common-sense view still holds that sociology is a superstructure built upon the substratum of the individual consciousness and that otherwise it would be suspended in a social vacuum" (1895:xlvii).

But, Durkheim continues, in other realms of nature, when elements combine and produce new combinations, these may be regarded as new phenomena and studied as a totality. A living cell contains nothing but atomic particles, but the particles do not explain the phenomena characteristic of life. Society, then, is composed of individuals, to be sure, but their combination yields a new kind of phenomenon. What about the "collective representations" which exist in the minds of the individuals? If every society is a synthesis of individuals yielding a new phenomenon, "then the social facts reside exclusively in the very society itself which produces them, and not in its parts, i.e., its members." They are "external to individual consciousnesses" in the same way that the characteristics of life are external to the mineral substances of which cells are composed (1895:xlviii).

This view of the new kind of reality which is social life suggests, therefore, who should study it: "Thus we have a new justification for the separation which we have established between psychology, which is properly the science of the mind of the individual, and sociology" (1895:xlix). Durkheim used the term *sociology* often to refer to problems, methods, and the kind of study of societies that Tylor and later British and American ethnologists would consider anthropological or ethnological.

If social facts—collective representations—are to be studied as though they were "external" to individual psychology, what is it that gives this evident priority to the social origin of these "things"? "The system of signs I use to express my thought, the system of currency I employ to pay my debts, the instruments of credit I utilize in my commercial relations, the practices followed in my profession, etc., function independently of my own use of them" (1895:2). Why do members of a society follow out such social ways of acting, thinking, and feeling? These types of thought and conduct are endowed with "coercive power" and impose themselves on the individual, independent of individual will.

For many people in society and for many kinds of acts and thoughts, the constraint is not felt at all, or only slightly. But for some few individuals, and with respect to some few acts, the coercion is direct in its surveillance and punishment. In other, lesser cases, such as not conforming in dress or courtesy patterns, the social punishment is made efficacious by ridicule or social withdrawal. Still more indirect is the constraint due to the prior teachings of morality or conscience.[3]

Durkheim further notes that social facts should be studied as though they were "objective reality" even when they are immaterial; above all, they do not depend on individual caprice but have uniform and orderly relations. There are, even in modern sociology, numerous survivals of the anthropocentric bias barring the way to science.

> It displeases man to renounce the unlimited power over the social order he has so long attributed to himself; and on the other hand . . . , if collective forces really exist, he is necessarily obliged to submit to them without being able to modify them. This makes him inclined to deny their existence. In vain have repeated experiences taught him that this omnipotence, the illusion of which he complacently entertains, has always been a cause of weakness in him; that his power over things really began only when he recognized that they have a nature of their own, and resigned himself to learning this nature from them. Rejected by all other sciences, this deplorable prejudice stubbornly maintains itself in sociology. Nothing is more urgent than to liberate our science from it, and this is the principal purpose of our efforts. (1895:lviii)

ROBERT H. LOWIE

In several works, beginning as early as 1915 with his article, "Psychology and Sociology," Robert Lowie stated his views on the locus of

---

[3]Critics evidently attributed to Durkheim a narrower, or more rigid, philosophy than he intended here. In his new preface he amended the above comments in a footnote: "The coercive power that we attribute to it is so far from being the whole of the social fact that it can present the opposite character equally well. Institutions may impose themselves upon us, but we cling to them; they compel us, and we love them; they constrain us, and we find our welfare in our adherence to them and in this very constraint" (1895:liv, Footnote 5).

culture with undeviating clarity. And, like Durkheim, he not only wrote theoretical, programmatic statements but turned out a solid corpus of empirical studies which conformed to his theory and illustrated it. In 1917 he published his first book, *Culture and Ethnology*, which Fred Eggan, editor of its paperback reissue, hails as "the best book he ever wrote." This is a very general work aimed at the "intelligent layman," somewhat in the same spirit as Durkheim's *The Rules of Sociological Method*. The subjects he deals with are culture and psychology, culture and race, culture and environment, and, finally, the determinants of culture. This is precisely the book we need for the present chapter.[4]

The opening chapter, "Culture and Psychology," begins with Tylor's famous definition, which, along with an illustrative list of cultural items, speaks of "capabilities and habits acquired by man as a member of society." Lowie then notes that there already exists a science dealing with man's capabilities and habits—the branch of knowledge called psychology. Why not simply merge the study of ethnological—that is, cultural—phenomena with the older science of psychology? Why insist that there should be a separate science to deal with culture as a distinct order of reality (1917a:7)?

Lowie goes to considerable lengths to explain that, while psychology is not irrelevant to human behavior, it can shed light only on certain aspects of it, the innate traits of the individual: it cannot explain the acquired traits characteristic of a society. A cross is *perceived* psychologically, true, but differently by Christian, Mohammedan, and Buddhist. The *acquired* significance of the symbolic cross cannot be explained by psychology. Lowie continues:

> . . . individual thought, feeling and volition are co-determined by social influences. In so far forth as the potency of these social factors extends we have culture; in so far forth as knowledge, emotion, and will are neither the result of natural endowment shared with other members of the species nor rest on an individual organic basis, we have a thing *sui generis* that demands for its investigation a distinct science. (1917a:17)

This does not mean that certain problems of society should not be referred to psychology or, indeed, to any of the other sciences. A Peruvian bronze implement has a cultural significance of its own, but the investigator might also want to know from a chemist what the proportions of copper and tin and trace elements were in the standard Peru-

---

[4]Also included in the book is a chapter on relationship terms, a very good and pathfinding one indeed, but we have already discussed Lowie's contributions to the study of kinship.

vian bronze items. There are architectural styles that vary greatly in the world, but none of them violate certain physical principles, such as gravitation. Yet the laws of gravitation, however inexorable, cannot explain the stylistic variations—nor can the science of psychology. "The capabilities and habits acquired by man as a member of society constitute a distinct aspect of reality that must be the field of a distinct science autonomous with reference to psychology" (1917a:26).

What are the determinants of culture? Psychology, race, and environment were all shown by Lowie, in successive chapters, to be inadequate suppliers of answers to crucial questions of human cultural differences. The answer is that to account for a given cultural fact one must refer it to a knowledge of other cultural facts. Most often, and importantly, the investigator tries to find its antecedents within the culture in which it is found or from where it may seem to have been imported. Quoting Tylor, Lowie says: "Civilization is a plant much oftener propagated than developed" (1917a:67).

Before societies can communicate cultural items to others, the items must somehow have been evolved. But Lowie finds no "laws of evolution" that can predict the stages of development of particular cultures. (This is the familiar Boasian injunction against the theories of "unilinear evolution.") "That a particular innovation occurred at a given time and place is, of course, no less the result of definite causes than any other phenomenon of the universe. But often it seems to have been caused by an accidental complex of conditions rather than in accordance with some fixed principle" (1917a:82).

Yet, the field of culture is "not a region of complete lawlessness." There are recurring phenomena, "parallelisms," in widely separated regions of the earth due to functional interconnections. (We should remember here his functional explanations of forms of kinship nomenclature, as discussed in Chapter 5.) In any case, functional parallelisms as well as unique developments have histories.

> In short, as in other sciences, so in ethnology there are ultimate, irreducible facts, special functional relations, and principles of wider scope that guide us through the chaotic maze of detail. And as the engineer calls on the physicist for a knowledge of mechanical laws, so the social builder of the future who should seek to refashion the culture of his time and add to its cultural values will seek guidance from ethnology, the science of culture. (1917a:97)

As Boas, Kroeber, and increasing numbers of subsequent students kept to the "history and psyche" (idiographic) approach to cultural phenomena, Lowie evidently steeled himself in later life to place ever-greater emphasis on the scientific (nomothetic) approach. By 1936, in an article appropriately called "Cultural Anthropology: A Science," he put it to them in no uncertain terms:

> There is a widespread but, in my opinion, vicious tendency to disassociate social from natural science. On the one side we hear that the social sciences must consider values, hence subjective elements that militate against an objective approach. Again, their data are said to be so complex as to preclude generalizations. Some also stress the impossibility of experiment, the absence of mathematics. (1936:302)

According to Lowie, these objections are based on a misconception of the nature of science—only some sciences do these things, others do not. Furthermore, the so-called subjective values can be as easily treated objectively.

> To sum up, ethnology is simply science grappling with the phenomena segregated from the remainder of the universe as "cultural." . . . Finally, it coordinates in terms of causality as the concept has been epistemologically purified; and by the demonstration of functional relationships it may attain the degree of generalization consistent with its own section of the universe. (1936:320)

A. L. KROEBER

Kroeber shared with Lowie, his longtime friend and colleague at the University of California at Berkeley, the same antireductionism, the same disposition to argue for culture as a reality *sui generis*, and a similar interest in distinguishing the "historical" from a "scientific" approach to cultural data. In the last respect, Kroeber was much more disinclined than Lowie to expect much success from the nomothetic perspective.

Kroeber's Ph.D. dissertation in 1902 (Columbia University) was on Arapaho art and exemplifies clearly his inclination to treat a culture as though it were like a work of art. It is made up of disparate parts and traits (which one studies minutely and carefully, and with pleasure), but they are all associated or interrelated in a context which is a style, a configuration—as is a work of art. Here are united what he frequently calls natural science (which seems to mean empirical data seeking or description) and the humanities, a unity different from, or opposed to, social science.

"Eighteen Professions" (1915) is Kroeber's first purely theoretical article devoted to the nature of culture (the "social"; "civilization") and his long-standing distinction between history and science. This distinction is obviously related (via Boas) to the distinction drawn by the Southwest German school between idiographic and nomothetic methods, but Kroeber is rather idiosyncratic in his view of what *history* is to mean. This early essay spells it out and insists that civilization (culture) is an entity or subject matter calling for a special aim and method. Of Kroeber's eighteen professions, we note only those few that have particularly direct bearing on the subject of this chapter. They are not discussed in the order of his presentation. Kroeber's essays were always characterized by considerable diffuseness and redundancy, which I shall try to minimize.

> *Civilization, though carried by men and existing through them, is an entity in itself, and of another order from life.*
>
> History is not concerned with the agencies producing civilization, but with civilization as such. The causes are the business of the psychologist. (1915:283)

In this passage, Kroeber has not departed from Boas at all, for here we meet the familiar assertion that the causes of civilization are psychological. But if they are psychological, then are they not reducible to the study of individuals? "Never forget the individual" was the oft-repeated ukase of Boas and his students Sapir and Benedict. But Kroeber goes out of his way to assert over and over, during his whole professional life, that the method of "history," regarding the study of culture, is to ignore the individual: *"The personal or individual has no historical value save as illustration"* (1915:284).

Now, one may define the *method* of history in any number of arbitrary ways, and if we choose to say that this method ignores the role of individuals, the statement is logically unassailable. So far so good, but we may wonder instead whether Kroeber feels that the actual nature of—the properties of—culture are such that the historical method is the only appropriate one: Is culture *itself* impervious to the causal actions of individuals? The answer is an unequivocal yes.

In fact, Kroeber speaks of history much of the time as though it were an inherent aspect of civilization rather than a perspective arbitrarily selected by himself. In this same "Eighteen Professions" we find this statement:

> *History deals with conditions sine qua non, not with causes.*
>
> The relations between civilizational phenomena are relations of sequence, not of effect. The principles of mechanical causality, emanating from the underlying biological sciences, are applicable to individual and collective psychology. Applied to history, they convert it into psychology. An insistence that all treatment of civilizational data should be by the methods of mechanical causality is equivalent to a denial of the valid existence of history as a subject of study. The only antecedents of historical phenomena are historical phenomena. (1915:287)

History, thus converted into *historical phenomena,* is not a perspective. So, culture *is* historical. Not only should it not be studied as though a causal, or psychological, approach were proper, but its course is not affected by the individual members. Years after the above was written, Kroeber made the same point, though somewhat differently, in his widely influential textbook, *Anthropology:*

> It is not grammarians that make languages, but languages that make grammarians. The analogous process evidently holds for culture. Lawgivers, statesmen, religious leaders, discoverers, inventors therefore only seem to shape civilization. The deep-seated, blind, and intricate forces that shape culture, also mold the so-called creative leaders of society as essentially as they mold the mass of humanity. Progress, so far as it can objectively be considered to be such, is something that makes itself. We do not make it. Our customary conviction to the contrary is probably the result of an unconscious desire not to realize our individual impotence as regards the culture we live in. Social influence of a sort we do have as individuals. But it is a personal influence on the fortune and careers of other individual members of society, and is concerned largely with aims of personal security, relative dominance, or affection among ourselves. This obviously is a different thing from the exertion of influence on the form or content of civilization as such.[5] (1923:133)

Here he is speaking, in his way, of culture as an entity with a nature ("historical"), which is, in reality, impervious to the purposes of individuals (but, one supposes, the will of the persons normally coincides with the direction the culture is taking). Is culture then characterized by the *necessity* of a historical approach, if one is to study it successfully? As we saw in a previous chapter, in his essay "The Possibility of a Social Psychology" (1918) Kroeber has concluded that the social (or cultural) level seems to reward the historical approach with some "understanding," but the nomothetic sciences such as psychology and sociology have had no success at all.

In 1952, when Kroeber published his major essays in book form, he took the opportunity to reassess his lifelong perspective. In the following passage, Kroeber is speaking of the levels of phenomena involved in total human behavior: the social and cultural, the individual or psychological, the biological, and the subhuman. There is a kind of finality, even weariness, in what he says:

> The level which I have personally chosen or become addicted to is the cultural one. This is not the only way of proceeding, but it is my way, and it seems the most consistent with an integrative–contextual or "historical" approach. It is hard to judge one's self, but I do seem more consciously and single-heartedly to

[5]This passage is taken from the original (1923) edition of *Anthropology* (chosen because of the date of writing; the 1948 revised edition is too close to his *The Nature of Culture* [1952], from which a final statement will be quoted).

separate out the purely cultural aspects of phenomena and to interrelate these among themselves, eliminating or "holding constant" the social and individual factors, than, for instance, my American colleagues [Boas *et al.*], or than British Anthropologists. (1952:7)

At first this passage sounds as though an arbitrary perspective toward behavior is possible and he has "chosen" or "become addicted" to one. But no—for it is a choice of *level*, the cultural one, and this level is the most consistent with the historical approach. So, no change, really, since 1902, for not only is culture real but it must be treated descriptively and contextually, in terms of its patterns or style—that is, historically. It is part of the nature of culture that this is so (even though other levels *can* be treated historically as well as scientifically).

But why cannot culture be treated scientifically, that is, in terms of determinable laws or causalities? Does this problem have to do with its locus? Kroeber answered this question most directly and specifically in a 1948 essay, "White's View of Culture." Leslie A. White had published an essay called "The Expansion of the Scope of Science" (1947) in which he extolled Kroeber's view of culture as a superorganic entity, explainable in terms of itself, but criticized him for falling short of being a complete "culturologist." White had said: "Professor Kroeber is not able to hold consistently to the culturological point of view, however. He appears to think that culturological explanations can be only historical; 'Anthropology belongs in the group of the historical sciences,' he says" (1947:91). Kroeber replied to this charge at some length; not, however, to deny it, but to justify it.

First of all we must remember that Kroeber does not use *history* in the normal sense of restricting it to temporal sequences alone. More important to *his* "history" is context, the relationship of traits or elements to each other in a pattern or configuration—and this is not a matter of causality. As so often, his best illustrative case is the analogy with linguistics:

Speech is a wholly human and wholly social phenomenon, but linguistics thrives by being completely anonymous and impersonal, with a minimum of reference to its carriers and their psychology, and by dealing with the relations of specific forms without serious concern for their specific productive causes. The relation of *d, T, Ts* in *deux, two, zwei* is a "law" in the sense of being a regularity of form, of consistent relation of pattern. But the linguist does not generally ask what made English have *t* where French has *d*. He could not give the answer, and he knows he could not. . . . Like language, culture exists only in and through human individuals and their psychosomatic properties; and, like language, it acquires a certain larger intelligibility and systematic significance in the degree that it takes these persons for granted and proceeds to investigate the interrelations of superpersonal forms of culture. . . . That a historical approach happens to be more fruitful with reference to culture, and a mechanical–scientific one more fruitful in regard to matter and energy, is the concession of a difference, not of an inferiority. (1948:115)

Kroeber, late in his life, collaborated with Clyde Kluckhohn and a host of researchers to assemble the monumental *Culture: A Critical Review of Concepts and Definitions* (1952). Evidently they felt that if they examined all the extant statements about the nature of culture they would know more about it. After gaining the utmost of this kind of sophistication, they concluded with the following definition of their own:

> Culture consists of patterns, explicit and implicit, of and for behavior acquired and transmitted by symbols, constituting the distinctive achievement of human groups, including their embodiments in artifacts; the essential core of culture consists of traditional (i.e., historically derived and selected) ideas and especially their attached values; culture systems may, on the one hand, be considered as products of action, on the other as conditioning elements of further action. (1952:181)

The concluding section of Kroeber and Kluckhohn's book makes it seem as though they had found out finally what culture really is by reviewing all the hundreds of statements of other people about what it is. But this assumes that there is some kind of identity between a natural phenomenon and a word used to designate it.[6] Kroeber and Kluckhohn frequently speak of what culture basically is instead of speaking of the possible utility of various arbitrary definitions for various kinds of questions. They are in thrall to the simplest (and most dangerous) of the characteristics of *real* definitions.

LESLIE A. WHITE

It should be noted at this point that the early evolutionists— Spencer, Tylor, Durkheim, Morgan—were talking about culture (or "society") in the general sense of the culture of mankind. If their talk about culture was more delimited, it was still about grand stages of culture (like savagery, barbarism, and civilization) and the discussion was carried on in terms of whole continents. Boas and his students, on

---

[6]My grandfather, a farmer, once said in disgust as we walked past some pigs wallowing in the muddy pen, *"Pigs.* It's a good name for them."

David Bidney's review of *Culture: A Critical Review of Concepts and Definitions* (1954) pointed out this confusion between a logical construct and an existential culture. Kroeber's latest discussion of his view of the nature of culture is in Kroeber and Parsons (1958), but it has not changed.

the contrary, were usually thinking about specific cultures—*the culture of a particular society.* Boas, and some of his German predecessors (especially Waitz), tried to get away from racial and subracial explanations of the characteristic behaviors of people in different societies. *Geisteswissenschaft* thus became a study of culture in this specific sense; it investigated the sociocultural determinant of the mentality of *a* society and sought to substitute a cultural psychology for a racial psychology.[7]

White, also an evolutionist at times, was at those times talking about culture in the general sense. But sometimes he was talking about specific cultural systems—functional entities. Sometimes, indeed, he was talking about "the individual" as a product of culture. But in all three perspectives the locus of culture was said to be outside the minds of the individual human "carriers" of culture—an entity *sui generis.* White is the latest of a distinguished line of American anthropologists to have said this.[8] Judging from the usual criticism of this kind of statement—that it is a "mystic entity" or an "abstraction reified"— we should consider what was probably meant by this. White, writing later than they and thus benefiting from longer consideration of the many criticisms, was very careful in talking about the locus of culture and what it really is.

To White, the locus of culture is of course in individual human beings, but it is also in human beings in social interaction, as well as in the institutional and material products of their behavior. Where else could it be? And that is what it really is, too. The problem, however, is that the science of psychology seems to have logical and historical priority in the study of the behavior of individual human beings. Obviously the nascent science of ethnology or cultural or social anthropology—whatever you want to call it—has proceeded in a way very different from psychology, asking different questions and finding many fruitful, even exciting, answers. We act, as scientists of culture, as though we agree rather well on our subject matter and how to deal with it. What is the trouble with our logic? If culture is behavior and if the "reasons" behind behavior are mental, then culture is in the mind,

[7]This culture-specific approach instead of the culture-general one is the source of the confused criticism of the evolutionists by Boas, who took them to be claiming that each culture had to go through the same general stages—obvious ethnographic and historical nonsense. Boas did not realize that the evolutionists were not talking about anything culture-specific at all. No evolutionist ever said that *each* culture had to go through all the stages.

[8]Including Lowie and Kroeber, already discussed, to which should be added such important contemporaries as Clark Wissler (1923) and G. P. Murdock (1932).

really, and belongs to psychology. Of late, many anthropologists have attempted to rescue their discipline's autonomy by saying that culture is not behavior exactly, but an *abstraction* from behavior.[9]

Culture is of course a word denoting a *class* of things and events; the concept is therefore an "abstraction." But this seems to mean to many that it is therefore vague and not concrete. But *all* things and events in the external world—things outside the mind of the observer—become sensed or experienced as percepts. They become concepts when they are manipulated in a process called thinking, and their validity is tested in a variety of ways in terms of prior thinking on the basis of other experiences with the external world. The things and events experienced are translated into concepts, which classify them. This process "abstracts" things and events by defining them, and it "thinks" about them by considering them in a context of other concepts. So what is the reality of such concepts? How real or unreal are they?

> A thing is what it is; "a rose is a rose is a rose." Acts are not first of all ethical acts or economic acts or erotic acts. An act is an act. An act becomes an ethical datum or an economic datum or an erotic datum when—and only when—it is considered in an ethical, economic, or erotic context. Is a Chinese porcelain vase a scientific specimen, an object of art, an article of commerce, or an exhibit in a lawsuit? The answer is obvious. Actually, of course, to call it a "Chinese porcelain vase" is already to put it into a particular context; it would be better first of all to say "a glazed form of fired clay is a glazed form of fired clay." As a Chinese porcelain vase it becomes an object of art, a scientific specimen, or an article of merchandise when, and only when, it is considered in an esthetic, scientific, or commercial context. (White 1959a:230)

An act of human behavior really is whatever it is. But the behavioral act of a man smoking a cigar can be considered in a great many contexts: physical, chemical, biological, psychological, or cultural. The act itself, as such, does not "belong to" any of the sciences dealing with the foregoing levels of reality. It is referred to a particular context for examination depending on the questions being asked.

White makes good use of the familiar language analogy at this point. The above distinction of two major contexts for a consideration of human behavior is precisely the same as linguists have been making for many years with respect to that quintessentially human–cultural behavior, talking, and cultural things, words.

---

[9]Radcliffe-Brown (1940:2) says that culture "denotes, not any concrete reality, but an abstraction, and as it is commonly used a vague abstraction." Kroeber and Kluckhohn (1952:155) say that culture "is an abstraction from concrete human behavior, but it is not itself behavior." Many others appear to have accepted this view, understanding it to mean not only that culture is not concrete but that it is abstracted from behavior by the ethnologist. The locus of the culture thus is in *his* mind.

> A word is a thing . . . or an act dependent upon symboling. Words are just what
> they are: words. But they are significant to scientific students of words in two
> different contexts: somatic or organismic, and extrasomatic or extra-
> organismic. This distinction has been expressed customarily with the terms *la
> langue* and *la parole*, or language and speech. (1959a:233)

Speech behavior is a form of human behavior, humans using words,
which may be referred to the somatic context. That is, the act of
speaking intelligible words can be studied in terms of the psychology,
physiology, and anatomy of the speaker. The concern is with how
words are spoken, with the meanings (symbolic and conditioned) of
words to individuals, with their attitudes, responses to words, and so
on. But in the "extrasomatic" context, speech behavior and "words"
are considered in terms of the relationship of the phonemes and mor-
phemes *to each other*—the varying human speech organs and mentalities and attitudes are averaged out and considered irrelevant to the
study of phonetics and phonemics, grammars, lexicon, historical
changes, and the evolution of language as such, considered as an entity
sui generis. It is now not just speech but language, *la langue*.

White continues:

> *The locus of culture.* If we define culture as consisting of real things and events
> observable, directly and indirectly, in the external world, where do these
> things and events exist and have their being? What is the locus of culture? The
> answer is: the things and events that comprise culture have their existence, in
> space and time, (1) within human organisms, i.e., concepts, beliefs, emotions,
> attitudes; (2) within processes of social interaction among human beings; and
> (3) within material objects (axes, factories, railroads, pottery bowls) lying out-
> side human organisms but within the patterns of social interaction among
> them. The locus of culture is thus intraorganismal, interorganismal, and extra-
> organismal. (1959a:235)

If culture exists, in part, within human organisms, then why say, as
is implied by the analogy of words to human behavior, that it is extrasomatic? "Wrong," White says. "We did not say that culture consists
of extrasomatic things and events, i.e., phenomena whose locus is
outside human organisms. What we said is that culture consists of
things and events *considered within* an extrasomatic context. This is
quite a different thing" (1959a:235; emphasis added). Even such subjective things as attitudes and sentiments, things whose locus is inside
the organism, are manifested as human behavior (including speech
behavior) and can therefore be considered in an extrasomatic context,
as culture, as well as in a somatic context, as psychology. Conversely,
such an objective, material thing as an axe can be considered in relation to individual organisms, its meaning can be considered in terms of
a person's conceptions of it; and so, of course, "intersomatic things"

like customs of social etiquette or patterns of social interaction can be considered in either the context of psychology or culture.

Opposed to the idea of culture treated as a reality *sui generis* has been another, very popular, version of the psychologistic or mentalistic argument to the effect that culture, an abstraction, does not act, grow, develop, or "do" anything, for it is *people* who do things. Boas (1928:236; and many other times) said that "the forces that bring about the changes are active in the individuals composing the social group, not in the abstract culture." Robert Lynd, a famous sociologist, stated firmly: "Culture does not 'work,' 'move,' 'change,' but is worked, is moved, is changed. It is people who do things. . . . Culture does not enamel its fingernails . . . but people do" (1939:39). Countless similar examples of such "realism" could be cited, but this should suffice, inasmuch as the argument is familiar. The misunderstanding here is not over whether people are involved in cultural processes, for of course they are. As White says, an item of human behavior can be viewed in the somatic context (i.e., in the context of the characteristics of people who are in reality doing things) or in the extrasomatic context of culture; it is a question of the relevance of the human biological–psychological characteristics to the question being asked. Albert Einstein was a living, breathing person doing things like thinking and writing about the theory of relativity. Let's say that he, a person, wrote a theory down, an act of human behavior. It can be referred to a somatic (biological–psychological) context to find out why it was Albert and not his sister who did it, or why his diet and physical condition and personal life history led him to do it when and where he did. But the theory of relativity can also be placed in another context, that of the previous, contemporary, and subsequent developments in the culture of mathematics and science itself—considered as an extrasomatic set of processes and events—to shed light on very different kinds of questions from those of Einstein's psychology and physiology.

White's final summation follows:

> Finally, our distinction [between psychology and culturology] and definition is in very close accord with anthropological tradition. This is what Tylor meant by culture, as a reading of *Primitive Culture* will make clear. It is the one that has actually been used by almost all nonbiological anthropologists. What is it that scientific field workers among primitive peoples have studied and described in their monographs? Answer: real observable things and events dependent upon symboling. It can hardly be said that they were studying and describing imperceptible, intangible, imponderable, ontologically unreal abstractions. To be sure, the field worker may be interested in things in their somatic context, in which case he would be doing psychology. . . . and anthropology, as this term is actually used, embraces a number of different kinds of studies:

anatomical, physiological, genetic, psychological, psychoanalytic, and culturological. But this does not mean that the distinction between psychology and culturology is not fundamental. It is. (1959a:247)

*   *   *

So what is the locus of cultural reality? Is culture really in the mind or is it an entitity *sui generis?* Culture is a concept, an abstract term which classifies a segment of reality. This reality is that human behavior which, by its classification (even if predefinitional), may be considered a cultural item when placed in the context of other knowledge of the same kind; it is psychological ("mind") or biological or chemical or physical in other contexts. A person's sneeze, covered by his Kleenex, and followed by a companion's cry, "Gesundheit!," obviously can be considered as a preeminently biological phenomenon (the nasal explosion). In the same way, it can be considered as psychological or cultural in other obvious respects, depending upon what questions one wishes to ask about it.

Evidently the arguments about the locus of cultural *reality* have been a terrible waste of ethnological debating time.

VII

A BROADER
CONTROVERSY

*The research and reporting in this book have been
carefully devoted to what may seem an impos-
sibility, an attempt to stay above the struggle between the various schools and individuals in order
to describe the issues and controversies themselves
as fairly as possible. It is not at all a presentation of
individuals as properly assessed in their full importance, nor is it an attempt to rate one above another; rather, the concern has been with the significance of particular contributions toward the
solution of certain major issues in the history of
ethnology. But for this very reason, other matters of
historical importance remain undone:*

*The rightful place of a Franz Boas cannot be as-
sessed in a book of this sort because it does not deal
directly with the significance—however great—of
such a man in his role as founder of an academic
school. Yet his influence echoes and reechoes in
works by several of his students discussed in these
pages. And, less obvious but more important, some
of his major ideas have been extended and refined
by people who were not his students nor even of his
nation or language (as in the notable case of Lévi-
Strauss).*

*There is another, almost opposite, kind of in-
justice that is done to individuals (or their
"schools") by considering only the works bearing
on what have been chosen as major issues. For example, the widespread influence of Bronislaw Mal-*

inowski's ethnological books is not discussed here because we are considering only his opinions on certain of the issues, and some, such as those dealing with kinship, were his poorest exhibitions by far. On the other hand, there are some writers who are virtually unknown in our day who were important contributors of ideas closely related to the grand issues: Fustel de Coulanges, Andrew Lang, A. M. Hocart, Spencer, Frazer, and others who had no academic posts or disciples deserve, because of their written efforts, more attention than they have lately received. Happily, too, there are some whose present renown in general ethnology is matched by important performances in the narrower contexts of the issues presented here. Readily to mind come such ethnologists as E. B. Tylor, Franz Boas, Émile Durkheim, A. R. Radcliffe-Brown, A. L. Kroeber, Robert Lowie, and Leslie White.

One of the strongest impressions resulting from the making of this book is how forgiving, or sympathetic, I now feel toward individuals with whom I once disagreed so heartily. This mellowing may be supposed to be a normal consequence of growing old; but more important now, though related to it, is an elementary discovery made when the present research was well under way. I began to doubt that the controversies had a necessarily right or wrong side, and this has given pleasure, finally.

19

Some Further
Conclusions

I have titled this concluding chapter in this way because each of the parts of this book tells its own story with its own conclusion. A summary of these seems unnecessary, but the book taken as a whole still has some implications worth discussing at this point.

I had long been confused by the lack of unanimity, or even consensus, about major issues in ethnology. The preparation of this book has largely dispelled the confusions, and I am anxious to impart my findings—even to those who do not admit to confusion. The findings have to do with the discovery that ethnologists seem to exhibit one of two basic kinds of attitudes and forms of thought and so are likely to misunderstand one another when addressing an issue or, frequently, to not even be interested in the same kind of issue.

THE MOIETY SYSTEM OF ETHNOLOGY

To say that there is an intellectual division in ethnology, one hastens to add, is not the same as to say that there are two kinds of *persons* (or personalities). Persons are rarely all of a piece, steady over a whole career or with respect to all problems. Some are; this story would be simple if everyone's works were so consistently characterizable as A. L. Kroeber's are as "Kroeberian" and Radcliffe-Brown's as "structural–functionalist." But few people knew so well "who they were" as those two; most of us are so uncertain as to be inconsistent, staggering after irreconcilable models at different stages of our careers.

The forgiving emotion was caused especially by the discovery that the controversies were rarely resolved in terms of one side's being right and the other wrong. Mostly, the controversies seem to come down to mutual incomprehension because of divergent aims and interests. Often, therefore, controversy is also a matter of different questions

being asked, which itself results in a lack of any confrontation whatsoever between important ethnologists. Not only do they sometimes
talk right past one another, often they are not talking toward one
another at all.

The absence of controversy over a particular issue suggests that
there really may be an implicit, broader controversy, a disagreement
over what is to be considered an issue and whether it deserves recognition. This is to say that sometimes the very lack of direct controversy
over a particular issue reveals an issue of another kind, just as a dead
silence may have resounding significance in a conversation.

There are some suggestive precedents in American ethnological self-
analyses that may help toward resolving the problem of this dichotomization. Perhaps the most noteworthy is Kroeber's article "History and Science in Anthropology" (1935), made more noticeable, perhaps, because Boas replied to it (1936).[1] Kroeber later wrote similar
articles on the subject: "The History and Present Orientation of Cultural Anthropology" (1952:Chapter 17) and "A History of the Personality of Anthropology" (1959). Ruth Benedict's address as retiring president of the American Anthropological Association, "Anthropology
and the Humanities" (1948), stresses the dual influence on ethnology
of natural science and the humanities, as did Robert Redfield (1953). In
all these cases, attempts were made to suggest some kind of duality in
ethnology between science (variously defined) and its opposite (variously named and defined).

It would seem that, inasmuch as these attempts at characterizing the
two-sidedness of ethnology were made by Boasians, it must be that
they were inspired by something implicit in and peculiar to the Boasian influence in America. (Redfield, to be sure, was not a student of
Boas, except indirectly at Chicago under Fay-Cooper Cole, but he
shared several Boasian characteristics.) This may be so: Boas and his
students were enthusiasts of a brand-new perspective in English-speaking ethnology, a conception of culture that kept it independent of
racial and biologistic connections, that was relativistic, and which
gave an important new dimension to the study of ethnic behavioral
differences (a kind of "comparative psychology") independent of the
behaviorist and various physioneurological–psychological schools of
the day. This new conception was difficult to convey in its manifold
significance; but it *was* different from all previous and contemporary
scientific attempts to study human behavior, at least in the English
and French literature. It may be that this is not only the main reason
why it was students of Boas who attempted to explain themselves in

[1]See also, in anticipation of these views, Boas (1887, 1908) and Kroeber (1915, 1918).

terms of their differences from their contemporaries but also, there-fore, why it was a dichotomization: There were only two main parties, *we*, the Boasians, versus the *others*, all others—appearing as a simple one-on-one confrontation.[2]

The controversies discussed in previous chapters were selected be-cause in historical perspective they seem to be the most important and difficult issues in ethnology from 1860 to 1960. That and that only was the reason for selecting them. But as the work progressed it seemed that more and more frequently the controversies were resolvable into the two sides mentioned above, and that each side (but not all of the individuals) seemed to maintain its pose through time in different contexts. Let us pursue this finding more fully to see if it is a useful way of talking about the development of ethnological thought.

First comes the problem of labels—surely not a surprise. As indi-cated above, precedents are involved (in America) by Kroeber's choice of *history* versus *science* and by Benedict's and Redfield's choosing *the humanities* to contrast with *natural science*. But although these words are suggestive of the problem of our bifurcated discipline, it may be useful to try out some others as well. This procedure may prove to be productive in another sense; the descriptive terms are not quite syn-onymous, but any of them may be appropriate epithets for certain works mentioned in our text—and they all do illustrate the bifurca-tion. Without further explication at this point let us simply list them, to be evaluated subsequently. The "moieties," if they may be called this, are labeled simply *A* and *B*, so as not to give any of the paired labels an untoward prominence by using them as major headings. The order in which they appear is not intended to reflect their relative importance.

A	*versus*	*B*
Natural Science		Humanities
Determinism		Free-willism (or Individualism)
Evolutionism		Relativism
Social Structure		Culture
Generalization		Particularism
Comparative Method		Holism
Environmentalism		Mentalism
Organismic Analogy		Language Analogy

[2]This seems accurate enough in explaining the American mood that influenced the dichotomization, but it should be added that Boas had precedents for this view much earlier in Germany (to be discussed below). Also, we shall see that some prominent Europeans shared some of the Boasian perspectives, notably Lévi-Strauss and the later Evans-Pritchard.

The reader may wonder why I do not discuss the opposition between the *materialist* and *idealist* schools that has been prominent for so long in philosophy (and political–historical theory). The reason is that I never found a true ethnological controversy between 1860 and 1960 that hinged on this particular theoretical dichotomy, although a few of the above come close. There are always a few people who claim to be materialists, but no idealists as such; the closest would be the B moiety's mentalism, discussed below.

NATURAL SCIENCE–HUMANITIES

Because this opposition seems to have been the most often used, and because it is the most generalized, it may well be the most difficult to discuss briefly. We should at least try to stay within the confines of the usual ethnological meanings of the terms rather than complicate the discussion with the more varying and recondite uses they have been put to in philosophy, literary criticism, intellectual history, and so on.

In the latter half of the nineteenth century the bifurcation in ethnology had not visibly begun. In those days a kind of "natural history" approach to the study of primitive peoples was predominant. The first note presaging the rise of Boasian ethnology in opposition was the (related) divergence of certain German philosopher–historians from the Anglo–French emphasis on positivism. This was the rise of the Southwest German school of thinkers in the 1860s, who separated their subject, the humanistic–cultural studies, from the natural sciences.[3]

The positivism of Comte (who popularized the use of this word, as he did the name *sociology*) was largely an attempt to erase all theological, mystical, and metaphysical traces from the new science. His model was physics, but at times there was also very much of a tradition of natural history in the beginnings of ethnology. There were the wide-ranging German ethnographer–geographers; the British collectors like Darwin, Wallace, and Douglas; and missionaries and "gentleman adventurers" of all sorts who were contributing ethnological information to the public.

Benedict's "Anthropology and the Humanities" (1948) readily acknowledges this natural science heritage while arguing that the hu-

---

[3]Apparently the most influential of these scholars on Boas was Wilhelm Dilthey, whose *Einleitung in die Geisteswissenschaften* (1883) argued strongly for the separation of the *Geisteswissenschaften* from the *Naturwissenschaften*. Boas acknowledged his indebtedness to Dilthey, as did Benedict (1932, 1934:49–50). As we have noted elsewhere, Windleband and Rickert were influential as well.

manities should be more fully utilized. Redfield's 1953 article makes much the same point. Why is modern ethnology to be considered by some as belonging importantly (if not wholly) to the humanities? Benedict emphasizes that the humanities and ethnology study the "mind of man." She then contrasts ethnologists who want to study culture divorced from the human organism with those who would include the organism. She maintains (1948:588) that "the great majority of present-day American anthropologists . . . include the mind of man within their definition of culture." The humanities, for this reason, should provide "our greatest resource." To Redfield, the ethnological method, which he calls "depictive integration," is what allies it to the humanities, particularly since it, like art, uses intuition, recognizes values, and treats ways of life as "wholes": "Humanity . . . ceases to be itself in so far as it is decomposed into parts or elements" (1953:732). This "holism" has also been much emphasized by A. L. Kroeber, as we have seen.

Kroeber (1959b:v) said of Boas' descriptive works, as opposed to theoretical statements of the sort discussed above:

> The great bulk of Boas' anthropological output is constituted of grammars, corpuses of texts, assemblages of tales, and ethnography—much of the last in the native language, whether it presents enumerations of customs or case histories. Altogether, these are the kinds of data that are dealt with in the humanities, except that the languages and cultures involved are Eskimo, Kwakiutl, Tsimshian, and Chinook instead of classical and European. (1959b:v)

So far it seems that the writings which are to be contrasted with natural science are mainly represented by prominent American students of Franz Boas (or influenced by them, as in Redfield's case), in opposition to the earlier traditions of ethnology. But this generalization is not wholly valid, even excepting the German forebears of Boas. Probably the foremost non-American, non-Boasian ethnologist to profess the humanistic tie is E. E. Evans-Pritchard,[4] who seems to have made this discovery in mid-career, all by himself, and in the academic context of the strongly scientistic British social anthropology (see also the discussion about Malinowski in the next section).

DETERMINISM—FREE-WILLISM

This pairing has been less frequently articulated than the foregoing, but it is closely associated with it, though not quite synonymous. For

---

[4]See Evans-Pritchard (1950). This profession of faith elicited an approving letter from A. L. Kroeber in *Man* (1951).

example, in the article just quoted we find Benedict saying that the anthropologists of the scientific–deterministic persuasion were forced "to leave out of account any consideration of human emotion, ethics, rational insight and purpose which had come into being within man's social life" (1948:588). And later, in our century, she finds that the culturologists and those engaged in certain kinds of historical reconstruction still exclude the "mind and purposes of man" from their definitions of culture (she is probably referring to White and Kroeber).

Redfield as well, in the above-cited article devoted to the relations of anthropology to the humanities, sees an important aspect of this revealed when anthropologists are interested in "the human individual as modifier and creator of his culture. . . . At this point anthropology has moved over into a field more often identified with the humanities: the study of the producers and the creative products of humanity" (1953:738a).

These statements of Benedict's and Redfield's are placed at the outset of the discussion in order to relieve what is otherwise likely to become a complex philosophical discussion and a considerable semantic confusion as well (when these are not the same thing). The statements reveal that the interest in individuals has somehow become allied with free will (or human creativity, design, and purpose). It may be supposed that this identification exists because the creativity of nonconforming genius, or for that matter the nonconformance of malefactors—Jack the Ripper as opposed to Einstein—is in its most notable aspects revealed in the activities of individuals. There is no logical reason for this parallelism, but for the moment we must leave freewillism unexamined, except as an aspect of individualism, because that is the way it appears in the writings both of determinists like Spencer, Tylor, Durkheim, Radcliffe-Brown, White, and Steward[5] and of individualists like most students of Boas and, of course, Malinowski and Evans-Pritchard (who as a convert to Roman Catholicism necessarily must have embraced free-willism).

No attempt will be made at this point to be exhaustive about the who's and where's of statements about determinism versus freewillism. The lines were well drawn and conclusively stated many times. The aim now is to describe and later to attempt to understand, if not resolve, a few complications. Again, the complications are largely that the lineup is not precisely or completely an opposition of Boasians and evolutionists–functionalists, although it is important to note how

[5]And others, of course, especially Marxists. A good example is Plekhanov's "The Role of the Individual in History" (1898).

nearly it comes to that; nor are certain of the important protagonists entirely logically consistent as individuals. These two problems will be addressed in turn.

The outstanding non-Boasian controversy that we noted earlier (Chapter 6) is between Radcliffe-Brown and Malinowski. Radcliffe-Brown expressed his determinism many times in different contexts, most strikingly in his insistence on "laws" and "principles." Malinowski, the artist,[6] put his concern for the individual in no uncertain terms. In one of his most noteworthy declarations, his introduction to Hogbin's *Law and Order in Polynesia*, he said:

> The tendency represented largely by the sociological school of Durkheim, and clearly expressed in Professor Radcliffe-Brown's approach to primitive law and other phenomena, the tendency to ignore completely the individual and to eliminate the biological element from the functional analysis of culture, must in my opinion be overcome. It is really the only point of theoretical dissension between Professor Radcliffe-Brown and myself, and the only respect in which the Durkheimian concept of primitive society has to be supplemented in order to be really serviceable in fieldwork, in theoretical studies, and in the practical application of sociology. (1934:xxxviii)

Aside from such statements of general policy, we have also seen how in practice Malinowski's individualistic perspective resulted in an analysis of Trobriand kinship systems almost exactly opposed to that of prominent British social anthropologists such as Fortes (1949) and Leach (1958).

The other major discrepancy is in the ranks of American students of Boas, wherein A. L. Kroeber made his stubborn argument against the significant place of the individual in culture history, and wherein Robert Lowie departed from his colleague Kroeber as well as other Boasians to align himself with the determinists on certain important issues in the study of kinship. We shall briefly review Lowie's thesis while reserving Kroeber for a longer discussion since his arguments (and those of his opponents) present some knotty problems of apparent inconsistency.

Lowie, it may be remembered, diverged markedly from Kroeber on the question of the meaning of kinship terms and their functional connection to forms of social organization. He did this quite successfully, it seems in retrospect, but the astonishing thing is that he did it as early as 1914 and 1915, years before anyone else, with the exception of Tylor's brief treatment (1888). (Rivers was making theoretical state-

---

[6]Who is reported to have said: "Rivers is the Rider Haggard of anthropology; I shall be its Joseph Conrad."

ments to this effect in 1915, but without successful demonstration.) It should be of interest now that Lowie saw his determinism and Kroeber's indeterminism as related to his own earlier training in chemistry and Kroeber's training in linguistics and the humanities (Lowie 1953). The two men were friends and were also longtime colleagues at the University of California at Berkeley, and they successfully defused their potential quarrel by relegating it to a matter of taste (which therefore one does not dispute). Yet it must have been uncomfortable for both: Lowie finding himself allied with Rivers and the irascible Radcliffe-Brown against Kroeber and Kroeber pursuing his lonely way for so many years, denying the social significance of kinship terms.

Kroeber's firmness about this is not so difficult to understand, since he, more completely (or more simply) than Boas, accepted an important aspect of Boas' theory of relativism, his ideas about culture, particularism, holism, and the language analogy. It is best, therefore, to review his thought on kinship terms again later as we discuss each of the above.

The other aspect of Kroeber, his antiindividualism, is also difficult to treat briefly. So far as our literature is concerned, his role in the controversy began with his 1917 article in the *American Anthropologist,* "The Superorganic." It was followed by a long letter from Edward Sapir, who approved of the article in general but took vigorous exception to one section of it. In this section Kroeber had stated, in effect, that the study of cultures by his historical method could dispense entirely with the preoccupation of most historians with the "great men"—generals, geniuses, rulers, messiahs—who were usually considered the focal points, if not the explanations of, grand historical epochs. In Kroeber's view, a true study of culture–history discovered (or devised) the *pattern* or *configuration* of the whole culture, not the peculiarities of individual persons.

Sapir's reply was: "It is always the individual who thinks, acts, dreams, and revolts" (1917:442). What would Western civilization be like had Jesus or Napoleon not been born? (The answer must be: Who knows? If *anything* had been different, subsequent history might be different; the anything including not only individual persons, great or small, but the quacking of the geese that saved Rome, the loss of the nail from the shoe of the horse . . . , etc.) Kroeber considered Sapir's (and others') disagreement with him to be an unprofitable discussion and a misunderstanding of his thought. He felt that he was talking about *culture,* not about the particular differences among persons: the plot of the play, not the performance of Bernhardt; the rules of the game of baseball, not Babe Ruth's digestion; Greek grammar, not the speech habits of Demosthenes. He felt particularly puzzled by Sapir, who, as a pathfinding linguist, had laid out the perspective of the study of language patterns, as such, rather than of the habits of particular speakers. Why could Sapir not see this as analogous to Kroeber's perspective on culture? (In fact, Sapir's later article, "The Unconscious Patterning of Behavior in Society," published in 1927, is an excellent summation of this basic perspective.) Kroeber's study of the patterned ways in which women's dress fashions changed (1919) was supposed to show the nonrational, unconscious aspects of human behavior despite the conscious attempts of designers, manufacturers, or even the purchasers of the dresses themselves to alter the patterned course of events. This is just like a grammar, "determining" the users' habits but itself undetermined by outside causes. Kroeber was also interested in the numerous historical cases of simultaneous inventions in order to show that the inventions (like the calculus, the steamboat, the telephone, etc.) were actually "in the works" of culture at the particular times that were so fortuitous for the "inventors" who got the credit. But American anthropologists too numerous to mention continued to cry: "Never forget the Individual!" as a sort of litany.

Yet a huge paradox ensued. Students of Boas, and of course Boas himself, continued to make distribution studies of culture traits and to describe whole cultures, the diffusion of culture, and acculturation as though individuals were irrelevant to the task at hand, just as Kroeber had specified they should. Probably the most noteworthy was Ruth Benedict's widely read *Patterns of Culture* (1934, published with an approving introduction by Boas himself). This book characterized the patterns of integration of whole cultures (Plains, Pueblo, Kwakiutl, and Dobu), making no reference to individual leaders, messiahs, chiefs, or innovators of any kind. A sort of anonymous selection of traits were accumulated into the "patterns." Very Kroeberian so far (or advanced Boasian, one might say), but Benedict soon found herself praising the free role of the individual (recall her 1948 article).

Ralph Linton, in *Acculturation in Seven American Indian Tribes*, made a statement very typical of American ethnologists of Benedict's generation when, after doing a rather usual analysis of culture change, work which could in no way be enhanced by reference to individuals, he said: "We talk glibly of the phenomena of culture change and are prone to forget that such change consists, in the last analysis, of changes in the attitudes and habits of the individuals who compose a society" (1940:125). Kroeber must have wondered what good it does to make such a statement which is gainsaid by the study itself, and which at least would appear to be wholly irrelevant.

Of the students of Boas, Kroeber seems to have stood alone on this issue of the individual. The only other prominent Americans who argued against individualism and free-willism were Leslie White and Julian Steward. But White was not a student of Boas and took a frankly anti-Boasian stance, and unlike Kroeber, he was a rousing determinist (1949:196). Steward, a former student of Kroeber's at Berkeley, differed from his mentor very directly on the deterministic side, holding firmly for "cultural causality and law" (1949). So Kroeber alone united what seemed to be contradictory characteristics: he was an anti-individualist who remained a nondeterminist. Arrayed against him because of his anti-individualism were all or most of the students of Boas; but on the other side, with mixed feelings about it, were White and Steward and most of their students, because of his nondeterminism. He seemed so near, yet so far: "You don't get mad at him, you just sigh," White once remarked. For a long time both sides seem to have felt that there was something illogical or paradoxical about Kroeber.

But it can be reasonably argued that the illogical and paradoxical stance belongs to Boas, Sapir, Benedict, Linton, Kluckhohn, Redfield, and the many other ethnologists who share their view. Kroeber took what was both explicit and implicit in Boas' view of culture, particularly the simple notion that, like a primitive people's grammatical and phonemic patterns, much of culture is unrecognized as such by those who are in it—it is patterned and it is often unconscious or "nonrational," in Boas' terms. The investigator teases out the patterns and that's it; he has done his culture–history, his "descriptive integration." No general cultural cause and effect is adduced, but neither is its character caused by the free will of individuals, of whom, perforce, one knows nothing. Who invented the Apollonian value patterns of the Zuñi Indians? Who invented the Kwakiutl grammar? Nobody or everybody. These are not sensible questions.

If it is Kroeber who was consistent and logical in this perspective that was so eminently Boasian, why was Boas himself, and seemingly all the rest of his students, so anxious to repeat endlessly the refrain about the ultimate worth of the individual? This confusion may have had something to do with the liberal–democratic political stance so characteristic of American ethnologists, particularly in the 1930s, 1940s, and 1950s. We wanted to *do* something about the world: stop fascism, combat racism, end unemployment, get out the vote, unionize heavy industry, stop imperialism, and so on. These attitudes and desires could have been related to two quite separate trajectories, both having to do with the question of individual free will.

First, and perhaps the more obvious, is that anthropology deals fundamentally with different races, ethnic groups, and cultural differences. And it seems that ethnology, the Boasian kind particularly, has had wider, deeper, and greater intellectual influence against racial discrimination and ethnic prejudices than any other academic discipline—thus its great political relevance. Above all, it was Boas' (and, earlier, Waitz') separation of race, language, and culture that was particularly important, with the continued refinement of our understanding of culture itself as the locus or source of a race's or ethnic group's distinctive modes of behavior—culture, not biology; nurture, not nature. This was a tremendous intellectual advance, but it provoked some unease. If we, as ethnologists, describe some cultural categories and say, "Those people act that way because of these unconsciously held cultural values and themes," have we said that they *all* have to act that way *all* the time, that none of them can help it, or change? No: because we have added our admonition, "Don't forget the Individual" (with his built-in freedom).

Boas once said that anti-Semitism was caused by putting individuals into a category (1945:77–78). Now, we do not have to agree that this was the cause of anti-Semitism, but we all feel distaste at being held responsible as individuals for the generalities attributed to a category we might belong to: WASP, Jew, Negro, Georgia cracker, used-car salesman, or absent-minded professor.

When Ruth Benedict, in *Patterns of Culture*, characterized Kwakiutl culture as "megalomanic," there were no Indians equipped in those days to object to the "anti-Kwakiutlism" caused by putting these Indians into a category; but if they had objected, what would it have availed Benedict to argue that she had stated many times that "one must never forget the Individual"?

Here is where Kroeber and White easily overmatched their critics. They both said, in effect: We are not talking about individuals and whether or not they are free to choose to do what they do. We are talking about cultural traits and patterns. For example, within the *same* society there can be many different patterns in the social drinking of alcohol: from wine tasting, cocktail parties, and beer brawls to prohibition, teetotalism, Mormonism, and the sip of communion wine. All of these exist, and they are legitimate items for an ethnologist to note. The fact that any individual person in this society may be caught in a complex field of forces consisting of any or all of these (and other) influences on his or her own psychological attitude toward drinking alcohol is another question entirely. Such a view as this may not be entirely satisfactory because it doesn't explain everything about individual human beings, or even their particular drinking behavior, but it does allow investigation to proceed about habits and customs *as such*, unencumbered by logical discrepancies.

The other possible source of paradox in cultural studies of the Boasian kind is more simply the classical sort of argument between determinism and free-willism. The modern dilemma of ethnology (or, for that matter, of all the social sciences) is that we are torn between scientific analysis of human behavior, which must be determined by laws of cause and effect if we are to succeed in our aim of understanding and successfully predicting it, and free-willism, which we must profess if we want to change anything or anyway encourage people to do so. We must say, in effect, that you are not bound (at least not entirely) to submit to the cake of custom or the iron frame of the past or any invisible hand or culture-bind. This is, of course, the classic dilemma of Marxism: an avowedly unswerving historical determinism that nevertheless swerves at times with a call to arms: "Workers of the world unite. . . ." Engels saw the solution in this form: All of past history had been determined by materialist forces, but in the future, armed by the powers of Marxist analysis, man would ascend to the mastery of those forces and become free to decide his own future (1880:82).

It is often stated by free-willist individualists that the determinists are fatalists, that their view of things, if prevailing, would result in inaction, lack of emotion, even acceptance of such an insane political force as Nazism—as though it were all in the historical works. Here again Kroeber and White seem to have been the only ethnologists of their generation in America to hold to a logical, one-pieced view against individualism. Again Kroeber was not a full-fledged determinist, although White was. But both shared one important characteristic: they were not political activists in the context of their ethnological studies. They may have done any number of political things as private individuals, but they never did so in the context of science. It is a problem to know how much to make of this, but it is certainly suggestive. At any rate, it does seem that the worries about free-willism and the powers of the never-to-be-forgotten individual must have been closely related to the desire to see the politically potent findings of ethnology used to benefit deprived ethnic groups and races.

American ethnology, largely of the Boasian slant, has been a kind of *moral* discipline of political relevance. The liberal, antifascist outlook found in its cultural psychology is an antidote to racism, but at the same time it has tended to lump individuals into categories. It also has wanted to get out the vote, muster the political strength of the poor, and so on. For both reasons, the freedom of individuals to change things had to be extolled. Or so one guesses.[7]

EVOLUTIONISM–RELATIVISM

A complication arises with this pairing because "evolutionism" is not a unitary conception. As examples: Spencer sometimes saw it in terms not only of the whole of society but also of whole individual societies (though not as cultures); Tylor often saw it as a progression of forms of particular kinds of cultural items—the improvement of weapons, art, language, religion, and so on; Morgan saw it as a mental–moral progression; much later, White united it with whole-cultural Marxist-like structural–functionalism; and Steward united it with ecology. These different aspects and emphases will have to be treated again, at least in part, under our rubrics "structural–functionalism," "generalization," "comparative method," "environmentalism," and "organismic analogy."

But all of these evolutionary schemes have one thing in common: they think of evolution as *directional* through time. That is, they all see cultures, or societies, or traits (such as communication or weapons) as successions of forms toward some evident end. Usually the changes are judged (often ethnocentrically) as improvements, as progress toward something better—somehow more efficient or more moral. Sometimes, especially in the cases of Spencer, Durkheim, and White, evolution is toward a larger and more complex society or culture. In these cases, improvement is not necessarily the issue. Our civilization, as a late one, is also larger and more complex than its predecessors, but this does not make it better in all senses—some of the ethnologists, White in particular, even vehemently disliked modern society and personally yearned toward something simpler and more honest.

Nevertheless, despite the fact that a perfectly sensible conception of evolution as temporally linked stages of directional changes (toward whatever: greater complexity of society or even greater simplicity, as with jet over reciprocating engines) does not necessarily convey a sense of ethnocentric preference of the modern over the earlier, this is nevertheless an obvious reading that can be given to some of the writings of Spencer, Tylor, and Morgan. In any case, however, evolution in their view could be measured in stages of progress toward something.

The opposition of relativism to evolutionism as it occurred in the

---

[7]For a skillful review of this problem see Elvin Hatch's *Culture and Morality: The Relativity of Values in Anthropology* (1983).

history of ethnology was simply that Boas and his students perceived evolutionism, as promulgated by the English-speaking leaders of that approach, to be largely and dangerously ethnocentric. Today most would agree: Boas felt that he needed to apply a corrective, and that corrective usually answers to the name of cultural relativity. Now it is true, as the phrase goes, that he threw out the baby with the bath water, and made the term *evolution* anathema to several generations of American students of ethnology who might otherwise have usefully cleaned up the theory, but Boas can hardly be personally blamed. Ethnology was in considerable disarray when he found it in America and he applied an antidote, relativism, and a "respect for native customs" that was necessary to the new emphasis on fieldwork among the remnants of aboriginal culture still to be found. It is not Boas who should be blamed for shortsightedness but his students, who, as students so frequently do, elevated his ideas to eternal, universal rules of order. (But perhaps they should not be blamed either. Perhaps we should see a *pattern* in the behavior of academic schools of thought—as Kroeber might have said.)

Relativity in the simple guise of antiethnocentrism has become natural and easy for well-meaning ethnologists to accept. We should look at culture traits as they are, record them accurately, try to understand them, no matter how bizarre, in the context of the whole culture and its setting. This is not only good science, especially in the original natural history sense of accuracy of description, but it is the way in which we try to obliterate our possible cultural prejudices and insensitivities. Sometimes this approach has been assailed as condonement or even approval. Do we condone cannibalism or head-hunting by describing them as objectively as possible as "culture traits," and are they therefore OK? Benedict's *Patterns of Culture* became the authoritative work on relativism and, therefore, the one most frequently criticized by those who say we should take a stand against cultures or traits we cannot approve of. This is not precisely to say that we should go back to early evolutionism and judge rates of progress in the cultural world, but nevertheless it has been a common liberals' worry about relativism. But this criticism is not fair to Boas, Benedict, and the other cultural relativists, for it far overextends their intention.

As evidenced by the lack of controversy in the 1950s over it, the concept of cultural relativity is well established in the methodological canons of modern ethnology, now that it has been finally grasped that trying to comprehend and accurately describe a culture trait is not to condone it. (*Tout comprendre est tout pardonner* is one of those pithy maxims that sound so good in French but can be very silly for all that.)

It would seem, then, that, if both sides could keep their theory–method from being overextended by the other, a highly desirable peaceful coexistence would be possible. The assumption of direction and the rating scale generally implicit if not explicit in a general evolutionary approach need not be ethnocentric and the criteria of advance or progress need mean nothing more than a measurement along an arbitrary scale—size, complexity, productivity, efficiency, and so forth—none of which needs to signify the investigator's or the reader's approval. Similarly, another set of questions, entirely different, could be fruitfully asked about the same cultures, embracing the relativistic view of the subjective function of the culture traits in their own context in a particular epoch. In neither case is ethnocentric praise or blame a necessary adjunct of the method. Nevertheless, such accusations played a large role in the development of ethnological method; though mistaken to some extent, they probably had a healthy result because they were not altogether mistaken. But today, it seems justifiable to hold these two perspectives to be complementary rather than antagonistic.

SOCIAL STRUCTURE–CULTURE

Structural–functionalism, in its most obvious and generally recognized sense, was created when Radcliffe-Brown used it to attempt to describe his organismic approach to the "natural science" kind of understanding of how a particular society, as such, works. That is the positive side; but he had also negative reasons, which were to distinguish his method from the reductionistic, psychologistic approach of Malinowski (the "structural" modifier was added because Malinowski's approach was also called functionalism); from the "conjectural history" diffusion studies of his teacher Rivers (and cohorts Smith and Perry); from the Vienna *Kulturkreislehre*; and from the more limited diffusionism of the Boasian students in America. Diffusion was, of course, diffusion of culture traits and complexes. Radcliffe-Brown objected to taking societies apart in terms of their traits, and finally dispensed with the concept of culture altogether, presumably in order to signify the magnitude of his break with all the diffusionist schools, as well as with Malinowski.

But there is another aspect or perhaps definition, of the concept "culture" that should be alluded to now. We have discussed it earlier as the Boasian school (and Southwest German school's *Geisteswissenschaften*). This school, in getting away from racial or biologistic explanations of peoples' behavior, posited an important *unconscious* patterning of values, habits, and attitudes—the "spirit" (cultural *gestalt*) of a society that is inherited by its members by virtue of participating in it. Radcliffe-Brown rejected this, too, as unscientific reification of an abstraction. This "abstraction" is Boasian in large part and altogether Kroeberian (Benedict, Sapir, Lévi-Strauss, and others share it as well). It was specifically on this point that Rivers and Radcliffe-Brown so magnificently misunderstood Kroeber about kinship terminologies. Kinship terms as a pattern of unconscious, mental, "cultural" constructs are a very different thing from the diffusible bits and patches view that Radcliffe-Brown was probably expecting to refute. Kroeber's actual argument produced not a single glint of understanding in him.

Radcliffe-Brown is reputed by one of his students to have said about "culture" in the above sense: "The trouble is that I can't *see* it." The idea evidently is that societies, or at least the structural parts, being visible, are *real*, not verbal abstractions or posited mental entities; and only real things are amenable to investigation by the methods of natural science. Of course there are things that nowadays we call culture traits and complexes that are eminently visible—a railroad, a football game, the stock market, courtesy patterns, a funeral ceremony—but these are the epiphenomena of society itself, Radcliffe-Brown says, and they serve societal (or structural) functions. But they are not basic; they are products, not the explanation of anything. Where is the locus of the *explanation* of behavior? It lies in the roles that traits, complexes—the parts of the society—play in maintaining the whole society. This is what is absolutely basic, the survival of the society as a structural entity. How do you find that out? The question leads directly to the next section.

GENERALIZATION–PARTICULARISM

In Radcliffe-Brown's model of natural science, the aim of analysis is generalization, ultimately in the form of some basic laws that would hold for all societies, anywhere. For other ethnologists, opposed to this, generalizations of any useful import would probably be impossible because each culture is a unique product of specific historical events. According to Boas, for example, to compare and generalize among cultures about a thing we name *totemism*, for example, is to compare incommensurables, for totem*ism* is an "artificial construct" created by ourselves. Its only reality is each single cultural manifestation in its own cultural–historical context, having its own meaning to its own members.

The idea of generalization as opposed to particularism goes much further back historically than Radcliffe-Brown, of course. Most of the earlier evolutionists were supreme generalizers; to talk about such grand stages as savagery and barbarism is to generalize mightily, far beyond what Radcliffe-Brown could countenance. But they talked about such general stages of things exclusively, rather than about whole societies and how they were constructed. Could we have some generalizations about *all* societies that would tell us, or predict for us, something about the structures of *a* society? Radcliffe-Brown had in mind some precepts that may seem a little naive or overly simple today, but in the context of the 1920–1930s they were quite revolutionary—and heady, to the new followers of such a charismatic personality.

Radcliffe-Brown's idea of law now might better be called descriptive generalization. He said a law would be of the order of "all male lions have manes." Such generalizations could be helpful to a science, of course, because if they are forthcoming from long research, and thus are likely to be "true," then you don't have to wonder what you are seeing when you see a lion with a mane (the law "predicts"). But this is not the sort of generalization that characterizes our best-known scientific laws. These typically state an invariant relationship between two or more classes of phenomena. Thus Boyle's Law states the relationship between heat and pressure of an enclosed gas. The relationship is invariant, however, not "in nature" (in the open air, that is) but under laboratory conditions that hold all other factors constant. Similarly, the law stating the relationship between mass and distance in a gravitational field (again, other factors are constant, as in a vacuum) is twofold. Radcliffe-Brown seems not to have envisioned this kind of law for societies. Instead he invented tautological "principles," as we saw in the examples of the "solidarity of the lineage principle" and the "equivalence of brothers principle."

However unsatisfactory may be Radcliffe-Brown's "laws," he was bent on making broad-scaled, basic statements about the nature of society. The opponents, particularly led by Boas in this regard, dismissed the idea of aiming at any such general statements about society. The first job for ethnology is to describe and "understand" with empathetic insight each unique, particular societal manifestation of human culture. Once those are accomplished (if ever), then it will be time to generalize and compare, and the general findings will have to do with the characteristics of the human mind, not society.

COMPARATIVE METHOD–HOLISM

This dichotomy is closely related to the preceding, if not merely another way of talking about it. Most of the important nineteenth-century evolutionists were, in one way or another, involved in comparing and classifying the data coming to their attention. Except for Morgan they did not do fieldwork, and they therefore missed the stimulus to see *a* culture or society as a self-contained entity of interconnected parts. The comparative method, against which the Boasian Americans reacted, was a further refinement of methodology and classification. Spencer employed clerical assistance in the "cut-and-paste" method of making his huge ethnographical files. It was Frazer, of course, who brought this method to its full fame. In the United States, in later times, G. P. Murdock (formerly a sociology student of A. G. Keller, Yale evolutionist) founded a corporation to employ researchers and to sell the resulting huge cross-cultural Human Relations Area Files. Julian Steward also initiated a kind of comparative method which he called "multilinear evolution." Radcliffe-Brown left one of his legacies at the University of Chicago in the restricted form called "the method of controlled comparison."

But mostly American ethnologists were not amenable to the comparative method. As noted in the previous section, Boas was opposed to tearing traits or complexes out of their natural cultural context—out of their associated pattern or configuration—and thus destroying their "meaning." The Americans who were also committed to culture-area and diffusion studies were wont to bring up another grave difficulty as well: how to correct for diffusion if you are simply counting the occurrences of a trait, for you might be counting the same "invention" several times.

Furthermore, are such a scattered people as "the Eskimo" one or several units? Even if all together they are only one unit, how does this unit compare with, say, "the Chinese"? A final criticism is the question of the validity of the data: Are they true just because someone wrote them down?

Basically, the comparative method was an attempt to put evolutionary and structural aims on an inductive scientific footing. And this largely consists of finding out what traits recur together. (Does the presence of the levirate imply patrilineal descent? Does totemism precede the development of anthropomorphic gods?) Tylor (1888) called such correlations "adhesions" and thought that scientific laws could be proved in this way by statistical means.

Nonevolutionists and nonfunctionalists felt no such need to validate the adhesions of items in *a* culture. Of course they "adhered," in a sense, for they necessarily participate in a *pattern* or *configuration*, so that things that fit the pattern would be more readily accepted, others rejected. But such statements of "descriptive integration" do not need to be proved by finding similar patterns elsewhere. The "Dionysian pattern," said to characterize the Plains Indians, does not depend for its veracity and interest on how many times it is found in different tribes, but only on the insight (or imagination) of a Benedict in portraying it. The comparisons made in *Patterns of Culture* of the three cultures were for the purpose of contrast, thus to highlight the *singularity* of each one.

A law, to the practitioners of the statistical comparative method, would be found and proved when invariably (or statistically significantly) two or more traits stayed together. To this general conception of law, the others, the "holists," counterposed *pattern* in their special sense. A distinction between the two, however, lay in the difference between what might be called induction as opposed to empathy. The "laws" were supposed to be *found in nature*; but the "patterns" were the analyst's empathetic description of the relationship of the parts to each other within the whole shared mental culture. The invented description of this *gestalt* was the aim of the research; it was not "found," exactly. It is evident, also, that we are faced here with two very different notions of the locus of explanation—or the whereabouts of the "greater reality." Is the reason for this connection of one thing to another (certain kinship terms and clan–lineage, for example) due to adaptive conditions and structural contingencies "out there"? Or is it due to some patterns of mental activity "in here" that means they must go together to avoid some kind of psychic strain? The earliest, and perhaps the clearest, example of this kind of controversy in ethnology is found in the Kroeber versus Rivers and Kroeber versus Radcliffe-Brown exchanges (Chapter 5), but it ran throughout the philosophical and methodological arguments of the nomothetic–idiographic proponents in Germany.

ENVIRONMENTALISM–MENTALISM

This pairing may remind the reader at first of the old materialism–idealism controversies, but there are some fundamental differences. *Environmentalism* here means simply the assumption that the direction of the causal arrow for human social behavior (in its differences from society to society) is from *outside–in* rather than *inside–out*. It does not mean necessarily that the causes are materialistic in the Marxist sense, though many would hold to that, but they simply are stimuli lying outside the minds of the people (Radcliffe-Brown and Durkheim, for example, saw them as largely social–integrational). On the other hand, *mentalism* refers not precisely to the causal powers or forces of ideas and ideologies but to the minds of the people of the society—and the mentation need not be overt, organized, conscious, or rational at all. This "unconscious," however, is not the entity posited by psychologists like Freud, nor are we facing precisely the problem of psychotic states, nor sentiments and emotions. It is something else, something never defined quite adequately. The environmental causality, the deterministic evolutionism, the comparative method, induction, the methods of a "natural science of society" (in Radcliffe-Brown's usual phrase) are less difficult to understand than the opposed cultural psychology of Boas and his students (and their most probable forebears, the *Geisteswissenschaften* historian–philosophers like Dilthey).

Consider these statements by Boas about the significance of the comparisons: "The frequent occurrence of similar phenomena in culture areas that have no historical contact suggests that important results may be derived from their study, for it shows that the human mind develops everywhere according to the same laws. The discovery of these is the greatest aim of our science" (1888:637). In the summary of "The Aims of Ethnology" he says: "We wish to discover the laws governing the development of the mind by a careful comparison of its varied manifestations" (1888:637). Again: "These laws are largely of a psychological nature. . . . They furnish, therefore, material for a truly comparative psychology" (1888:624). (Note: Boas early used "law," but soon he and his students stopped using it.) Much later, in a summary statement at the end of his introduction to the text *General Anthropology*, we read:

> The principle problem [is] that of understanding a culture as a whole. Neither history nor sociological laws are of considerable help in its solution. . . . Sociology may teach us the morphology and general dynamics of society; it will give us only a partial insight into the complex interaction of forces, so that it is not possible to predict the behavior resulting from the historical events that made the people what they are. *This problem is essentially a psychological one and beset with all the difficulties inherent in this investigation of complex mental phenomena of the lives of individuals.*[8] (1938:5–6; emphasis added)

In the previous section we referred to the Boasian preoccupation with "a culture as a whole." For example, in his introduction to *Patterns of Culture* Boas approved Benedict's emphasis on the "integration of culture." What does this mean? The basic message of *Patterns of Culture* was not at all about the integration of culture traits or complexes or institutions, either with respect to each other or as integrated by some objective institutional means such as social networks

---

[8]See also his lecture "Anthropology" (1908).

or political organization—the way an evolutionist or structural–functionalist would have it. Rather, the overall pattern of "integration" was simply the psyche, the *geist*, an unconscious creation of a mental connection which selects behaviors that fit the subjective *gestalt*. Thus, this pattern is not an integrated *system* of differentiated parts; it is only the sharing by the people of a common subjective pattern, of a sense of coherence that is more felt than understood by them.

Kroeber seems to have written more programmatically about the patterning of culture, and more often, than anyone else. Over and over in his collection of essays, *The Nature of Culture* (1952), he states that "pattern and style" are the structuring property of culture as they are in language (1952:148). Pattern is what ought to be the basic focus of cultural anthropology: "I am convinced that, on the cultural level and in any 'historic' approach . . . , recognition of pattern is the suitable and fruitful aim of nearer understanding" (1952:9).

Where is this pattern located? It is in the minds of the people as a shared "unconscious logic" (1952:172).

ORGANISMIC ANALOGY—LANGUAGE ANALOGY

It should be noted at the outset that although this section comes last, it is not because it is the least important. It might appropriately be argued that it should come last because it seems to inform all the others in various ways and therefore may somehow help to tie them all together. These two analogies may well have been the governing factors in the methodological thought of such leaders as Spencer, Durkheim, and Radcliffe-Brown on one side and Boas, Sapir, Kroeber, Benedict, and Lévi-Strauss on the other. All of the above, at least, attributed intellectual powers to their chosen analogies. Latecomers, such as these writers' students and students of the students, are not themselves necessarily guided very strictly by these analogies, but they must have been influenced by them, nevertheless, however indirectly and unconsciously.

The organismic analogy had its most forceful champion, though not its first, in Herbert Spencer. Spencer *was* the first to argue for organic and societal evolution from the perspective of general, or cosmic, evolution, so that the analogy of an organism, with its "physiological division of labour," was implicit for society. In 1857 he said this:

> The advance from the simple to the complex, through a process of successive differentiations, is seen alike in the earliest changes of the Universe to which we can reason our way back; and in earliest changes which we can inductively establish; it is seen in the geologic and climatic evolution of the Earth, and of

every single organism on its surface; it is seen in the evolution of Humanity, whether contemplated in the civilized individual, or in the aggregation of races; it is seen in the evolution of Society in respect alike of its political, its religious, and its economical organisation; and it is seen in the evolution of all . . . [the] endless concrete and abstract products of human activity. (Carneiro 1967:xviii)

Later Spencer came out more explicitly and more vehemently in favor of the analogy. In fact, this analogy, converted into identity by his critics, caused this to become one of the most useful arguments against Spencer's thought. To the charge that he "based Sociology upon Biology," Spencer replied:

Here let it once more be distinctly asserted that there exist no analogies between the body politic and a living body, save those necessitated by the mutual dependence of parts which they display in common. Though in foregoing chapters [of *Principles of Sociology*, Vol. 1], sundry comparisons of social structures and functions to structures and functions in the human body, have been made, they have been made only because structures and functions in the human body furnish familiar illustrations of structures and functions in general. (Carneiro 1967:xli)

But the most trenchant critique of Spencer's organic analogy was not of the above sort. Durkheim's *The Division of Labor in Society* (1893) singled out Spencer's (and other British rationalists') notions of the causes of the human social division of labor because he thought that Spencer attributed too much force to the role of individuals and their thought in creating *anything* in society. He singled out the "division of labor" aspect of the organismic analogy because it seems to sociologists, at first glance, to be such an obvious *good thing* for both society (creating interdependence and cohesiveness) and the individuals in it (creating greater productivity via specialization).

Durkheim held that the self-interest of individuals does not draw them together to form an organic society, but the opposite—it drives them apart. Rather, cooperation and cohesion are created because the individuals of a society are under the control of a system of beliefs and sentiments, a collective conscience, which both rewards and constrains their behavior. This system regulates and modifies, rather than expresses, the individual ego's self-interest.

Neither Durkheim nor Spencer used the general concept "culture," although both came very close to it in describing its specifics. Durkheim, I think, exaggerated and thus somewhat misrepresented Spencer's thought, in particular, but he was quite correct in his criticisms of the British "Utilitarians" and "Economists." Durkheim was not so far from Spencer, however, as he thought. (Spencer and Durkheim also shared the fate of being grossly misrepresented by later sociological and anthropological commentators.)

Radcliffe-Brown closely followed Durkheim's organismic analogy in his conversion of so many British anthropologists into structural–functionalists in the 1920s and 1930s. (He did not subscribe to Durkheim's evolutionism, however.) His earliest statement of the organismic analogy was in 1914, in his monograph *The Andaman Islanders*, completed in that year: "Every custom and belief of a primitive society plays some determinant part in the social life of the community, just as every organ of a living body plays some part in the general life of the organism" (1922:229).

Probably the most distinctive contribution of Radcliffe-Brown's view of the organismic-like society is his theoretical characterization of "social strucure," differing from Durkheim's general conceptions of "the social" and "society" in being more precisely definable, consistent in usage, and easier to understand. Often, as we have seen, Durkheim seems to have been trying to talk about a *sui generis* something, much like the Whitean concept of culture, as determining human behavior rather than holding that society is simply the sum of individual behaviors, or an "abstraction" from behavior. But Radcliffe-Brown's concept of "social structure" explicitly separates it from "culture," which he deemed an abstraction and an epiphenomenon, being those "habits and mental characteristics" an individual acquires in adapting *to* social life (1952:9). This culture is thus related to social structure, but in a subsidiary way. Social structure is the study of groups in their interrelationships in a social system. Differentiated social institutions (like marriage rules and kinship statuses) and social positions generally are all related to, and derive from, the basic social structure (1952:193). Analysis and interpretation of traits and institutions proceed by attempting to discover the role, or function, they play in contributing to the successful working of the coherent system.

Radcliffe-Brown, like Spencer before him, had been often criticized not only for his organismic analogy, but also for his uses of the terms *morphology* and *physiology* as applied to societies. He replied to these charges in much the same form as did Spencer:

> In using the terms morphology and physiology, I may seem to be returning to the analogy between society and organism which was so popular with medieval philosophers, was taken over and often misused by nineteenth century sociologists, and is completely rejected by many modern writers. But analogies, properly used, are important aids to scientific thinking and there is a real and significant analogy between organic structures and social structures. (1952:195)

There was a language–linguistics analogy of sorts early in the history of ethnology. Fustel de Coulanges, Max Müller, and other famous comparative philologists had already influenced greatly the ethnohistorical aspects of ethnology. But this was by way of a method of recovering historical data from past ages; it was not a methodological analogy for ethnology. E. B. Tylor may have been the first to propose the usefulness of the actual analogy of language to culture when he said: "The study of languages has, perhaps, done more than any other in removing from our view of human thought and action the ideas of chance and arbitrary invention, and in substituting for them a theory of development" (1871:17). Tylor had spent some time on the problem of the evolution of language, from gestures to full-fledged speech. His use of the analogy was thus not precisely what was to come later; his was not the analogy of *a* language to *a* culture and the corresponding analogy of a linguist's methodology to that of an ethnologist.

To use the simplest and most obvious example, the ethnologist (like Boas) is faced with the problem of describing the grammar of a people who do not know they have one. So, out of a great many examples of speech-behavior taken down as text, the ethnologist–linguist extracts (or abstracts) what seems to be the morphology and phonemic pattern of the language. This is an important point: he has no precedent or experience to give him any clues as to how to proceed. The student of an Indo–European literate language has already acquired some notions of the matters of gender, case, tense, syntax, and so forth, but in the case of the Kwakiutl all the rules have to be discovered or invented by the ethnologist. (The new methods of discovery, as though the language were previously completely unknown, eventually became an important part of modern structural linguistics applied to the re-study of the Indo–European languages.)

If, out of speech behavior, rules (or "patterns") of language can be discovered, it must mean that other rules of other shared behaviors can be similarly probed for and portrayed—and they will be unconscious *mental* rules of some sort. Boas said:

> Its [ethnology's] main object may be briefly described as the discovery of the laws governing the activities of the human mind. . . . [These laws are largely of a psychological nature.] . . . they furnish, therefore, material for a truly comparative psychology. The results of the study of comparative linguistics form an important portion of this material, because the forms of thought find their clearest expressions in the forms of language. (1898:624)

Boas referred often to the significance of the language analogy for ethnology, but it may be that certain of his followers have expressed in their own work, more strikingly and directly, the powerful influence of the language analogy. Many could be mentioned, but it may be better to cite only those few who have attracted the most attention: Kroeber, Benedict, and Lévi-Strauss should suffice (Edward Sapir deserves to be included, but since he was primarily a linguist, it should not be surprising that he leaned heavily on the language analogy).

Kroeber has argued many times for the utility of the culture-as-language analogy (1928:491; 1952:86, 107–109, 115, 126–127, 148). It is more relevant now simply to point out the salient researches which exemplify this preoccupation. First of all, there is his refrain that the task of the ethnologist is "descriptive integration"; that is, to find the "pattern," "fashion," "style," "configuration" of cultures—in short, their structure. "So the structure of cultures, like that of languages, also seems potentially describable in terms of an over-all patterning." The very titles of his major works illustrate the point: *Style and Civilizations* (1957), *Configurations of Culture Growth* (1944), "On the Principle of Order in Civilization as Exemplified by Changes of Fashion" (1919), "Basic and Secondary Patterns of Social Structure" (1938).

Once Kroeber's intense preoccupation with the culture–language analogy is accepted, the seeming paradox of his nondeterminism coupled with anti-individualism is resolved. If the main thing (or most interesting thing, to him) about human behavior is its cultural patterning, and if this is like the morphology of language, then why talk of individuals (either "great men" or "little men")? But then, also, why talk of cause and effect? If *pattern* is the basis, then one part "selects for another" in the sense that the parts must be appropriate for one another, but that is all. Changes in culture are like changes in language; a "drift" in a certain direction maintains, despite historical changes, the essentials of the pattern, but it is not a causal chain.

Very similar remarks can be made appropriately about Benedict's "Configurations of Culture in North America" (1932) and *Patterns of Culture* (1934). She endorses the language analogy, with particular reference to phonemic patterning (how, out of the "great arc" of possible behaviors to emphasize, only a limited number are chosen, just as phonemes are a limited number of the much greater number of possible phonetic sounds). But nothing is explained; just when the reader is saying to himself how easy it should be to explain the *why* of the differences between Plains Indian "Dionysian" culture and Pueblo Indian "Apollonian" culture, she retires, as though *purposely* leaving nothing explained.[9] In Aberle's words: "She takes essentially the posi-

---

[9] I knew her fairly well, and therefore I feel that I can risk my own personal addendum here. It seemed to me that she actually took satisfaction in *not* explaining; as a humanist she simply did not want anything about humans to be scientifically explained. Rather than argue, I submitted to her a long paper contrasting the ecology–economy of the Plains Indians with that of the Pueblos (mainly the differences between aggressive,

tion I have ascribed to the linguist: she observes the pattern and its power to rework materials over time, but does not attempt to account for differences of patterns between cultures" (1960:24).

Lévi-Strauss has tried many times to explain his work in terms of the analogy to structural linguistics, to uncover, as Boas often put it, "the unconscious activity of the human mind."[10] He differs from the others mainly in the greater amount of time and effort he devoted to this single task, and in the amount of confusion and contention created in the ranks of his students and readers. We have seen some examples of the explanatory application of his conception of the unconscious presence of "binary opposition" to marriage exchanges, totemism, and the incest taboo. Except for such specific applications of the structural principle, it is difficult to find any actual deviation from the general Boasian view discussed above—although it could be said that Lévi-Strauss has carried it further and applied it far more widely. That is, although Boas had expressed an early interest in laws of *the* human mind, in practice he and his students restricted themselves to members of particular cultures and culture areas.

Lévi-Strauss himself does not claim any more than simple, straightforward adherence to the principles enunciated by Boas and exemplified by Kroeber, Benedict, Sapir, and others.[11] It would seem that the main ideas borrowed are "patterns" (in his own version, "models") and the distinction between conscious and unconscious varieties of them. Lévi-Strauss says, for example: "In the history of structural thought, Boas may be credited with having introduced this distinction. He made clear that a category of facts can more easily yield to structural analysis when the social group in which they are manifested has not elaborated a conscious model to interpret or justify them" (1953:526). Further on he refers to "Kroeber's studies of women's dress fashions, a landmark in structural research" (1953:528). Kroeber's point, one should recall, is that the *conscious thought* of the clothing's designers, manufacturers,

---

mobile, mounted, predator—hunters and defensive, sedentary, close-knit agriculturalists tied down to their little fortresses, and so on). She read it, I guess, and said, "Very interesting. Thank you." I said: "But . . . but . . . don't you agree with me as to *why* the Pueblos are like this, and . . ." She gave her sweet, kindly smile and said, "You just don't understand, do you?" And she was right: I did not understand.

[10]Especially prominently displayed in the last four pages of the "Conclusions" of *Structures élémentaires de la parenté* (1949:493–497). See also Lévi-Strauss (1945, 1951, 1953).

[11]If it is not unprecedented, then why the turmoil his work has created in France? It may be due to the fact that this Germanic—American view of culture—language was unprecedented there in a sociology—ethnology so long dominated by Durkheim's school.

and wearers had no explanatory value whatsoever in regard to the actual long-term patterns of change and persistence in the fashions of women's clothing.

The organismic analogy is the opposite of the language analogy with respect to the form that explanation takes. Explanation of similarities and differences among societies is the explicitly desired aim of research: *why* this or that is always being asked. Naturally enough, this grand difference in the aims has an important effect on the way a society is investigated in the field, how the monographs will be organized and written, and even the kind of emphasis that will be given to some over others of the several aspects of primitive life. In fact, this characterization applies readily to the whole problem of the *A* and *B* moieties of ethnology, and it seems to be reflected as much by striking silences as in the noise of the controversies.

PEACE AND QUIET

On the *A* side a number of topics are analyzed and related questions asked which are often ignored by the *B* side, and vice versa. Thus controversy is rare between the two when side *A* asks questions about evolutionary processes, integrative institutions, and religious organizations, and as the structural causes and functions of these things are proposed. Similarly, quiet prevails on that side when side *B* asks about art styles, componential analysis of kinship semantics, periodic changes in women's hemlines, personality-and-culture, "covert values" and "thematic apperceptions," national character, and other aspects of the "unconscious activity of the human mind." As noted in Chapters 12 and 13, for example, the major scientific figures contributing to one of the most long-standing and important questions ever asked about human history or cultural evolution, the matter of the origin of the state and civilization, include not a single side *B* ethnologist. (To be sure, Lowie was a student of Boas, and he wrote a book called *The Origin of the State*, but its main purpose was to show that the evolutionists were wrong. Additionally, the most prominent members of side *B* who were not actual students of Boas—Malinowski, Evans-Pritchard, Lévi-Strauss, and Redfield—did not address the question either positively with research or negatively by criticizing the research of others.[12]

---

[12]In 1947 Julian Steward made a concluding synthesis of a Wenner–Gren symposium on culture growth in Peru and Mesoamerica. His manuscript was exciting (it led to his classic 1949 paper, "Cultural Causality and Law") and I showed it to Kroeber and Benedict. Neither indicated any interest in it.

Redfield came the closest with his *Folk Culture of Yucatán* (1941), in which he described four societies as representing way stations, or social stages, along the folk-to-urban continuum of communities. Although this was not exactly an attempt to account for the "origin of the state," it could have been put into an evolutionary context, or a structural–functional one, and the dependence of social type on politics, technology, and economics explored. Instead, something terribly frustrating for a side *A* student to note, Redfield accounts in typically Boasian fashion for this folk–urban continuum in terms of "increasing individualism" and "communication"—*mentalism* again (recall Redfield's definition of culture: "A set of common understandings . . .").[13]

There are other topics on which we find similar silences. In Chapter 9, on social structure, we find very little representation from side *B*— only a bit from Lowie, who was, in the topic of social organization, quite a maverick. The major controversy concerned the clan–gens problem and there the opposing views seem to have been caused by a kind of minor dichotomization within side *A*, there being differences in perspective between modern structural–functionalists and earlier evolutionists. On the major question of primitive economics, a question concerned with property and exchange systems, there was not a word from side *B*. Herskovits' *Economic Anthropology* (1952) would seem to be an exception, but it actually departs little from Boasian conceptions. Benedict's "Marital Property Rights in Bilateral Society" (1936) is an interesting exercise from the *B* side, for here she treats a primary aspect of economics, property, in an interesting way. But although Benedict's concern with property in this case sounds like an interest in "primitive economics," she is really making a sociological point. By showing how weak are the claims of a spouse in inheritance compared to the claims of the deceased's consanguineal kin in bilateral society, she indicates that the bilaterality in primitive society actually has within it the *subjective* basis for a unilateral society. Thus the "clan" is only nascent, but "felt" in primitive bilateral society. It is a good point, but it is not really about economics, nor about objective social structure.

On the other hand, the many problems having to do with the con-

---

[13]The state of Yucatán was then a "monocultural" plantation economy, nearly entirely dependent on the export of henequen (sisal). But almost nothing is said of this important fact in Redfield's book, nor are the communities placed in their obviously varying relationships with this economy. It is reminiscent of Benedict's reluctance to have anything explained by economy, ecology, or anything outside the subjective "common understandings."

cept "culture" itself were bypassed by most of the evolutionists, and yet this concept is the key to the many questions regarding behavioral differences asked by side B. E. B. Tylor addressed himself to the definition of culture and its deterministic aspects, but not in the Boasian mentalistic sense. Leslie White wrote of the "evolution of culture," to be sure, but his major writings on the concept of culture were essentially Boasian (especially Kroeberian–Boasian), with the addition of deterministic proposals. It may be, by the way, that here lies the greatest distinctiveness of White's contribution to ethnology—his cultural determinism.

So, the silences were sometimes as meaningful as the direct controversies between the A and B moieties in ethnology. On the face of it, the dichotomization seems a weakness. Can, or should, anything be done about it?

A MODEST PROPOSAL

It is too bad, really, about the silences. The cause seems to be, simply, that the moieties really do exist and one of their features is a frequent lack of interest (by each side) in the questions the other side typically asks. I have two proposals for rectifying the situation.

One is to welcome the distinctiveness of the moieties in the spirit of cultural relativity; diversity is interesting. Were the differences to be better understood and perhaps even sharpened, we might have a more sophisticated theory–method overall that could ask questions more carefully and have a modest expectation of mutual understanding. One of the intentions of this book has been to point up how messy ethnology has been, especially in its lack of epistemological rigor. But a related feature, I hope, is the demonstration that the *recognition* of the moieties could help us understand better the nature of the disagreements. So one proposal might suggest sharpening the moieties in order to learn how to address the related issues more successfully.

Another obvious proposal related to the recognition of the moieties is to *unsharpen* the distinction in the interest of greater eclecticism. This perhaps does not need to be proposed and worked at, for it seems likely to happen here and there willy-nilly. At any rate, this is what usually occurs through a few generations of students in the academic school-of-thought phenomenon. The measures advocated by Durkheim, Radcliffe-Brown, Malinowski, Boas, and others typically become oversimplified by their major followers in the first years ("Disciples betray the Master"). But following generations modify the measures and theories as history casts a clearer light on what has happened; it is as though a mellowing takes place simply as a function of time.[14]

But the silences are not such a difficult thing to correct or repair as the noisy controversies. So many of them have been dubious as true issues because of logical confusions. The trouble over definitions is a case in point: What *is* culture? A related problem is the confusion between the real and nominal types of definitions. A good example is Kroeber's (and many others') inability to distinguish between the actual properties of the thing defined and the definer's personal, often idiosyncratic preferences of theory or method in dealing with it (e.g., "Culture really is history").

Other confusions are related to perspectives, such as the evolutionary view of religions, totemism, primitive communism, and the state as arranged in stages; this view was opposed to the flat perspective of the Boasians. Both sides were mystified by the other, because the *data* did not seem to be at issue very often. (Sometimes it was, along with perspective, as in the Speck–Leacock disagreement over family hunting territories.) The clan–gens confusion was again an evident difference in perspective: the evolutionary versus the flat perspective of the structural–functionalists. A small but very neat controversy was again a matter of perspective (though different from the foregoing): The Dumont–Radcliffe-Brown disagreement over Dravidian marriage. But these were not differences over evolutionary versus flat perspectives, but differences over structure and what it is. This argument was so instructive and interesting because at first it *was* regarded as factual matter, with Dumont finally figuring out that the real trouble lay with the perspectives.

Another obvious problem, as always with arguments, is that each side thought it was right about the true nature of the phenomenon being addressed. Who was right about kinship terms, Radcliffe-Brown or Kroeber? Each one probably went through the remainder of his years convinced of the other's mental incapacity. Could it be that there is no complete right or wrong in this and countless other cases that deal with human social behavior, since that behavior is somehow *both* subjectively patterned *and* objectively institutionalized? Human social behavior must be visible and objectifiable, amenable, in other words, to gross scientific analysis; but it also must have its subjective, mental, individualistic side as well, being not so predictable, and

---

[14]This, at any rate, is what has happened to me, as I confessed in the opening pages of this book. I would like to think it is caused by a fuller knowledge of the issues rather than the weariness of advancing age.

changeable even without obvious cause. Furthermore: Is behavior "patterned"? Yes and no—it all depends on the meaning of *pattern*, and where the pattern is located. The simple way out is to decide what it is you want to know, whether it is discoverable, and by what means.

At this point, there has been an important shift in outlook. To ask what you want to know about a phenomenon is different from arguing about what it is. Kroeber and Racliffe-Brown were not saying to one another: "*You* want to know this about kinship terms, but *I* want to know more about this other, different aspect." They each were saying: "My view of kinship is what kinship *really is*."

What *is* a "thing" like kinship terminology, or totemism, or a symphony concert, or a man smoking a cigar? If it is what it *is*—including all the chemical and physical ingredients, and the mass, weight, and volume, number, shape, age, and color—then any of the above cultural traits is infinitely complex, and in the present state of science unknowable in the full or absolute sense. But really we should not be asking such ultimate questions, though often it sounds as if we are. The trick is to make certain that the question is asked properly.

Our attention is called to an act of human behavior; let's say to tobacco smoking. Who is the kind of scientist to study it, a Radcliffe-Brown or a Kroeber? For that matter, should it be studied by an ethnologist, sociologist, psychologist, physiologist, or chemist? All of these could presumably cast some light, from their different prisms, on the behavior. But this is a bad question: we do not want to find out "all about" the behavior, what it is in an absolute sense, but just something new which we deem important. What something do we want to know? How can we find out? Pose the limited question properly, then decide whether economics, ethnology, history, psychology, medicine, or whatever is the scientific context to which the behavior should be referred for diagnosis. Asking how much cigars cost is very different from asking why they make you sick or what the psychology and physiology of tobacco addiction is. Radcliffe-Brown would probably think the question not worth asking except in the form of the relation of the tobacco industry to the general economy and polity of the society. To Kroeber, perhaps, the interest would be in the swings in fashion from cigars, snuff, and pipes to cigarettes; he might ask why so many women in Western society today smoke cigarettes but not pipes, or chew Red Man. (Once in the classroom he attributed the predilection of south European men for cigars and cigarettes and north European men for pipes to the history of European colonization of the Americas. The English and Dutch colonized North America; they acquired the pipe-smoking custom of the North American Indians. The Spanish and

Portuguese colonized the Caribbean area and South America; they acquired their cigar- and cigarette-smoking custom from the Indians there. After adoption of the customs by Europeans, the patterns persisted to this day.)

It may seem unsatisfactory to propose that we not aim for such grandiose explanations nor attempt such complete answers as our ethnological forebears, particularly the evolutionists, thought possible. But a quick review of the major questions discussed in this book suggests that ethnology has not really progressed very far, as measured against the claims. There is today still no clear-cut or generally accepted opinion about the "meaning" of kinship terms, or the basic forms of social structure and totemism, or the origins of the state, law, primitive property and forms of economic exchange, or even of the very key concept of culture itself. To be sure, as individuals most of us have taken sides, each convinced that we have an answer to many of these issues, but the point has to do with the lack of clear consensus. What does this mean? Does it mean that we have had 100 years of intellectual drought in our beloved land of ethnology? In a sense, it does. But is this discouraging? Does it mean that our ethnological science is a failure, proceeding from incorrect premises and assumptions? Well, it is no more a failure than any of the other social sciences, is it? Indeed, it is a less conspicuous failure than economics, sociology, or social psychology, most of us would claim.

Perhaps the fault lies not so much with the various social science disciplines as with their subject matter, human beings. The ancient dictum *Know thyself* is fine, as a project, but how many achieve it? Perhaps on a different scale—of societies instead of individuals—we are faced with the same problem, the recalcitrance of human societies to be understood (and managed) by themselves or somebody like themselves. It could be argued that the intellectual progress of ethnology lies largely in an increased sophistication and greater knowledge about human societies—and above all in refuting the huge supply of false or dubious information and misleading generalizations that societies have always made about themselves and their neighbors and enemies.

There is a very important sense in which ethnology's significance has lain in its negativism. This seems to be because the *onus probandi* is so often put on us, making us argue the negative, when it logically belongs elsewhere. Take the enormously important problem of race versus culture as the cause of grand ethnic differences in behavior. The answer to this had been "known," as an aspect of folk knowledge, for a long time. In its simplest form it often went like this, in Western Europe and America: There are three (or four) races, white, yellow, black (and red, sometimes). Behavioral differences, the most important of which were thought to be caused by different degrees of intelligence, are due to these racial differences. Thus there arose the widespread notion that there is, in effect, an inborn connection between skin color and intelligence (and thus with degrees of civilization). This was a most improbable proposition from a scientific point of view, and certainly one on which the burden of proof should have been directly placed. But it was not. It was anthropology that had to attempt to show that the proposition was false; in short, to prove the negative. And of course it cannot be *proved* to be false, so what has happened is a substitution of other, more likely and more sophisticated propositions (usually having to do with the powers of culture over biology as a better explanatory device for the presence of certain behavioral characteristics of social groups).

This kind of limited progress, fitful, often negative, piecemeal, and difficult to state easily or briefly to the public, is still real and very important. It comes this way—backwards, so to speak—again because of our difficult subject matter. People, in the union of society, already know the answers to all of the questions they consider basic. The same symbolic capacity that enables them to pose questions also enables them (or some of them—a priest, prophet, philosopher, Uncle Remus) to give answers. Unlike the natural sciences, which at first were called on simply to fill the dark void of ignorance with increasingly sure, or testable, knowledge (and which were likely to be the ones asking the question), the behavioral sciences faced questions that had already been asked *and* answered by the culture itself. The consequence was the largely negative and difficult role of ethnology in locating itself as an aspect of its subject matter and trying to free itself enough to say something not already received as "wisdom" from its own culture.

Bibliography

Where two dates follow the author's name, the first is the identifier used in the text. The second date (within brackets) denotes the edition actually used. It is felt that the date for the original edition gives readers a better sense of the author's temporal place, since they come upon it in the historical contexts in our discussion.

ABERLE, DAVID F.
1960   The influence of linguistics on early culture and personality theory. In *Essays in the science of culture in honor of Leslie A. White*, edited by Gertrude E. Dole and Robert L. Carneiro, pp. 1–29. New York: Thomas Y. Crowell.

AGINSKY, B. W.
1935   Kinship systems and the forms of marriage. *American Anthropological Association, Memoir* 29.

ANONYMOUS
1875   Review of Lubbock's *Origin of Civilisation*. *Nature*, March 25:401–403.

BACHOFEN, JOHANN J.
1861   *Das Mutterrecht*. Stuttgart: Krais and Hoffman.

BAGEHOT, WALTER
1872   [1956] *Physics and politics: thoughts on the application of the principles of "natural selection" and "inheritance" to political society*. Boston: Beacon Press.

BARNES, J. A.
1961   Physical and social kinship. *Philosophy of Science* 28:296–299.
1964   Physical and social facts in anthropology. *Philosophy of Science* 31:294–297.

BASEDOW, HERBERT
1945   *The Australian aboriginal*. Adelaide: F. W. Preece and Sons.

BEAGLEHOLE, ERNEST
1932   *Property, a study in social psychology*. London: Macmillan.

BEATTIE, J. H. M.
1964   Kinship and social anthropology. *Man* 64:130.

BECKER, HOWARD
1950   In defense of Morgan's "Grecian Gens": ancient kinship and stratification. *Southwestern Journal of Anthropology* 6:309–339.

BENEDICT, RUTH
1923   The concept of the guardian spirit in North America. *American Anthropological Association, Memoir* 29.
1930   Psychological types in the cultures of the Southwest. *Proceedings: Twenty-third International Congress of Americanists*. New York (1928):527–581.

1932   Configurations of culture in North America. *American Anthropologist* 34:1–27.

1934   [1948] *Patterns of culture.* New York: Mentor Books.

1936   Marital property rights in bilateral society. *American Anthropologist* 38:368–373.

1938   Religion. In *General anthropology,* edited by Franz Boas, pp. 627–665. New York: D. C. Heath.

1948   Anthropology and the humanities. *American Anthropologist* 30:585–593.

BENDYSHE, THOMAS

1865   The history of anthropology. *Memoirs of the Anthropological Society of London* 1:335–458.

BIDNEY, DAVID

1954   Review of Kroeber and Kluckhohn's *Culture: a critical review of concepts and definitions. American Journal of Sociology* 59:488–489.

BOAS, FRANZ

1887   [1940] The study of geography. In Boas 1940:639–647.

1888   [1940] The aims of ethnology. In Boas 1940:626–638.

1898   [1940] Advances in methods of teaching. In Boas 1940:621–625.

1908   Anthropology. *Columbia University Lectures on Science, Philosophy, and Art* 1:1–10. New York: Columbia University Press.

1910   [1940] The origin of totemism. In Boas 1940:316–323.

1911a   Introduction. In *Handbook of American Indian languages* edited by Franz Boas, pp. 1–83. Bureau of American Ethnology, Bulletin 40.

1911b   [1929] *The mind of primitive man.* New York: Macmillan.

1928   *Anthropology and modern life.* New York: W. W. Norton.

1932   [1940] The aims of anthropological research. In Boas 1940:243–259.

1934   Introduction. In Benedict, *Patterns of culture.* New York: Mentor Books. Pp. unnumbered.

1936   [1940] History and science in anthropology: a reply. In Boas 1940:305–311.

1938   *General anthropology.* New York: D. C. Heath.

1940   *Race, language, and culture.* New York: Macmillan.

1945   *Race and democratic society.* New York: Augustin.

BOHANNON, PAUL J. AND JOHN MIDDLETON (editors)

1968a   *Kinship and social organization.* Garden City, N.Y.: Natural History Press.

1968b   *Marriage, family and residence.* Garden City, N.Y.: Natural History Press.

BURLING, ROBBINS

1964   Cognition and componential analysis: God's truth or hocus–pocus? *American Anthropologist* 66:20–28.

BURROW, J. W.

1966   *Evolution and society: a study in Victorian social theory.* London: Cambridge University Press.

BURROWS, EDWIN G.

1940   Culture areas in Polynesia. *Journal of the Polynesian Society* 49:349–363.

CARNEIRO, ROBERT

1967   Editor's introduction. In Spencer, *The evolution of society: selections from Herbert Spencer's principles of sociology.* Chicago: University of Chicago Press. Pp. ix–lvii.

CHILDE, V. GORDON

1950   The urban revolution. *Town Planning Review* 21:3–17.

CODERE, HELEN
   1959   The understanding of the Kwakiutl. In Goldschmidt, The anthropology of
            Franz Boas, *American Anthropological Association, Memoir* 89. Pp. 61–75.
COOPER JOHN M.
   1937   Lafitau. *Encyclopaedia of the Social Sciences* (Vol. VIII) , pp. 697–698. New
            York: Macmillan.
   1939   Is the Algonquian family hunting ground system pre-Columbian? *American
            Anthropologist* 41:66–90.
COSER, LEWIS A.
   1956   *The functions of social conflict.* Glencoe, Ill.: The Free Press.
CRAWLEY, ERNEST
   1902   [1965] *The mystic rose.* London: Spring Books.
DARWIN, CHARLES
   1871   [1930] *The descent of man and selection in relation to sex* (second ed., re-
            vised). New York: Appleton.
DAVENPORT, WILLIAM
   1959   Nonunilinear descent and descent groups. *American Anthropologist* 61:557–
            572.
DAVIDSON, BASIL
   1959   *The lost cities of Africa.* Boston: Little, Brown.
DILTHEY, WILHELM
   1883   *Einleitung in die Geisteswissenschaften.* Leipzig: Duncker and Humbolt.
DOLE, GERTRUDE E.
   1957   *The development of patterns of kinship nomenclature.* Ph.D. dissertation,
            University of Michigan. Ann Arbor: University Microfilms.
DRIVER, HAROLD
   1968   Ethnology. *International Encyclopedia of the Social Sciences,* pp. 178–186.
            New York: Macmillan and The Free Press.
DUMONT, LOUIS
   1953a   Dravidian kinship terminology. *Man* 53:224.
   1953b   The Dravidian kinship terminology as an expression of marriage. *Man*
            53:34–39.
   1957   Hierarchy and marriage alliance in South Indian kinship. *Occasional Papers of
            the Royal Anthropological Institute,* No. 12. London: Royal Anthropological
            Institute.
DURKHEIM, ÉMILE
   1893   [1964] *The division of labor in society,* translated by George Simpson. New
            York: The Free Press of Glencoe.
   1895   [1938] *The rules of sociological method,* translated by Sarah A. Solovaz and
            John H. Mueller. Edited by George E. G. Catlin. Glencoe, Ill.: The Free Press.
   1897   [1963] *Suicide: a study in sociology,* translated by John A. Spaulding and
            George Simpson. Glencoe, Ill.: The Free Press.
   1898a   Review of J. Kohler's *Zur Urgeschichte der Ehe. L'Année Sociologique*
            1:306–319.
   1898b   [1963] La prohibition de l'inceste et ses origines. *L'Année Sociologique* 1:1–
            70. Reprinted as *Incest: the nature and origin of the taboo,* translated by
            Edward Sagarin. New York: Stuart.
   1912   [1963] *Les formes élémentaires de la vie religieuse: le systéme totemique in
            Australie.* Paris: Félix Alcan. English edition: *The elementary forms of re-*

ligious life, translated by J. W. Swain. New York: The Free Press.

DURKHEIM, ÉMILE AND MARCEL MAUSS
 1903   [1963] *Primitive classification,* edited and translated by Rodney Needham. Chicago: University of Chicago Press.

EGGAN, FRED
 1937a   [1955] The Cheyenne and Arapaho kinship system. In *Social anthropology of North American tribes,* (second ed., revised), edited by F. Eggan, pp. 35–98. Chicago: University of Chicago Press.
 1937b   Historical changes in the Choctaw kinship system. *American Anthropologist* 39:34–52.
 1960   Lewis H. Morgan in kinship perspective. In *Essays in the science of culture in honor of Leslie A. White,* edited by Gertrude E. Dole and Robert L. Carneiro, pp. 179–201. New York: Thomas Y. Crowell.
 1968   Kinship. *International Encyclopedia of the Social Sciences,* pp. 390–401. New York: MacMillan and The Free Press.

ELKIN, A. P.
 1933–1934 Studies in Australian totemism. *Oceania* 4:113–131.

EMBER, MELVIN
 1959   The nonunilinear descent groups of Samoa. *American Anthropologist* 61:573–583.

ENGELS, FRIEDRICH
 1880   [1965] Socialism: utopian and scientific. In *Essential works of Marxism,* edited by Arthur P. Mendel, pp. 45–82. New York: Bantam Books.
 1884   [1942] *The origin of the family, private property, and the state.* New York: International Publishers.

EVANS-PRITCHARD, E. E.
 1937   Anthropology and the social sciences. In *Further papers on the social sciences,* edited by J. E. Dugdale, pp. 5–20. London: Le Playhouse Press.
 1950   [1962] Social anthropology: past and present (the Marett Lecture). In *Social anthropology and other essays,* edited by E. E. Evans-Pritchard, pp. 139–157. New York: The Free Press.

FERGUSON, ADAM
 1767   [1966] *An essay on the history of civil society,* edited by Duncan Forbes. Chicago: Aldine.

FIRTH, RAYMOND
 1929   *Primitive economics of the New Zealand Maori.* London: Routledge.
 1930   Totemism in Polynesia. *Oceania* 1:291–321; 377–398.
 1936   *We, the Tikopia.* London: Allen and Unwin.
 1939   *Primitive Polynesian economy.* London: Routledge.
 1957b   The place of Malinowski in the history of economic anthropology. In Firth (editor) 1957a:209–227.

FIRTH, RAYMOND (editor)
 1957a   *Man and culture: an evaluation of the work of Malinowski.* London: Routledge and Kegan Paul.

FISON, LORIMER AND A. W. HOWITT
 1880   *Kamilaroi and Kurnai, group marriage and relationship, and marriage by elopement.* Melbourne: George Robertson.

FLETCHER, ALICE
 1897   The import of the totem. *Smithsonian Annual Report,* pp. 577–586.

FORTES, MEYER
1949   *The web of kinship among the Tallensi.* London: Oxford University Press.
1953   The structure of unilineal descent groups. *American Anthropologist* 55:17–41.
1957   Malinowski and the study of kinship. In Firth, *Man and culture: an evaluation of the work of Malinowski,* pp. 157–188. London: Routledge and Kegan Paul.
1966   Totem and taboo. *Proceedings of the Royal Anthropological Institute,* pp. 5–22.
1969   *Kinship and the social order: the legacy of Lewis Henry Morgan.* Chicago: Aldine.

FORTES, M. AND E. E. EVANS-PRITCHARD (editors)
1940   *African political systems.* London: Oxford University Press.

FORTUNE, REO
1932   Incest. *Encyclopaedia of the Social Sciences,* pp. 620–622. New York: Macmillan.

FRAZER, SIR JAMES G.
1887   *Totemism.* Edinburgh: Adams and Charles.
1890   [1955] *The golden bough: a study in magic and religion* (13 volumes). London: Macmillan (one-volume edition, abridged paperback).
1910   *Totemism and exogamy.* London: Macmillan.

FREUD, SIGMUND
1913   [1918] *Totem and taboo,* translated by A. A. Brill. New York: Dodd, Mead.

FRIED, MORTON
1957   The classification of corporate unilineal descent groups. *Journal of the Royal Anthropological Institute* 87:1–29.

FUSTEL DE COULANGES, NUMA DENIS
1864   [n.d.] *The ancient city: a study on the religion, laws, and institutions of Greece and Rome,* translated by William Small. Garden City, N.Y.: Doubleday Anchor Books.

GALLATIN, ALBERT
1836   Archaeologia Americana. Cambridge, Mass.: *Transactions and Collections of the American Antiquarian Society* 2.

GELLNER, ERNEST
1957   Ideal language and kinship terms. *Philosophy of Science* 24:235–243.
1960   The concept of kinship. *Philosophy of Science* 27:187–204.
1963   Nature and society in social anthropology. *Philosophy of Science* 30:236–251.

GENNEP, ARNOLD VAN
1908   [1961] *The rites of passage,* translated by Monica B. Vizedom and Gabrielle L. Caffee. Chicago: University of Chicago Press.

GIFFORD, E. W.
1922   California kinship terminologies. *University of California Publications in American Archaeology and Ethnology* 18:1–285.
1940   A problem in kinship terminology. *American Anthropologist* 42:190–194.

GOLDENWEISER, ALEXANDER
1910   Totemism: an analytic study. *Journal of American Folklore* 23:179–293.
1917a   The autonomy of the social. *American Anthropologist* 19:447–449.

1917b   [1965] Religion and society: a critique of Émile Durkheim's theory of the origin and nature of religion. Reprinted in *Reader in comparative religion*, edited by William L. Lessa and Evon Z. Vogt, pp. 65–72. New York: Harper and Row.

1918   Form and content in totemism. *American Anthropologist* 20:280–295.

1931   Totemism: an essay on religion and society. In *The making of man: an outline of anthropology*, edited by V. F. Calverton, pp. 363–392. New York: Modern Library.

1934   Totemism. *Encyclopaedia of the Social Sciences* (Vol. XIV), pp. 602–606. New York: Macmillan.

GOLDSCHMIDT, WALTER (editor)

1959   The anthropology of Franz Boas. *American Anthropological Association, memoir 89.*

GOODENOUGH, WARD H.

1955   A problem in Malayo–Polynesian social organization. *American Anthropologist* 57:71–83.

1956   [1968a] Componential analysis and the study of meaning. *Language* 32(1):195–216. Reprinted in Bohannan and Middleton, *Kinship and social organization*, pp. 93–124. Garden City, N.Y.: Natural History Press.

GOODY, JACK

1958   Developmental cycles in domestic groups. *Cambridge Papers in Social Anthropology*, No. 1.

1968   Descent groups. *International Encyclopedia of the Social Sciences*, pp. 401–408. New York: Macmillan and The Free Press.

1970   Cousin terms. *Southwestern Journal of Anthropology* 26:125–142.

GRABURN, NELSON

1971   *Readings in kinship and social structure.* New York: Harper and Row.

GREY, GEORGE

1841   *Journals of two expeditions of discovery in north-west and western Australia.* London: T. and W. Boone.

GRUBER, JACOB

1966   In search of experience. In *Pioneers of American anthropology: the uses of biography*, edited by June Helm, pp. 3–27. Seattle: University of Washington Press.

HADDON, A. C.

1910   *History of anthropology.* New York and London: G. P. Putnam's Sons.

HALLOWELL, A. IRVING

1928   Recent changes in the kinship terminology of the St. Francis Abenaki. *Twenty-second Proceedings: International Congress of Americanists* 2:97–145.

1943   The nature and function of property as a social institution. *Journal of Legal and Political Sociology* 1:35–45.

1949   The size of Algonkian hunting territories: a function of ecological adjustment. *American Anthropologist* 51:35–45.

1960   The beginnings of anthropology in America. In *Selected papers from the American Anthropologist, 1899–1920*, edited by F. de Laguna, pp. 1–90. Evanston, Ill.: Row, Peterson.

HARRIS, MARVIN

1968   *The rise of anthropological theory.* New York: Thomas Y. Crowell.

HATCH, ELVIN
   1983   *Culture and morality: The relativity of values in anthropology.* New York:
            Columbia University Press.
HEINE-GELDERN, ROBERT
   1964   One hundred years of ethnological theory in the German-speaking countries:
            some milestones. *Current Anthropology* 5:405–418.
HERSKOVITS, MELVILLE J.
   1952   *Economic anthropology.* New York: Knopf.
   1953   *Franz Boas: the science of man in the making.* New York: Scribner's.
HILL-TOUT, CHARLES
   1901–1902 The origin of the totemism of the aborigines of British Columbia.
            Transactions of the Royal Society of Canada 7:Section 2.
HOBHOUSE, L. T.
   1913   The historical evolution of property in fact and in idea. In *Property, its duties
            and rights,* pp. 1–31. London.
HOCART, A. M.
   1928   The Indo–European kinship system. *Ceylon Journal of Science, Section G*
            1:179–210.
   1933   *The progress of man.* London: Methuen & Co.
   1936   [1970] *Kings and councillors.* Chicago: University of Chicago Press.
   1937   Kinship systems. *Anthropos* 32:345–351.
HOMANS, GEORGE C.
   1941   Anxiety and ritual: the theories of Malinowski and Radcliffe-Brown.
            American Anthropologist 43:164–172.
HUBERT, HENRI AND MARCEL MAUSS
   1897–1898 Essai sur la nature et la fonction du sacrifice. *L'Année Sociologique* 2:29–
            138.
   1904   [1960] Esquisse d'une théorie générale de la magie. *L'Année Sociologique* 7.
            Reprinted in Marcel Mauss, *Sociologie et anthropologie* (second edition), pp.
            1–141. Paris: Presses Universitaires de France.
KARSTEN, RAFAEL
   1935   *The origins of religion.* London: Kegan Paul, Trench, Trubner.
KHALDUN, IBN
   1377   [1958] *The Muqaddimah: an introduction to history.* New York: Pantheon.
KIRCHHOFF, PAUL
   1955   [1959] The principles of clanship in human society. *Davidson Journal of
            Anthropology* Vol. 1, No. 1. Seattle: University of Washington. Reprinted in
            Readings in anthropology, edited by M. H. Fried 2:259–270. New York:
            Thomas Y. Crowell.
KLEMM, GUSTAV F.
   1843–1852 *Allgemeine Culturgeschichte der Menschheit* (10 volumes). Leipzig:
            Leubner.
   1854–1855 *Allgemeine Culturwissenschaft* (2 volumes). Leipzig: Leubner.
KOHLER, J.
   1897   *Zur Urgeschichte der Ehe, Totemismus, Gruppenehe, Mutterrecht.*
            Stuttgart: Entke.
KROEBER, A. L.
   1909   [1952] Classificatory systems of relationship. In Kroeber 1952:169–181.
   1915   Eighteen professions. *American Anthropologist* 17:283–288.

1917a   California kinship systems. *University of California Publications in American Archaeology and Ethnology* 12:163–213.

1917b   [1952] The superorganic. In Kroeber 1952:22–51.

1918   [1952] The possibility of a social psychology. In Kroeber 1952:52–56.

1919a   On the principle of order in civilization as exemplified by changes of fashion. *American Anthropologist* 21:253–263.

1919b   Zuñi kin and clan. *American Museum of Natural History, Anthropological Papers* 18:39–205.

1920   Totem and taboo: an ethnologic psychoanalysis. *American Anthropologist* 22:48–55.

1923   *Anthropology.* New York: Harcourt, Brace.

1928   The anthropological attitude. *The American Mercury* 13:490–496.

1935   History and science in anthropology. *American Anthropologist* 37:539–569.

1936   Kinship and history. *American Anthropologist* 38:338–341.

1938   [1952] Basic and secondary patterns of social structure. In Kroeber 1952:210–218.

1939   Totem and taboo in retrospect. *American Journal of Sociology* 45:446–451.

1944   *Configurations of culture growth.* Berkeley: University of California Press.

1948   [1952] White's view of culture. In Kroeber 1952: 110–117.

1949   The concept of culture in science. *Journal of General Education* 3:181–196.

1951   Letter to the editor. *Man* 51:33.

1952   *The nature of culture.* Chicago: University of Chicago Press.

1957   *Style and civilizations.* Ithaca: Cornell University Press.

1959a   A history of the personality of anthropology. *American Anthropologist* 61:398–404.

1959b   Preface. In Goldschmidt, The anthropology of Franz Boas, American Anthropological Association, Memoir 89. Pp. v–vii.

KROEBER, A. L. AND CLYDE KLUCKHOHN
1952   Culture: a critical review of concepts and definitions. *Papers of the Peabody Museum of American Archaeology and Ethnology* 47(1). Cambridge, Mass.: The Museum.

KROEBER, A. L. AND TALCOTT PARSONS
1958   The concepts of culture and of social system. *American Sociological Review* 23:582–583.

KUPER, HILDA
1947   *An African aristocracy: rank among the Swazi.* London: Oxford University Press.

LAFITAU, JOSEPH
1724   *Moeurs des sauvages Amériquains, comparées aux moeurs des premiers temps* (2 volumes). Paris: Saugrain L'aîné.

LANE, ROBERT AND BARBARA LANE
1959   On the development of Dakota–Iroquois and Crow–Omaha kinship terminologies. *Southwestern Journal of Anthropology* 15:254–265.

LANG, ANDREW
1878   Family. In *Encyclopaedia Britannica* (ninth edition). 9:17–24.

1887   [1899] *Myth, ritual and religion* (second edition, 2 volumes). London: Longmans.

1903   *Social origins* (Including T. J. Atkinson, *Primal Law*). London: Longmans.

1905   *The secret of the totem.* London: Longmans.

1909   *The making of religion.* London: Longmans, Green.

LAVELEYE, ÉMILE DE
  1878   *Primitive property*, translated by G. R. L. Marriott. Introduction by T. E. Cliffe Leslie. London: Macmillan.
LEACH, EDMUND R.
  1945   Jinghpaw kinship terminology. *Journal of the Royal Anthropological Institute* 75:59–72.
  1951   [1961] The structural implications of matrilateral cross-cousin marriage. In *Rethinking anthropology*, by E. R. Leach, pp. 54–104. London: University of London, The Athlone Press.
  1954   [1964] *Political systems of highland Burma*. Boston: Beacon Press.
  1958   Concerning Trobriand clans and the kinship category *tabu*. In *The developmental cycle in domestic groups*, edited by Jack Goody, pp. 120–145. Cambridge: Cambridge University.
LEACOCK, ELEANOR
  1954   *The Montagnais "hunting territory" and the fur trade. American Anthropological Association, Memoir*. 78.
  1963   Introduction and annotations. In Lewis Henry Morgan, *Ancient society*. Cleveland and New York: World Publishing, Meridian Books.
LESLIE, FRANK
  1878   *Illustrated Newspaper*, July 27.
LESSA, WILLIAM A. AND EVON Z. VOGT.
  1965   *Reader in comparative religion: an anthropological approach*. New York: Harper and Row.
LETOURNEAU, CHARLES
  1892   *Property, its origins and development*. London: W. Scott.
LÉVI-STRAUSS, CLAUDE
  1943   The social use of kinship terms among Brazilian Indians. *American Anthropologist* 45:398–409.
  1945   L'analyse structurale en linguistique et en anthropologie. *Word* 1:1–21.
  1949   [1969] *The elementary structures of kinship* (revised edition), translated by James Harle Bell, John Richard von Sturmer, and Rodney Needham. Edited by Rodney Needham. Boston: Beacon Press.
  1951   Language and the analysis of social laws. *American Anthropologist* 53:155–163.
  1953   Social structure. In *Anthropology today*, edited by A. L. Kroeber, pp. 524–554. Chicago: University of Chicago Press.
  1956   The family. In *Man, culture and society*, edited by Harry L. Shapiro, pp. 261–285. New York: Oxford University Press.
  1958   [1967] *Structural anthropology*, translated by Claire Jacobson and Brooke Grundfest. Garden City, N.Y.: Anchor Books.
  1962   [1963] *Le totémisme aujourd'hui*. Paris: Presses Universitaires de France. English edition: *Totemism*, translated by Rodney Needham. Boston: Beacon Press.
LINTON, RALPH (editor)
  1940   *Acculturation in seven American Indian tribes*. New York: Appleton.
LONG, J.
  1791   [1968] *Voyages and travels of an Indian interpreter and trader*. New York: Johnson Reprint.
LOUNSBURY, FLOYD G.
  1956a   A semantic analysis of the Pawnee kinship usage. *Language* 32:158–194.

1956b   [1964] The structural analysis of kinship semantics. *Proceedings of the Ninth International Congress of Linguists*, edited by Horace G. Lunt, pp. 1073–1093. The Hague: Mouton.

1965   Another view of the Trobriand kinship categories. *American Anthropologist* 67:142–185.

LOWIE, ROBERT H.

1915a   Exogamy and the classificatory systems of relationship. *American Anthropologist* 17:223–239.

1915b   Psychology and sociology. *American Journal of Sociology* 21:217–229.

1916   Historical and sociological interpretations of kinship terminologies. In *Holmes anniversary volume*, pp. 293–300. Washington, D.C.: J. W. Bryan Press. Reprinted in Graburn, *Readings in kinship and social structure*, New York: Harper and Row. Pp. 72–76.

1917a   [1966] *Culture and ethnology*. New York: Basic Books.

1917b   The kinship systems of the Crow and Hidatsa. *Proceedings: Nineteenth International Congress of Americanists*, pp. 340–343.

1920   [1947] *Primitive society* (second edition). New York: Liveright.

1922   The origin of the state. *The Freeman*, July 19 and 26:440–442; 465–467.

1927   *The origin of the state*. New York: Harcourt, Brace.

1928   A note on relationship terminologies. *American Anthropologist* 30:263–267.

1936   Cultural anthropology: a science. *American Journal of Sociology* 42:301–320.

1937a   *History of ethnological theory*. New York: Farrar and Rinehart.

1937b   Kinship. *Encyclopaedia of the Social Sciences*. New York: Macmillan.

1947   Biographical memoir of Franz Boas: 1858–1942. *National Academy of Sciences* (Vol. 24). Ninth Memoir:303–322.

1948a   *Primitive religion*. New York: Liveright.

1948b   *Social organization*. New York: Rinehart.

1953   Ethnography, cultural and social anthropology. *American Anthropologist* 55:527–534.

LUBBOCK, SIR JOHN

1870   [1882] *The origin of civilisation and the primitive condition of man* (fourth edition). London: Longmans.

1875   Letter. *Nature* 12:124–125.

1876   Review of McLennan's *Studies in Ancient History*. *Nature* 15:133–134.

LYND, ROBERT

1939   *Knowledge for what?* Princeton: Princeton University Press.

MCLENNAN, JOHN F.

1865   *Primitive marriage*. Edinburgh: Adam and Charles Black.

1869–1870 The worship of animals and plants. *Fortnightly Review*, New Series 4:407–427, 562–582; 7:94–216.

1876   [1886] *Studies in ancient history comprising a reprint of primitive marriage*. London: Macmillan.

1885   *The patriarchal theory* (edited and completed by Donald McLennan). London: Macmillan.

MACLEOD, WILLIAM CHRISTIE

1924   *The origin of the state, reconsidered in the light of the data of aboriginal North America*. Philadelphia: William Christie MacLeod.

MAINE, SIR HENRY SUMNER
   1861   [1931] *Ancient law: its connection with the early history of society and its relation to modern ideas* (introduction by C. K. Allen). London: Oxford University Press.
   1871   [1890] *Village-communities in the East and West, to which are added other lectures, addresses and essays* (second edition). London: Murray.
   1883   [1886] *Dissertations on early law and custom.* New York: Henry Holt.

MALINOWSKI, BRONISLAW
   1913   [1963] *The family among the Australian aborigines.* New York: Schocken.
   1922   [1961] *Argonauts of the Western Pacific.* New York: E. P. Dutton.
   1923   The problem of meaning in primitive languages. In *The meaning of meaning,* by C. K. Ogden and I. A. Richards, pp. 451–510. London: Kegan Paul.
   1925   [1948] Magic, science and religion. In Malinowski, *Magic, science and religion and other essays,* pp. 17–92. Glencoe, Ill.: The Free Press.
   1929a   [1962] *The sexual life of savages in northwestern Melanesia* (third edition). New York: Harcourt.
   1929b   Kinship. *Encyclopaedia Britannica* (fourteenth edition), pp. 431–439. New York: The Encyclopaedia Britannica Company.
   1929c   Marriage. *Encyclopaedia Britannica* (fourteenth edition), pp. 601–608. New York: The Encyclopaedia Britannica Company.
   1930a   Kinship. *Man* 30(17): 19–29.
   1930b   Parenthood: The basis of social structure. In *The new generation,* edited by V. F. Calverton and S. D. Schmalhauser, pp. 113–168. London: Macaulay.
   1931   Culture. *Encyclopaedia of the Social Sciences* (Vol. IV), pp. 621–646. New York: Macmillan.
   1932   [1962] Special Foreword. In Malinowski 1929a: xix–xliv.
   1934   [1961] Introduction. In *Law and order in Polynesia,* by H. I. Hogbin, pp. xvii–lxxii. Hamden, Conn.: Shoe String Press.
   1935a   [1965] *Coral gardens and their magic* (2 volumes). Bloomington: Indiana University Press.
   1935b   *The foundations of faith and morals, an anthropological analysis of primitive beliefs and conduct with special reference to the fundamental problems of religion and ethics.* London: Oxford University Press.
   1944   [1960] *A scientific theory of culture and other essays.* New York: Oxford University Press.
   1967   *A diary in the strict sense of the term.* New York: Harcourt, Brace and World.

MARETT, ROBERT R.
   1900   [1929] *The threshold of religion* (fourth edition). London: Methuen.
   1907   Is taboo a negative magic? In Thomas et. al., *Anthropological essays presented to E. B. Tylor,* pp. 219–234. London: Oxford University Press.

MAUSS, MARCEL
   1923–1924 [1967] *Essai sur le don, forme archaïque de l'echange.* English edition: *The gift,* translated by Ian Cunnison. New York: W. W. Norton.

MORGAN, LEWIS H.
   1851   [1954] *League of the Ho-de-no-sau-nee, or Iroquois.* New Haven: Behavior Science Reprints.
   1858   Laws of descent of the Iroquois. *Proceedings: American Association for the Advancement of Science* 11:132–148.
   1859   System of consanguinity of the red race, in its relation to ethnology. Read

before the American Association for the Advancement of Science. Manuscript in the University of Rochester Library.

1862   Circular in reference to the degrees of relationship among different nations. *Smithsonian Miscellaneous Collections* II. Washington, D.C.: Smithsonian Institution.

1868a   *The American beaver and his works.* Philadelphia: J. B. Lippincott.

1868b   A conjectural solution to the origin of the classificatory system of relationships. *Proceedings: American Academy of Arts and Sciences* 7:436–477.

1870   *Systems of consanguinity and affinity of the human family.* Washington, D.C.: Smithsonian Institution.

1872   Australian kinship, from the original memoranda of Rev. Lorimer Fison. *Proceedings: American Academy of Arts and Sciences,* 8:412–438.

1875   Letters. *Nature,* June 3:86 and August 10:311.

1876   [1950] Montezuma's dinner. *North American Review* 122:265–308. Reprinted as a pamphlet by the Socialist Labor Party, New York: New York Labor News.

1877   [1964] *Ancient society.* Introduced and edited by Leslie A. White. Cambridge, Mass.: Harvard University Press, Belknap Press.

1881   [1965] *Houses and house life of the American aborigines.* Contributions to North American Ethnology, Washington: Government Printing Office (with an introduction by Paul Bohannan). Chicago: University of Chicago Press.

MURDOCK, GEORGE PETER

1932   The science of culture. *American Anthropologist* 34:200–215.

1947   Bifurcate merging: a test of five theories. *American Anthropologist* 49:56–68.

1949   *Social structure.* New York: Macmillan.

1959   Evolution in social organization. In *Evolution and anthropology: a centennial appraisal,* pp. 126–143. Washington, D.C.: Anthropological Society of Washington.

NADEL, S. F.

1942   *A black Byzantium.* London: Oxford University Press.

1957   *The theory of social structure.* Glencoe, Ill.: The Free Press.

NEEDHAM, RODNEY

1960   Descent systems and ideal language. *Philosophy of Science* 27:96–101.

OBERG, KALERVO

1940   The kingdom of Ankole in Uganda. In Fortes and Evans-Pritchard, *African political systems,* pp. 121–162. London: Oxford University Press.

1955   Types of social structure among the lowland tribes of South and Central America. *American Anthropologist* 57:472–487.

OLSON, RONALD L.

1934   Clan and moiety in native America. *University of California Papers in American Archaeology and Ethnology,* pp. 351–421. Berkeley: University of California Press.

OPPENHEIMER, FRANZ

1907   [1926] *The state: its history and development viewed sociologically.* New York: Vanguard Press.

PALERM, ANGEL

1967   *Introducción a la teoría etnológica.* Mexico, D.F.: Instituto de Ciencias Sociales, Universidad Iberoamericana.

PARKMAN, FRANCIS
    1851   Indian antiquities in North America. *The Christian Examiner* 50:424.
PARSONS, TALCOTT, AND ROBERT F. BALES
    1955   *Family, socialization and interaction process.* New York: The Free Press of Glencoe.
    1961   Introduction. In *The study of sociology* (new edition), by Herbert Spencer. Ann Arbor: University of Michigan Press.
PLEKHANOV, G.
    1898   [1940] *The role of the individual in history.* New York: International Publishers.
POLANYI, KARL
    1944   [1957] *The great transformation.* New York: Beacon.
    1947   Our obsolete market mentality. *Commentary* 13:109–217.
    1953   [1959] Anthropology and economic theory. In *Readings in anthropology* (Vol. II), edited by M. H. Fried, pp. 161–184. New York: Thomas Y. Crowell.
POLANYI, KARL, CONRAD M. ARENSBERG, AND HARRY W. PEARSON (editors)
    1957   *Trade and market in the early empires.* Glencoe, Ill.: The Free Press.
POWELL, J. W.
    1880   Sketch of Lewis Henry Morgan. *Popular Science Monthly* 18:121.
RADCLIFFE-BROWN, A. R.
    1914   Review of *The family among the Australian aborigines* by B. Malinowski. *Man* 14:31–32.
    1922   [1948] *The Andaman Islanders.* Glencoe, Ill.: The Free Press.
    1923   The methods of ethnology and social anthropology. *South African Journal of Science* 20:124–147.
    1929   [1952] The sociological theory of totemism. *Java: Proceedings of the Fourth Pacific Science Congress* 3:295–309. In Radcliffe-Brown 1952:117–132.
    1930–1931 The social organization of Australian tribes. *Oceania* 1:34–63, 206–246, 426–456.
    1935   Kinship terminologies in California. *American Anthropologist* 37:530–535.
    1939   [1952] *Taboo* (the Frazer Lecture). In Radcliffe-Brown 1952:133–152.
    1940   [1952] On social structure. In Radcliffe-Brown 1952:188–211.
    1941   [1952] The study of kinship systems. In Radcliffe-Brown 1952:49–89.
    1944   Meaning and scope of social anthropology. *Nature* CLIV, No. 3904 (August 26, 1944):257–260.
    1945   [1952] Religion and society (the Henry Myers Lecture). In Radcliffe-Brown 1952:153–177.
    1946   A note on functional anthropology. *Man* 29,30:38–41.
    1949   Functionalism: a protest. *American Anthropologist* 51:320–323.
    1951   Letters to the editor. *Man* 50:198.
    1952a   *Structure and function in primitive society.* Glencoe, Ill.: The Free Press.
    1952b   The comparative method in social anthropology. Huxley Memorial Lecture for 1951. *Journal of the Royal Anthropological Institute* LXXXI:15–22.
    1953   Dravidian kinship terminology. *Man* 53:169.
    1957   *A natural science of society.* Glencoe, Ill.: The Free Press.
RADIN, PAUL
    1937   *Primitive religion.* New York: Viking Press.
    1939   The mind of primitive man: eighth of the "Books That Changed Our Minds." *The New Republic* April 19:300–303.

RECLUS, ELIZÉE
   1910   Ethnology and ethnography. *The Encyclopaedia Britannica* (eleventh edition). Vol. IX, pp. 849–851. New York: The Encyclopaedia Britannica Company.
REDFIELD, ROBERT
   1941   *The folk culture of Yucatán.* Chicago: University of Chicago Press.
   1953   Relations of anthropology to the social sciences and to the humanities. In *Anthropology today,* edited by A. L. Kroeber, pp. 728–738. Chicago: University of Chicago Press.
RESEK, CARL
   1960   *Lewis Henry Morgan: American scholar.* Chicago: University of Chicago Press.
RIVERS, W. H. R.
   1900   A genealogical method of collecting social and vital statistics. *Journal of the Royal Anthropological Institute of Great Britain and Ireland* 30:74–82.
   1907   [1924] On the origin of the classificatory system of relationships. In Rivers 1924, Appendix 1:175–195.
   1914a   *The history of Melanesian society* (2 volumes). London: Cambridge University Press, Publication No. 1.
   1914b   [1968] Kinship and social organization (with commentaries by Raymond Firth and David M. Schneider). *London School of Economics Monographs on Social Anthropology* 34. London: The Athlone Press.
   1924   *Social organization.* London: Kegan Paul, Trench, Trubner.
ROMNEY, A. K. AND P. J. EPLING
   1958   A simplified model of Kariera kinship. *American Anthropologist* 60:59–74.
SAPIR, EDWARD
   1917   Do we need a superorganic? *American Anthropologist* 19:441–447.
   1924   [1966] Culture, genuine and spurious. In Sapir 1966:78–119.
   1927   The unconscious patterning of behavior in society. In *The unconscious: a symposium,* edited by Ethel S. Drummer, pp. 114–124. New York: Knopf.
   1932   [1966] Cultural anthropology and psychiatry. In Sapir 1966:140–163.
   1937   Custom. *Encyclopaedia of the Social Sciences,* pp. 658–662. New York: Macmillan.
   1966   *Selected writings of Edward Sapir in language, culture and personality,* edited by David G. Mandelbaum. Berkeley: University of California Press.
SCHMIDT, WILHELM
   1931   *The origin and growth of religion: facts and theories.* New York: Lincoln MacVeagh.
SCHNEIDER, DAVID M.
   1964   The nature of kinship. *Man* 64:217.
   1965   Some muddles in the models: or, how the system really works. In *The relevance of models for social anthropology,* pp. 25–80. *Association of Social Anthropologists of the Commonwealth Monographs* 1. London: Tavistock Publications.
SERVICE, ELMAN R.
   1960   [1971] Kinship terminology and evolution. *American Anthropologist* 62:747–763. Reprinted in E. R. Service, *Cultural evolutionism: theory in practice* pp. 95–114. New York: Holt, Rinehart and Winston.
   1975   *Origins of the state and civilization.* New York: W. W. Norton.
   1981   The mind of Lewis H. Morgan. *Current Anthropology* 22(1):25–43.

SIMMEL, GEORG
1908   [1958] *Sociologie: Untersuchungen über die Formen der Vergellschaftung.* Berlin: Duncker and Humbolt.
SIMOONS, F. J.
1961   *Eat not this flesh.* Madison: University of Wisconsin Press.
SMITH, W. ROBERTSON
1886   Sacrifice. *Encyclopaedia Britannica* (ninth edition). 21:132–138. Edinburgh: Black.
1889   [1927] *Lectures on the religion of the Semites* (third edition). New York: Macmillan.
SOARES DE SOUZA, GABRIEL
1587   [1851] Tratado descriptivo do Brasil em 1857. *Revista do Instituto Histórico e Geográphico do Brasil* 14:1–423. Rio de Janeiro.
SOLIEN, NANCIE L.
1959   The nonunilineal descent group in the Caribbean and Central America. *American Anthropologist* 61:578–583.
SPECK, FRANK G.
1915   The family hunting band as the basis of Algonkian social organization. *American Anthropologist* 17:289–305.
1926   Land ownership among hunting peoples in primitive America and the world's marginal areas. *Proceedings: Twenty-second International Congress of Americanists* 2:323–332.
SPECK, FRANK G. AND LOREN C. EISELEY
1939   The significance of the hunting territory systems of the Algonkian in social theory. *American Anthropologist* 41:269–280.
1942   Montagnais–Naskapi bands and family hunting districts of the central and southern Labrador peninsula. *Proceedings of the American Philosophical Society* 85:215–242.
SPENCER, HERBERT
1873   *The study of sociology.* New York: D. Appleton.
1876   [1967] *The evolution of society: selections from Herbert Spencer's Principles of Sociology,* edited by Robert L. Carneiro. Chicago: University of Chicago Press.
1885   *Principles of sociology,* (3 volumes, revised edition). New York: D. Appleton.
SPENCER, ROBERT F.
1954   The humanities in cultural anthropology. In *Method and perspective in anthropology,* edited by Robert F. Spencer, pp. 126–144. Minneapolis: University of Minnesota Press.
SPIER, LESLIE
1959   Some central elements in the legacy. In Goldschmidt, The anthropology of Franz Boas, *American Anthropological Association, Memoir* 89. Pp. 146–156.
SPOEHR, ALEXANDER
1947   Changing kinship systems: a study in the acculturation of the Creeks, Cherokee and Choctaw. *Field Museum of Natural History Anthropological Series* 33 (4):151–235.
STARCKE, CARL NICOLAI
1889   [1901] *The primitive family in its origins and development.* New York: D. Appleton.

STERN, BERNHARD J. (editor)
1930   Selections from the letters of Lorimer Fison and A. W. Howitt to Lewis
          Henry Morgan. *American Anthropologist* 32:257–279.
STERN, BERNHARD J.
1931   *Lewis H. Morgan, social evolutionist.* Chicago: University of Chicago Press.
STEVENSON, ROBERT F.
1968   *Population and political systems in tropical Africa.* New York: Columbia
          University Press.
STEWARD, JULIAN H.
1949   [1955] Cultural causality and law: a trial formulation of the development of
          early civilizations. Reprinted in Steward 1955:178–209.
1955   *Theory of culture change.* Urbana: University of Illinois Press.
STIGGINS, GEORGE
n.d.   A historical narration of the genealogy, traditions and downfall of the Ispo-
          coga or Creek tribe of Indians written by one of the tribe. Ms. on file.
          Madison: Wisconsin Historical Society. (Written about 1830–1835.)
SWANTON, JOHN R.
1904   The development of the clan system and of secret societies among the North-
          western tribes. *American Anthropologist* 6:477–485.
1905   The social organization of American tribes. *American Anthropologist* 7:663–
          673.
TAX, SOL
1955   From Lafitau to Radcliffe-Brown: a short history of the study of social organi-
          zation. In *Social anthropology of North American tribes*, edited by Fred Eg-
          gan, pp. 445–481. Chicago: University of Chicago Press.
TERRAY, EMMANUEL
1972   *Marxism and "primitive" societies.* New York: Monthly Review Press.
THOMAS, N. W.
1906   *Kinship organization and group marriage in Australia.* Cambridge:
          Cambridge University Press.
1907   The origin of exogamy. In Thomas et al. 1907:343–354.
THOMAS, N. W. et al. (editors)
1907   *Anthropological essays presented to E. B. Tylor.* London: Oxford University
          Press.
THOMSON, GEORGE D.
1949   *Studies in ancient Greek society.* London: Lawrence and Wishart.
TITIEV, MISCHA
1943   The influence of common residence on the unilateral classification of kin-
          dred. *American Anthropologist* 45:566–573.
TYLOR, EDWARD B.
1863   Wild men and beast-children. *Anthropological Review* 1:21–32.
1865   *Researches into the early history of mankind.* London: J. Murray.
1871   *Primitive culture: researches into the development of mythology, philoso-
          phy, religion, language, art and custom* (2 volumes). London: J. Murray.
1877   Mr. Spencer's "Principles of Sociology." *Mind* 2:141–156.
1878   Review of L. H. Morgan's *Ancient Society. Academy* July 20:67–68.
1888   On a method of investigating the development of institutions; applied to
          laws of marriage and descent. *Journal of the Anthropological Institute*
          18:245–272.
1894   On the Tasmanians as representatives of Paleolithic men. *Journal of the
          Anthropological Institute* 23:141.

1896 The matriarchal family system. *The Nineteenth Century* 40:81–96.
1899 Remarks on totemism, with especial reference to some modern theories respecting it. *Journal of the Anthropological Institute* 1:138–148.
UNWIN, J. D.
1929 The classificatory system of relationship. *Man* 29:124.
1930 Kinship. *Man* 30:61.
URRUTIA, BENJAMIN
1974 Lévi-Strauss and Mormonism (discussion and debate). *American Anthropologist* 76:342–343.
WAGLEY, CHARLES
1940 The effects of depopulation upon social organization as illustrated by the Tapirapé Indians. *Transactions of the New York Academy of Science* (n.s.) 3:12–16.
WAITZ, THEODOR
1858–1871 [1863] *Anthropologie der Naturvölker* (Vol. I). English edition: *Introduction to anthropology*, edited and translated by J. F. Collingwood. London: Longman, Green, Longman, and Roberts.
WALLIS, WILSON D.
1939 *Religion in primitive society.* New York: F. S. Crofts.
WESTERMARCK, EDWARD A.
1891 [1921] *The history of human marriage* (3 volumes, fifth edition). London: Macmillan.
WHITE, LESLIE A. (editor)
1937 Extracts from the European travel journal of Lewis H. Morgan. In *Rochester Historical Society Publications* 16:219–389.
1940 *Pioneers in American anthropology: the Bandelier–Morgan letters, 1873–1883* (2 volumes). Albuquerque, N.M.: University of New Mexico Press.
WHITE, LESLIE A.
1944 Morgan's attitude toward religion and science. *American Anthropologist* 46:218–230.
1947 [1949] The expansion of the scope of science. In White 1949:55–117.
1948 Lewis H. Morgan: pioneer in the theory of social evolution. In *An introduction to the history of sociology*, edited by H. E. Barnes, pp. 138–154. Chicago: University of Chicago Press.
1949 *The science of culture.* New York: Farrar, Strauss.
1957 How Morgan came to write *Systems of Consanguinity and Affinity. Papers of the Michigan Academy of Science, Arts, and Letters* 42:257–268.
1959a The concept of culture. *American Anthropologist* 61:227–251.
1959b *The evolution of culture.* New York: McGraw-Hill.
1964 Introduction. In Morgan, *Ancient society*, edited by Leslie A. White, pp. xiii–xlii. Cambridge, Mass.: Harvard University Press, Belknap Press.
1968 Lewis Henry Morgan. *International Encyclopedia of the Social Sciences*, pp. 496–498. New York: Macmillan and The Free Press.
WISSLER, CLARK
1916 Psychological and historical interpretations for culture. *Science* 43:193–201.
1923 *Man and culture.* New York: Thomas Y. Crowell.
WITTFOGEL, KARL A.
1957 *Oriental despotism: a comparative study of total power.* New Haven: Yale University Press.
WORSLEY, P. M.
1955 Totemism in a changing society. *American Anthropologist* 57:851–861.

Index

Dates in italic index cited publications.

A

Aberle, David F.
  1960, 264, 311, 312
Abnaki, 103
Aborigines, Australian, 29, 79, 80, 82
Academy of Arts and Sciences, 24, 34
Acculturation, 102, 110
Adams, Henry, 16
Adhesions, 304
Adoption, 5
Affines, 19, 29, 30, 39, 90, 92, 95, 96, 99,
  106
Age-grades, 126, 191
Agricultural Revolution, 185
Agriculture, 198
  field, 204
Albania, 37, 115
Algonkian, 103, 142, 205, 211–213
Alliance, 93
American Association for the
  Advancement of Science, 17, 19, 21,
  34
American Historical School, 70
American Indians, 18, 26, 37, 44, 70, 206
  Asian origin, 44
  race, 21
  system, 20, 71
Ancestor worship, 160
Andaman Islanders, 102, 148, 192
Animism, 160, 164, 165
  coined, 158, 160
  vs. materialism, 159
Ankole, 181
Anthropomorphic gods, 135, 160
Anti-evolutionism, 47, 161
Anti-functionalism, 255
Anti-reductionism, 76, 241, 254, 259, 269,
  270, 274

Apollonian culture, 311
Arandas, 194
Arapaho, 103, 104, 274
Arensberg, Conard M.
  1957, see Polanyi, Arensberg, and
  Pearson, 221
Aristocracy, 110, 119, 122, 124, 189, 204,
  206
Aristoi, 127
Aristotle, 38, 174
Art, 253, 274
  history of, 184
Aryan, 30, 42, 46, 48, 60, 100, 188, 203,
  see also Descriptive kinship system
Aryan–Semitic, 23, 25, *see also*
  Descriptive kinship system
  founded on monogamy, 23, 100
Associations, as used by Lowie, 190
Aul, 206
Australia, 26–29, 68, 95, 140, 141, 148,
  150, 164, 165, 169, 170, 191
Australian system, 36
Avebury, Lord, *see* Lubbock, Sir John
Aversion theory of incest, 153–155
Avunculate, 208
Aztec, 37, 115, 131

B

Bachofen, Johann J., 4, 7, 8, 11, 15,
  113–115
  1861, 7, 13, 37, 45, 114
Baden School, 230
Bagehot, Walter, 232
  1956, 178
Bandelier, Adolph, 116, 131
Banyanole, 197
Barbarism, 182, 183
  upper status, 204

339

STUDIES IN ANTHROPOLOGY

under the consulting editorship of E. A. Hammel,
UNIVERSITY OF CALIFORNIA, BERKELEY